A JOURNEY TO FREEDOM

THE HENRY ROE CLOUD SERIES ON AMERICAN INDIANS AND
MODERNITY

Series Editors: Ned Blackhawk, Yale University; Joshua L. Reid, University of
Washington; Kate W. Shanley, University of Montana; and Kim TallBear,
University of Alberta

Series Mission Statement
Named in honor of the pioneering Winnebago educational reformer and first
known American Indian graduate of Yale College, Henry Roe Cloud (Class of
1910), this series showcases emergent and leading scholarship in the field of
American Indian Studies. The series draws upon multiple disciplinary
perspectives and organizes them around the place of Native Americans
within the development of American and European modernity, emphasizing
the shared, relational ties between indigenous and Euro-American societies.
It seeks to broaden current historic, literary, and cultural approaches to
American Studies by foregrounding the fraught but generative sites of
inquiry provided by the study of indigenous communities.

KENT BLANSETT

A Journey
to Freedom

RICHARD OAKES, ALCATRAZ, AND THE
RED POWER MOVEMENT

Yale UNIVERSITY PRESS   NEW HAVEN AND LONDON

Published with assistance from the foundation established in memory of Philip Hamilton
McMillan of the Class of 1894, Yale College.

Yale University Press books may be purchased in quantity for educational, business, or
promotional use. For information, please e-mail sales.press@yale.edu (U.S. office) or sales@
yaleup.co.uk (U.K. office).

Set in Scala type by IDS Infotech, Ltd.
Printed in the United States of America.

Library of Congress Control Number: 2018933962
ISBN 978-0-300-22781-9 (hardcover: alk. paper)

A catalogue record for this book is available from the British Library.

This paper meets the requirements of ANSI/NISO Z39.48-1992 (Permanence of Paper).

10 9 8 7 6 5 4 3 2 1

This book is dedicated to Jewel Blansett, 1936–2014

For Kelie and Maya

CONTENTS

ACKNOWLEDGMENTS

This book is dedicated to my father, Jewel Blansett, who passed away a few years before *A Journey to Freedom* was published. Despite coming of age in the Jim Crow south, my dad persevered against overwhelming obstacles as an Indigenous man. In ways that I will never fully know or understand, he developed a unique outlook on life during his years living in the southern Ozarks. My best memories are helping my dad restore antique furniture in the garage where, between the silences, he shared the stories of his life. From my earliest memory, he made certain to instill value and pride in our Cherokee ways. My mother, Connie Rank, grew up in Sedalia. This well-known central Missouri town, labeled the birthplace of ragtime and Scott Joplin, is located among cattle cars, juke joints, and state fairs. My mom dreamed of becoming a writer and, like her own mother, was inspired by the power of story. The value of a college education was understood by both my parents, for in their own lifetimes it was the one dream that was unattainable. They encouraged my brothers and me from a young age to strive for success in all of our educational pursuits. In a good way and with a full heart, I offer thanks to all my relatives, communities, and ancestors for their untold sacrifice, support, and inspiration.

I extend gratitude to editors Chris Rogers, Laura Davulis, Erica Hanson, and Adina Berk and all of the publishing staff at Yale University

Press for assisting in the final completion of this book. The feedback from reader reports also strengthened the overall manuscript. I especially want to thank Ned Blackhawk, Josh Reid, and Kate Shanley for their dedication and support in securing *A Journey to Freedom*'s inclusion in the Henry Roe Cloud Series on American Indians and Modernity.

I am incredibly grateful to my academic family at the University of New Mexico. I appreciate all of their support, time, detailed edits, thoughtful comments, insightful critiques, patience, and advice that has brought this project to fruition. I am especially indebted to my dissertation advisor Margaret Connell-Szasz, whose unwavering belief in my research and scholarship was immeasurable and life-changing. Other committee members were also invaluable sources of wisdom and encouragement. The research for this book started almost twenty years ago for a research paper during Frank Szasz's graduate seminar on biography. I am thankful to Frank, who, like many of the faculty at UNM, has inspired me to become a better writer, historian, and person. His guidance undoubtedly changed my life. I am thankful to Cathleen Cahill for taking the time to provide direction, critical feedback, workshops for early drafts, and vast support for my work. I also benefited from the advice of Paul Hutton, whose gift for historical narrative and the power of story continues to inspire me. Finally, David Farber's books, lectures, and seminars motivated me to write about the history of the 1960s. As a graduate student at UNM, it is not hard to find excellent mentors outside of your dissertation committee: Virginia Scharff, Beverly Singer, Ann Massman, Sam Truett, Andrew K. Sandoval-Strausz, Durwood Ball, Richard Etulain, Melvin Yazawa, Tim Moy, and Robert Kern challenged me and fostered my intellectual growth in the historical profession.

No one can survive graduate school without a solid support network of fellow graduate students and friends. At UNM I was fortunate to form a network of lifelong friendships with Alden Bigman, Adam Kane, Lincoln Bramwell, B. Erin Cole, Sarah Grossman, Meg Frisbee, Jim Ersfeld, Shawn Wiemann, Jason Strykowski, Sonia Dickey, Colin Snider, Erik Loomis, Brandon Morgan, Amy Scott, Katie McIntyre, Maurice Crandall, and many others. The University of New Mexico offered generous resources in the form of scholarships, grants, and fellowships from the Native American Studies department, the Office of Graduate Studies, and the UNM-Mellon program.

I am lucky to have colleagues and friends around the country who lent their support during the manuscript revision process. Jennifer Kolpacoff Deane, Ben Narvaez, Bert Ahern, and Ed Brands provided advice and wonderful conversations during my time at the University of Minnesota, Morris. Ed's skillful knowledge and dedication resulted in the beautiful maps used throughout this book. At the University of Nebraska at Omaha, I joined a talented faculty in the history department and throughout the university, a group that includes Mark Scherer, Danielle Battisti, Sharon Wood, Elaine Nelson, Denny Smith, Moshe Gershovich, John Grigg, Martina Saltamacchia, Mark Celinscak, Maria Arbelaez, Charles King, Jeanne Reames, Bruce Garver, Mike Tate, Beth Ritter, Lyn Holley, Brady DeSanti, Gina Robbins, Alan Osborn, Amy Schindler, Jason Heppler, Mark Walters, and my dean, David Boocker, has offered valuable encouragement and assistance since I arrived in 2014. Both institutions provided generous grants that funded research travels and the expense of acquiring maps and photograph permissions.

I owe gratitude to several archivists and librarians from around the country whose research and expertise were crucial to this manuscript. As the Katrin H. Lamon Fellow at the School for Advanced Research, I had the privilege of collaborating with an exceptional assortment of scholars. From our workshops to our late-night potlucks, I watched us grow into an extended family. Thank you to James Brooks, Amy Lonetree, Jon Daehnke, Jason De León, Abigail Bigham, Islah Jad, Philippe Bourgois, Lori Hart, He Li, Deborah Boehm, George Karandinos, Will Wilson, Joan Kane, Jordan Wilson, Elle-Máijá Apiniskim Tailfeathers, Trish Cecil, and Chris Cecil for encouraging my professional endeavors and offering me personal support in the wake of my father's passing in 2014. A research fellowship at the Newberry Library connected me with Scott Stevens (former director of the D'Arcy McNickle Center of American Indian and Indigenous Studies), who has had a lasting impact on my research. I was fortunate that Scott connected me to his aunt and uncle, Jackie and Dave Mitchell, who then introduced me to Leonard Oakes. My interviews with Richard's brother were vital to this book, and I thank Leonard for his kindness, patience, and honesty during our conversations. A special thank you to Craig Glassner and the Alcatraz Island National Park Service staff for the wonderful help and support. There are additional individuals who offered their expertise and feedback on my publications throughout this journey. I am particularly indebted to Troy Johnson, whose seminal work on the Alcatraz occupation influenced my own work. Robert Warrior also graciously shared his research with me during the earliest stages of this project. Their dedication to telling the story of Red Power activism sparked my interest in this pivotal era in American Indian history, and I hope that my work builds on theirs and others in a productive way.

Researching and writing can be isolating activities, so it is crucial to maintain connections with friends and mentors. My research has bene-fitted from so many people, including Don Fixico, David Edmunds, Jeani O'Brien, Ned Blackhawk, Sterling Evans, Josh Reid, Phil Deloria, Richard White, Sherry Smith, Bob Conley, Don Birchfield, Kurt Kinbacher, María Muñoz, Akim Reinhardt, Dave Neshiem, Taylor Keen, Doug Kiel, Karen Cockrell, Linda Warner, Phil Arnold, Maureen Konkle, Carol Anderson, Grace Gouveia, Beth Castle, Brian Collier, Andy Fisher, Kathy Brosnan, Fred Hoxie, Brianna Theobald, John Wunder, Linda Waggoner, and Alessandra Robert Link. I deeply appreciate Mike Childers and Leisl Carr Childers for our conversations on the historical profession and our friendship, which has meant the world to me. My longtime friend William S. Yellow Robe Jr. provided me with a creative outlet through the Wakiknabe Theater Company. Acting and writing plays helped me grow as a Native scholar, writer, and teacher. Finally, for the meaningful conversations on contempo-rary Indigenous issues and Native Nationalism, I thank my best friend and brother Steve Sexton, who helped inspire me to create, revise, and complete this manuscript.

This book would not have been possible without the support from many of the veterans from the Red Power movement. Their generation sacrificed much of their time, much of their energy, and many of their lives to protect Indigenous sovereignty for the future. I consider it an extreme honor to have worked with them in some capacity throughout this journey. I thank them for their time and their memories, which they generously shared with me: Dean Chavers, Grace Thorpe, Robert Free, Mary Lee Johns, Ramona Bennett, Hank Adams, Sid and Suzette Mills, John Vigil, John Fadden, Reaghan Tarbell, and the dozens of additional activists who spoke with me about this biography. Ramona Bennett's hospitality and enthusiasm were particularly helpful. I thank her for welcoming me into her home, for inviting me to participate in several ceremonies, and for driving me throughout Washington state for interviews. Finally, I extend my deepest gratitude to Leonard Oakes and the Oakes family for sharing their family history and memories about Richard Oakes, in addition to the dozens of Mohawk ironworkers and community members who shared their memories with me at Akwesasne's annual Ironworkers Festival.

Family is a crucial part of anyone's life journey. Thank you to all my family, who have been so patient and supportive. I have always looked up to my brothers Keith and Kevin and appreciated their support. To all the Nelsons and Hoffmans, I offer my deepest gratitude, especially to Gayle and Angie Nelson, who provided so much love and support over the years, as well as to Deanna, Kristen, and Matt, who treated me like a brother from the moment we met.

Finally, I owe the most gratitude to my beautiful wife Elaine. You are the love of my life, my colleague, my favorite traveling companion, and my best friend. This book is also dedicated to you, for without your guidance, your willingness to read countless versions, and your patience when tackling a new research lead, this book would not have been published. While our first argument involved the current state of the field of American Indian History, this was also the moment when I fell in love with you. It has been a great voyage with you over the years through multiple conferences, research adventures, and road trips (with our dog and cat, Luka and Zoey). No matter how much our lives have changed, your love remains my constant. Thank you for all the times you listened to me carry on about Richard Oakes or comforted me through the challenging experience of writing—and then completing—a book. Your calmness, laughter, passion, intellect, support, and patience helped tremendously. You bring amazement to my life. You are also the best mother and role model to our beautiful daughters. To my daughters, Kelie Nokisi Blansett and Maya Marie Jewel Blansett: Always follow your hearts, no matter what obstacles are placed before you, and take strength from your Indigenous heritage. Be strong, honorable, and kind. Remember that I love you and that I am extremely proud to be your dad.

A JOURNEY TO FREEDOM

IT WAS A CRISP FALL DAY in 1969 when Richard Oakes and others stepped onto dock number 40 in the San Francisco Bay. A crowd of reporters had gathered to witness the Indian "takeover" of Alcatraz Island. The reporters snapped photos of Oakes holding up strips of red cloth and beads, mocking, with a smile, an attempt to purchase the island from the government. Finally, a boat was found to take the "occupiers" to the island. One by one, people climbed on board the *Monte Cristo* (a triple-mast vessel commissioned by Canada and built in New Zealand to resemble the *Endeavor*, the ship of eighteenth-century explorer Captain James Cook) and started out. Harnessing the power of the wind, the boat sliced through the rough currents; the faces of the passengers reflected the excitement. As the winds picked up, many glanced back at the pier and the enormous crimson superstructure of the Golden Gate Bridge.

Eventually, the focus returned to the weathered concrete of "the Rock." Dressed in blue jeans, a sweater, and a cherished pair of cowboy boots, Richard Oakes made his way to the side of the boat. Looking over at the waves and the island, he turned to the crowd and motioned, "Come on. Let's go. Let's get it on!" Within a few seconds, his shirt was off; his large frame disappeared into the chilled November waters, his boots still on as he swam for the land.

Oakes never looked back. He continued to swim through wave after wave. He seemed to lack fear. The danger of being swept out to sea or, worse yet, drowning never entered his consciousness. After two hundred and fifty yards, he was pushed in by the waves. He reached for the shore, pulling himself up on the sea-stained rocks. A lone dog approached and began to lick the salt from his exhausted body. Richard Oakes had started the final chapter in his long journey to freedom.[1]

The life story of Akwesasne Mohawk Richard Oakes is crucial to any discourse on contemporary American Indian leadership. Oakes helped organize the highly publicized Alcatraz, Fort Lawton, and Pit River take-overs. His assassination in 1972 galvanized the Trail of Broken Treaties march on Washington, D.C., and unified a movement that eventually ushered in the era of Native self-determination in the mid-1970s. Oakes's life served yet another purpose: it inspired and enlightened future generations of Native leaders. This book explores the life of Richard Oakes and illustrates how his actions reflected the unique voice of Indigenous leadership within the Red Power movement of the 1960s and 1970s.

The 1969 occupation of Alcatraz Island by the Indians of All Tribes served as the catalyst for the Red Power movement. While the "Red Power" concept existed long before the occupation itself, Alcatraz became a critical turning point, a place where the term found its true meaning—and became more than just a slogan. Along the way, Richard Oakes never lost or discarded his Mohawk Nationalism or heritage. His leadership and participation in the Alcatraz and Pit River takeovers reinforced his identity as a Mohawk citizen *and* as a Red Power activist in defense of Native Nationalism. Understanding Richard Oakes's story depends on a close examination of his Mohawk Nationalism, which is rooted in his ancestral histories of Akwesasne and Kahnawà:ke; is connected to the Indian Cities of Brooklyn, San Francisco, and Seattle; and inspired the birth of the Red Power movement that forever transformed contemporary politics throughout Indian Country.

A Journey to Freedom is the biography of Richard Oakes, Indigenous leader and activist. The first published biography of Oakes, this book represents an entirely new perspective on the Red Power movement and its impact on American history. Previous scholarship has often interpreted the Red Power movement through a narrow lens as a common narrative of two political organizations, either the National Indian Youth Council (NIYC) or the American Indian Movement (AIM). Countering convention, this biography moves the discussion beyond these organizations, introducing new research and theoretical approaches through the perspective of biography. Oakes's life exposes a unique form of populism, one essential to 1960s activism, as a coalition of diverse individuals, organizations, and Indigenous movements collaborated in order to inspire, shape, and define Red Power as a political movement, for this movement arose out of an intellectual and philosophical connection to nonviolent civil disobedience and direct action. Oakes's life highlights the historical development of Native Nationalism and reveals the inherent political complications that surround the definitions, origins, and legacy of the twentieth-century Red Power movement. Recent Indigenous political coalitions, from the Idle No More movement to the Water Protectors' rejection of the Dakota Access Pipeline at the Standing Rock Reservation, can trace their historical roots back to the abandoned prison within the heart of San Francisco Bay, an island where Native Nationalism awakened a great vision of Red Power.[2]

In order to understand Richard Oakes and the political foundations of the 1969 occupation of Alcatraz Island, it is important to consider how Native Nationalism inspired the philosophical, ideological, and political origins of the Red Power movement.[3] *Native Nationalism* is a term that covers a long history of efforts to promote and protect the explicit rights of an Indigenous nation's governance, lifeway, language, community, land, law, and peoples. It is based firmly on a foundation of Indigenous sovereignty. *Native Nationalism* is a non-exclusionary term that describes a concept that has always inherently existed in Indigenous nations throughout North America, from ancient times to first contact with European peoples. Tribes have employed Native Nationalism to defend and promote their historic rights to maintain their distinct sovereignty from one another and to uphold their sovereign status apart from the interference of any colonial power or nation-state (such as the United States or Canada). Their relationships with these entities evolved over time and included the development of a unique status (or trust) as defined by historic negotiations, political interactions, and treaty rights. As recognized by Canada and the United States, treaties are legally binding documents that required debates, negotiations, signatures, and approval between two equal governments. While these treaties changed the legal definition of Indigenous nations in relation to these colonial nation-states, Native Nationalism remained a force that served to protect and uphold the rights of Native peoples and Indigenous sovereignty.

The narrative of Richard Oakes's life highlights the existence of Indigenous sovereignty, a core component to my definition of *Native Nationalism*. Indigenous sovereignty is dependent on the concept of relationality—or the ties that bind Native nations, communities, families, spaces, places, and peoples together. Indigenous sovereignty throughout the Americas is unique, and its existence is not dependent on nor granted through federal recognition or bestowed by a colonial power—as a term and concept, it is entirely different from the simple term *sovereignty*. It transcends geopolitical borders and states, and it has always honored all life. It is a significant part of Native Nationalism, as it recognizes Indigenous individuals, families, clans, bands, genders, sacred spaces, societies, communities, marine space, and lands. Throughout Oakes's lifetime, the reciprocal relationships that emerged from Indigenous sovereignty and Native Nationalism molded his character and shaped his brand of leadership. Oakes's story reveals how Native Nationalism and Indigenous sovereignty transformed throughout the twentieth-century, especially with the advent of Red Power.[4]

So, how is *Red Power* defined? I define *Red Power*, rich in meaning and historically distinct, as an Intertribal movement that emerged from Native Nationalism. By the 1960s Red Power leaders, thinkers, and activists like Oakes employed nonviolent direct action to gain greater recognition of Indigenous sovereignty. Deeply rooted in Indian self-determination, Red Power called for the restoration of treaty lands, lifeways, and Indigenous human rights. In previous scholarship, Red Power is often compared to civil rights movements of the time. Such comparisons oversimplify Red Power and dismiss a long legacy of Native Nationalism and resistance. Red Power was never about civil rights or equal integration into the colonial nation-state; rather, it was about protecting Indigenous human rights, especially as part of independent and sovereign nations. *A Journey to Freedom* showcases how, situated within the much longer history of Native Nationalism, Red Power advocated for Indigenous peoples to fight beyond colonial forms of recognition and to protect their Indigenous sovereignty. Richard Oakes and other leaders believed that if they succeeded in their fight for Indigenous land reclamation on a tiny island in the Bay Area, then the Red Power movement could ignite a new cause across the Western Hemisphere. In 1969, Richard Oakes stated, "Alcatraz is not an island, it's an idea." This idea transformed Red Power into a movement of direct action as Native peoples championed the causes of land reclamation, liberation theory, treaty rights, federal and Tribal reform, cultural revival, education, health care, economic justice, and an Indigenous sovereignty that linked reservation, urban, and rural populations. Ultimately, Oakes served as a spokesperson, leader, and symbol for the next chapter in Native Nationalism, which came to be known as Red Power. The life of Oakes highlights the historical connection between Red Power and Native Nationalism, a connection that forever altered the modern Indigenous experience.[5]

For the American public and media, militancy emerged as the most popular stereotype for Red Power, yet violent resistance never served as a founding principle for Red Power organizations, leadership, or strategy. Conservative forces in America touted the "militant" label as a way to discredit the varied foundations of Red Power. Despite the nonviolent origin of Red Power politics that emerged in the 1960s, other incidents encouraged the media to cast a violent shadow over all Red Power movements, such as the BIA takeover in 1972 and the standoff at Wounded Knee between the Independent Oglala Nation and the U.S. military in 1973. Likewise, images of Black Panthers marching in military formations with unloaded guns in front of California's Capitol, the terror bombings by the Weather Underground, and gun battles with the Chicano Brown Berets fueled further misperceptions of Red Power activists. Contemporary studies on Red Power activism often mislabel the Alcatraz takeover and other movements with a violent or militant overtone. Irrevocably linked in the public's mind with other power movements of the time, Red Power in fact developed outside of these movements to successfully change federal Indian policy and promote modern Indigenous sovereignty.[6]

One crucial aspect of the Red Power movement was its reliance on Intertribalism. In his 1973 book *Native American Tribalism*, Salish author, historian, and anthropologist D'Arcy McNickle argued that "Indian nationalism, pan-Indianism, Red Power ... indicate a growing sense of shared problems, shared goals, and a shared heritage ... the new voices avow . . . [America] will have to contend with an integrating tribal people, not with isolated individuals lost in anonymity."[7] McNickle's words revealed the true nature of Red Power as an Intertribal movement through "integrating tribal people." Indigenous peoples could only achieve this goal if they unified and promoted Native Nationalism without abandoning their individual Tribal citizenship. Oakes demonstrated this through his brand of leadership. As a Mohawk citizen he was also bound to the Haudenosaunee Great Law of Peace. This is a confederacy of six autonomous Haudenosaunee nations (Mohawk, Cayuga, Onondaga, Oneida, Tuscarora, and Seneca) in one centralized governing structure. Taken further, Oakes's Mohawk Nationalism is a function of the complex application of Native Nationalism, which was comprised of three parts: he was beholden first to the Mohawk, second to the Haudenosaunee Confederacy, and finally to the thousands of recognized and non-recognized Indigenous nations and communities across Turtle Island. Oakes as a Mohawk citizen frequently lent his activism to Indigenous peoples and nations outside of the Haudenosaunee Confederacy. Such actions of Oakes and other activists underscored the significance of Intertribalism and how Red Power evolved as the Intertribal extension of Native Nationalism.[8]

One organization, Indians of All Tribes (IAT), was essential to the success of the Alcatraz takeover. Beginning in 1969, Indians of All Tribes sparked hundreds of similar occupations across America, from the takeover of Wrigley Field in Chicago to the occupation of Ellis Island in New York. Especially at Alcatraz, their actions represented a blueprint for the growing tide of nonviolent American Indian activism that has continued well into the twenty-first century. From its inception, IAT elected Richard Oakes as its spokesperson. Oakes's political activism and embrace of coalition politics inspired several other Bay Area organizations like the Black Panther Party, the Third World Liberation Front, the Brown Berets, Aztlán, and the American environmental movement. The construction of these coalitions inspired Indians of All Tribes and Oakes to lend their leadership to major demonstrations between two coasts and throughout the American West. At the forefront of leadership in dozens of key occupations, Oakes routinely organized mass media, political, and legal campaigns that championed Indigenous land rights, self-determination, treaty rights, human rights, resource rights, economic independence, cultural revitalization, and the development of sustainable ecological practices.[9] His efforts were reinforced by a vast network of Intertribal political coalitions connecting reservation, rural, and urban spaces. The advent of Red Power evolved into a new Indigenous political movement, structurally distinct from, but inherently tied to, Native Nationalism.

Intertribalism as a core ingredient within Red Power politics is represented by two 1970s events. At the 1970 takeover of Fort Lawton, a military base in Seattle, Washington, Oakes and other Native leaders showcased the possibilities of utilizing Intertribalism within the Red Power movement. That same month, scholars and Tribal leaders sponsored the First Convocation of American Indian Scholars at Princeton University in March 1970. Through a series of meetings, roundtables, and conference papers, participants crafted a theoretical lens for Red Power. Proceedings from this convocation were subsequently edited by a married activist couple, Cahuilla citizen Rupert Costo and Eastern Cherokee citizen Jeannette Henry Costo, and published by the Indian Historian Press, based out of San Francisco. Lakota anthropologist Bea Medicine's convocation speech, entitled "Red Power: Real or Potential," emphasized the importance of Intertribalism as a defining characteristic of Red Power: "Pan-Indian forces which had been prevailing for some time had formed into feelings of 'inter-tribalness' in one organization on a national scale . . . transcending tribalness in existing organizations . . . in my estimation, [is] a cornerstone for this movement . . . we cannot achieve the goal of equal opportunity for all unless we can accept a significant redistribution of power in all aspects of our social, political, economic, and intellectual, as well as our legal existence."[10] Medicine's speech echoed the core principle of Red Power—Intertribalism as a tool of political reform. To achieve such ends, Medicine suggested a redistribution of power: Federal reform would mean little without Tribal reform and the strength to accept total change. Thus, she called on Indigenous peoples and Tribal governments to decolonize.

The term *Intertribalism* advances a transnational history by looking at the intersection of thousands of distinct Native individuals, communities, and cultures. I argue that previous terminologies, ranging from *pan-Indian* to *supratribal*, are misleading and fail to capture the history of Red Power. The "pan-Indian" notion began in the early twentieth century as a byproduct of the assimilation and acculturation movements sponsored by the U.S. federal government, salvage anthropologists, and other

Gilded Age reform organizations. These movements sought to racialize, integrate, and transform Native peoples into American Indians, thereby joining the larger mainstream ethnic-Americanization process. Under this canon reformers used racialization to suppress Native Nationalism and Indigenous sovereignty; they declared that distinct Tribal peoples belonged to a single race rather than to individual Nations. Anthropologists and other scholars coined *pan-Indian* as a means to explain how individuals are no longer Tribal (detribalized) but should be perceived as collectively racialized into "American Indians."[11]

In distinct contrast to this terminology of the early twentieth century, Intertribalism centers on the power of place and Native Nationalist definitions of shared culture. This (as both McNickle and Medicine suggested) enables Native peoples to retain their Tribal identity, yet create a political, legal, and Intertribal identity and culture as American Indians. Native peoples do not willingly give up their Tribal affiliations (with its political, national, and cultural meanings) to become American Indian. Rather, they protect these Tribal affiliations and reinforce them within Intertribal coalitions. This shared connection and identity directly counters a "pan-Indian" identity. It encourages the wholesale acceptance of an American Indian identity for the promotion of political, cultural, and legal gains for Tribes.

While this is an Intertribal story, it is also an urban history and biography. *A Journey to Freedom* operates as an interpretive lens into the sophisticated politics of Indian Cities. When Richard Oakes entered San Francisco in the late 1960s, he entered an Indian City. His urban experience was defined by the institutions, structures, community, and organizations that comprised the Indian City within the City by the Bay. As increasing numbers of Native peoples relocated to urban environments throughout America during the twentieth century, each city with a substantial Native population fostered its own Indian City, a distinctively new urban space. By the 1970s, roughly half of the total population of American Indians resided in major U.S. cities. Kiowa author N. Scott Momaday's Pulitzer Prize–winning first novel *House Made of Dawn* (1969) exposes a deep-seated division between reservation and urban communities. Momaday's main character, Abel, is portrayed as a victim of the city, as he is unable to adjust or adapt to urban life in Los Angeles—also called the "concrete prairie." At the end of the novel, Abel leaves Los Angeles to return to the reservation, his traditional teachings, and lifeways. While Momaday's work has been heralded by literary scholars for deserved reasons, the storyline created a set of popular beliefs about the urban Indian experience: that Indians had become victims of the city and its modernity and technology, while the urban landscape remained void of any Tribal identity. The logic was, mistakenly I believe, that the city had become a "concrete prairie" in opposition to and without the influence of Native worldviews. *A Journey to Freedom* counters this misperception by revealing how Native peoples actively Tribalized (or Indigenized) urban space and fostered the growth of Indian Cities. This was both a result of physical spaces as well as social and intellectual ties. Spaces within certain neighborhoods and various urban organizations brought the community together. In those spaces, Native residents of Indian Cities utilized Intertribalism to protect Tribal identity by politicizing entire communities of urban Native peoples. These communities became a major stepping-stone in the development of Red Power because they created shared experiences that would connect urban, reservation, and rural spaces.[12] By placing an individual like Richard Oakes at this intersection, such an approach reveals how Native peoples constructed communities in these urban spaces and used these institutions to dismantle systems of oppression. What follows moves beyond a history of injustice. This is a story about our struggle for justice and freedom.

The concept of the Indian City also has historiographic implications. Since World War II, modern American Indian history has undergone significant historiographical and theoretical changes. While scholars of American Indian history have experimented with a host of different methods and theories, the field has focused largely on the writing of Tribal histories. Scholars have written multiple volumes, many of which detail the history of a single Native nation: Comanche, Cherokee, Lakota, or Diné. Using the concept of the Indian City and its Intertribalism places these histories in communication with one another. They reveal that Tribal history does not evolve in a vacuum. Instead, new scholarship that explores the intersections and cross-cultural exchanges between Tribes and Native peoples show how these histories are incredibly rich, complex, and significant to the twentieth-century U.S. narrative. The history of Intertribalism is part of the mortar of modern American Indian history, and it deserves further exploration. *A Journey to Freedom* is an Intertribal history, as Oakes's life story provides a window through which the historian can explore the peoples, organizations, institutions, nations, places, and spaces that define Intertribalism.

Eagle and "FREE" shield carving located above the entrance to the Administration Building on Alcatraz Island, 2011. Photo courtesy of the author.

Oakes's leadership emerged out of Native Nationalism and came to symbolize Red Power, and it was also driven by the tenets of freedom. Scholars eager to discuss the Red Power movement as critical to Native history often neglect to mention one of its most significant foundations: American Indian freedom. Early in the occupation of Alcatraz, the abandoned federal prison emerged as the ultimate symbol for two different Americas—justice for whites and a different form of justice (mostly injustice) for Indigenous peoples. Evidence of this dual sense of justice is still apparent to tourists who visit Alcatraz Island. The political statements that blanket the walls and superstructures of this national park continue to tell a complicated story to thousands of visitors every year. One of the most photographed symbols on the island is an elaborately carved eagle carrying a large shield, located at the entrance to the Administration Building. The seven vertical red stripes on the shield resemble the bars of a jail cell. During their time on Alcatraz, occupiers used paint to transform the red bars into a single word—*FREE*. This one act of defiance offered a powerful critique about American colonization, issues of equality, and the duality of justice for Indigenous peoples. Most Alcatraz Island visitors glance at the shield and may never notice the word *FREE*. American symbols of nationalism are so common that most recognize the symbol before their eyes process the actual image. To see the *truth,* Americans must recognize their own colonization and decolonize their minds to discover freedom. Political slogans found throughout the island transformed the crumbling federal prison into an enormous protest sign. For example, the water tower for Alcatraz Island proclaims "Peace and Freedom, Home of the Free," and the concrete cylinder from the incinerator declares "Freedom, Peace on Earth." Freedom is the most frequent reoccurring message displayed on the isolated rock.

Throughout the 1960s, Native peoples like Richard Oakes challenged concepts of freedom and asked: is freedom granted or inherent? What must change for Native nations to be free? What does a "free" Indian look like? Can Indigenous peoples ever truly be free in America? How does freedom impact Indigenous sovereignty, peoples, and lifeways? For Oakes and other Indigenous men and women in the Red Power movement, the dialogue on freedom dismantled the colonial apparatus and rejected systems that perpetuated oppression. Today, ideas of Indigenous sovereignty and freedom remain an essential component in the process of understanding the modern Indigenous and American experiences. In the Indian City, the strength of Intertribalism sparked the Red Power movement and resulted in one of America's most harrowing and courageous chapters. Richard Oakes remains at the heart of this monumental story of Native resistance and the modern fight for Native nations to reclaim their lands and freedom.

Akwesasne, Kahnawà:ke, and "Little Caughnawaga"

[Akwesasne is] a big reservation, six miles square, with three thousand people and three thousand problems. My growing up was hard, as it is for most Indians. The hopes were there, the promises were there, but the means for achieving them weren't . . .

Richard Oakes, 1972

Thomas Richard Oakes—Ranoies (which means "A Big Man") or Tharih-wasátste ("He Has Strong Beliefs")—better known as Richard George Oakes, an Akwesasne Mohawk of the Bear Clan, was born to Arthur Oakes and Irene Foote on May 22, 1942, on the St. Regis Mohawk Reservation in northern New York.[1] St. Regis, also known as Akwesasne, "the land where the partridge drums its wings," is located between the U.S. and Canadian border along the southern provinces of Ontario and Québec.[2] Akwesasne is the home of the Kanien'kehá:ka (Mohawk) Nation, meaning "People of the Flint," and is a sovereign Nation within the Great Iroquois Confederacy, known collectively as the Haudenosaunee, or "the People of the Longhouse."[3] The reservation comprises twenty-eight thousand acres, including forty-nine islands—the largest being Cornwall Island—within the mighty St. Lawrence River and contains two additional rivers, the St. Regis and the Raquette. The diverse geography is accented by rolling hills and dense foliage, which blend gradually into a center of fertile lowlands containing several water inlets or marshlands. Akwesasne is split by State Highway 37 between the New York towns of Massena to the west and Malone to the east. South of Akwesasne are the lush green Adirondack Mountains. To the north, Akwesasne territory extends sixty miles (composed of 49 islands in the St. Lawrence River) into the Canadian provinces of Ontario and Québec.

Approximately 120 miles east on the Canadian side is Akwesasne's "sister" community, Kahnawà:ke, meaning "By the Rapids." Kahnawà:ke Reserve was formerly called Caughnawaga, an Anglicized and mispronounced colonial title bestowed upon the First Nation. The twelve-thousand-acre reserve moved three times before 1719, when it was located across the St. Lawrence River from the booming Canadian metropolis of Montreal, in the Québec Province.[4] The community, as its meaning suggests, is in every aspect tied to the St. Lawrence River through economy, culture, socialization, and politics. For hundreds of years its uninhibited flow served as the lifeblood of both Mohawk Nations. The geographic division between the two communities occurred in the mid-1700s, when the French established a separate Oswegatchie Mission at Akwesasne to relieve the overcrowded Caughnawaga Mission.[5] While these Nations are both predominantly Mohawk, their mission history points to an Intertribal past, as both communities were made up of minority populations of French, British, Abanaki, Onondaga, and other Iroquoian Nations.[6] Growing up in the Haudenosaunee Confederacy acculturated Oakes to the traditional sensibility of living in an Intertribal world. This Intertribal way of life in Oakes's formative years became a key political component of victories in modern Indian politics. One part of Oakes's Intertribal world was an understanding of the geopolitical borders that divide Haudenosaunee communities.[7] To understand Richard Oakes, we must first understand the environment and world that he was born into and how this world influenced his life as a Native leader.

The center of Haudenosaunee life is the Great Law of Peace, a set of laws that was woven in wampum after the year 1100 by the individual known as the Peacemaker. These laws, or wampum, tie all Nations within the Kaianere'kowa (Longhouse) together, offering shelter and protection to each Nation. As an alliance the Haudenosaunee were a powerhouse of the northeast that relied on successful Iroquois diplomacy that played the French and British off each other in the Seven Years' War. Later the Confederacy refined this power during the American Revolution. The Haudenosaunee, despite constant warfare and the threat of removal, continued to grow. In times of crisis, the Haudenosaunee relied on the teachings and laws from the Great Law of Peace, and the Longhouse flourished throughout the 1800s. Two of the most memorable leaders to emerge in the nineteenth century were Union General Ely S. Parker,

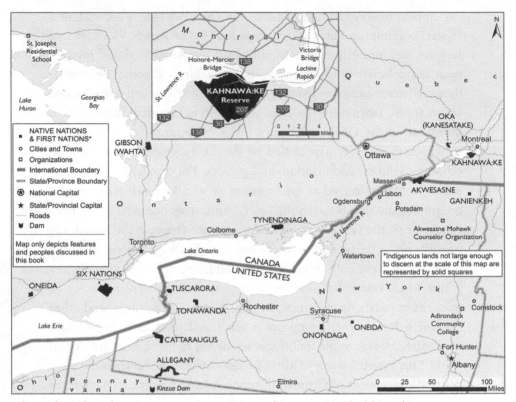

Kahnawà:ke and Northeastern Iroquois Reservations and Reserves. Map by Ed Brands.

Seneca, aide to General Ulysses S. Grant, and his great-nephew, Arthur C. Parker, the famed Seneca anthropologist and a leader in the Society of American Indians (SAI), an Intertribal organization founded in 1911.

By 1918, the Iroquois had independently declared war against Germany and enlisted as allies with both the United States and Canada in World War I.[8] Mohawk peoples served gallantly in both Canadian and American regiments. The Great War would have a lasting and profound effect on Indian Country as a whole. An entire generation of fathers, brothers, and sons as well as intellectuals and future leaders quickly signed up for military service on both sides of the international border. At government-run Indian Schools, almost every male student was recruited or encouraged to enlist for military service.[9] Hundreds of Mohawk women and men worked in ammunition plants or war factories in Toronto and New York City.[10] Many Akwesasne and other Native nations from the American side also enlisted for service in Canada, because America entered the war much later than its northern neighbor.[11] As a result, over seventeen thousand American Indians registered for the draft, of which 55 percent were inducted. This was almost twice as high as the national average for other American populations.[12] The casualties from the war also had a transformative impact on smaller Native communities with a high number of enlistments. A significant number of young Indian men were lost to the battlefields of Europe, and yet many American and Canadian Indians were not even legal citizens of their representative countries. Why did these non-citizen Indians fight for either America or Canada?

Many members of the press and generations of scholars have identified several characteristics in connection with Native people's service in the Great War. These attributes included fearlessness, adventurous spirit, a general disposition for warfare, the extension of Native masculinity through continued warrior societies and traditions, and the identity of noble savage—noble off the battlefield but savage in the face of war. For Mohawks and Haudenosaunee in particular, these attributes were a far cry from their inherent political objectives in the war as allies. Yet, service in the war effort was implicitly tied to Haudenosaunee Nationalism and the protection of treaty rights. Defeat to a foreign power warring against Canada or the United States would have jeopardized the diplomatic interests for all of Indian Country. The Society of American Indians (SAI) relied on the rhetoric of patriotism—on the American Indian's equality with white America. With this rhetoric the battlefields of Europe became a great ideological equalizer—or, as President Woodrow Wilson termed it, "a war to end all wars"—for Indian Country. Arthur C. Parker, first president of SAI, offered a striking definition of wartime Native Nationalism:

> The Indian fights because he loves freedom and because humanity needs the defense of the freedom-loving man. The Indian fights because his country, his liberties, his ideals and his manhood are assailed by the brutal hypocrisy of Prussianism. Challenged, the Indian has responded and shown himself a citizen of the world and an exponent of an ethical civilization wherein human liberty is assured.[13]

Parker's words capture the core issues of the day—Native Nationalist desires, freedom from oppression, equal citizenship in the world, and preservation of treaty rights.

Parker was instrumental in authoring the Iroquois Declaration of War. In 1918, Parker penned a note to fellow Seneca Walter Kennedy in which he asserted that it is "your independent right to act as a Nation and not as a ward-bound tribe that had no powers of a Nation. The Senecas have lost none of their sovereignty since 1812 and a war declaration would serve to emphasize your status."[14] Both quotations point to another understanding of American Indian veterans during the Great War, that protecting America's sovereignty was equal to protecting Indigenous sovereignty/treaty rights—a "double V" campaign (that is, victory abroad is victory at home).

During the war, Mohawk soldiers, like other Native peoples, served in integrated regiments for both Canada and the United States. In addition to serving in the military, many Akwesasne and Kahnawà:ke Mohawk citizens also worked in integrated ammunition plants around Toronto.[15] This was deemed by most contemporary observers to be progressive military policy, despite the mandate that black Americans serve in segregated units. American Indian service in integrated units allowed soldiers to forge unique bonds, to act as ambassadors for their respective Nations, and to establish new Intertribal networks. Those who returned home brought with them a new awareness about Europe, a common bond with other Native veterans, through a shared experience of modern warfare. Many Iroquois who returned home discovered that they were not entitled to military bonuses because they were not legally recognized as citizens of the United States. Through a concerted campaign by Haudenosaunee leaders and the New York press, Iroquois soldiers received their bonuses in 1921.[16] New challenges to Haudenosaunee sovereignty were just around the corner, however, as the 1920s and 1930s gave way to the Indian New Deal. The Iroquois fight for veterans employed a refined and highly organized political tactic, a strategy of Haudenosaunee Nationalism that Richard Oakes would mimic in future occupations.

The Haudenosaunee unilaterally rejected the provisions outlined in the Citizenship Act of 1924 because they wanted to protect their sovereign status as an Indigenous nation. Iroquois feared that approval of the measure translated into an acceptance of a federal control over their lives.

Haudenosaunee leaders believed that a vote in favor of the act might also grant the U.S. government the authority to revoke federal trust responsibilities with the Six Nations. Growing frustrations over this debate flourished in 1934, as John Collier, Commissioner of Indian Affairs, was able to get his "ground breaking" Indian Reorganization Act (IRA) passed by Congress.[17] Arguably it was one of the most significant pieces of Indian policy passed in the twentieth century. For Richard Oakes's parents and grandparents the fight against the IRA quickly evolved into the central issue in Akwesasne politics. This act called for an end to the old allotment policies under the Dawes Act of 1887; it also advocated that a restricted measure of home rule be restored to Native nations through a referendum.[18] Akwesasne would act as the epicenter for the Iroquois campaign against the IRA, as it was scheduled to be the first Haudenosaunee community to vote on the act.

Collier's understanding of Haudenosaunee opposition to the Citizenship Act led him to enlist the help of Ho-Chunk citizen Henry Roe Cloud, who later served as superintendent of the Haskell Institute; anthropologist and Indian Service community worker William N. Fenton; and W. K. Harrison, New York's Colonial Agent. All of them conducted meetings to explain the provisions of the IRA at Akwesasne. As a Nation, Akwesasne is made up of three governments: the traditional Life Chiefs of the Longhouse; the New York state–sponsored Akwesasne Tribal "elected" Council/Chiefs (chosen by only a quarter of the population); and a separate Mohawk government, called the St. Regis Band Council, on Cornwall Island to deal with Canadian affairs.[19] On the opposite side of the forty-fifth parallel, the Mohawk of St. Regis, the Canadian name for the Reserve, was divided further between the traditional Life Chiefs (appointed by Clan Mothers) and the "band council" popularly elected by the terms of the Indian Act (1876).

The transnational politics of Akwasasne consistently reinforced the importance of protecting the traditional Longhouse government. Through solidarity and Intertribalism, Akwesasne Mohawk citizens could overcome the policies of two colonial governments. Well before the IRA, Akwesasne had a long history of resistance against any federal control over their lives. The Canadian Indian Act of 1876, which had four main parts, had a direct impact on Richard's family, as his mother Irene Foote was from the Canadian side and his father Arthur Oakes the American side of Akwesasne. First, the act defined who was Indian. Women who

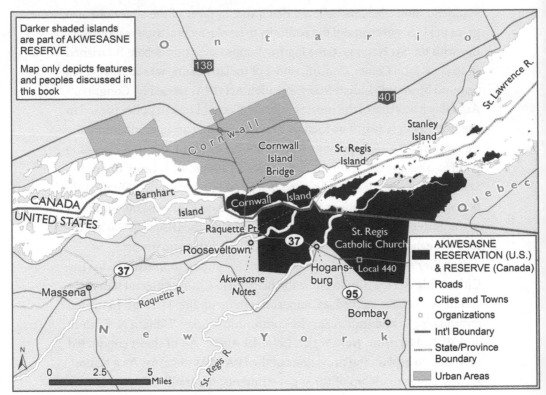

Akwesasne (St. Regis) Mohawk Reservation and Reserve. Map by Ed Brands.

"married outside" (that is, married other nationalities outside the Reserve) were denied status/identity as a "Canadian" Indian, yet for Native men, it worked the other way around. This gendered part of the act attacked the institution of the Haudenosaunee family through citizenship. It robbed Iroquois women of their freedom of choice, despite their prestigious Clan Mother status. Next, this legislation established a system of services for the Reserve, mainly rooted in education. Third, the act called for a formalized system to manage Native lands and resources. Finally, the most disruptive measure of the Indian Act allowed for Canadian provincial governments to abrogate Indigenous treaty rights.[20] Since its inception, Indigenous leaders and Akwesasne citizens in particular have debated the prospects of repealing the Indian Act.

Fittingly, Richard Oakes once described the politics at Akwesasne as "a big reservation, six miles square, with three thousand people and three thousand problems. My growing up was hard, as it is for most Indians. The hopes were there, the promises were there, but the means for achieving them weren't."[21] Oakes's statement hints at the complexity of Akwesasne politics and identifies their unique political reality as a sovereign in constant negotiations of their independence between two colonial governments and policies. From the 1890s to the 1930s, despite these very real challenges, Akwesasne Nationalists remained highly organized against colonial threats to their sovereignty.

In the 1890s, this legislation pushed the Canadian side of Akwesasne to revolt. Mohawk Clan Mothers wrote to the governor general on June 2, 1899, and explained that Akwesasne refused the governance provisions of the Indian Act in favor of their traditional government:

> We have considered the elective system as not being intended
> for us Indians, and we would therefore return to our old method
> of selecting our life chiefs, according to our Constitutional
> Iroquois Government. As Your Excellency must know, the
> ancient custom of creating life chiefs is that they are selected
> according to the different clans, there being three from each
> clan, and also three women who select her special chief from
> among her clan. Of these chiefs, one is considered the head
> chief, the second is "the big man" and the third is the "crier." As
> there is four distinct clans, there is twelve life chiefs, who hold
> their office for life.[22]

This announcement met with fierce resistance from Canadian authorities. Dominion Police were sent to the Québec side of Akwesasne to force an election of an Indian Act band council. Over two hundred Akwesasne protested against the election, confiscating arms from the Dominion Police and placing the Colonial Agent George Long under house arrest at the schoolhouse. Embarrassed by their defeat, Canadian officials mounted a devastating counter-strategy by secretly arresting the Life Chiefs. It is important to note that after the public execution of Métis leader Louis Riel in 1885, Ottawa remained in a constant state of paranoia in reaction to any whispers of rebellion among First Nations.

On May 1, 1899, Colonial Agent Long sent word that he wanted to meet with the Rotinonkwiseres (which translates to "They Have Long Hair") or Life Chiefs about job opportunities and community matters.

Upon their arrival at the agent's office, a large police force headed by Lieutenant-Colonel Percy Sherwood served arrest warrants on the unsuspecting Mohawk diplomats. Saiowisakeron ("The Ice Is Floating By"; also known as "Jake Ice"), a traditional follower of the Longhouse, had heard about the arrests, as news quickly spread throughout the Reserve. Ice, a brother of one of the Life Chiefs known as Ohnehtotako ("Pine Tar") was well respected in the town of Kanatakon. Ice and his wife Two Blankets had only recently invested some of his earnings to construct a new schoolhouse for the community. He was met by Colonel Sherwood, who in the struggle shot the unarmed Jake Ice twice in the chest, killing him instantly. All of this occurred without any protest from the other police or George Long, the Colonial Agent on site.

Towns close to Akwesasne wrote scathing editorials denouncing the police action and the Indian Act. The Life Chiefs arrested by provincial police were held in the Beauharnois jail for over a year before facing trial. Beyond serving a long-term jail sentence without trial, the majority were released except for two to three individuals who were to stand trial as examples for challenging colonial authority. The Life Chiefs ordered to stand trial were forced to pay for their prosecution and defense. Each of the defendants was set free with further warnings. The agent eventually gathered a few individuals to hold a mock election, and the first twelve chiefs of the band council were elected. For Akwesasne, the memory and story about the imprisonment of Akwesasne Life Chiefs and the murder of Jake Ice would always remain connected to the band council and the Indian Act.[23]

By the 1930s, leaders at Akwesasne were well aware of the devastating impact of the Canadian Indian Act, and this facilitated powerful suspicions about the long-term effects of the American policy as outlined under the Indian Reorganization Act. Caught between geopolitical borders, Akwesasne retains three different forms of representative government as established by Haudenosaunee, Canadian, and U.S. policies.[24] Historically, this complex assortment of competing colonial and traditional forms of governance has attempted to undermine and divide the overall political authority of Akwesasne. As a territory it straddles both the Canadian and American border. The borderland location is advantageous in some respects. Rival external laws and systems between borders have forced the community to rely more extensively on their traditional government. The competing colonial governments established by federal policies and borders were forged as a direct assault upon Akwesasne's sovereignty. Based on sheer numbers alone, Mohawk citizens minimized the power of these competing modes of colonial governance by limiting the power of the franchise (voting) and gradually redirecting policy/ enforcement matters toward the consensus politic of traditional Life Chiefs.[25] More distinctly, the band council is elected by the Akwesasne populace, a power held exclusively by the people. At Akwesasne the band council is held in check by the governance of the people and by competing American and Canadian systems.[26]

Despite Canada's Indian Act and the threat of the Indian Reorganization Act, Akwesasne leaders employed the power of the vote in order to reject the relinquishing of any further federal controls over their lives. On June 8, 1935, acceptance or rejection of the IRA came down to a vote. Akwesasne women representing the views of the Longhouse gathered together at the polls to let their voices and opinions be heard. As the crowd of mothers and daughters came together, they attempted to confiscate the ballot boxes from Foresters' Hall and the Mohawk Indian School in Hogansburg. In all, out of 800 eligible Mohawk voters, about 517 refused to vote. This offered clear proof that Akwesasne women, like the traditional Clan Mothers, continued to hold the ultimate veto in political matters. Richard Oakes was raised in a community of strong and politically active women in a Native nation that honored a woman's political convictions and voice.

At the end of the day, only forty-seven people had voted for the act, and about two hundred and thirty-seven had rejected it. Many Mohawk citizens regarded voting on a federal act as tacit acceptance of colonial citizenship and a federal mandate over their lives. On both sides of the border, Mohawk peoples solidified their sovereignty by outright refusal to vote in national elections in Canada and the United States.[27] The political activism of Akwesasne women inspired a showing of solidarity, as all Haudenosaunee Nations within New York followed their lead in rejecting the IRA. In the end, Collier was dismayed by the vote, but he respected the Iroquois view of home rule by not forcing the Haudenosaunee to accept the act by default.[28]

By 1933 the United States was at the height of the Great Depression. Over 40 million Americans found themselves out of work, and the national unemployment rate had reached a staggering high of 29 percent.[29] At this moment, Richard Oakes's parents, Irene Foote and Arthur Oakes, made calculated decisions for their physical and economic survival.

Richard's parents grew up on Cornwall Island, a location that is literally bisected by the U.S./Canadian border. His father, Arthur Richard Oakes, the son of Richard and Margaret (née Brown) Oakes, was born in 1920.[30] Arthur attended the St. Regis Island School before moving to Buffalo, New York, in the 1930s. Arthur Oakes continued his education in the New York public school system, earning his diploma from Central High School in Syracuse, New York. His future wife, Irene Foote, also born in 1920, was the daughter of Thomas and Cecile (née Sharrow) Foote. Her father, Tom Foote, had been a star lacrosse athlete on the celebrated Cornwall Island Indians lacrosse team, known widely as the "Islanders," from 1918 to 1935. Summer lacrosse ultimately became a major pastime in Canada.[31] At an early age, while her father endured an intense lacrosse schedule, Irene's parents enrolled her in the Sisters of Mercy Indian Girls Industrial School managed under the Bureau of Catholic Indian Missions on the American side of the reservation. Originally founded in 1880, by 1903 the boarding school situated in a small off-reservation border town of Bombay, New York, had become a federal Indian boarding school.[32] While attending the small school, which was managed by six Catholic nuns, Richard Oakes's mother received training related to managing a household economy. The school numbered around fifty students and trained Mohawk girls to become efficient housewives and domestic laborers. By 1932, Irene and her three siblings transferred to the St. Joseph Indian Residential School in Spanish, Ontario. The school was divided by gender into two separate campuses. The girls' dormitory, where Irene and her sisters lived, was managed by nuns of the Jesuit organization the Daughters of the Heart of Mary. Irene's brother William (Bill) Foote, who attended the school from 1932 to 1940, described the harsh abuse that many of the kids at the Residential School faced: "They called us little heathens, pagans, savages and ignorant. . . . Every night [Father Bleu] would come and get another boy and taken him into his bed. . . . We were all being physically assaulted and battered by the staff, which included being stripped and then beaten. They would pull our hair, our ears, and hit us with leather straps made out of horse harnesses and sticks." The actual numbers of First Nation children who died from abuse or neglect in Canadian Residential Schools remains unknown, but conservative estimates have placed the tally at over four thousand children. Over 150 girls attended St. Joseph and lived in an entirely separate dorm. Little is known about their experiences at this isolated school, which was located near the shore of Lake Michigan. One survival story about the student experience reveals how regularly the girls snuck out of their dorm at night to hold secret powwows, speak their Indigenous languages, and share Intertribal dances and songs to the muffled beat of an overturned metal pail.[33]

When the Indian Act was amended in 1927, it required all First Nations children between the ages of seven and fifteen to attend a Residential School. Considering that Irene Foote and her three younger siblings were all born on the Canadian side of Akwesasne, it is very plausible that this 1927 amendment to the Indian Act precipitated their arrival at St. Joseph after 1930.[34] It is also possible that the Bureau of Catholic Indian Mission school had closed its doors in Bombay, New York, due to lack of funds. It was hard enough for most families to survive the economic downturn, but most children never experienced the severe trials of life at a Residential School that the Foote and Oakes families endured.

At the height of these most trying times, Americans questioned whether their country would survive. Akwesasne felt the full force of the Depression's impact. In nearby Massena, the aluminum plant first laid off Mohawk workers in a string of layoffs. Akwesasne's main sources of income, farming and dairy cattle, sturgeon fishing, and the Mohawk Lacrosse Stick Manufacturing Company, saw the futures market slide to a near halt. The Mohawk Lacrosse Stick Manufacturing Company on Cornwall Island employed a number of Mohawk men and women laborers—as lacrosse evolved into a national sport in Canada with eventual inroads in America as well. The Great Depression saw the rise in popularity of box lacrosse via amateur teams. Founded by Frank and Alex Roundpoint along with Scottish teacher Colin Chisholm, the Mohawk Lacrosse Stick Manufacturing Company offered direct competition with the Lally Factory located directly across from Akwesasne in Cornwall, Ontario. Mohawk stick makers traveled long distances to harvest wood from forty-year-old hickory trees—allowing the wood to cure for several months before carefully steam-bending each individual stick. Mohawk women often took home bundles of lacrosse sticks to lace them with leather webbing. By the 1960s the factory at Akwesasne was manufacturing 95 to 97 percent of all wood lacrosse sticks in the world.

During prohibition both Akwesasne and Kahnawà:ke served as smuggling centers for organized crime bosses in New York City. In addition to the multiple dangers inherent in bootlegging liquor from Canada into the United States, the job provided unstable employment and to only a few.[35] Fewer and fewer white people had expendable money to purchase the exquisite Mohawk beadwork or locally manufactured lacrosse sticks that the Tribes' economy depended upon. Jobs became scarce, and survival began to dominate the actions of many American Indians. The Emergency Conservation Work Act of 1933 created the Indian Division of the Civilian Conservation Corps (CCC-ID). In the beginning, the Haudenosaunee did not support New Deal programs, and the Canadian side of Akwesasne refused to support CCC-ID projects for fear of future flood damage.

Despite community and international objections, the CCC-ID called for three massive building projects—the West Ditch along the St. Regis River in 1935; the Frogtown Ditch, half completed by 1936; and the East Ditch, some one-and-a-half miles long, that linked to the St. Regis River. These projects were created to drain the flooded marshlands located in the center of the reservation, opening them for future development by the Mohawk. The CCC-ID work employed a total of one-quarter of Akwesasne's available workforce or roughly 300 out of 1,219 Mohawk citizens.[36] Along with government assistance in employment, the Indian New Deal championed educational opportunities for Mohawk youth.

In the mid- to late 1930s Mohawk educator Ray Fadden (Aren Akweks or Tehanetorens) founded a new organization called the Akwesasne Mohawk Counselor Organization (AMCO). The efforts of Fadden and others in AMCO to impart traditional teachings and Mohawk culture provided future Iroquois leaders like Richard Oakes an opportunity to be proud, informed, and grounded in their traditions. Fadden's commitment to American Indian and Iroquois education was dynamic and contagious. His first teaching job at the Tuscarora Indian School on the Tuscarora Reservation (located not far from Niagara Falls) lasted for three years. After leaving the Tuscarora Indian School, Fadden was employed by the Mohawk Indian School. At Akwesasne most of the schools were located off the reservation with Mohawk children divided between multiple schools on the U.S.

and Canadian sides. In addition to breaking up the Mohawk family (by removing children from their families), such policies promoted disunity among the subsequent Mohawk generations. These schools included the St. Joseph Residential Schools; the Indian Girls Industrial School; Thomas Indian School; Mohawk Institute Residential School; Carlisle Indian Industrial School; Massena High School; St. Regis Mohawk School; Salmon River Central (which Richard Oakes was rumored to have attended); Cornwall Island High School; Cornwall Island Elementary; Chenial, Québec Elementary; and St. Regis, Québec Elementary.[37] Although many of these schools were located on or near Akwesasne, the non-Indian community exclusively controlled their administrations. Much of the curriculum taught to young Mohawks, as Ray Fadden discovered, ignored Mohawk and Native cultures, language, and histories. As a Mohawk teacher, Fadden challenged these constructs when he created the Akwesasne Mohawk Counselor Organization. It was a bold attempt at a new form of Indian education, one administered and controlled by the community.

Patterned after the Boy Scouts of America, AMCO fostered a uniquely Haudenosaunee learning environment. Fadden stressed that this "organization is the first of its kind and was organized to train young Indian boys and girls in the history, traditions and crafts of their people, the Six Nations of Iroquois of New York state and Canada."[38] Fadden aggressively sought to foster an Intertribal awareness among the membership, traveling to local and distant Indian communities, such as Qualla Boundary (Eastern Cherokee Reservation, North Carolina) or the Six Nations Reserve in Canada. Each of these trips, which coincided with Indigenous guest lecturers from Crow, Lakota, Tuscarora, Narragansett, Anishinaabe, Seneca, and other Tribes, were scheduled to inspire its young participants. Tours of educational centers like Carlisle Indian School and Dartmouth revealed the varying lengths Fadden explored to promote Indian education. Future Iroquois leaders like Mohawk Ernest Benedict and Tuscarora Mad Bear Anderson learned under Fadden's tutelage and AMCO. By the early 1970s, Mad Bear Anderson became a teacher, confidant, and traditional guide for Richard Oakes in the White Roots of Peace movement.

By the late 1930s, impressed by the success and strategy of AMCO, future Commissioner of Indian Affairs Louis R. Bruce Jr., a Mohawk and Lakota citizen, created an Iroquois branch of the National Youth

Administration (NYA) under the Works Progress Administration (WPA). An extension of AMCO, the NYA had federal funding and employed Iroquois youth to build trails, parks, and new reservation community centers. Encouraged by Fadden's design, Bruce employed camp counselors to act as role models for younger camp members. Many of these camp counselors were already counselors under AMCO. Summer camp was headquartered out of Fadden's camp retreat, which was located in the Adirondack Mountains. Together both organizations encouraged the collection of oral history, the study of Native medicine and arts, language revitalization, an appreciation for the outdoors, and a solid knowledge of Tribal governance and treaty rights. Although the government phased out the NYA due to lack of funding during the Second World War, AMCO continued to inspire and enlighten future generations of American Indian educators.[39]

One of the most significant New Deal agencies to impact both Akwesasne and Kahnawà:ke during the Indian New Deal was the Works Progress Administration. The WPA provided much needed employment, despite borders at Akwesasne and Kahnawà:ke. In the beginning, Kahnawà:ke and the Canadian side of Akwesasne residents were excluded from participation in American New Deal programs. Through pressures exerted by lawyers and the press, President Franklin Delano Roosevelt and his administration buckled under the pressure. By 1940, "Canadian" Mohawk were allowed to participate fully in all New Deal programs.[40] This decision established an important precedent because it acknowledged that despite the geopolitical border and reserve/reservation boundaries, Mohawk are Mohawk and are also an independent Nation with different borders. Out of the WPA building projects, Akwesasne and Kahnawà:ke Mohawk laborers forged a unique bond in their WPA days that was born out of a shared profession—ironwork—that employed a young Richard Oakes as well as his father and uncles before him, and it was this labor that molded his ideas of organization, structure, detail, perseverance, and leadership.

As an industry and an occupation, ironwork completely transformed the political economy of both Akwesasne and Kahnawà:ke. Its beginnings can be traced back to the mid-nineteenth century when, in 1851, Kahnawà:ke Mohawk men were first trained and employed to construct the Victoria Bridge, a timber-framed railroad bridge across the St. Lawrence near Montreal. While construction of the bridge brought to a halt the once-prosperous steamboat trade at Kahnawà:ke, it was soon replaced by bridgework and, later, ironwork. As iron bridges increasingly replaced timber frames, Mohawk laborers quickly adapted and learned this new trade. By the late 1880s, Kahnawà:ke agreed to a new iron-framed railroad bridge to be constructed on reserve lands. The agreement with Dominion Bridge Company called for the employment of local Mohawk men for the completion of the bridge. These crews were then trained onsite during the construction of the new iron-clad bridge. With each new contract through Dominion, Kahnawà:ke Mohawk crews trained more and more Mohawk men in ironwork.[41]

The date August 29, 1907, will forever remain a tragic moment in the history of Kahnawà:ke. On opposite sides of the Reserve, still visible today, stand two large steel crosses built to memorialize what became known as the Quebec Bridge Disaster. Work on the bridge, designed to stretch out across the St. Lawrence River as the largest cantilever span in the world, began in 1900.[42] Work came to a halt on the bridge for a short time in 1907 as inspectors noticed that the steel beams were beginning to twist under the enormous weight of the expanse. Workers like Tom Deerhorse and Harold Diebold, members of Kahnawà:ke's famed lacrosse team, eagerly resumed work when the stop-work order was lifted in August. A young "punk," a rookie recruit just learning the trade, John Montour (Kahnawà:ke Mohawk) remembered, "Everything was going OK when suddenly I could hear the sounds of the rivet heads shearing and popping like gun fire. Then there was this tremor like an earthquake and a roar. Then this bad grinding sound and a thunder as the bridge fell into the water."[43] The mass entanglement of steel and men fell into the St. Lawrence. Shock waves and screams were heard from residents at Kahnawà:ke as members of the community gathered around the Reserve's only phone at the community store. Loved ones ran to the inhuman scene of twisted metal and the terrified voices of loved ones still trapped below. A priest was called to the scene to administer last rites, as the tide slowly began to rise, drowning the few remaining survivors. After this horrific incident, which claimed the lives of ninety-six workers (including thirty-three Kahnawà:ke Mohawk citizens), women in the community gathered with Kahnawà:ke Clan Mothers and instituted a new community directive. In an effort to avoid future disasters, all Mohawk ironworkers were prohibited from working the same construction site.

The loss of the thirty-three men on the Quebec Bridge Disaster impacted every facet of the small community as wives lost husbands, mothers lost sons, and children lost fathers and uncles. The tragic disaster forced Kahnawà:ke citizens to come to grips with their commitment to the profession and true risk with ironwork. Eventually, in an effort to increase their numbers, Kahnawà:ke ironworking veterans began to recruit and train their relatives at Akwesasne in the trade. By the 1920s, ironwork saw a boom with the development of the skyscraper. The Roaring Twenties ushered in a dynamic growth spurt in New York's famed skyline, and Mohawk peoples represented a sizable percentage of the ironworkers recruited for such undertakings. Mohawk citizens, especially those from Kahnawà:ke, found themselves caught between an economic boom and America's rampant nativism and obsession with scientific eugenics. As a movement, nativism strove to set limits on immigration to preserve a larger proportion of Anglo-Saxons in America. Much of this movement stemmed from a growing fascination and genetic determinism that strove to use the study of science to position the Anglo-Saxon race as the "superior" race in a hierarchy of races.[44] As these political movements garnered national attention, evidenced by the national immigration acts passed in 1921 and 1924, Kahnawà:ke faced a new legal challenge about their employment in America.

In a shocking turn of events, Kahnawà:ke Paul Kanesto Diabo and his family were cited as illegal aliens and deported to Canada. Mohawk citizens quickly rallied behind the Diabo family, determined to press for their legal rights to work across the border, a freedom established by the Jay and Ghent treaties of 1794 and 1814, respectively. The legal case, managed by a top team of Philadelphia lawyers, challenged the very constructs of not only the 1924 Citizenship Act for American Indians but also of the 1921 and 1924 Immigration Acts, which established further restrictions and quotas on U.S. citizenship. Founded only one year prior to Diabo's arrest in February of 1925, this case captured the attention of the Indian Defense League of America, which was led by Tuscarora leader Clinton Rickard and Mohawk David Hill.[45] Soon Mohawk workers and the Indian Defense League of America rallied behind the Diabo family, determined to press their legal right to work without restriction across the international border as outlined under both the Jay and Ghent treaties. Ironworkers pulled all their money together in order to build a defense fund for Diabo's mounting lawyer fees. Akwesasne and Onondaga Nations both contributed funds and engaged in fundraising for Diabo's defense. Ironworkers pulled their money together to create a defense fund for Diabo's lawyer fees. Mohawk ironworkers donated approximately one-quarter of their earnings to support the case. Diabo's case went before a federal court, which overturned Diabo's illegal alien status and supported the provisions of the Jay Treaty of 1794.[46] The U.S. Immigration Department appealed the case to the Circuit Court level, and once again, on March 9, 1928, the court ruled that Mohawks have the right to free passage across the border. Judges Buffington, Woolley, and Davis backed the lower court's decision, stating that the "Mohawk nation was a 'separate dependent nation,' separate from and dependent on both Canada and the United States."[47] More importantly, the court echoed Chief Justice John Marshall's famed opinion in *Worcester v. Georgia* (1832), stressing that Kahnawà:ke remained a nation within a nation bound by treaties, impervious to the geopolitical borders between the United States and Canada. This was a significant legal victory for Mohawk ironworkers during a growing fervor of American nativism; the verdict forever linked the Mohawk ironwork trade to the protection of Iroquois sovereignty and treaty rights. Increased Iroquois participation in the occupation of ironwork became an extension of enforcing one's collective and individual political rights as representatives of a sovereign Native nation.[48] The victory in the Diabo case worked its way into the oral tradition of Mohawk ironworkers and possibly influenced young Richard Oakes's fascination with the trade.

Having won a decisive victory in the courts, during the 1920s and 1930s Kahnawà:ke and Akwesasne Nations found that employment and wages in ironwork remained increasingly steady. Mohawk crews worked alongside others to create the modern marvels that set Manhattan's famed skyline apart to this day: the Fred F. French Building, Graybar Building, One Fifth Avenue, Empire State Building, Bank of Manhattan building, RCA Building, Chrysler Building, Waldorf-Astoria Hotel, Rockefeller Center, Triborough Bridge, Bayonne Bridge, Pulaski Skyway, Henry Hudson Bridge, George Washington Bridge, and the Bronx-Whitestone Bridge.[49] Ironworkers used to joke that the first meal at the luxurious Waldorf-Astoria Hotel was enjoyed by Mohawk steel workers during their lunch break. Some of the greatest photographs of ironworkers dangling from solitary beams at extreme heights featured Mohawk men.

Work in the high steel industry is one of the most dangerous professions and, consequently, one of the highest-paid.[50] Mohawk men were
attracted to this trade not because of any "superhuman ability" but rather
because few people applied for this dangerous work, thus leaving a large
job market open to them.[51] Randy Horn from Kahnawà:ke commented on
the danger: "The height didn't even bother me. . . . I could go a hundred
and twenty at the time; you think twice now when you're walking on the
steel, walking on the steel with the wind . . . some gusts . . . could throw
you right off . . . suddenly the wind picks up and you just try to balance
yourself. You would have to jump from the top of the beam onto the
bottom of the beam and grab the top and hold on . . . you crouch down
and you grab the flanges of the beam so you won't fall off, and when the
wind dies down you get back up and keep going."[52] Ironworkers had to
adjust to an occupation that required them to deal with the anxiety of
injury or instant death. Every day a worker left home, his family was
constantly reminded that it might be the last time they would ever see
their husband, father, son, or brother. It was an anxiety that created a
bond between families and ironworkers, an unspoken silence that was
acknowledged in the community. When tragedy did occur, Mohawk families and ironworkers came together and raised funds for the victims'
families. At Indian bars in New York, workers held wakes and drank in
silence to honor the fallen. Each ironworker had to contend with the
concrete realities of life and death in this occupation.

By the 1930s, Mohawk ironworkers had constructed some of the
most famous buildings of the Manhattan skyline. These jobs, along with
the CCC-ID, the WPA, and the NYA, transformed the community and
allowed Akwesasne and Kahnawà:ke to survive the depths of the Great
Depression. Ironwork in New York also gave way to the creation of an
Indian City within North Gowanus, Brooklyn. Since Mohawk peoples
wanted to live beside other Mohawk, they formed their own Mohawk City
in Astoria, Queens. By 1922, the community relocated from Queens to
Brooklyn due to its easy commute into Manhattan and closer proximity to
employment opportunities. Eventually this largely Mohawk City would
earn the nickname "Downtown Caughnawaga" or "Little Caughnawaga."[53]

Mohawk peoples also settled in Brooklyn because of its proximity to
Ironworkers Local 361 of the International Association of Bridge,
Structural, Ornamental, and Reinforcing Iron Workers. This was

comprised mostly of Akwesasne and Kahnawà:ke ironworkers. The Union Hall itself became the center of Mohawk life, likened to a "Longhouse" in Brooklyn.⁵⁴ One of the most significant annual events occurred at the Ironworkers Ball, often held at the opulent Manhattan Center. The event drew the Mayor of New York, and hundreds of single Mohawk women traveled from Akwesasne and Kahnawà:ke for the ball. Back at Akwesasne, most ironworkers were also members of the Local 440, which was based in Hogansburg. Ironworkers were an increasingly migratory community; families often moved back and forth between the Indian City and their home communities upstate. Children who came back in the summers were often referred to as "Brooklyn Bums," a title that Richard Oakes had to contend with at a young age as his family often moved between Akwesasne and Brooklyn.

The Mohawk population in Brooklyn had always remained high. At its peak the Mohawk population in the 1940s was over seven hundred.⁵⁵ By the 1970s, the total American Indian population in New York City was estimated at ten to twelve thousand people.⁵⁶ For over fifty years, Mohawks created and maintained a distinctly Mohawk neighborhood that stretched across "Nevins, Dean, State, Schermerhorn, Hoyt, Smith and Bond Streets" and "along Pacific Street, Fourth Avenue and Sixth and Seventh Avenues."⁵⁷ This area of North Gowanus, now known as Boerum Hill or Red Hook, was comprised of ten square blocks of primarily Mohawk residents. The streets that connected this Mohawk City also connected a young Richard Oakes to his heritage. Joseph Mitchell's essay in Edmund Wilson's book *Apologies to the Iroquois* captures a brief, eloquent description of the area: "North Gowanus is an old, sleepy, shabby neighborhood. . . . There are factories in it, and coal tipples and junk yards, but it is primarily residential, and red-brick tenements and brownstone apartment houses are most numerous."⁵⁸ Tom LeClair from Kahnawà:ke remembered his first visit to Brooklyn thus: "When I was 19 years old, in 1966, I came to State Street. It was the best. It was the most beautiful place in the world."⁵⁹ Like previous immigrant groups, other Mohawk thought New York City would be made out of gold. Those expectations failed to last long, but the community was a transplant from their homelands. Myrtle Bush stated that Mohawk citizens differed from immigrants as the "need was to leave the reservation to bring back a better way of life. We want to take out and bring back."⁶⁰ Out of this bustling community,

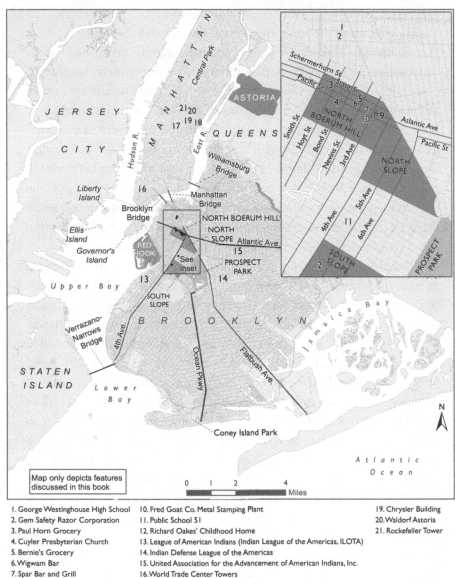

1. George Westinghouse High School
2. Gem Safety Razor Corporation
3. Paul Horn Grocery
4. Cuyler Presbyterian Church
5. Bernie's Grocery
6. Wigwam Bar
7. Spar Bar and Grill
8. Doray Tavern
9. Brooklyn Local 361
10. Fred Goat Co. Metal Stamping Plant
11. Public School 51
12. Richard Oakes' Childhood Home
13. League of American Indians (Indian League of the Americas, ILOTA)
14. Indian Defense League of the Americas
15. United Association for the Advancement of American Indians, Inc.
16. World Trade Center Towers
17. Empire State Building
18. United Nations
19. Chrysler Building
20. Waldorf Astoria
21. Rockefeller Tower

Brooklyn Mohawk City. Map by Ed Brands.

Mohawk peoples formed their own organizations, institutions, businesses, and centers that became the foundations for a unique Mohawk Indian City.

Indian bars were one of the first institutions of the Indian City in Brooklyn: examples included the Wigwam Bar on Nevins Street, the Spar Bar and Grill on Nevins Street and Atlantic Avenue, and Doray Tavern in Boerum Hill. The Wigwam was owned by Kahnawà:ke Mohawk Irene Vilis. Her husband, Manuel Vilis, who was a veteran of the Normandy invasion of World War II, purchased the bar shortly after his discharge from service. The bar was often smoky and dimly lit and hosted a jukebox in the corner. The walls were decorated with the posters of famous Indian leaders, including a large poster of renowned Sac and Fox athlete Jim Thorpe. Above the entrance a sign read, "THE GREATEST IRON WORKERS IN THE WORLD PASS THRU THESE DOORS."[61] One wall also contained the hard hats— likened to a modern Gustoweh (the Haudenosaunee headdress)—of those who had lost their lives while on the job.[62] It was a vivid memorial that served as a constant reminder about life and danger within the industry. The bar was also a place where ironworkers could relax, kick back, cash paychecks, find rides back home, and tell stories of their adventures.

For many, Indian bars were the social hub of the community, a place to gather information, talk politics, and find affordable solutions for urban life in Brooklyn. By the early 1950s, the Spar Bar and Grill, located at 491 Atlantic Avenue, was managed by Kahnawà:ke Josephine Diabo, well known throughout the community for cooking exclusively Mohawk meals on Sunday evenings. Many of these meals of home consisted of cornbread and steaks, meat pies, or corn soup. The Spar Bar and Grill frequently pulsed with life in the evenings and nights, including lively conversations spoken in both Mohawk and English. Over this bar hung drawings of famous Lakota peace and war leaders, and by the early 1960s a portrait of John F. Kennedy also graced a wall of prominence beneath an elaborately carved Northwest Coast crest pole.[63] One floor up from the bar, the owners always had six beds available for rent to ironworkers. Clearly, the Spar Bar and Gill served as another type of institution, one that echoed the political aspirations and commitments of its loyal clientele.

These serene moments at the Wigwam or Spar Bar were sometimes interrupted by fights. In 1946, the *New York Times* reported the death of one Mohawk ironworker, Stephen Staceys, outside of Tom's Cafeteria on Nevins Street. The short article referenced the negative forces that sometimes emerge with bar culture: "A dozen men, chiefly Mohawks, were in the brawl, throwing sugar bowls, crockery, glassware and chairs, the police said. Angus Deerhouse of 459 Pacific Street saw Staceys collapse, led him outside and got help, but it came too late."[64] While this episode was rare, bar fights did occur on occasion. Many fights were led by competing factions of Mohawk riveting gangs, each working to secure the next job contract.

Some memories of the bar were fondly recalled by the children, many of whom were sent by their mothers to fetch their dads at suppertime. Future Mohawk and Native activist Kahentinetha Horn reflected on her childhood and the bar:

> We used to live on the third floor, of this tenement, and it was right across from the Wigwam Bar. My mother would tell us, "you know to watch to see what was happening." If there was a big outburst of screaming and hollering we'd go look to see if our father was a part of it, and they would come rolling out of there and land right out on the sidewalk. Then we would watch, it was a lot of fun. We didn't have television in those days—we eventually got a television but it was never as interesting as what was going on at the Wigwam Bar.

Horn's remembrance pinpoints a key factor in how the Mohawk community viewed the bar culture. The bar culture was not a progenitor of self-destructive behavior as such. Nor was it necessarily the promoter of habitual alcohol abuse. Rather, the emphasis was on entertainment. The Spar, Wigwam, and Doray stocked a particular Montreal ale as a way to reinforce the substantial Kahnawà:ke ties to Canada. The Indian bars served another function, namely as a place for dating. Couples on date night were able to go dancing, listen to stories from those who had recently returned from Akwesasne or Kahnawà:ke, and enjoy a drink reminiscent of home.[65]

Beyond the Indian bars, Mohawk peoples assumed a large presence in the community, and their presence began to transform the tiny district. On Sundays, a majority of the Mohawk citizens in Brooklyn frequented Cuyler Presbyterian Church on Pacific Street. On one Sunday, Dr. David

Monroe Cory, the minister of Cuyler Presbyterian, overheard the Mohawk language being spoken by members of the congregation. Dr. Cory began to take language lessons from members of the Mohawk community; he eventually hosted church services exclusively in the Mohawk language. Despite the Catholic faith of the community, Mohawk citizens began to fill up the pews of Cuyler Presbyterian by the hundreds. The minister hosted an annual powwow and even went so far as to challenge the non-Indian church opinions. As an institution of the larger Indian City, Cuyler Presbyterian quickly became assimilated into Mohawk custom and culture. The church became more than a place of worship or a gathering place for Mohawk families; it emerged as an institution that promoted the continued use and practice of the Mohawk language. Like so many of their generation, Richard and his brother Leonard Oakes never became fluent in the Mohawk language, even though they had been raised by an older generation of Mohawk residential and boarding school graduates who struggled to keep the language alive. Several Mohawk parents refused to teach their children the language out of a fear that their own children would confront discrimination in American schools or that the language might hinder access to equal educational opportunities in English-speaking schools.[66]

Local grocery stores also met community needs. A shop called "Bernie's," on Atlantic near Nevins, and Kahnawà:ke Paul Horn's family-owned store carried a specific brand of cornmeal, "Quaker White Enriched and Degerminated Cornmeal," that could be used to make a traditional *kanata* (a boiled corn and bean bread often served as a side dish to steak or sausages). This particular cornmeal was also a primary ingredient for making *onensto* (corn soup). Every grocery store competed for Mohawk business; eventually, every Gowanus store carried this partic-ular brand of cornmeal.[67]

Beyond fulfilling their traditional matriarchal roles, Mohawk women quickly emerged as the economic center of the community. On payday ironworkers were notorious for handing their paychecks immediately over to their wives, who managed the bills, meals, and expenses for the entire family. In addition to managing the financial affairs of their fami-lies, Mohawk women also took employment in the many industries around Gowanus, such as the metal stamping factory of Fred Goat or the Gem Safety Razor Corporation.[68] Other Mohawk women owned their

Dr. David Monroe Cory preaching to a Mohawk congregation at Cuyler Presbyterian Church in Brooklyn, New York. This photo appeared in the July 1952 edition of *National Geographic Magazine* under the article "Mohawks Scrape the Sky." Photo: B. Anthony Stewart/National Geographic Creative.

own businesses, such as local boarding houses that took in new Mohawk residents or ironworkers.[69] During the 1920s and 1930s, Mohawk women relied on an older tradition of beadwork that they sold at state fairs and boardwalks during the off-season of ironwork.[70] Most Mohawk peoples purchased their beading supplies at the Plume Trading and Sales Company located on Lexington Avenue in downtown Manhattan.[71]

One of the first photos of a Mohawk family in New York City appeared in social reformer Jacob Riis's *How the Other Half Lives,* originally published in 1890. The photo features a Mohawk family Riis identified as having the name "Mountain Eagle." Perhaps the strangest photo in the publication, the image of the windowed apartment is a rare showcase of affluence in a book primarily about the epidemic of poverty and squalor in tenement housing—the son plays a fiddle while the father, mother, and smiling sister work on raised beadwork at a nearby kitchen table. The subtle and yet stark affluence captured in Riis's photo stands in sharp contrast to the broader subject matter of the book—as Riis strove to expose social ruin and decay within tenements and flophouses. The

"Mountain Eagle and his Family of Iroquois Indians—One of the few Indian families in the city, found at no. 6 Beach Street, Dec. 1895." Photo: Jacob A. (Jacob August) Riis (1849–1914)/Museum of the City of New York. 90.13.4.287.

Mountain Eagle family in Riis's photo has a window, wallpaper, carved furniture, and the largest luxury, space.[72] With the benefit of a dual income, many Mohawk families became prosperous, but, like the Oakes family, they were also quick to uphold social and cultural ties to their extended family both in Brooklyn and back at home.

While the Gowanus, Brooklyn, community was largely Mohawk, most of the Native organizations that emerged were Intertribal. One of the most significant of these urban organizations was the Indian League of the Americas (ILOTA). Headquartered out of Brooklyn, only half of its membership was Mohawk.[73] Founded in 1951, the League, originally called the Intertribal American Indian Council, sponsored an annual powwow and was instrumental in founding the first Indian center in New York City.[74] ILOTA was also part of a growing number of Native organizations that found their home in New York. The United Association for the Advancement of American Indians, Inc., for example, sponsored an annual American Indian Day in Brooklyn's Prospect Park. The many powwows and pageants these organizations introduced played a central role in curbing discrimination and educating the public about Native politics, customs, culture, and history.[75] At the local YMCA, often frequented by Richard Oakes and his brother, Hopi and Ho-Chunk descendent Louis Mofsie founded the Thunderbird American Indian Singers. In 1968 Mofsie explained that the Thunderbirds "started primarily to get younger children interested and exposed to their rich background."[76]

Powwows were more than a commercialized public display of nationalism. They were also designed to showcase Native children as active participants in learning about their distinct cultures. Intertribal by design, these powwows brought together the larger community of Native peoples from New York's five boroughs. Eventually, these organizations spurred the founding of the American Indian Women's Service League, which sponsored a series of monthly lectures for the larger Indian community in the 1960s.[77]

Richard Oakes's father, Arthur Oakes, was an ironworker. Like most Mohawk ironworkers, he had to live close to the work site in Brooklyn or other places, as he worked jobs throughout the New England area. Despite their father's absence for a majority of their childhood, Irene Oakes managed to keep her two sons engaged in a lively Mohawk-centered community in New York. This Indian City was built and maintained by a community that strove to protect their political and cultural identity as Mohawk citizens. While the institutions of this Mohawk city have faded in the early twenty-first century, the community still represents an important dimension of Mohawk history. Former residents often reminisce about life during the height of the Mohawk City during the 1940s and 1950s. In one interview in the *New York Times,* a Mohawk woman identified as "Ms. White" recalled the roaring days of the Mohawk City:

> The talk over the beer mugs at the Spar Bar and the Wigwam was always of the latest job: the Verrazano-Narrows Bridge, the hangars at Kennedy International Airport, the Seagrams Building, the Time & Life Building. "There were a lot of skyscrapers built over those two bars back in those days. . . . It was like I didn't leave home because they were there, my people were there, and I felt safe."[78]

Understanding the political, historic, and economic relationships linking Akwesasne, Kahnawà:ke, and Brooklyn is crucial to understanding Richard Oakes's childhood.

Oakes's worldview was undoubtedly influenced by a rich and politically active community. Akwesasne was a largely Intertribal nation that imparted a long history of resistance and Native Nationalism to Oakes. The teachings of the Longhouse and the politics of a borderlands Nation forced to deal with both Canadian and American policy complicated his political views. Each member of the community from traditional Life Chiefs, Mohawk Clan Mothers, ironworkers, teachers, storytellers, and veterans fought to protect the sovereign rights of the Mohawk Nation and the Haudenosaunee Confederacy. In the years to come, Richard Oakes increasingly relied on Mohawk teachings and community as the foundation for his unique understanding of Native Nationalism.

CHAPTER TWO

The Emergence of a Leader

I quit high school in the eleventh grade and went into iron work.
My father and uncle taught me the trade. They passed it down, and
when I was sixteen, I just started working. I worked all over, living
on the reservation and off the reservation. I lived in New York,
Massachusetts, the New England states. . . . I went where the work
was. I was an iron worker for eleven years. I made good money, but
beyond that there was nothing.

Richard Oakes, 1972

It is important to note that in our Indian language the only translation
for termination is "to 'wipe out' or 'kill off.'" We have no Indian
words for termination. . . .

Earl Old Person, Blackfeet, 1966

Richard Oakes's childhood was split between the bustling Mohawk communities of Brooklyn and Akwesasne. Each community and lifeway had
an adverse effect on Oakes's political and social development. His education was tied to several complicated and distinct issues that emerged in
the 1950s and 1960s. Termination legislation, the St. Lawrence Seaway
Project, and the disruptive force of gang life were all a part of Richard
Oakes's Mohawk awakening. During these years America was emerging
as an economic and diplomatic superpower in an era of dynamic social
change.

Five months before his birth, the war in the Pacific tragically crept up
on the Pacific Fleet in Hawaii, culminating in the Japanese attack on Pearl
Harbor on December 7, 1941. The attack on Pearl Harbor added intensity
to the Haudenosaunee fight to preserve the sovereign powers of the
Longhouse throughout the war. One month after Richard's birth on June

12, 1942, several Iroquois leaders visited Washington, D.C., where they issued the following statement on the footsteps of the U.S. Capitol: "Now, therefore, we do resolve that it is the sentiment of this council that the Six Nations of Indians declare that a state of war exists between our Confederacy of Six Nations on the one part and Germany, Italy, Japan, and their allies against whom the United States has declared war."[1] This declaration of war followed a long courtroom battle over the right of the United States government to draft non-citizen Iroquois through the Selective Service Act.[2] President Franklin Delano Roosevelt and the media heralded the Iroquois declaration, which quickly erased public and political scrutiny over Iroquois draft resistance. American and Canadian Mohawk citizens faced the difficult legal decision between the acceptance of conscription or selective service. To allow either government the right to draft Mohawk soldiers was a breach of sovereignty and acceptance of federal mandate. Eventually both countries would change their draft or conscription policies to accommodate Six Nations political rights. Several Akwesasne and Kahnawà:ke Mohawk peoples eventually contributed honorably to the war effort, serving gallantly in both the European and Pacific theaters. A select group of Mohawk in the American campaign would also serve as code talkers, a covert group who used their Native language to create a code that baffled Japanese code breakers.[3]

In New York Mohawk ironworkers used their collective skills to promote wartime industry. In the *New York Times* Mohawk Paul Horn commented on Mohawk labor at the Brooklyn Navy Yard: "Many of his Mohawk brothers, who have long been known as skilled ironworkers, are working the Navy Yard. . . . Eighteen hundred Indians of several tribes are filling defense jobs in this city, and about 5,000 through the country."[4] Mohawk adults turned out by the hundreds to work in wartime industries. Many Mohawk women also began working in the wartime factories; they learned riveting and ironwork, an occupation dominated by Mohawk men.[5] In general, Mohawk families also profited from the desegregation of the wartime industries and in turn relied on ironwork to promote the war effort. Some estimates place the number of American Indians who served in the wartime industries at forty thousand, about 10 percent of the total American Indian population.[6] In Canada, First Nations service is documented at around four thousand enlisted, and small numbers of First Nation women also enlisted in the Canadian Women's Army Corps.[7]

Approximately, over eight hundred American Indian women served in the armed forces, representing fully one-quarter of the entire Indian wartime labor force.[8] As a whole, American Indian service and participation in the war effort proved exceedingly high. Like many Americans, Richard Oakes and his family were greatly affected by the Great Depression and the Second World War.

Before the war, Richard Oakes's father, Arthur, struggled to find steady work, often locating seasonal labor as a lumberjack. In between lumber jobs, Arthur Oakes trained as a boxer to earn extra income. His first recorded fight appeared in the sports section of *The Citizen-Advertiser*, published out of Auburn, New York. In the November 18, 1938, edition, a preliminary match occurred between Arthur Oakes of Syracuse, New York, and Mike Giovanazzo, a.k.a. the "Rome Bearcat," at the Auburn Athletic Club. The following spring, the 150-pound middleweight Arthur Oakes, who had earned the name "the Cortland Leather Ladler" from the local press, challenged local favorite Joe Kinch. The Oakes/Kinch fight was scheduled to go between four to eight rounds in order to warm up the crowd for the main event. In the first round, Oakes leveled the middleweight Kinch with his noteworthy long right fist. Kinch managed to last another five tortuous rounds before the final bell rang in Oakes's favor.[9]

After some success in the ring, "Art" or "Artie" Oakes, as the local newspapers called him, weighed in at 152 pounds and had won central New York's middleweight boxing title. Four months later, his name appeared as the headlining fight at the City Hall Auditorium in Ogdensburg, New York, where he faced the rock-like fists of Frank Brenno. Before a packed house, their fight picked up steam in the third round. Oakes had carried the previous rounds; in round two he briefly knocked Brenno off-balance with a stiff right to the head. Brenno's corner quickly changed up the fight strategy as he stormed out of his corner, raging at Oakes with an unrelenting barrage of hard lefts and rights. One final left to the midsection and a hard right to Oakes's head quickly sent the middleweight champ to the mat. As the referee's count reached seven, Oakes tried to stand and braced himself on one knee, but just as he shook off the blow from his head the official had reached ten. The Friday edition of the *Ogdensburg-Advance* celebrated Brenno's knockout of Oakes in the third round. The top sports story for March 10, 1939, featured a photo of the referee towering over Oakes as he knelt on a single knee peering back into the flash of the camera. The caption read, "No Stout Oak was Art Oakes." Arthur, despite the devastating loss, refused to relinquish his title. In the local papers, Oakes's manager labeled Brenno's victory a complete fluke. Oakes and his managers quickly pressed Brenno's people for a rematch. Oakes claimed that he had failed to hear the actual count from the referee.[10]

On the heels of their famed rematch, the local press labeled Brenno as the front-runner with an almost guaranteed advantage over Oakes. Interestingly, for the first time, the editors of the *Ogdensburg-Advance* highlighted Arthur Oakes's heritage as a Mohawk from St. Regis. The *Ogdensburg-Advance* played on local politics in an effort to publicize the main attraction, an attraction billed squarely on local race and politics, as they labeled Oakes the "copper-skinned destroyer."[11] Considering Ogdensburg's close proximity to Akwesasne, the underlying tone of the article pinpointed a different set of stakes for this match—border town versus reservation, white versus Indian. While such undertones hid beneath the marketing of the featured match, Oakes struggled to fight for more than a paycheck—it was also about the honor of his nation. The billing for the fight put both communities into the ring. Like Joe Louis and many other boxers of color before him, this was his fight to win. Oakes's performance could serve either to disrupt or to reinforce regional misperceptions about Native peoples. Actively squaring off in the ring against border town discrimination also protected him from being arrested for open and physical resistance. While this boxing match remains relatively unknown in the history of boxing, it is significant for a host of reasons; for our purposes the fight showed Oakes's tenacity and fortitude, creating a legend that shaped his son's future.

The Thursday night fight card for the Veterans of Foreign Wars buzzed with excitement as a sold-out crowd entered into the packed Ogdensburg City Auditorium. Six days before the scheduled match, Arthur Oakes had defeated Vic Raymond of Binghamton, New York, at an amateur boxing exhibition. While the local press still favored Brenno, Oakes arrived with the momentum. After his first loss to Brenno, Oakes and his managers adjusted his training and strategy. The much-anticipated fight lasted only three minutes before the official decision was called in Oakes's favor. The next day, Ogdensburg reporters slammed the fight as a dull display of Oakes's rapid footwork. Rather than trading blow for blow, a tack that would have put Oakes at a disadvantage, he and his managers waged a defensive strategy to wear down and outlast the powerful punch of the town favorite. Future fighters like Muhammad Ali may have been celebrated for their fancy footwork and defensive strategies, but Arthur Oakes was reviled by the press for it. Interestingly, after Oakes's victory, the local press failed to mention St. Regis or his Mohawk heritage. Instead, reporters identified Arthur Oakes as the "Indian fighter from Syracuse," not Akwesasne, robbing their Mohawk community of a fully recognized victory.[12]

Securing a paid bout at any New York venue was a challenge for most amateur fighters, but especially for Native boxers due to discrimination. In the summer of 1940, the Onondaga Nation had sponsored their own boxing and wrestling tournament featuring a bout between Art Oakes and Onondaga Nation boxer Chuck Honyoust. Arthur Oakes's brother-in-law Angus Papineau, along with future Chief of the Haudenosaunee Confederacy or Tadadaho, Leon Shenandoah, also squared off against such wrestling characters as "Wild Bill" Worley. The match itself brought boxing and wrestling under the authority of the Onondaga Nation rather than Syracuse or other non-Native venues. Aside from promoting Native fighters, Onondaga organizers used the match to boost revenue and to provide fighters with a larger take from the house. The tournament itself undercut the Syracuse boxing markets, which had a reputation for keeping a larger percentage of revenues from the Onondaga.[13] By creating their own venues, they provided an alternative to Syracuse, one that could offer fairer competition and better pay. Thus, Onondaga was able to keep a larger percentage of the profits inside their own community.

Between training and fights throughout New York, Arthur Oakes began to date Irene Foote. How they first met is unknown, but they soon fell in love and became engaged to be married. On November 23, 1939, on the First Nations side of Akwesasne, Catholic priest Michael Karhaienton Jacobs from Kahnawà:ke performed their wedding ceremony at St. Regis Village. The year before their marriage, Father Jacobs had moved to Akwesasne, a relatively new pastor for the St. Regis Catholic Church, which was made out of light grey stone and overlooked the point between the St. Regis and St. Lawrence Rivers. Jacobs's ordination through Ottawa afforded him with the proper credentials to conduct services at Akwesasne. Many of these church services, due to the location of the

church, occurred almost exclusively on the Canadian side of the reservation. Known as an avid lacrosse fan, Reverend Jacobs had inevitably
followed the box scores of Thomas Foote (bride's father) and Mitchell
Oakes (groom's uncle) with the Cornwall Island Indians. Despite his
talent in the sport of boxing, Arthur Oakes gradually left the ring to gain
more reliable employment in order to provide for his family.[14]

In 1935, before they were married, Arthur had lived with his parents
in Syracuse, and Irene resided in Colborne, Ontario. Arthur's older sister,
Bernice Papineau, had filled out the census document for the family.
Bernice was married to Angus Papineau, a construction worker, who later
influenced Arthur along with his brother and father to seek out employment in the construction industry. During the Great Depression, finding
steady work and pay was next to impossible. Both Arthur and Irene Oakes

Father Michael Karhaienton Jacobs after his ordination by
Archbishop Guillaume Forbes as a priest in the Roman
Catholic Church in St. Francis Xavier Church at Kahnawà:ke.
The original caption read: "first time that an Indian had ever
been ordained." Photo courtesy of Getty Images, Bettmann
Collection 665582698.

had earned their high school degrees, however, which afforded the young couple greater opportunities. Arthur earned his diploma from Syracuse and Irene completed the St. Joseph Residential School after the tenth grade. By 1935, Arthur lived with his parents in Syracuse, New York, and Irene worked as a maid in Ontario.[15]

After they married in 1939, Irene and Arthur Oakes moved in with Arthur's parents, who were renting a home for ten dollars a month in Lisbon, a small town in northern New York, located eleven miles northeast of Ogdensburg. The main employer in Lisbon was a powdered milk factory, and Arthur's father most likely worked as a farm laborer for the factory. Living with her in-laws, another married couple (Angus and Bernice Papineau), and five more of her husband's brothers and sisters must have made for a cramped household without much privacy. Employment for Irene Oakes meant utilizing her Canadian Residential School training to locate a domestic position in a private home while her husband searched for part-time work in the nearby lumber industry. The economic hard times had forced most families to conserve, save, and sometimes rely on neighborly kindness from strangers in order to survive. By the 1940s, every member of the Oakes household had secured steady work, either in or around Lisbon.[16]

While joy occurred after the birth of Arthur and Irene's first child, whom they named Leroy, tragedy loomed around the corner. A year later, in 1941, the young couple lost their second child at birth. By the 1940s, for a majority of American women, childbirth was largely occurring outside of the home, without midwives, and more and more frequently within hospitals. Women during birth were most often subjected to the practice known as twilight birth—medical doctors dosing women into a drug-induced semiconscious state that resulted in a birth without the memory or "pain" of actual childbirth.

One can only speculate how the loss of the second child affected the young couple. Certainly it took a deep personal toll on each of them and ultimately their marriage. Historically, for Mohawk women and Haudenosaunee peoples in general, children represent a direct gift, a blessing from Creator. A Mohawk child completes a sacred bond between the spiritual and physical worlds and serves as a spiritual and physical continuation and affirmation of Mohawk lifeways. In 1943, two years after the loss of their second child, Leroy passed away at the age three.

A new beginning arrived on May 22, 1942, when Irene Oakes gave birth to her third child, Thomas Richard Oakes. One year later, she and her husband welcomed their fourth child, Leonard Oakes, into their world. For their third child, Irene and Arthur selected a very special name. Perhaps it was for protection, as this name combined the first names of both of their fathers, Thomas Foote and Richard Oakes. Of course, as their third son grew older, he spent long summers with his Oakes relatives back at St. Regis and chose to go by the name of his paternal grandfather, Richard Oakes. All of Irene Oakes's children were born a year apart and conformed to the larger historical phenomenon known as the Baby Boom.[17]

In 1941, one year after the birth of Leroy, Arthur Oakes enlisted in the military. Initially, he continued to box locally for the Navy, but in March of 1943, he received his active military orders to join a naval crew as a boatswain's mate for the war in Europe. Struggling on the home front, with her husband called to war, Irene Oakes was left alone to care for her two sons. On June 6, 1944, Arthur Oakes took part in the legendary D-Day invasion on a troop transport ship for the beaches of Normandy, France.

Unbeknownst to Arthur, the night before the beach offensive, his younger brother Alex Oakes (member of the 82nd Airborne Division) had parachuted behind enemy lines into the town of Sainte-Mère-Église in one of the largest and most tragic airborne raids of the war. Due to a fire at a nearby farmhouse, the slowly descending U.S. paratroopers were easy targets for the Nazi troops. The few who survived, like Alex Oakes, helped liberate the town and capture the center of German communications. Arthur's brother later saw action at the Battle of the Bulge.[18]

After the war, many Mohawk veterans, like Alex Oakes, kept their service records a secret. While Richard Oakes and others might have overheard stories about their relatives' wartime service, one story remained hidden. As recently as 2013, Mohawk soldiers finally gained official recognition for their service as code talkers in the European campaign. During World War II, the United States military relied on the Mohawk language, along with several other Native languages, to create an unbreakable communications code to help win the war in Europe and the Pacific. While Alex was recognized for his service within this elite group, the participation of Arthur and Harold has never been officially corroborated. At the conclusion of the war, Alex received two Purple Hearts and a

Bronze Star for valor. Another brother, Thomas Oakes, who served in the Marines was wounded in action. Only Abraham "Archie" Oakes, Arthur's cousin, never returned home from the war. He was killed in action on July 1, 1944, in northern Italy. One final casualty of the war was Irene and Arthur's marriage, which, like so many other World War II marriages, ended in divorce in 1946.[19]

Accompanying the divorce, Irene Oakes, now a single mother of two, faced the death of her eldest sister, who was killed in a gruesome accident. Late one evening at Onondaga, Olive Sullivan and her companion were hit by a car and killed as they walked home.

It is well known that in the wake of World War II, the United States saw a sharp spike in marriages, which led to the Baby Boom. But few scholars have highlighted the enormous spike in the divorce rate that also followed the war. Due to enlistment or draft, thousands of young fathers were forced to abandon their wives or children, in some cases for several years. Those fathers lucky enough to return from the horrors of war often reunited with children or wives who hardly knew them. Some estimates from 1947 place the divorce rate at 43 percent after the war. Throughout the war, Irene managed to survive day by day living off war rations and her husband's wartime income. It was barely enough to support herself and two small children. The divorce added to Irene Oakes's struggles to keep her family out of poverty and left her with few options.

Orphanages throughout America struggled to keep their doors open, especially in larger cities, due to an astronomical increase in the national divorce rate and recent widows. More troubling for divorced mothers after the war, many industries shifted back to hiring men only. Irene and other single moms like her faced unemployment and greater competition for only a handful of jobs. In Brooklyn most of the want ads for women were advertised in the Brooklyn-Eagle under the heading "Girls Wanted." American women in general, particularly women of color and most especially Indians, faced an uphill battle in the pursuit of equal pay, opportunity, and job equality. Irene Oakes's complicated situation as a single mother highlights the extreme wage inequality that thousands of American women experienced after World War II. With no husband, no money, and dwindling job prospects, Irene Oakes had few options in the winter of 1947, and she made the tough decision. She turned her two sons, Richard and Leonard, over to the care of strangers at a New York orphanage.[20]

Late in 1946, when Leonard and Richard were respectively three and four years old, Irene enrolled her two sons at St. Mary's Angel Guardian Home for Orphans in Brooklyn, New York. Once they were old enough, her children were transferred from St. Mary's to the House of Providence, located on 1654 West Onondaga Street in Syracuse, New York. Living in the enormous five-story dome-topped building with three hundred other boys, Leonard Oakes remembered that the worst aspect of the orphanage had little to do with actual physical abuse; rather, the hardest days for them occurred every visitor's day. On these particular days, not one family member or parent ever showed up at the orphanage. Cut off from their family and community, the two young boys were taught by nuns. They quickly learned that in order to survive they had to keep their heads down and their mouths shut and follow orders without complaint—maintaining this trinity was far easier than fighting it.

By 1950, overcoming both gender and racial discrimination, Irene landed a new job as a factory worker at a Brooklyn tool and dye factory. Her new home, along with evidence of steady employment, had proved sufficient grounds for the orphanage to release her two sons from their care. Irene Oakes, with limited resources and a shoestring budget, worked hard to provide her children with a fresh start—a chance to experience a different childhood from her own. Their roomy two-story Brooklyn row house was located in the South Slope neighborhood, which earned its name from the topography of the area, as the terrain "slopes" uphill from Gowanus and Boerum Hill. Constructed around 1899, their new home was situated at 219 14th Street between 4th and 5th Avenues near Prospect Park, one of Brooklyn's most popular public spaces. Brooklyn, unlike any other major city in the state, meant more than just an economic opportunity or a fresh start; it meant keeping her children closely tied to their culture within a thriving Mohawk City.[21] Meanwhile, as Irene and her children embarked on a new life in Brooklyn, Indian Country faced the startling new prospect of a postwar anti-Indian movement, known ominously as "termination."

Throughout World War II, the Bureau of Indian Affairs had suffered several setbacks: Funding for the agency was cut for the war effort, offices were relocated from Washington to Chicago, and staff depletions nearly paralyzed the entire agency. Programs such as the CCC-ID and NYA lost all funding, and by 1949 the BIA office in Buffalo, New York, and many

Left: Richard Oakes's childhood home at 219 14th Street between 4th and 5th Avenues in the South Slope neighborhood of Brooklyn, New York, in 2012. Photo courtesy of the author. Right: Richard Oakes (front), Leonard Oakes (back), and Irene Oakes (Foote) holding young Pamela Sullivan and seated next to Teresa Sullivan inside their Brooklyn home. Photo credit: James Clarke and the Sullivan family.

others had officially closed their doors. While Mohawk soldiers fought under the U.S. flag in foreign lands, opposition to Native sovereignty and Treaty Rights had slowly been cultivated in Congress by Nebraska Senator Hugh A. Butler. The senator's campaign for termination utilized the slogan of "freeing Indians from the chains enslaving them to the federal bureaucracy."[22] By the end of the war, Akwesasne soldiers and wartime laborers who had allied against European fascism now faced a new enemy. Termination legislation, as we shall see, was meant to terminate federal recognition and trust responsibilities with individual Indigenous nations.

Officially, termination began in 1947, when Senator Butler introduced three bills, known jointly as the Butler Bills, which transferred civil and criminal jurisdiction over the Iroquois to New York state courts and challenged the Canandaigua Treaty of 1794 with a lump-sum payment. Iroquois leaders organized several protests outside the United Nations building in New York and employed the help of the press and the three-year-old National Congress of American Indians (NCAI) to help overturn the legislation. At Akwesasne the fight intensified as the elected tribal chiefs, empowered by the state of New York, fought with the traditional Life Chiefs of the Longhouse. This political "factionalism" at Akwesasne was taken up by Senator Butler and others as evidence that the state should intervene in Haudenosaunee affairs. Despite fierce debate and public opposition to the bills, they successfully made their way through Congress, leaving the Iroquois in limbo between federal and state authority. In effect, this new legislation sidestepped federal protections by granting the state of New York new legal authority and jurisdiction over Haudenosaunee peoples. Before the Butler Acts, the federal government had the exclusive power to make civil and criminal arrests or prosecute Tribal citizens on sovereign Tribal lands.

Overturning termination legislation ended up commanding most of Richard Oakes's political life. In 1953, the same year that saw the passing of famed Sac and Fox athlete Jim Thorpe and the end of the Korean War, Congress passed Public Law 280 and House Concurrent Resolution 108, which highlighted Butler's attempt to terminate the federal trust status of federally recognized nations (or every Native nation represented under the 1934 IRA).[23] Both of these legislative measures of the "Red Scare" era sought to hand civil and criminal jurisdiction of Tribes over to the state and to terminate treaty and trust responsibilities with more than one hundred Tribes, including all Tribes within California, New York, Florida, and Texas.[24] The real-life impact of terminating federal jurisdiction was enormous: (1) Mohawk citizens could be arrested, tried, and prosecuted in biased state courts; (2) Mohawk businesses faced further regulations by state laws and jurisdictions; (3) millions of acres of Indian lands were stripped of federal protection or trust status; and (4) the privatization and exploitation of Indigenous resources and lands would be greatly acceler- ated. While the mid-1950s was a time of intense debate over civil rights and desegregation, the adverse effects of this mood had a devastating impact on Indian policy. Lawmakers viewed reservations as federally sponsored segregation and a haven for communists. The elimination of federal trust status, or termination, was championed under the banner of national civil rights reform and anticommunism.[25] Nevada Senator George Malone followed the influence of McCarthyism when he supported termination measures with these words: "While we are spending billions of dollars fighting Communism . . . we are at the same time . . . perpetuating the systems of Indian reservations and tribal governments, which are natural Socialist environments."[26] By the early 1950s, the state of New York had taken full advantage of the Butler Bills by enforcing the right of eminent domain for the construction of the St. Lawrence Seaway Project.

Just as menacing as termination legislation, American Indians faced yet another imminent threat—a national boom in mineral consumption and hydroelectric construction. While most Americans were experiencing postwar economic affluence, Tribal governments and citizens had little time to celebrate postwar prosperity. Instead they battled the military-industrial complex, which included multinational corporations as well as state and federal governments, in order to protect against further land loss and erosion of their precious few natural resources:

> The Allegany Senecas lost one-third of their reservation to
> flooding by the Kinzua Dam. . . . Tuscaroras found themselves
> 550 acres poorer by the time the Niagara Reservoir was
> completed in 1961. . . . The Sioux of Standing Rock, Cheyenne
> River, Lower Brule, Crow Creek, and Yankton reservations, and
> the Mandan, Arikara, and Hidatsa at the Fort Berthold reserva-
> tion were the most devastated. The Shoshone, Arapaho, Crow,
> Cree, Chippewa, Blackfoot, and Assiniboine were forced to give
> up land for the [Pick-Sloan] project . . . in total 550 square miles.
> In western Canada, the Swampy Cree at Cumberland House
> and Easterville and the Rocky Cree at South Indian Lake, as well
> as the James Bay Cree in northern Quebec, were all dispos-
> sessed in favor of hydroelectric projects. . . . The tragedy is not
> that Kahnawake's case was unique, but that it was all too
> common.[27]

The hydroelectric crisis weighed most prominent in New York as Iroquois leaders again pulled their legal resources together to challenge America's growing need for increased energy consumption.

The St. Lawrence Seaway Project was designed as one of the largest canal projects in North America, implemented by a joint effort of Canada and the United States. The seaway dwarfed the Panama and Suez Canals, making it one of the world's largest canal endeavors. It "consisted of a twenty-seven-foot deep channel, dug through dry land and dredged lake bottoms, stretching from Montreal to Lake Erie, and capable of lifting ships 600 feet above sea level as they sailed inland. The new waterway with its fifteen locks replaced a fourteen-foot deep system of canals and thirty time-consuming locks."[28] The proposed construction of the seaway adversely affected the political, social, economic, and cultural life at Akwesasne and Kahnawà:ke.

Research by Kahnawà:ke anthropologist Stephanie Phillips pinpoints the socio-cultural effects and power of place that emerged before the Seaway Project: "In wintertime people skated and sledded on the frozen water, but the river truly came alive in the summer months. Women brought their laundry (few people had running water at the time), hung it on the trees, and then waded into the water. People brought their lunches, cooked by the shore, and swam until dark. The river was also a rich source of food: frog legs, berry bushes, and fish almost all year round."[29] The Seaway Project ended this lifeway for hundreds of Akwesasne and Kahnawà:ke residents. Ultimately the Seaway Project transformed the very movement and flow of the river and threatened migrating fish populations.

This international development threatened a fragile ecosystem and the treaty and human rights of Mohawk citizens in the United States and Canada. In 1947, Mohawk leaders and other First Nations people called a special joint committee to investigate the repeal of the Indian Act of 1876. And while this protest to abolish the Indian Act waged, the political outcry from First Nations leaders over a lack of representation created a new set of reforms to the 1951 Indian Act that ended restrictions on cultural and religious ceremonies but also promoted oppressive regulations on First Nation women's voting and Indigenous citizenship. It was a very minor victory that officially curtailed some provincial authority and laws over First Nations. It is important to note that not all First Nation peoples had sought to abolish the Indian Act, as several moderates had lobbied against abolishing the Indian Act. Many, in this moderate faction, feared that the Indian Act might be replaced by a Canadian policy of termination.[30]

As a precursor to Richard Oakes's battle to reclaim Alcatraz Island, a similar fight for another island took place at Akwesasne when he was eight years old. In November of 1954, a significant confrontation ensued that had a lasting impact on the young Richard Oakes. The state of New York claimed Barnhart Island through eminent domain for the building of the Seaway Project. The Iroquois claim to Barnhart Island involved several treaties and renegotiations of treaties that had occurred from the late eighteenth century to the middle of the nineteenth century. After the War of 1812, the island changed hands from Canada to the United States under the second Treaty of Ghent of 1822, which stated that all Mohawk rights with regard to the island were to be honored. With this legal precedent in mind and through the power of treaty, the Iroquois filed suit against the state of New York for compensation. In *St. Regis Tribe v. State of New York* the Court of Appeals eventually dismissed the case, and in 1959 the Supreme Court refused to hear the case.[31]

In March of 1959, Iroquois leaders announced their intention to march on Washington, D.C., in order to take their case to the people and government in person. They scheduled meetings with retired Brigadier General Herbert C. Holdridge to discuss strategy. The meeting was attended by Akwesasne, Tuscarora, and Onondaga leaders. On March 18, 1959, over one hundred Haudenosaunee, led by the Tuscarora leader Wallace "Mad Bear" Anderson, picketed outside the White House.[32] During the previous year, Mad Bear had visited Cuba to meet with Fidel Castro and to promote Cuban sponsorship of the Iroquois joining the United Nations.[33] The delegation of Haudenosaunee leaders also demanded an audience with President Dwight D. Eisenhower about the illegal confiscation of Iroquois lands. Recuperating from the fallout over McCarthyism, Eisenhower's administration, aware of recent Cuban and Iroquois ties, refused an audience with Haudenosaunee leaders. For Eisenhower's Vice President, Richard M. Nixon, whose career was largely built on being tough on communism, the fact of the coming election in 1960 was salient. Having failed at the White House, the delegation focused their energies on Glenn L. Emmons, the Indian Affairs Commissioner. Two days later, on March 20, the remaining force of one hundred Iroquois leaders failed to serve a citizen's arrest on Commissioner Emmons. While their protest failed to achieve its expressed intent, Iroquois leaders successfully secured support from members of Congress. William Langer, a Republican senator from North Dakota, told the *New York Times* that "President Eisenhower should have received the Indians. . . . They really had a just complaint."[34] More importantly, this singular event reveals that Haudenosaunee leaders were adept at utilizing the media as an alternative lobby for political change.

On September 16, 1955, back at Kahnawà:ke, Canadian authorities unveiled a plan to confiscate 1,262 acres of Reserve land for the seaway. Within one month of the decision, eviction notices were sent to Kahnawà:ke residents. With construction of the seaway well underway, Kahnawà:ke homeowners lacked any figures for just compensation. In a series of back-room negotiations between the Indian Affairs Department and the Seaway Authority, property values were negotiated. Kahnawà:ke protested this negotiation, hired lawyers, and began to fight the eviction notices the Seaway Authority leveled on families. Like Akwesasne, Kahnawà:ke tried to protect their land rights through the courts. By 1957, the Montreal Superior Court overturned Kahnawà:ke's appeal against the seaway. All told, by the time the seaway was completed in 1959, Akwesasne had lost 130 acres and Kahnawà:ke a total of 1,262 acres of riverfront land. Over 6,500 Akwesasne and another 9,000 Kahnawà:ke citizens were forced to abandon their homes, as whole families were uprooted and their villages disappeared beneath the floodwaters from project.[35]

Along with the seaway came the New York Power Authority, who operated the FDR Power Project along the St. Lawrence. Several large corporations like Alcoa, Reynolds Metals, Domtar, and General Motors moved into the area, lured by the prospect of lower energy costs. While some Mohawk citizens gained employment in these factories, Akwesasne lost much more than its land base. By the twenty-first century, after years of illegal dumping of dioxin, releasing toxic wastes like PCBs (polychlorinated biphenyls) into the river, and pumping heavy metals into the air, part of Akwesasne was destroyed and turned into an environmental Superfund site where no humans were permitted to live because of pollution. The battle against the seaway was the first in a long series of pitched political battles that Richard Oakes witnessed at an early age. Despite the loss of Akwesasne and Kahnawà:ke land to the St. Lawrence Seaway, another battle ended in a short-lived victory on the Tuscarora Reservation in southwestern New York.[36]

In 1958, Tuscarora leaders took on Robert Moses and the New York State Power Authority.[37] Moses sponsored plans to build a storage reservoir that would confiscate 1,383 acres, amounting to nearly one-quarter of Tuscarora lands. Approximately 124 Tuscarora families lived in the area, and the agriculture harvests from its rich fields were the cornerstone of their economy. Chief Henry Patterson, who also protested against the draft, stated, "We cannot sell it. . . . That's against the rules of the six-nation confederacy. We cannot sell the land to a private concern."[38] One year later, Patterson's strong rhetoric was challenged by the lump-sum figure of three million dollars, in addition to home relocation, the right to clear the harvest, construction jobs for Tuscarora citizens, and the option to purchase 1,200 more acres to curb the land lost by the hydroelectric project. The compromise represented a significant change from the New York State Power Authority's original offer of $1,000 an acre.[39] The final offer proposed by Moses was weighed in Tribal council and, eventually, the Federal Power Commission decided in favor of protecting Tuscarora land. Moses and the New York State Power Authority would be obliged to build a much smaller reservoir and were prohibited from taking any Indian land. It was a decisive victory that would propel future traditional leaders like Tuscarora Mad Bear Anderson into the national spotlight. Eventually, despite the legal victory, Tuscarora lost 550 acres of land to the reservoir project.[40]

Back in Brooklyn, brothers Richard and Leonard Oakes shared an upstairs bedroom with their boxer, named Rocky, who provided the young boys with companionship, an occasion to learn responsibility, and an added bit of security from strangers on the street. With pride, Irene's sons took turns walking their dog throughout the neighborhood. Often they competed with one another for the exclusive rights to this one chore, as walking the dog afforded the young boys a reason to escape house confinement when grounded. Irene Oakes operated a strict regimen over all the household responsibilities, a trait most likely carried over from her Residential School days. In a recent interview, First Nations Anishinaabe sisters Ida Embry and Blue Cloud Woman, both survivors of Spanish Residential School, recalled how the trauma of that experience forever altered their relationships as well as their parenting: "The nuns never referred to the students by name, only by number. . . . My number was 44 and Ida's was 107. . . . We didn't know how to raise [our own children], we didn't know parenting because of the school."[41] Their mother timed every phone call; long-distance calls were limited to three minutes (the first minute was free) to keep the household on budget. Rules such as the restricted phone time pressured her sons to learn the art of talking fast, making a point, and sticking to the facts. Their mother had to maintain an ordered household, one that Leonard Oakes later commented made boot camp in the Marines a pleasant vacation.[42]

The corner of 14th Street and 4th Avenue, across from Romeo's Wine and Liquor and the local laundromat, was a favorite spot for the two brothers. Leonard Oakes remarked that as the two brothers grew older, they often spent less time at church and more time on the street corner. A candy store on the same block specialized in chocolate egg creams—a well-known Brooklyn concoction that consists of chocolate syrup, milk, egg, and seltzer water, all combined by an electric shake mixer. When the three-story Public School 51 rang the last bell, Leonard and Richard, like many other kids, made a speedy exit to the myriad of adventures awaiting children on the streets of Brooklyn. Without the supervision of teachers or the watchful eye of a parent, kids played, invented, and discovered new worlds. The two brothers often stayed out late playing games of stickball, handball, or touch football, activities that were popular pastimes for a majority of Brooklyn youth. Stickball in particular became a favorite pastime for Richard and Leonard Oakes, as the kids on their block challenged other neighborhoods on 11th and 12th Streets to compete for a dollar a game. While pockets of the streets filled with shouts of excitement, every kid dreaded the distinct whistle or call from a parent to come home. Aside from street games, the inseparable brothers frequented the Police Athletic League facilities or the local YMCA because they offered training in the sport of boxing. It is no surprise that participation in boxing offered them a long-distant connection to their father. Most importantly, participation in these organizations imparted guidance and support from older male role models and coaches. Learning boxing taught them self-defense, personal fitness, and survival from the rough and tumble of Brooklyn's bullies and street gangs.[43]

On special occasions, Irene Oakes took her two boys to the beach as a convenient escape from the city. On these rare outings the family of three soaked in all the sights and sounds of the Coney Island boardwalk. Located right off the beach, the boardwalk offered unlimited adventures like the 250-foot-high parachute jump, mysterious sideshows, games, and treats, while distant screams and laughter filled the background. Such weekend vacations provided an outlet for entertainment, excitement, and leisure for generations of New York families.

By the early 1950s, aside from rare visits to Coney Island, Leonard Oakes recalled one outstanding memory: the day their mother purchased their first television set. For Irene Oakes and her sons, this purchase became a major milestone in their family history. Every Wednesday night at 7:45 p.m. the two boys gathered in the living room with their mother to watch Irene Oakes's favorite television series, *The Perry Como Show*. Everything in their small two-story home came to a stop, and with a twist of a dial, their black and white television screen jumped to life, projecting big band sounds and celebrity appearances from the comedy of Bob Hope to the urbane sounds of Dean Martin. For most Americans, the purchase of a television set had all but replaced the radio and topped even movie going as a major source of family entertainment and leisure. Most holidays the Oakes family traveled northwest to Syracuse, New York, in order to visit Irene's sister Theresa Sullivan and her brother William "Bill" Foote. Bill had a lasting impact on Leonard and Richard as he often took his nephews to Longhouse meetings at Onondaga. Some holidays, Irene Oakes's other sister, Cecilia Stacey, and her family came down from Kahnawà:ke to Syracuse for a Foote sibling reunion.[44]

Bill Foote, like Arthur Oakes, worked as an ironworker in Syracuse with the local 333. He was a skilled lacrosse player who played for the dynamic Onondaga Warriors, a professional box team. He was also a devoted member of the Longhouse at Onondaga. Bill Foote anchored his life to the teachings of the Great Law of Peace, learning its history, songs, stories, language, sports, and dances from the central fire of the League located at Onondaga. Their uncle imparted family stories to an impressionable Leonard and Richard Oakes, involving them in ceremonies at the Longhouse and reciting stories about their Foote relatives with his sisters. One story probably included the lacrosse exploits of their grandfather Thomas Foote, who played for the champion Cornwall Indian Islanders. In the Longhouse for the Onondaga Nation, Bill Foote gradually rose to a place of honor, serving as an official Runner for the Onondaga Longhouse. This Longhouse position was only granted to certain individuals who exhibited a respect and knowledge of the Great Law of Peace: Runners were often tasked with carrying and delivering important wampum belts to other Longhouses throughout the Haudenosaunee Confederacy. These rare family visits fostered in the young men a greater sense of purpose, belonging, and identity—an awareness about their unique lifeways as Mohawk and Haudenosaunee peoples.[45]

Growing up in Brooklyn, both Leonard and Richard Oakes had to contend with many different neighbors and neighborhoods. The brothers knew only a few other Mohawk kids from their school. Catholic parochial schools claimed the largest attendance of Mohawk students throughout Brooklyn. Many parents feared bad influences in the Brooklyn public school system. As a minority among minorities, the boys quickly learned how to mask their Mohawk identity. They found themselves "passing" when they could as dark-complexioned Italians, when in Italian neighborhoods, or as Puerto Ricans, when in other ethnic neighborhoods. Leonard reflected that certain jackets and colors identified the wearers as gang members, and Richard once wore an Onondaga Warriors lacrosse jacket that on one occasion was mistaken for gang colors. The only discrimination the brothers confronted emerged from Irish kids, who often attacked the brothers once they learned of their Indian heritage. In fights or neighborhood brawls, when Leonard got into a bad situation, he quickly signaled his older brother, who always jumped in to end the fight. Of course, as Leonard Oakes remembered, Richard determined the outcome of any street fight, and he always emerged victorious.[46]

During the summer, Irene often sent her sons back to Akwesasne to visit with their Oakes grandparents and family living on Cornwall Island. They usually stayed at their Aunt Bernice Papineau's (an Oakes relative), who enjoyed traditional basket making and owned a motel which contained one bedroom in America and another in Canada—the international border split their aunt's property between two separate countries. Everyone who visited the motel shared in the joke, the simple act of moving between rooms required guests to cross the border multiple times. The family often laughed about the situation, a joke that highlighted the everyday reality of Akwesasne's unique political status as a border nation straddling the United States and Canada. While all Mohawk citizens, through treaty rights, maintain both First Nation (Canadian status) or American Indian (U.S. federal recognition) legal status, such dual citizenship at Akwesasne remains a distant second to that of Mohawk citizenship.[47]

As Richard and Leonard Oakes spent valuable time with their relatives at Akwesasne, they also grew closer to their cultural heritage as young Mohawk citizens. A sense of pride in and acceptance of their heritage and abilities stemmed from their long summers on the reservation and interaction with the Mohawk community in Brooklyn. Leonard Oakes recalled one of these summers before the seaway, when Richard challenged a man in a rowboat to a race across the swift channels of the St. Lawrence River to St. Regis Island. The most significant detail of the bet: Richard Oakes had to outswim the man in the rowboat and be the first to make it to the three-mile-long island. From one shore to another, the distance of the swim amounted to over a thousand feet against the added force of the mighty current of the St. Lawrence River. In a standard gymnasium-type pool this would amount to about seven laps. Leonard Oakes and his companion's cheers grew louder and louder from the shore as his brother's arms and legs battled through the stiff current, and before too long, Richard began to outpace the rowboat. Pulling himself up onto the shore, he had accomplished a victory his friends had thought impossible. Through pure physical determination, he had won the bet and claimed St. Regis Island. While that swim lives on in the memory of those who experienced it, this was only the first purposeful swim of his life.[48]

As he was growing up, Richard was known for being adventurous. He was encouraged to follow the ways of his people. One prominent legend Leonard Oakes described as pure fiction involves a mythic journey. This disputed story is worth mentioning to understand how meaningful Richard Oakes's activism was to Haudenosaunee peoples. His political awakening was imagined as a small but significant part of the protest against the seaway. In 1954, when he was only twelve years old, Richard stowed away on a bus taking Iroquois leaders to Washington, D.C., for a meeting. After the bus pulled away from Akwesasne, Richard emerged from his hiding spot. It was far too late to turn the bus around, so the leaders on the bus made room for the young man. He supposedly rode all nine hours with the delegation, from Akwesasne to Maryland, listening to stories and speeches. Such a tale capitalizes on this key moment, linking Oakes's youthful emergence and self-determination to the greater Haudenosaunee and American Indian political landscape. This was an extremely fortunate opportunity to become immersed in Iroquois politics, if it did indeed happen.[49] Oakes had asserted himself politically and gained a unique educational experience about the politics of protest. Despite his Nation's repeated protests over the seizure of Barnhart Island, construction on the St. Lawrence Seaway Project began in the summer of 1954, an event that Richard witnessed in his youth.[50]

In 1957, conflict over the removal of families from an eighty-acre site along the Raquette River found its voice in the leadership of Standing

Arrow (Francis Johnson), a Mohawk ironworker and Navy veteran who was in his mid-twenties. Standing Arrow led a group of protesters who were occupying land at Kahnawà:ke to protest construction of the seaway. After eviction by the seaway authorities, Standing Arrow relocated the encampment on acreage along Schoharie Creek, located next to the New York Thruway near Fort Hunter, New York.[51] The occupiers, totaling around four hundred families, sought just compensation for the land and challenged the court's refusal to hear Iroquois demands. This takeover in action publicly challenged Canadian and U.S. law that used the right of "eminent domain" to evict Mohawk families for seaway construction. The occupation lasted almost two years, until March 1958, when the occupiers were evicted by a court order.[52]

The protest and eviction, however, fueled frustration and resentment in the life of Richard Oakes. As he himself said, "I was involved in the 1959 struggle to blockade the building of the Lawson [St. Lawrence Seaway] Dam, the seaway project which was taking parts of our reservation without compensation. Also the building of a bridge from the U.S. to Canada on the reservation and the building of facilities to house the maintenance men and the various aspects of the bridge, all on Indian Land without just compensation, so it has really been a big part for me to try to rectify some of this."[53]

These events may have also molded his adamant rejection of school. Despite the opportunity for learning, Richard was dissatisfied with the education offered in Brooklyn. "All they wanted me to do was to become a part of the machinery, to make me into what they wanted: a white Indian. I wanted to do something for my people," Oakes said, "But I didn't know what."[54] He eventually dropped out in the eleventh grade and began to learn the trade of ironwork. Richard Oakes had grown up overhearing stories of danger and brotherhood in the trade from his relatives. It was an industry that held an aura of mystery, as young men were often disciplined if they were caught even touching their father's ironworking tools. The reasoning behind this was to protect the ironworker from distraction on the job, as a misplaced tool might lead to tragedy on the job.

Richard's father and his relations had worked as ironworkers for most of their lives, and Richard continued in this Mohawk tradition. In 1958, the Oakes brothers took a bus to Potsdam, New York, located about thirty minutes southwest of Akwesasne. This event marked the first time that either of them had seen their father since the divorce. At the time, Richard was only sixteen years old. Arthur's sister Charlotte ran a bakery there, which made it a suitable place to meet their father. With barely a memory of their father before the divorce, the anticipation surrounding this first encounter surely elicited feelings of nervous excitement, if not all-out awkwardness, for the two young men. Shortly after meeting their father, he had his sons accompany him to an ironworking job site in Providence, Rhode Island. Arthur and others were constructing the new Prudential Building, and he used the moment as an opportunity to introduce his two boys to the ironworking trade.

Except for spending summers with their Oakes relatives at Akwesasne, one of the rare stories they knew about their father involved a deadly barroom brawl. The fight took place at a bar in Rochester, New York. An altercation grew dangerous when another patron grew increasingly agitated with Arthur Oakes. As their exchange grew more heated, this man threatened and then physically charged Arthur Oakes. With a single punch, Arthur knocked his assailant to the ground. His attacker, eager to get a piece of the former boxing champion, quickly regained his footing and charged a second time at Arthur Oakes, and again he leveled his attacker with another powerful blow. The strong and long right from Oakes sent his attacker crashing to the floor. His head slammed against a barstool, which killed the guy on contact. Having killed a man, Arthur Oakes faced arrest, jail time, or worse, but after a short investigation Oakes escaped prosecution for reasons of self-defense. After the incident, Arthur left Rochester and moved back to Syracuse.[55]

Reunited with his sons in Rhode Island, Oakes assigned them the back-breaking task of hauling wooden planks (the average plank weighed between 100 to 125 pounds) for all the ironworkers at the construction site. It was a critical job, as ironworkers' lives depended on the planks supporting their collective weight. Leonard Oakes recalled lasting about two weeks on that job, but his brother stayed on, as he grew quite fond of the business. When the school year at George Westinghouse High School in Brooklyn drew near, Leonard departed Rhode Island without his brother. Richard dropped out of school at this time and elected to stay on the job site, learning and working with his father. Passionate about the trade, like his father and other relatives, Richard Oakes was a full-time ironworker at the age of sixteen.[56]

Despite this bond between Arthur and his son, a powerful tension soon came between them. Tempers flared as Richard Oakes lived with his father—maybe he expected too much of his father or brought up the touchy subject of his mother. In the beginning he tried to defend himself, but he was no match for his father's skill and training as a former boxer. Leonard Oakes remembered the lasting effect of this physical abuse— Richard Oakes continued to work out, lifting weights, performing endless pushups, until one day Richard fought back against his dad and finally won. After this last fight Arthur kicked him out of the house. Richard left, and they never spoke again. Arthur Oakes then traveled the world working numerous construction jobs for the American Bridge Company, including Venezuela, Portugal, Bermuda, and Alaska. Not until the late 1960s did Arthur Oakes reunite with his other son, Leonard Oakes, when they discovered that they were building separate towers of the World Trade Center in New York City.[57]

Ironworkers often competed for bragging rights over working the greatest number of stories. Through ironwork, Richard entered a new world of an elite brotherhood. Oakes had started working iron at sixteen (the average age for entering the profession was seventeen). To join the

Left to right: Allan Delaronde (Mohawk, Kahnawà:ke), Doc Alfred (Mohawk, Kahnawà:ke), and Arthur Oakes (Mohawk, Akwesasne) on the 110th floor of the World Trade Center, North Tower, April 1971. Photo courtesy of Kanien'kehá:ka Onkwawén:na Raotitióhkwa Language and Cultural Center, Kahnawà:ke.

Local 361 in Brooklyn, members had to be at least eighteen years old. Arthur Oakes was most likely a "pusher," or foreman, which would explain how Richard could have entered the profession at such a young age. (It was customary for foremen to vouch for their sons so that they could start the occupation in an apprentice role at an earlier age.) When he first joined the trade he was called a "punk." As a rookie Oakes had to learn the ropes of the profession.

Older and more experienced ironworkers often played pranks on the new recruits. These pranks taught the "punks," or rookies, valuable lessons that could save their lives and mold them into valuable workers. In such an apprenticeship position, Oakes learned invaluable skills, like licking the sulfur end of a matchstick and using it to remove a piece of metal from the surface of an eye. Another reason for the nickname of "punk" was to make every work crew aware of your lack of experience; in this way other ironworkers kept an eye out for you.[58]

Oakes gained a physical presence in ironwork and would be known later as "A Big Man," one who had influence in the Longhouse. Ironwork is one of the most dangerous professions in the world. But, Oakes learned to cope with fear as he managed to work twenty to forty stories above the earth. Three separate types of crews worked in tandem on any given job site: derrick operators, connector gangs, and rivet gangs. The derrick operation relied on a set of electronic signals or sound bursts transmitted from the top of the structure to the crane operator, as much as forty stories below. The connector gangs set the mobile beams into place with spud wrenches, bullpens, and large bolts. Such an assembly and tools emerged after the "flyboys" of the industry, the riveting gangs. Throughout the 1950s, stories about Mohawk ironworkers were popular and featured in magazines like *Readers Digest, National Geographic,* and *The New Yorker.* The media exploited their masculinity in ads, selling products like cigarettes and televisions.[59]

One of Richard's main duties was serving as a catcher in a riveting gang. The riveting process lasted up to 1960, when it was replaced with bolts and spud wrenches. A riveting gang usually consisted of four ironworkers who divided the tasks of the heater, catcher, sticker-in, bucker-up, and riveter. Hundreds of feet high in the air, each ironworker had a very specific task or combination of tasks to accomplish in assembling steel beams one by one into an enormous superstructure for a skyscraper or bridge. The first job went to the heater, whose duty it was to heat dozens of five-inch metal rivets (they look like giant metal mushrooms) until they are glowing red hot. His job starts by stacking and leveling large wooden planks across several support beams, as the structure supports the weight of a large portable coal furnace. After the rivets are nice and hot, the heater, wearing long protective gloves, reaches into the furnace and retrieves a rivet with a pair of three-foot iron tongs. Before the rivet cools, the heater quickly tosses the molten rivet in the air to the catcher, who is standing near the enormous steel beam they are ready to attach. The catcher's job involves using a cone-shaped metal bucket to catch each scorching hot rivet thrown by the heater, one at a time. Afterwards, the catcher takes over the task of the sticker-in and places the stem or rod end of the rivet through two pre-molded holes from two steel beams. On the same side as the sticker-in is the bucker-up, who utilizes a dolly bar to hold the mushroom head of the rivet in place. On the opposite side of the beams from the bucker-up is the riveter. Riveters have the most dangerous job, as they risk getting their feet tangled up or tripping over the big bulky cord attached to the pneumatic hammer. Once the rivet is held in place by the bucker-up, the riveter forms a steady grip on his pneumatic hammer. With a flip of a lever he pounds the protruding stem of the rivet into a mushroom cap, sealing the beam. Every rivet shrinks as it cools, forming an airtight welded bond—effectively joining the two formerly detached beams into a permanent framed structure. Once completed, the process starts all over again with another rivet.

Speed was everything. The average riveting crew took less than two and a half minutes to set a new hot rivet, at a pace averaging 400 to 600 rivets a day. Few words were spoken, as danger lurked with every breath—one false step, reach, or glance could rob an ironworker of his life.[60]

Often these iron gangs worked under blistering conditions of 95-degree heat. To fight the sweltering heat, men took off their shirts to cool down while working. Accidents happened. Richard occasionally missed some rivets, catching them only after they seared his upper torso, inflicting permanent scars.[61] Oakes proudly carried the scars from this industry for the rest of his life. For some, it was a rewarding trade; for others, it was just hard, muscle-grinding work. Riveting gangs competed with other riveting gangs to be the fastest and best on a job site. Each gang earned not only a wage but a reputation that would potentially generate

A Mohawk ironworking gang heating and driving rivets at a construction site in New York City. These photos appeared in the July 1952 edition of *National Geographic Magazine* in the article "Mohawks Scrape the Sky." Photos: B. Anthony Stewart/National Geographic Creative.

more work in the future. Each member of the riveting gang depended on the skill and concentration of their fellow members. They depended upon each other to remain safe. The loss of even one member was devastating. The pressures and stresses that Richard Oakes inherited from the industry had to take their toll at times. While he was employed in iron-work, Oakes began running with a street gang in New York, possibly as a way to vent the frustrations of his profession and the tense relationship with his father.[62] Ultimately, as was often the case, Richard ran into conflict with the law. Gang life at this time was confined to turf wars of young men who sought proof of their perceived masculinity and some kind of respect of their peer group.[63] Many of these wars were fought over access to public space, such as parks, entertainment, and municipal services.

During the 1950s, gang violence in Brooklyn steadily increased as the number of juvenile arrests more than doubled. Gangs in Brooklyn, as in the rest of America, were divided along racial lines as each neighborhood youth assembled his own means of protection. Richard Oakes gained a physical presence in ironwork, but by the early 1960s he had earned street cred as well. Such credibility was gained in turf battles between rival district gangs; often these scrimmages were tests of endurance, and many ended in bloodshed. These battles were waged with chains, bats, broken bottles, and bare knuckles. Death was rare in these street brawls; it was an unwritten rule that gang violence targeted other gangs almost exclusively. As a minority population among Brooklyn gangs, Indian gangs were often outnumbered and struggled to maintain their street credibility. In 1960, a reported sixty-two gangs existed in Brooklyn alone. The violence between racially segregated gangs mirrored the larger racial conflict that was brewing in many American cities.[64]

Between 1958 and 1959, while protests flared over construction of the St. Lawrence Seaway, Oakes was arrested several times; one time the charge was petty theft, and in 1962 it was for assault and robbery. In March of 1959, a few months before he turned eighteen, Richard Oakes and two associates stole a meat truck in Syracuse. Instead of claiming both the truck and its contents for themselves, they acted as traditional warriors stealing from an enemy—counting coup on a butcher (touching an enemy during battle but not killing them). In their getaway, they drove the meat truck fifteen minutes south to the Onondaga Reservation. Not long after their arrival, word quickly traveled back to Syracuse and soon sheriff's deputies were dispatched to Onondaga. By the time law enforcement got to the scene, Oakes's friends had split on him. Oblivious to his surroundings, Richard Oakes remained in the back of the truck, still handing out meat to Onondaga citizens. He had no defense. He was caught in the very act of committing a crime. Because of his young age and altruistic intentions, he received a light sentence for the charge of petty larceny. As a juvenile at the time of his arrest, he was sent first to the

Elmira Recreation Center in Elmira, New York, for processing. Elmira held the dark reputation of being more of a prison than a school. Elmira Reformatory School was noted for its repressive environment that fostered more aggression from its pupils.[65]

After his release from Elmira, Oakes quickly fell in with the wrong crowd. In Brooklyn, Irene Oakes was dating a Mohawk man who had two sons. Leonard Oakes described the father and sons as "wise guys." In 1962, Richard Oakes was arrested for assault and robbery—after being targeted by a crooked cop who had a reputation for beating on Indians. As he tried to defend himself from the cop, backup arrived and he was suddenly outnumbered. He surrendered. Oakes received a three-year sentence at Comstock, a maximum-security prison also known as "Great Meadow." Akwesasne Mohawk Dave Mitchell, who was at Comstock with Richard Oakes, remembers that very few inmates messed with Oakes. Standing in the lunch line at the prison, one inmate began to throw insults at Oakes thinking the cell bars would shield him. Mitchell recalls that Oakes threw one hard punch and knocked out his tormenter through the bars of his own cell. Within the first year of serving his sentence, Oakes's initial charges were reduced to carrying a dangerous weapon, so he left Comstock on parole. While in prison, his brother Leonard Oakes enlisted with the Marines and served in the failed Bay of Pigs invasion of Cuba.[66]

Once released from prison, Richard went right back into ironworking. Often between construction jobs, he returned to Akwesasne to see family and friends or to cruise for dates. He drove multiple "Indian cars," vehicles that had once been discarded. A certain pride and Indian humor went into reclaiming these automotive misfits throughout Indian Country. Indian cars typically contain special features that provide a unique automotive statement, ritual, and personality. Features ranged from bumpers and fenders secured by baling wire to an ignition that required a certain flathead screw driver. On one particular drive from Syracuse to Akwesasne, Richard drove three hours with a Ho-Chunk friend in a car without a windshield. He gained a reputation among his Akwesasne peers for his charismatic swagger and as a fighter who confronted injustice. Several of his former girlfriends at Akwesasne remembered him as handsome, gentlemanly, and always full of excitement. Oakes had a personality that could easily win over the trust of a perfect stranger, a trait of a natural leader. Once at Bear's Den (a popular hangout), he reportedly lay across the top of a car occupied by several young Mohawk women. Armed only with his charm, he convinced them to offer him a ride. In the early 1960s, the two biggest night spots at Akwesasne were either the Bear's Den, for ice cream, pizza, or burgers, or Tooties Bar, which was a smoky dance hall located off Highway 37 in Rooseveltown to the west of town. Stories about this era and Richard Oakes still circulate throughout Akwesasne.[67]

One of the greatest legends still told about Richard Oakes involves a fight between him and a local tough named Peter Burns. His adversary had a reputation for winning every fight. Most at Akwesasne knew enough about Burns's reputation to keep their distance.

On Monday, May 25, 1963, three days after his twenty-first birthday, Richard Oakes was out late celebrating with a group of friends. He and Herbert Mitchell snagged a car ride with George Laffin and his cousin.

Mohawk activists test their custom-free border crossing rights as recognized by the 1794 Jay Treaty, in Cornwall, Ontario, on January 5, 1969. The Canadian customs official had confiscated $12.94 worth of groceries because Mohawk citizens refused to pay any customs tax, as such a tax conflicted with their treaty rights. To the right of the customs officer are Akwesasne leader Mike Mitchell, young Alex Burns, and Peter Burns wearing a Caughnawaga lacrosse jacket. Photo courtesy of Getty Images, Bettmann Collection 660778710.

Before they reached the international border to Canada, Laffin stopped his car and dropped both Mitchell and Oakes off by the side of the road. The taillights of Laffin's car soon disappeared, and both Oakes and Mitchell recalled exploits and shared stories while they waited for Laffin's return. After he crossed the border and dropped his cousin back off at his home, he picked up a few more friends. It must have taken quite a while on Laffin's part, for as he headed back to the American side of Akwesasne he had picked up four new passengers: Thelbert Bigtree, Irene Loran, Laure Laughing, and Alen King. The five of them drove back across the border to pick up Laffin's two friends, who were waiting by the side of the road. Some time passed, and Mitchell grew impatient and excited. As Laffin's car approached, Mitchell jumped out into the road waving his hands. Trying to avoid hitting Mitchell, Laffin's car swerved left, but it was too late. The car went off the road, landing in a ditch. The impact of the collision sent Mitchell's body over the top of Laffin's car. As Richard Oakes ran to the scene and passengers exited the car, they found that Mitchell had been impaled on a spike protruding from a nearby telephone pole. Over six feet off the ground, the spike had completely punctured Mitchell's right shoulder.[68]

In a panic and out of sheer horror, everyone tried desperately to reach his lifeless body. Only after the state police arrived were they finally able to remove Mitchell's body from the pole. Much later, the county coroner revealed that Mitchell had died from the initial impact with Laffin's car. But in the moment, the police blocked off the road and soon a crowd of people gathered at the gruesome scene. Peter Burns, a spectator in the crowd, grew increasingly agitated by the delay. Richard Oakes, having witnessed the tragic death of his friend, immediately stood up to Burns's impatience and disrespect. Before too long, Burns shoved Oakes. One of the state troopers at the scene stepped in to prevent a fight and to calm the crowd. The trooper ordered Oakes and Burns to take their fight across the border and out of their jurisdiction.[69]

Word traveled fast across the reservation. In a short while, a large crowd assembled near Edith Hemlock's store; rumor has it that someone in the crowd began selling popcorn to the spectators. While Burns was bigger in size and height, Oakes remained resolute. After several rounds of hard lefts and rights, Oakes knocked Burns to the ground. As he offered his hand, Burns threw a wild sucker punch, just missing Oakes. As the fight continued, when he finally sent Richard Oakes to the ground, Burns, rather than extending a hand, began to lay into Oakes's body with a series of relentless kicks. Bloody and swollen, Oakes fought to rise again and never extended another hand to Burns. The fight continued, their bodies swollen and bloody and wracked from sheer physical exhaustion. Spectators watched in disbelief as Oakes and Burns fought until they both fell to the ground simultaneously. The fight resumed again only when one of them started to rise. The battle continued until about the third hour. Burns, barely able to stand, tossed in the towel.

For the first time, someone had stood up to Peter Burns and emerged victorious. The crowd, despite the tragedy that had drawn them together, celebrated Richard's victory. The win was short-lived but well remembered, as Akwesasne prepared to grieve the loss of close friend and relative Herbert Mitchell. While Oakes struggled with the immediacy of Mitchell's death, he also sacrificed himself to defend his community from a reservation bully. Today, the story of the Oakes/Burns bout has reached legendary status, as several different versions of the fight still circulate at large gatherings like the annual Ironworkers Festival held each year at Akwesasne.[70]

Three months later, on Friday, September 13, 1963, Richard's grandfather, Richard Oakes Sr., passed away in Cornwall, Ontario. The fact that his grandfather was in the hospital of course makes it quite plausible that Richard Oakes had traveled back to Akwesasne in order to visit with his grandparents. The Oakes family gathered together at the home of Mitchell Oakes, his grandfather's brother. Services were held at the St. Regis Catholic Church officiated by Reverend Jacobs. Within a year, on March 3, 1964, Richard Oakes's grandmother, Margaret Oakes, followed her late husband in death. The loss of both grandparents within a year must have taken an emotional toll on the entire Oakes family and the wider community in which they lived.[71]

Ultimately, the passing of Richard Oakes's grandparents are like bookends around the violent public death of America's thirty-fifth president. The assassination of President John F. Kennedy in 1963 provoked many Americans to question their service and their role in life. Like so many in his generation, Richard confronted the typical tribulations of his age group but also took on the troubles of his people as well as the dangers of his profession. So Oakes sought another outlet for his frustrations—education.

By the early 1960s, he had completed his requirements for a high school degree. Despite his troubles with the law, Oakes earned a reputation as a skilled laborer and was recruited for construction jobs throughout the New England area.

During the summer of 1964, a race riot erupted in Harlem and Rochester, leading New York Governor Nelson Rockefeller to call up the National Guard. Risking parole violations in 1965, Richard continued to live a migratory life, moving between various construction sites and visiting family in Brooklyn and at Akwesasne. He witnessed an America battling over civil rights on the streets and in the courtroom. On television the world sat on the edge of their seats as they witnessed a Lakota runner named Billy Mills come from behind in the 10,000-meter race to take gold at the 1964 Olympic Games in Tokyo. Mills's victory symbolized more than a gold medal. His come-from-behind win signaled a new era of determination throughout Indian Country. As Richard Oakes traveled between job sites, he learned about Malcolm X's assassination. By March 1965, the nightly news was featuring coverage of peaceful civil rights demonstrators being beaten in the streets of Selma, Alabama, and American troops setting fire to Vietnamese villages. One year later, Student Nonviolent Coordinating Committee (SNCC) leader Stokely Carmichael, who had recently taken part in James Meredith's March Against Fear, issued a national call for Black Power (as opposed to Freedom Now).[72]

While the civil rights movement struggled between ideas of nationalism and integration and between defense and nonviolence, American Indian leaders also struggled to redefine Native political and human rights. In 1961 the Chicago Conference, organized by anthropologist Sol Tax and assisted by Salish-Kootenai historian D'Arcy McNickle, and members of the National Congress of American Indians (NCAI) produced the Declaration of Indian Purpose; the meeting also gave rise to a political organization known as the National Indian Youth Council (NIYC). The Declaration of Indian Purpose called for the repeal of termination legislation and the promotion of Indian sovereignty or home rule.[73] The NIYC promoted Intertribal conferences and chartered organizations of American Indian college students from across the country. The organization hosted conferences and offered variant forms of support to Native Nationalist causes.[74] In 1967, Vine Deloria Jr., the executive director of the NCAI, sanctioned the use of the term *Red Power,* one that would hold crucial meaning throughout Oakes's life.[75]

Soon Richard pursued higher education by moonlighting at Adirondack Community College. From there, he enrolled in night classes at Syracuse University, amidst rumors of a selective service draft for Vietnam.[76] While working on a bridge in Rhode Island, Oakes must have reflected on the growing protests throughout the country and his Nation's role in protecting Indigenous human rights. In 1968, he spontaneously quit his job, sold his ironworking tools, and made plans to move across the country to San Francisco, where he hoped to see the world.[77]

Before he left for San Francisco, Oakes had been working long hours, taking on sixteen-hour shifts on the Newport Bridge in Rhode Island. While living in Rhode Island, he fell in love with a woman from Bethel, Rhode Island. After a fast romance the young couple got married. Despite their whirlwind nuptials, their marriage ended quickly, but not before his wife gave birth to a son. Oakes's father-in-law was a high-ranking law enforcement officer, and as Leonard Oakes remembered it, he never approved of Richard Oakes or the marriage. Perhaps it was the quick marriage, Oakes's criminal record, or maybe even his Mohawk heritage, but whatever the reason, the father-in-law arranged for the break-up and end of their marriage. Divorced and now estranged from his firstborn son, Richard Oakes had to start over.[78]

The 1960s was the season of "love and revolution," which began in San Francisco. By the late 1960s, San Francisco was awash with counter-culture philosophy. College students experimented with LSD, listened to Janis Joplin's smashing vocals, chanted Black Panther slogans like "fight the power," and immersed themselves in the Haight-Ashbury "tribal" aura of nonconformity. Richard Milhous Nixon was about to upset Hubert H. Humphrey in the 1968 presidential election. The world that Oakes entered in California soon provided new horizons to his once-hectic life.

In the summer of 1968, he packed his few belongings, left his family and everything he had known in New York, and headed west for San Francisco, driving a 1965 Rangoon Red Ford Mustang. As he shifted into gear and the miles increased, New York gradually disappeared from his rearview mirror. Oakes, like so many Americans in this era, envisioned moving west as a chance for redemption, a new start on life. By the late 1960s, the lure of the west had been embraced by a radical and diverse

Richard Oakes on Alcatraz Island in 1969. Photo courtesy of
Stephen K. Lehmer/www.stephenlehmer.com.

generation of Americans. The powerful myth of the American West came
to symbolize endless possibilities, innovation, revolution, and greater
independence. For Oakes in 1968, the California dream meant absolute
freedom and offered a cultural and political awakening that radiated from
the steep streets of San Francisco.[79]

CHAPTER THREE

Better Red Than Dead

SAN FRANCISCO AND THE EMERGENCE
OF AN INDIAN CITY

They discovered, as we did, that the "better life" the BIA had
promised all of us was, in reality, life in a tough, urban ghetto. Many
people were unable to find jobs, and those who did were often offered
only marginal employment. Urban Indian families banded together,
built Indian Centers, held picnics and powwows, and tried to form
communities in the midst of large urban populations.

Cherokee Principal Chief, Wilma Mankiller, 1993

Along his route across Indian Country, Oakes stopped at several reservations and made inquiries into local Native issues and politics. Oakes's
lived experience as an Indigenous person complicates standard interpre-
tations about the countercultural movement, as he dropped out of America and fell into Indian Country. Oakes's road trip across Indian Country
ignited a pursuit that commanded the remaining years of his life. During
this time, he uncovered the *true* history and culture of America from an
Intertribal perspective, which later emerged as a guiding principle for
founding the discipline of Native American Studies.[1] At each stop, he listened closely to other Native peoples and discovered a vast community
with many shared issues and experiences. Despite distinct Tribal differences between traditions, language, and culture—the facts of a common
oppressor and a recognizable system of colonization would often bind
Native peoples. Before his trip west, Oakes read about other Nations and
absorbed the history of Turtle Island, but like most young people, he
sought the truth. For many youth at that moment, the answers were radi-
ating from San Francisco.

The urban environment of San Francisco inspired a unique utopian
Intertribal vision of Tribal sovereignty. It was a vision that forged a new

awareness of Native empowerment and independence. From the early 1920s, San Francisco was home to a vibrant and politically active Intertribal community. Over the next several decades, the Bay Area Indian population doubled, and it eventually tripled in size by the 1970s. This twentieth-century mass exodus from reservations and rural communities to western cities represented one of the greatest per capita internal migrations of a people in the United States.

Several external factors influenced this great migration: World War II, the controversial Bureau of Indian Affairs (BIA) relocation program, and the destructive federal policy of termination. Each successive generation of new Indian migrants into San Francisco and other U.S. cities faced extraordinary odds: discrimination, isolation, inadequate public housing, police brutality, and unemployment in addition to the inherent challenges of assimilation and acculturation. Indigenous San Franciscans collectively challenged these overwhelming odds by forming political, economic, social, and cultural coalitions supported by community organizations, centers, and institutions that lent their services to political objectives.

Community leaders struggled to draw enough media and public attention to unmask the truth behind relocation and termination. Bay Area activists competed with a counterproductive bureaucratic utopian vision that consistently enforced paternalistic "father knows best" policies. The best-known of these policies was the BIA's relocation program, which systematically and geographically segregated Native peoples throughout San Francisco—a form of de facto gerrymandering. Through these programs the federal government disenfranchised Native peoples from their Tribal communities while systematically sponsoring relocation into distant cities and districts to prevent a solid Native voting bloc from forming. Whereas termination policy was established to destroy Tribal governments, relocation was forged under the guise of terminating individual connections to Tribal communities.

Ultimately, Native peoples transformed what appeared to be the failed experiment of urban migration and developed a new cultural and political vision—Intertribalism. The San Francisco Indian community formed institutions, chartered organizations, enrolled at college campuses, established business networks, and politicized an entire community. By operating through these new community institutions and organizations,

Native peoples erased old identity questions and stereotypes and formed a new consensus politics.

As thousands of individuals from different Tribal backgrounds created political coalitions to challenge destructive government policies, a more populated Intertribal community altered the urban Americanization experiment. Migrants who typically found themselves at the bottom of the Red Ghetto, located in the North Mission District, strove to protect and reinforce their Tribal identities by accepting an Intertribal identity as "American Indians." This process of Intertribal community building is what I define as creating an Indian City, because it served as a localized model and pattern for other urban Indian communities. By exploring this historical phenomenon, one can better understand the roots of the Red Power movement in the late 1960s. This was a movement that fused together a powerful voice on a tiny island in the Bay Area. The 1969 occupation of Alcatraz became more than just a social experiment; it was an idea. This idea of full independence or home rule, known collectively as sovereignty, ushered in a new era of Native politics that emphasized self-determination.

San Francisco's 1960s Indian community has received little attention from scholars. This chapter explores the complicated invention of the Indian City: a city that both opened and closed doors to Native peoples but also gave birth to a movement where assimilation took a back seat to intense Native Nationalism and Intertribalism.[2]

The urban environment did not turn Native peoples into victims but instead inspired urban Indians to build Intertribal institutions and a community that forever altered their political relationship with the federal government. The cultural, political, social, and economic relationships that Native peoples developed in San Francisco during the 1960s raises several important questions: How did the urban space of San Francisco facilitate the growth of Intertribal identity? How was the city transformed by the newly politicized Indigenous activists? What created the "Red Ghetto"? How did American Indians adapt and survive in this new space? How did Native peoples maintain distinct nationalities while creating Intertribal spaces such as cultural and political organizations, Indian bars, and Indian centers? By creating alternatives to a life of assimilation or Tribal disaffiliation, Richard Oakes and other Indigenous activists transformed their urban neighborhoods and public and private spaces into an Intertribal Indian City.

THE GREAT NATIVE MIGRATION

The majority of historical scholarship that discusses internal migration of ethnic groups in the United States in the twentieth century focuses on African Americans. However, excluding the Depression years, Native peoples migrated to urban centers at a rate of four times that of African Americans.[3] Economic necessity constituted the primary reason that Native peoples moved to cities, particularly in the postwar period. During the 1960s the average annual income on Indian reservations totaled $1,500 per family versus $2,850 per family in cities.[4] A high unemployment rate compounded this situation, reaching well above 90 percent in some communities.[5]

The top industries within reservation communities were agriculture, timber, and mining. Sociologist Joseph G. Jorgensen analyzed BIA reports from 1968 and estimated that Americans grossed $170 million from agricultural products. Of that amount, Indian agriculture accounted for only $16 million. Similarly, of 803 million board feet of lumber harvested from Native lands, Indian communities received only $15 million (this amounts to a little more than $0.18 per board foot of lumber removed from Native lands compared to an average national price between $0.60 to $0.75 per board foot). Mineral leases yielded $31 million to select Indian communities, yet only ten thousand jobs were created for a total Indian population of 764,000.[6] Most reservation communities lacked a stable economic infrastructure to keep these profits within their borders. Additionally, much of the profits that accrued to Native peoples via agricultural and extractive industries were derived through the leasing of lands, which stripped most Tribal governments of their right to control the production of resources on Indian land.

Depopulation led to further economic disparity for many reservation communities. In the twentieth century, three major events led to an increase of migration from the reservation to the city: World War II, the Bureau of Indian Affairs relocation program, and the federal termination policy, which was passed into law in 1953.[7]

The first migration of Native peoples to urban centers took place during and after World War II, as a result of the approximately 44,500 Native men and women who enlisted in the armed forces. Many of these troops were exposed to other worlds in their platoons and travels. The military proved through desegregated regiments that Indians could actively compete on the battlefield among soldiers from different back-grounds. The regimented life of the military and service in wartime industry mobilized thousands of American Indians to pursue opportuni-ties in an urban setting after the war. Like thousands of their comrades, many Native veterans took advantage of the GI Bill to secure loans and an education, while others applied for Veterans Administration (VA) loans to purchase homes or start businesses in western cities. Some even relo-cated to the burgeoning suburbs. For some veterans the urban environ-ment was a place that would enrich their newfound foreign and domestic wartime experiences.[8] For others, the city represented the ultimate escape, a place where one could get lost in the crowded streets, delight in window-shopping, and experience new foods and sensations. It was a different and exciting reality, far from the pace of reservation life or life within the many rural non-reservation communities of Oklahoma.

Enlisted men started the flow of Native peoples to western cities during World War II, but others soon followed, looking for semi-skilled factory jobs in wartime industries.[9] Both Indian men and women helped to desegregate industry in American cities, and many of them achieved an economic prosperity that was unprecedented in Native life. Native women by the thousands championed the call to factories in the aircraft industries, and scholars estimate that women workers constituted about one-quarter of the Native population that left the reservation during World War II.[10] Many men and women were recruited directly from local boarding schools to work in the factories. Overall, around forty thousand Native peoples relocated to urban environments to acquire employment in wartime industries.[11]

As soldiers returned home and the war came to a close, demand for workers decreased. Native peoples were usually the first to be laid off from their newfound employment: "By 1950 the unemployment rate for urban Indians had reached fifteen percent nearly three times that of whites."[12] As quickly as opportunity had come to Indian wartime laborers, tragedy was just around the corner. Despite increased financial savings from the wartime years, many Native peoples survived on dual incomes—supporting family and relations back home or on the reservation while subsisting in the city. Many lacked the flexible savings to deal with the sudden loss of employment. Those who could afford it returned to their home communities, while those who lacked such funding sought affordable housing and semi-skilled jobs and continued to fight for better jobs and living conditions.

During the war, the first wave of Native migrants to San Francisco settled in Hunter's Point, a district formed among the shipyards of Little Tokyo—a district that had recently witnessed the forced removal of thousands of Japanese Americans who were sent to internment camps. Soon thereafter, much of the Native community was dispersed throughout Greater San Francisco.[13] The majority who settled in Hunter's Point were African American families who sought employment in the shipyards, and eventually former Little Tokyo became known by outsiders as Harlem West.[14] Former Cherokee resident Wilma Mankiller recalled, "Jobs started to become more and more scarce in the 1960s . . . the housing area became little more than a ghetto. . . . We found a few Native Americans living at Hunter's Point, including another Cherokee family. . . . My Mother also became friends with people from different backgrounds. . . . Sometimes it seemed like a war zone when rival gangs clashed on the streets. . . . Living in Hunter's Point also gave me an insight into cultures I otherwise might not have ever known."[15] Soon, Native and African American families began to compete for skilled and semi-skilled employment, housing, and economic mobility.

Housing in Hunter's Point proved a more affordable solution for the thousands of laborers who relocated to San Francisco for employment during the war. Without the advantages of the VA loan, Native laborers were forced to stick to a tight budget, so many latched onto affordable rentals throughout Hunter's Point. Due to the huge influx of laborers relocating into the Bay Area during the war, this sudden population boom created a severe housing shortage and pushed the value of real estate far beyond the grasp of many Native families. Despite official numbers, Native peoples faced de facto discrimination and redlining when applying for mortgages, especially when buying homes in all-white neighborhoods. Coupled with high unemployment, many found themselves at the end of a very short economic stick.[16]

While military service and the promise of jobs drew many Indigenous peoples to U.S. cities during World War II, federal Indian policy determined the nature of the migrations during the postwar years. By 1952, the BIA launched one of the most dramatic projects in its history: the relocation program. The program began in 1948, with the BIA using the

Hopi and Navajo Tribes as test cases.[17] In 1956 Congress passed the Indian Vocational Training Act (Public Law 959) to provide job training to migrants. Along with job training, relocatees received a one-way bus ticket to one of six relocation centers located in Chicago, Cleveland, Dallas, Denver, Los Angeles, and San Francisco. The federal government also provided temporary housing, supplementary income for furniture and household necessities, and job counseling for one year after arrival.[18] Within that year most migrants received a monthly check of $140; if they found work, then the monthly stipend was cut off. Rarely did the BIA provide migrants with the promised retention-based services. Many Natives, such as Shoshone/Bannock citizen LaNada Means, an Alcatraz occupation leader, had experienced relocation in her twenties, and found that the promises made by the federal government were only lies:

> The only programs the BIA has are vocational training for
> menial jobs, and I didn't especially want to be a beautician.
> Actually, I wanted to try college again, but when I told this to a
> BIA counselor, he said they didn't have any money for that and
> told me I was being "irrational and unrealistic." All types of
> problems develop when you're on relocation. The Indian who
> has come to the city is like a man without a country. Whose
> jurisdiction are you under, the BIA's or the state's? You go to a
> county hospital when you're sick and they say, "Aren't you taken
> care of by the Indian Affairs people?" It's very confusing. You
> hang around with other Indians, but they are as bad off as you
> are. Anyway, I started sinking lower and lower. . . . I married. . . .
> I got pregnant again . . . things didn't work out in the marriage.
> . . . I ended up in the San Francisco General psychiatric ward for
> a few weeks. I was at the bottom. . . . Indian people get to this
> point all the time, especially when they're relocated into the big
> city and are living in the slums. At that point, you've got two
> choices: either kill yourself and get it over with—a lot of Indians
> do this—or try to go all the way up, and this is almost
> impossible.[19]

Native peoples who participated in the relocation program were promised housing, jobs, and financial assistance. Most found these few options to be a dead end; as a result, relocation was viewed by Indigenous critics as a failure. Economist Alan Sorkin calculated that "from 1953 to 1957 . . . three out of ten who were relocated returned home during that same fiscal year in which they migrated."[20] On the other hand, some, like Quechan, Mojave, and Maricopa citizen Yvonne Lamore, found her experience to be quite rewarding in the end: "The group I was in was made up mostly of single women who were either going to attend some kind of business school or cosmetology school. It was fun getting to know each other, but by the end of the week we would all scatter to different parts of the Bay Area: some would remain in Oakland, others would go to San Jose or Hayward, and some of us to San Francisco. Our paths would cross again over the years at one Indian bar or another. In the 1960s, there were Indian bars everywhere, and they all seemed to be doing a very lucrative business."[21]

The experiences of LaNada Means and Yvonne Lamore offer a glimpse into the complex associations that Indigenous peoples forged with the relocation program. For some, the program and living situations in the "Red Ghetto" were far better than conditions in their homelands. Additionally, the opportunities for some Native women greatly increased once they left paternalistic and corrupt Tribal governmental systems. For couples, the economic gain was twofold: now Indian couples could enjoy the financial rewards of a double income. For Native children it meant new horizons and public education, through which they avoided boarding schools. Such benefits often brought families closer together.

The advantages for many Indian families outweighed the costs of relocation, which was strictly voluntary, and the BIA screened all applicants and searched out those they believed would adjust to urban living. Applicants were ranked on age, previous work experience, police record, marital status, and education. The program, for instance, preferred married applicants over single individuals, for relocation officers assumed that family connections increased a migrant's chances for success. Veterans held a good chance of being selected for relocation. In fact, almost half of the Indigenous peoples who relocated to San Francisco were World War II veterans. Although the relocation program convinced many Native peoples to move to San Francisco, about one-third of the total Native population relocated without government assistance.

There is no doubt that relocation was a force of transformation to Indigenous populations. Oakes relocated to San Francisco voluntarily. After he arrived in the Bay Area, Oakes stayed away from construction work, but in a twist of irony he landed a job as a delivery driver—years earlier, Oakes had done time in prison for stealing a delivery truck. Not long thereafter, he secured permanent work as a bartender at Warren's Slaughterhouse Bar, which was located in San Francisco's Mission District and owned by Klamath bar owners Ruby and Frank Loureiro. He lived in a single room occupancy (SRO) at the Star Hotel located at 2176 Mission Street.[22] An SRO offered affordable urban living options for new urban arrivals, as it was typical for residents to share a single kitchen and bathroom.[23] Having met several people who had relocated to San Francisco, in 1969 Oakes commented of the program, "The San Francisco Bay Area has been, as have many urban centers, recipient of a large scale Native American migration. Because of the relocation program of the Bureau of Indian Affairs, there are representatives of most of the major tribes residing here. Many are facing urban situations for the first time and find it an unknown and disruptive experience. The variety of tribal identities, the lack of communication between these, and public images of the 'Indian' which are culturally undefined and often confusing in institutional application . . . have added to the stress of urban 'adjustment' and the formation of self-identity."[24]

By 1972, the relocation program had resettled a hundred thousand Native peoples out of a total U.S. population of 764,000 Indigenous Americans. In 1960 local Native organizations estimated that the San Francisco Indian population was around ten thousand.[25] Nationally, in 1960, about 27 percent of Indian Country lived in urban enclaves; by 1977, cities were claiming almost 50 percent of the total Native population throughout America.[26] This mass movement of Native peoples also had the effect of displacing other Indigenous communities local to San Francisco. For some, such as the Ohlone Nation, relocation complicated their fight for greater visibility and recognition. While invisibility remained a critical issue, California Tribes, also called rancherias, competed for far fewer resources within their state. Many more California Tribes championed their cause for Native Nationalism by incorporating the ideology, tactics, and philosophies of Red Power into their fight for greater treaty and human rights.[27]

The House Concurrent Resolution 108 (passed in 1953), commonly known as the Termination Act, affected the Native migration experience by ending federal trust responsibilities with 109 Indigenous nations throughout America. Termination policy devastated many Native communities, overturning the protection of Tribal land; negating treaty rights, including health care and education; and threatening a way of life for thousands. Statistics on those moving into the city because of termination legislation are lacking, but this legislation in effect accounted for a large proportion of the one-third of the Native peoples who relocated to San Francisco and other cities at their own expense.[28]

One major criticism of the relocation and termination era was that the government sought to exploit a large unskilled labor force, and this strategy weakened the already meager labor force on many reservations. Some statistics indicate that as much as 25 percent of the U.S. mineral wealth is located solely on Native lands.[29] Compounding this was the government's increasing dependence on uranium for atomic weapons and energy, which demanded an exploitable labor force (and smaller populations to limit the extent of exposure) and diminished the powers of some Tribal governments against multinational corporations.[30] By September of 1969, BIA Division Director Prentice Mooney published an article in *Nation's Business* magazine which declared, "Indian Country Is a Frontier Again." Coupled with the BIA's relocation program, large tracts of land were taken out of trust status when individuals left their reservation communities. These large plots of land created a checkerboard effect and ripped Tribal control of these lands from their respective Tribal governments.[31] Relocation and termination legislation accelerated suspicions of resource exploitation across Indian Country and promoted the systematic economic and diplomatic destruction of Tribal governments.

MISSION DISTRICT

Before 1906, the Mission District was primarily comprised of worker tenements and the famed Mission Dolores dating back to 1776. After the devastating earthquake and fire of 1906, working-class Irish families moved into the area in search of cheaper lands for housing. Tenements were promptly built in the district for workers helping to rebuild the city. Eventually, because of the high numbers of working-class people, unions relocated their headquarters into the district. Following the unions were other ethnic laborers, primarily Italians, Germans, Russians, and Scandinavians. Throughout the 1930s, the Mission District was at the center of organized labor, which successfully sponsored strikes around the Bay Area.

By World War II the population in the area had nearly doubled.[32] As older emigrant groups moved out, new migrant workers, including African Americans, Mexican Americans, Samoans, and Native Americans replaced them. Neighborhoods like the Mission were typically characterized by low-income housing (left over from the early 1900s), high unemployment, and crime—residents referred to this part of town as "the Little Rez."[33] As the incoming Native populations grew in number, they competed with other ethnic groups for services, housing, and jobs. By the 1960s, the Mission District—especially the North Mission—was home to the largest concentration of Native peoples in the city and was the site of the San Francisco Indian Center.[34] LaNada Means recalled, "Whenever Mayor Alioto went to the Mission District where many of us lived, he would meet with the Latino and Spanish groups, the Mission Rebels (Blacks) and the Indians. . . . We were recognized as a political unit and gradually we became politicized."[35] These coalition politics were critical to the unification of the Mission District, as Wilma Mankiller remembered: "My spirits were buoyed in the mid-1960s whenever I heard more news from the San Joaquin Valley about the National Farm Workers Association, led by Cesar Chavez. . . . I attended several of their benefits and consciousness-raising events held throughout the Mission District."[36] Forming alliances with the National Farm Workers Association and creating powerful coalitions was a focus for many Native peoples in the Mission District. Despite competing for scarce urban resources, coalitions could bolster municipal reform. Seminole citizen Al Miller, later instrumental in the formation of Native American Studies (NAS) and the Alcatraz takeover, collected the local paper *Nuestra Misión de San Francisco*, a publication put out by the League of United Latin American Citizens.[37] The periodical was a way to organize the diverse citizenry of the Mission District into a voting bloc. Several of the articles suggested forming a separate and unique "worldwide" municipal government independent from San Francisco's City Hall. These types of coalition politics created institutional and organizational support for Native peoples throughout the Mission District.

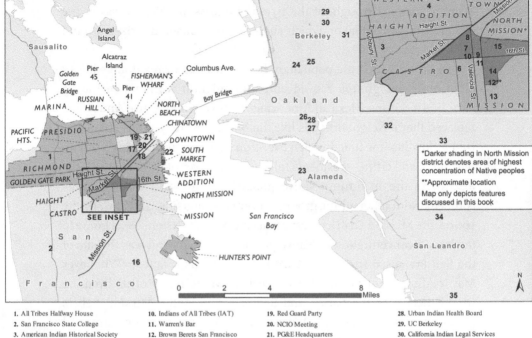

San Francisco Indian City. Map by Ed Brands.

1. All Tribes Halfway House	10. Indians of All Tribes (IAT)	19. Red Guard Party	28. Urban Indian Health Board
2. San Francisco State College	11. Warren's Bar	20. NCIO Meeting	29. UC Berkeley
3. American Indian Historical Society	12. Brown Berets San Francisco	21. PG&E Headquarters	30. California Indian Legal Services
4. Friendship House	13. La Raza Legal Defense	22. Alcatraz Receiving Depot	31. Far West Laboratory
5. Black Panther Party Office, SF	14. Mission Rebels	23. BIA Office	32. Brown Berets Oakland Office
6. Mission High School	15. Mission Tenants Union	24. Pacific Automotive Training	33. Merritt College
7. Mission Area Community Action Board	16. American Indian Baptist Church	25. Black Panther Party Headquarters	34. Oakland American Indian Baptist Church
8. SNCC	17. Glide Memorial Church	26. Oakland Inter-Tribal Friendship House	35. United Bay Area Council of Indian Affairs
9. SF American Indian Center	18. NAACP	27. BANAC	

National movements, like the La Raza Unida Party, which emerged out of California in 1969, initially sought to divest from the Democratic Party and build an alternative political party consisting of a voting bloc between Mexican Americans and Native peoples throughout the American Southwest.[38] This political shift mirrored a larger demographic shift in San Francisco's population. In 1960, San Francisco was estimated at 82 percent Anglo, and a decade later only 57 percent of the city remained Euro-American; much of this shift has been attributed to the phenomenon known historically as white flight.[39] Political activists like Rodolfo Corky Gonzales from Crusade for Justice initially advocated for a greater Indigenous Nationalism that could transform American leadership, law, and policy. The La Raza Unida Party represented a unique brand of coalition politics and a form of political organizing that was embraced by Richard Oakes and other Red Power activists.

The Mission District built a strong core by utilizing coalition politics; with Model Cities financing in 1968, local community activists founded Community Action Programs like the Mission Coalition Organization (MCO). This particular organization forged together a diverse alliance of community activists, which included a Lakota executive officer named Elba Tuttle. The MCO incorporated in an effort to regulate and reform urban renewal programs. They supported tenant rights through the formation of the Mission Housing Development Corporation. Most of the efforts of the MCO went towards curbing the dramatic fallout from gentrification, a process where large-scale middle- to higher-income development occurs in a lower-income neighborhood, which has the effect of spiking property values and living expenses. For the most part gentrification fosters the gradual eviction and removal of lower-income resident populations. The potential loss of four thousand apartments in and around the San Francisco Indian Center on 16th Street for a new BART station acted as a spur to bring these groups together under the MCO.[40]

The Mission District also saw the rise of power politics with Los Siete de la Raza, an organization that published its own underground newspaper *Basta Ya!* and facilitated a joint Chicano/Latino social justice movement to overturn the conviction of six Latino men slated to be executed for the killing of a San Francisco police officer.[41] A principal organizer of Los Siete was a Cahuilla Indigenous woman named Judy Drummond, who worked alongside key representatives from the Red Guard Party in Chinatown, the Black Panther Party, and the Third World Liberation Front.[42] The Brown Berets began in Los Angeles in 1968 but soon established an office on 16th Street near the San Francisco Indian Center. Many of the leaders of the Brown Berets abandoned their Mission offices to lend greater support to the Third World Liberation Front. Despite the closing of their office in 1969, the Brown Berets also maintained a larger office in Oakland near Merritt College and the Black Panther Party headquarters.[43]

In 1960 local Native organizations estimated San Francisco's Indian population to be around ten thousand; ten years later San Francisco contained the third-largest urban Indian population in the United States, numbering around twenty thousand and hosting more than a hundred

different Indigenous nations.[44] Unfortunately, the majority of this population found themselves in the Mission District after a string of broken
promises from the relocation and termination era. The development of a
new infrastructure and political awareness was crucial for turning back
the tide of destructive federal policies toward Indigenous peoples. An
Intertribal awareness and creation of institutions that politicized Native
concerns at the local, state, and national levels culminated with the advent
of a new city—an Indian City.

Soon after he arrived in the politically active Mission District, Oakes
met a young woman who frequented the San Francisco Indian Center
named Anne Delores Marrufo, a twenty-seven-year-old Kashaya Pomo
from Stewart's Point Rancheria in northern California. Marrufo was a
single mother with six children: Yvonne, Rocky, William, Tanya, Joseph,
and Leonard. Born on April 7, 1941, Annie was one of six kids—three
sisters and two brothers. Her parents, Leonard and Lillian Marrufo, maintained a strong presence in Kashaya politics. Her home was Stewart's
Point, a forty-acre rancheria located just off the jagged coastline near Sea
Ranch and nestled in among the giant redwoods, a forest that absorbs all
sound. Annie has often been described by those who knew her as resil-
ient, quiet, shy, reserved, and extremely protective of her family. Over
time, Oakes loved Annie's kids as his own, and her kids clung to him.[45]
She would become the counterbalance to Richard Oakes, and at times she
was the only one who could cool his tempered frustrations. They quickly
fell in love and were married by 1968.[46]

SAN FRANCISCO INDIAN CITY

Although the North Mission District most closely represented an urban
American Indian ethnic neighborhood, a vast majority of the Native
population was widely dispersed throughout the greater San Francisco
area. Therefore, Native peoples were typically mobile, juggled multiple
jobs, and were increasingly migratory between urban and reservation
communities. The Indian City or Native neighborhood was created and
defined by Indian institutions and businesses. In San Francisco, the first
institution that characterized the development of an Indian City was the
bar culture. The most famous "Indian Bar" was the Klamath-owned
Warren's Slaughterhouse Bar in the North Mission District.[47] Warren's
had also provided Richard Oakes with one of his first jobs shortly after he

arrived in San Francisco. Like in Brooklyn, Indian bars served as an entry point to San Francisco and were the first stop on the road to urban survival for many Native peoples. At neighborhood bars individuals and families learned about opportunities for housing, jobs, and Tribal politics. This atmosphere fostered much-needed Intertribal interactions. These bars often cut across class lines, as the necessity arose to interact with other Natives who possessed a shared history and a common background. Bars were also places that promoted social interaction through dating or "cruising" for dates. For newcomers to the city, bars were places where they met or located people from their community and established networks of friends. These networks were crucial for sustaining and building an Intertribal community, in that they imparted survival skills to new migrants within the urban environment. Political organizers in the community took advantage of these networks for lobbying purposes. Warren's was the first place that future American Indian Movement leader Russell Means, a Lakota citizen, learned about the policy of termination.[48] Ultimately, an important function of these bars was to foster atmospheres of entertainment, relaxation, and refuge from the pressures of the concrete prairie. In particular, Warren's was also a place of employment for Native peoples, hiring managers, bartenders, and waitresses, which accented its cultural atmosphere.

On the other hand, joints like Warren's sometimes fostered a hostile social setting and encouraged the habitual dependency of some of its clients. Lumbee citizen Dean Chavers described Warren's as "the grungiest bar in the history of the world. . . . I went there only about once or twice, no more than that, it was a rough bar."[49] Police typically patrolled the bars of the North Mission District. They relied on racial profiling and stereotypes, which led to higher arrest rates for Native peoples.[50] A 1977 study revealed that arrest rates for Indians were seven to twenty-two times greater than the arrest rate for African Americans for alcohol-related offenses.[51] The study also revealed that the arrest rate for urban Indians was four times higher than any other ethnic group in the city, the total arrest rate being 27,535 per 100,000.[52] Despite the threat of racial profiling by police outside the bar or violence inside the bar, Native peoples continued to frequent Warren's. In 1972, Oakes remembered his time as a bartender at Warren's: "Drinking seems to fill a void in the life of many Indians. It takes the place of the singing of a song, the sharing of a song with another tribe, the sharing of experiences that another tribe member might have had. Drinking is used as a way to create feelings of some kind where there aren't any. It fills a void, that's all."[53] Within the Mission District, as competition among different ethnic groups increased over housing, jobs, and limited resources, so did crime between groups. Contemporary researchers have concluded that the high arrest rates were the product of simple discrimination, because Indians represented one of the most visible populations within the city.

On September 14, 1968, Oakes got into an altercation with police officers in downtown San Francisco near the popular shopping destination of the Embarcadero Center. He had been in a fight and assaulted a police officer who was trying to restore order. Upon his arrest, the officers witnessed something in Richard that many would come to recognize: his potential for leadership.[54] The San Francisco Police Department had been working to curb violence between Native Americans and Samoans in the Mission District. After Richard's arrival, they began to look to Oakes to help resolve their difficulties with community relations. Much of the rivalry between the two groups in San Francisco was over turf, dating, and competition over the meager resources in the district. Street gangs emerged within the Samoan and Native communities to enforce "street laws" and protect their relations.[55] Oakes found himself caught in the middle. With his prior record, he was all too aware of the consequences for his involvement in this contentious situation. He was no longer single—he had responsibilities to his wife and children. Instead of a long jail stint, the police department offered him work as a community organizer. His job was to calm differences between the two groups and help to restore peaceful relations in the Mission.[56]

Indian centers coexisted with the bar culture as important institutions that facilitated a more formalized networking system. The San Francisco Indian Center, also located in the North Mission District, was a focal point for bringing the community together socially and politically. Much like the bar culture, Indian centers served a function of networking and supplied information about jobs, housing, and health care for the Bay Area community. The Indian center was originally established in the early 1950s by the Society of St. Vincent De Paul, a Catholic organization. By the mid-1960s, however, the society turned over the management of the center to the American Indian Council of the Bay Area, an Intertribal political group that offered aid to migrants in the Indian City, sponsored the Annual Indian Day Picnic, and lobbied against relocation and termination.[57] Wilma Mankiller recalled what the San Francisco Indian Center meant for her: "Located upstairs in an old frame building on sixteenth street on the edge of the very rough and tough Mission District, the Indian Center became a sanctuary for me. . . . For me, it became an oasis where I could share my feelings and frustrations with kids from similar backgrounds."[58] Mary Lee Johns described it as a beautiful place. The upstairs had a massive hardwood dance floor (dances occurred once a week, powwows every month), meeting rooms, and a sewing room where the older women worked on everything from quilts to dance regalia. The main level contained a small restaurant with several dining tables and chairs off of the kitchen as well as various offices for staff members. She recalled fondly several plush red-velvet chairs that graced an elegant room on the main level.[59]

The Indian center established programs to aid in job counseling, social work, and health outreach programs and served as a distribution center for food and clothing. After relocatees were cut off from the aid provided by the federal program, many took refuge in the programs administered by their local Indian center.[60] Eventually, Indian centers throughout the country competed for grants from the federal government to cover their operating expenses and program budgets. The San Francisco Indian Center created a governing board of directors responsible for appointing a director and maintaining the annual budget for the institution. For many migrants to San Francisco, the center was an organization that located temporary housing and assisted in their overall adjustment.[61]

In 1969, the San Francisco Indian Center was destroyed in a suspicious fire. Most Native peoples blamed this catastrophe on the Samoan community, illustrating the depth of interethnic rivalry in the district. A temporary Indian center was established in a makeshift office on 16th Street that eventually served as the mainland office for Indians of All Tribes—which later would be responsible for the nineteen-month occupation of Alcatraz Island.

By 1971, the San Francisco Indian Center hosted an estimated forty or more local organizations.[62] These disparate cultural and political organizations and associations became the third component in the development

Left: Unidentified Indian family standing in front of the temporary location of the San Francisco Indian Center on Valencia Street in the Mission District in 1972. Top right: Three unidentified American Indian teenagers at the entrance to the Oakland Indian Friendship House in Oakland, California. Middle right: Two unidentified students from the Pacific Automotive Center, a school for training American Indian mechanics in Oakland, California, in March 1972. Bottom right: Eldy Bratt, a Quechua/Aymara citizen, on Alcatraz Island in May 1970. The Bratt and Oakes families remained close friends before and well after the occupation of Alcatraz Island. In addition to participation in the Alcatraz Island takeover, Eldy later participated in the 1970 Puyallup Encampment. © Ilka Hartmann 2018.

of the Indian City's infrastructure. Organizations ranged in function from Tribally specific (Navajo, Eskimo, Chippewa, and Tlingit-Haida clubs) to a wider range of Intertribal associations. The Tribally specific clubs emphasized language revitalization and contact with relatives and were usually quite small in attendance. Intertribal organizations of the Bay Area were vital to the longevity of the urban Indian community, from churches to alumni associations. A total of six or more Indian churches were located in the Bay Area, including the American Indian Baptist Church to the Native American Church. The Native American Church in San Francisco operated under a confederacy of roadmen devoted to Grandfather Peyote.[63] Church culture served as the meeting ground for families and individuals that cut across Tribal and class differences.[64]

A host of different activities were arranged by organizations, which provided a recreational purpose, ranging from baseball and basketball teams to dance clubs that hosted local powwows. Sponsored by the San Francisco Indian Center once a month, powwows served to facilitate an Intertribal awareness. On reservations powwows were strictly Tribal in nature, but as the Intertribal community increased in numbers, new Intertribal dances and songs were created. Beyond Indigenizing public spaces and cities, powwows sponsored a new consensus politic, an institution that respected both Tribal difference and Intertribal unity. Powwows were overt demonstrations of how American Indian peoples employed tradition, public action, and commerce to bolster the Indian City.[65]

Powwows became another source of income for many Indians in the city, as traders were able to sell traditional crafts to the general public, and Indian business owners used sponsorship of these cultural activities to advertise. In California a total of 450 Indian-owned businesses were located primarily in urban areas. These businesses eventually formed a statewide association called the United Indian Development Association, which aided other Native peoples when seeking loans for commercial development.[66] Two of the most notable businesses in the San Francisco area included Adam Nordwall's termite business and Warren's. Nordwall served on the American Indian Council of the Bay Area and was president of the local Chippewa Club. Nordwall used profits from his business to fund organizational development in the Bay Area, to support agencies of protest within the community, and to provide jobs for those who sought employment. Warren's Slaughterhouse Bar was owned by a member of the Klamath Nation from Oregon who also utilized Indian employment and circulated money back into the Indian community. Both business owners, however, lived outside of the Mission District and Hunter's Point, which was typical of middle-income individuals but robbed the district of a much-needed tax base for redevelopment and financial infrastructure.[67]

Every Indian City relied on the formation of neighborhoods with high concentrations of Native peoples. Indian neighborhoods like the Red Ghetto in the Mission District were typically characterized by low-income housing, high unemployment, and crime. As the Native population increased in the district, Native peoples increasingly found themselves competing with other ethnic groups for municipal services, housing, and jobs. One particular immigrant group that the Native community was in constant disagreement with were the Samoan peoples. Much of this rivalry started between street gangs of Samoan citizens and the Native gang, better known as the "Thunderbirds" in the Mission District.[68] These gangs competed for dates and women and ultimately over turf rule within the district. It is hard to pinpoint a sole cause for this interethnic rivalry, but Mary Lee Johns, who relocated to San Francisco from the Cheyenne River Sioux Reservation, recalled that the tensions stretched back to a murder that had occurred before 1964. The conflict originated with a Lakota who killed another Samoan for which vengeance was leveled against any Indian in the Mission. More importantly, Johns connected the rivalry to municipal politics, as the BART (Bay Area Rapid Transit) line after 1966 sought to construct a station where the Indian center and Warren's were then located. More specifically, San Francisco mayor Joseph Alioto's office solicited Samoan gangs to target and pressure the Native community into surrendering their opposition to the BART expansion into the Mission District. A third source for conflict might have involved a piece of legislation, proposed in 1965 by Daniel Inouye, that sought to identify Samoan peoples as Native Americans. This measure would surely have eroded the already fragile relationship between leaders of the Native and Samoan communities. Given that any new classification of Samoan peoples as Native Americans would have the effect of increasing the number of people entitled to federal services, Native peoples viewed the bill as an assault on trust responsibilities and meager funding resources through the already-strapped Bureau of Indian Affairs.[69]

Neighborhoods instituted their own forces of stability as families like the Oakeses came together for civic activities such as powwows or picnics at the San Francisco Indian Center. Much of the housing was substandard, with high rents and landlords who discriminated against Samoans or Natives. As a result many families were highly mobile, often moving three to four times a year because of eviction or other setbacks.[70] This increased mobility within the community necessitated a growing dependence on the institutions that constituted San Francisco's Indian City. Most families that came from the reservation typically had either a poor credit rating or no rating at all and represented large families, which gave some landlords the legal justification to discriminate.

If the Mission District was so ghettoized, why did so many Native peoples choose to stay there? Many Natives refused to live in these conditions and returned back to their home communities, but for others their communities at home were often worse: "In 1970, 46 percent of all rural Indian housing had inadequate plumbing facilities compared to 8 percent for urban Indians. . . . 19 percent is considered crowded (more than one resident per room), compared to 44 percent for rural Indians."[71] Eventually, as federal funding for urban Indians began to rise in the late 1960s, it caused competition for reservation communities. This was one of the sparks that began a political and cultural split between urban and rural or reservation Indians.[72]

On April 4, 1968, the Reverend Dr. Martin Luther King Jr. was assassinated outside his hotel room in Memphis, Tennessee. His death shocked and stunned the nation. His funeral became a portrait of his life, as television images displayed over a hundred thousand people marching behind his casket. His coffin was carried through the streets of Atlanta on an old farm wagon pulled by two Georgian mules. During his lifetime he led one of the country's most powerful civil rights movements. His nonviolent tactics for peaceful demonstration would influence generations to come. Just two years prior to King's death, a young Fort Peck Assiniboine activist named Hank Adams, who was part of the five-year-old National Indian Youth Council, had listened to King deliver his powerful anti-Vietnam address in a small crowded church in Riverside, New York.[73] Haudenosaunee leaders had worked with King on his Poor People's Campaign and would now march beside Ralph Abernathy in the assassinated leader's memory. To say that the Native community felt a loss would be an understatement. Following King's death, riots broke out in over one hundred cities. Americans watched as hatred and racism dismantled their cities and the National Guard arrived to "restore order." For Native peoples, the signs of revolution and change were everywhere.

Two months later, in June 1968, yet another event stunned the nation when presidential nominee Robert Kennedy was assassinated after delivering his victory speech for the California Democratic primary. The act was captured by camera crews anxious for an interview with the presidential hopeful. A young disgruntled man named Sirhan Sirhan who had taken offense at Kennedy's Israeli policies pushed through the crowd and fired several rounds from a handgun. This chaotic and cowardly act triggered tears of disbelief in almost every American. Richard Oakes and the rest of Indian Country witnessed the tragedy unfold on national television. Only a few months earlier Kennedy had visited the Pine Ridge Reservation. He had listened to testimony about its issues from both young and old. While there, accompanied by South Dakota Senator George McGovern, the two politicians paid their respects at a large grey stone memorial that sits atop a mass grave. Etched into the memorial are the names of the Lakota Ghost Dancers—men, women, and children— who were massacred in 1890 by the U.S. military at Wounded Knee. With Robert Kennedy's passing, Indian Country lost a potential champion for Indian Rights. Before his death, Kennedy had been researching and drafting new legislation to reform federal Indian policy.

As the country continued to mourn, the city Richard Oakes had entered was different from the rest of San Francisco, it was a city unrecognizable to most of its residents—it was an Indian City. Having grown up in the largely Mohawk Indian City of Brooklyn, New York, Richard Oakes understood the politics of the Indian City. He had a unique insight into the institutions, organizations, and built environment of this diverse concrete prairie. Oakes would eventually make an enormous historical impact on this vibrant Indian space and in Indigenous cities throughout North America.

THE BIRTH OF NATIVE AMERICAN STUDIES

Another major element of the Indian City was the development of Native American Studies programs and student organizations. While serving as a community organizer in the Mission District, Richard Oakes met with Dr. Samuel Ichiyé Hayakawa, the president of San Francisco State College

(SFSC).[74] Both Oakes and Hayakawa had very strong personalities, and Hayakawa immediately grew attached to Richard. Dean Chavers remembers, "He loved Richard . . . he let it be known that . . . Hayakawa loved this guy, he was like a son." Shortly after their first meeting, Hayakawa recruited Richard for the coordinator position in the newly established Native American Studies program for the spring semester of 1969.

While attending San Francisco State College, Oakes and Annie moved their family into the dorms, known popularly by students as "Gatorville." The dorms were constructed during World War II to house workers employed by the Navy. In between the box-like military grey apartments was a large playground with jungle gyms, slides, and swing sets for the kids. The two-story apartment complex was an economical choice for Richard and Annie. They could rent a two-bedroom apartment for about fifty-five dollars a month.[75] This was a cheap alternative compared to the average cost of about two hundred dollars a month for one-bedrooms in inner-city San Francisco. Another positive aspect for the young couple was the free cooperative babysitting program that freed time for Annie and for Richard's studies.[76] He continued to work part-time at Warren's and as a community organizer curbing gang violence for the city.

Prior to Oakes's enrollment, San Francisco State was engulfed in one of the most heated campus strikes to date. In September of 1968, a strike was called by the Black Student Union around the controversial firing of an African American faculty member named George Murray, who had connections with the Black Panther Party and who made several rousing speeches on campus.[77] Not long after, BSU strikers combined forces with the Third World Liberation Front and American Federation of Teachers as they fought together to establish one of the first Ethnic Studies departments in the country. By the end of the strike, "more than 700 arrests, countless beatings, and daily occupation of the campus" had produced negotiations.[78] The negotiators for the Mexican-American Student Alliance also represented Native student interests and convinced the university to create a Native American Studies department.[79] Richard Oakes had arrived at San Francisco State College with the recommendation of the Third World Liberation Front and the ear of the college president. Many of the tutors that worked for the San Francisco Indian Center were connected to the strikes at SFSC, and had known Richard Oakes, having tutored his and Annie's children at the Indian center.

S. I. Hayakawa, president of San Francisco State College, in a Japanese Zero with California Governor Ronald Reagan as they drop police bombs on college students. Reagan favored Hayakawa's early no-compromise tactics during the SFSC strikes. The phrase "Remember Hayakawa" and December 7 are in reference to Pearl Harbor and the surprise attack by Japan on American forces that propelled the United States into World War II. Cover of *Berkeley Barb*, vol. 7, no. 24 (Dec. 5–12, 1968). *Berkeley Barb* permissions courtesy of Raquel Scherr.

On January 23, 1969, San Francisco police trapped and arrested 380 demonstrators at San Francisco State College for an "illegal rally." Some strikers reportedly hurled rocks, bottles, and heavy posts at the police before being hauled off in patrol wagons. This was the first pitched battle between student strikers and police since the college had reopened seventeen days earlier. Photo courtesy of Getty Images, Bettmann Collection 640119074.

As a result of the strike, by the spring semester of 1969, Richard Oakes and eight other students were admitted to the first Native American Studies (NAS) department at San Francisco State.[80] Oakes described the events: "The college was going through a lot of changes itself in the Third World Liberation strike. In the turmoil, an Ethnic Studies Program was being explored. When I went out there, they asked me to enroll. Through my job in the bar and my contacts in the community, I was able to recruit other students. . . . I felt that Indians needed attention . . . not tomorrow or the week after, but today."[81] San Francisco State used federal funds from the Office of Equal Opportunity (OEO) to recruit more than thirty Native students from the Bay Area for its first NAS class.

Across the bay a similar situation was playing out at the University of California at Berkeley, where LaNada Means was instrumental in developing Berkeley's first Native American Studies department. Like San Francisco State, Berkeley was in the wake of the free speech movement and knee-deep in its own third world liberation movement. In 1968, Means found her own voice in campus politics when she established Berkeley's first Native American Student Association. She took over an abandoned section of a campus building. Alone, she petitioned the university for squatter's rights to the property and was granted the building for the purpose of a campus Indian center.[82] By January of 1969, she and other students were caught in the middle of the third world strikes at Berkeley:

> 1969 was the most expensive of Berkeley campus riots because they assembled the largest force of Berkeley police and National Guard ever. They marched on campus with their unsheathed bayonets and fogged the campus with pepper gas. Every class on campus was interrupted and stopped. All of the Third World Leadership was arrested during the strike for various alleged charges. After the gas cleared away, I was one of the coalition leaders on the four-man negotiation team for our Third World College. We arouse victorious with our own Department of Ethnic Studies consisting of all four departments Black, Chicano, Asian and Native American Studies Programs.[83]

In response to Means's participation in the strike, the university suspended her for one semester, but she continued to organize Berkeley's Native American Studies department.

While on academic suspension, she worked with Lenape and Renape historian Jack Forbes at the Far Western Regional Labs, which students nicknamed the "Far Out Lab." At one point representatives from the National Indian Youth Council managed a small office in the same building. Repeatedly, Paiute citizen Mel Thom and the enigmatic Ponca, Clyde Warrior, both famed NIYC leaders, hung out at the lab and interacted with students and leaders from the Bay Area.[84] Forbes and Hoopa educator David Risling of the California Indian Education Association assisted the local university students in developing a course curriculum for their unique programs. Together with students from Berkeley and San Francisco State, they launched a conference at the University of California at Davis to discuss curriculum options.

It was at this conference that Richard Oakes would mention the idea of Alcatraz for the first time. Oakes stood before the students and proposed that they occupy the abandoned Alcatraz Island. Oakes's announcement was met with a few snickers, then uncertainty, and finally hope. After a brief silence, an elder from the community slowly stood up and said, "All you young people listen: We have been looking forward to this day when there would be something for you to do. You are our leaders."[85]

Richard Oakes was in this first class of students and became the first coordinator for the NAS department at SFSC. In a statement of purpose Oakes wrote,

> The courses which are proposed as community oriented will offer the community and the student opportunity for interaction with a philosophy of self-help based on group identification. As noted above, the San Francisco Bay Area offers a situation wherein the student might expand his studies, possibly innovate worthwhile constructive programs, seek reform and otherwise contribute to the solution of pressing urban problems.[86]

From this single moment everything changed for Oakes and other Native students in the Bay Area as they began researching their claim to Alcatraz Island. They relied on recommendations from Forbes and Risling, and the Berkeley students had selected Lakota citizen Lehman (Lee) Brightman, the fiery local president of United Native Americans (UNA), and another Berkeley student to be the co-chairs of Berkeley's new Native American Studies program.

On April 12, 1969, the Nixon administration's National Council on Indian Opportunity (NCIO) sent a committee chaired by Diné leader Peter McDonald to San Francisco to gather testimony on the urban Indian experience. Committee members such as Mescalero Apache President Wendell Chino heard stark testimony about police brutality, job discrimination, inadequate housing, poor health care facilities, high unemployment, and meager educational opportunities. The San Francisco Native community had been up in arms since March over the failure of federal programs and the palpable local apathy on Indian issues. The marchers picketed outside of federal buildings in San Francisco and Oakland, holding handwritten cardboard signs that read, "BIA Is a Flop." Richard Oakes, Al Miller, Mary Justice, Walter Johns, and Earl Livermore (Blackfeet) then brought these issues and concerns to the attention of NCIO.[87]

The work of the NCIO was spearheaded by Comanche LaDonna Harris, wife of Oklahoma Senator Fred Harris. (Senator Harris chaired the Senate Committee on Indian Affairs.) LaDonna Harris was stunned by each of the testimonies. After the meeting, Richard Oakes and Mary Justice invited her to see the Mission District for herself, suggesting that she and some staffers accompany them for a brief tour of the Red Ghetto. After working out the details, Harris secured a ride with Mary Justice to the Mission. After parking on 16th Street, they walked to the San Francisco Indian Center. Once there, they met Earl Livermore, who provided Harris with a tour of the building and the services available to Indians throughout the Bay Area.[88]

After they exited the Indian center, LaDonna Harris was spotted by a young Alaskan Native woman from the hearings who invited her into Warren's for a drink. Oakes entered the bar first and announced, "Hey, everybody, LaDonna Harris is here. She's a Comanche and her husband is a senator!" After his announcement, he was confronted by a group of six Samoan men, some carrying knives, who immediately laid into Oakes and any other Indian in the bar. Sonny Lao, a Native Hawaiian and Lakota man who tended the bar part-time, was known for tipping off the Samoan gangs, especially when certain Native community leaders were at the bar. Mary Lee Johns later noted in an interview that Lao also kept a machete under the bar. Soon a Samoan gang leader, adopting a traditional Malietoa role, raised the machete and shouted a Samoan war song, or "Ailao," as he encouraged his soldiers to victory. Several organizers, having spotted a rear exit door, quickly grabbed Harris and hurried her to the back of the bar. The exit, however, was locked. Trapped between a violent bar brawl and the exit at the front of the bar, Harris's two aides surrounded her. Walter Johns, known for his martial arts skills, quickly joined the battle helping out as his friend Richard Oakes was knocked to the ground by the Samoan gang. Johns drew their attention and divided the attackers; within moments he cleared a path and pulled Oakes to safety.

The first echo of police sirens sent the Samoan gang members crashing out the back door (either they possessed a spare key or it was unlocked by Sonny Lao). After recovering their bearings from the fight, they surveyed the damage: one purse and one silver watch stolen. In addition, one Delaware student had his clip-on tie stolen—which quickly shifted the mood of Warren's into laughter. While she remembered laughing, LaDonna Harris also recalled being overcome with fear and panic.[89] After this experience, Harris used all of her political capital to contact San Francisco mayor Joseph Alioto about police conditions and other concerns raised at the NCIO meeting. Soon she received letters of apology from top municipal figures and a continued assurance of reform. The NCIO committee later made their recommendations to President Nixon, but little action came from the administration based on NCIO's final report.[90]

Six days after the fight at Warren's on April 18, 1969, Lee Brightman and Earl Livermore, director of the American Indian Center, held a joint press conference to voice their concerns over police brutality and misrepresentation by the press.[91] Some police officers were known to wait outside Warren's and harass patrons on their way home, encouraging an arrest. Dressed in a dark suit, Brightman, a former Oklahoma A&M football star, denounced the press coverage of a recent arrest involving two Native Americans stereotypically dubbed "a pack of wild Indians." Brightman commented, "If there were Indians involved, they should be punished. . . . You've once again made it difficult for all Indians. Who the hell will hire an Indian without remembering things like this?" Twenty-seven-year-old SFSC student Al Miller, who also served on the board of directors of the Indian center, took a determined stance and silenced the press with his own challenge: "What do white people really know about us?" They left the meeting unified but with many more unanswered questions and a burning desire for resolution.[92] Meanwhile, Oakes continued in his effort to create a viable Native American Studies department at San Francisco State.

By mid-April 1969, Oakes and several other Native American students created SCAN, the Student Coalition of American Natives. The organization aimed to bring Native American students together to aid in the development of Native American Studies and to serve as a voice for the Native student population at San Francisco State. On April 21, SCAN released the following statement:

> We of SCAN . . . are familiar with the structures. . . . We are
> concerned with the lack of response and outright hostility on the
> part of government-assigned "specialists." . . . We are aware of a
> country that spends plenty in the name of humanity elsewhere.

... We are acquainted with the poor wisdom of the educators in failing to realize the importance of our language, culture and dignity. . . . We are alarmed at the government policy of Tribal termination. We are a proud and strong assortment of tribes with an equally strong sense of survival. In the past we fought with these encroachers, for we flatly refused to be enslaved. The path was one of dignity and the losses sustained were justified by our strong belief in death to dishonor and death to enslavement! Genocide happened . . . and later, after its failure. . . . They shelved the problem! "Let sickness overtake them!" the oppressor said, "Starve them!" shouted the farmer. Then later: "There is no such thing as a full-blooded Indian," whispered the acculturist authoritatively. The Indian has not weakened, nor has he capitulated his awe-inspiring cultural heritage; he lives! This Dawn will bring forth a new struggle, a new battlefield and a new Native American Indian![93]

With this prophetic tone, the twenty-seven-year-old Oakes released his frustrations into a new direction—education. The organization quickly elected Oakes to be its president and Miller, a Seminole, as vice president.[94] Cheyenne River Lakota citizen Mary Lee Johns (formerly Justice) was a former student at SFSC and recalled Oakes and Miller being inseparable. She described both leaders as highly intelligent, intense, and always engaged in heavy conversations. Through SCAN Oakes and others provided an established network for new Native students enrolling at the college. Soon members of SCAN created the building blocks for another organization in conjunction with the San Francisco Indian Center called the Movement of American Native Youth.[95]

MANY was a "non profit corporation dedicated to helping American Indians through the implementation of action programs initiated by American Natives."[96] One idea that was mentioned was to establish a Native retail outlet in which community members could sell their artwork and traditional crafts. The outlet would train members of the community in how to run and operate their own businesses. Sales from the outlet were to return to the community, helping relocatees with supplemental income during their transition. One positive outlook for the program was to draw community members together into an economic force and in the process develop a Native arts district. Art existed as a bridge connecting outside communities and neighborhoods with an appreciation for Native culture.

A third program that Oakes established was *Native American Critic and Review,* a newsletter for Native students at San Francisco State to use as a forum to publicize their views on any issue. Oakes urged students to take action and responsibility for their future:

> It is the duty of the Native American student to become of necessity the critics of their own programs that are shaping their destiny and to evaluate it as if their life depended on it. . . . The criticism should never localize itself entirely and should reach out into whatever environment it feels strong on. The student should not feel that their own organizational names are barriers and not subject to criticism, for this is an injustice to himself and others who are interested in the same. . . . Be critical of the Indian and the non-Indian (More So) working on your future so it represents you! You have a right as a Native American to speak out![97]

Slowly, NAS gathered student support for SCAN and other organizations. Oakes had a visible presence in the community as he worked among its members and expanded the enrollment numbers for the Native American Studies department.

At the beginning of May, after devoting countless hours to developing Native American Studies, Richard Oakes received the shocking news that his mother had passed away. Early on a Thursday morning, Irene Oakes, at the age of forty-nine, had died in her two-story Brooklyn home. She departed this world with her two boys on opposite shores. A strong Mohawk woman, she had overcome great odds in order to provide her sons with a better life. While Richard had struggled to find his way in New York, she left this world a grandmother, with the knowledge that her son would attend San Francisco State College. Irene Oakes's last rites and funeral service were administered by Reverend Jacobs at the St. Regis Catholic Church as her body was laid to rest at Akwesasne.

A vast emptiness must have washed over Oakes after losing his mother. Far more than anyone else, Irene, a strong Mohawk woman, had shaped and guided Oakes into the leadership role he was about to claim. While it is impossible to know for sure, her loss must have triggered

something in him. After her death, he began to assert himself as an
Akwesasne Mohawk Nationalist and as a father and leader.[98]

During Oakes's first semester at SFSC in the fall of 1969, he and
other students also participated in the search committees for faculty positions and attended various conferences throughout California. In May of
1969, Oakes led a committee meeting to create a seminar with the title
"The American Indian in an Era of Social Change." Members of the
committee who gathered at the Chautauqua House on Masonic Avenue
(home of the American Indian Historical Society) included educators,
other community members, and students from campuses around the Bay
Area. One of the pamphlets handed out at the meeting came from the
Organization of Native American Students (ONAS), an East Coast group
that unified Native students throughout the New England area. Richard
had to grin when one of the students on the list caught his eye. At the end
of a long list appeared the name Bruce Oakes, one of his cousins. Bruce
had just graduated from the exclusive Pomfret School in Connecticut.
From Pomfret he was sent by Hank Adams of the United Scholarship
Service to Havre, Montana, where he engaged with other youth among
the communities of Rocky Boy and Fort Belknap. Richard Oakes and the
seminar committee hammered out the logistics for the program and
handed out assignments for the next meeting. Oakes scheduled the
lodging at SFSC dorms and participated in open discussions on promotion, registration, and funding. By this point, he had gained the necessary
skills to organize and prepare for large events.[99]

One of the most important decisions that Oakes made was the
establishment of an NAS community advisory board, which linked the
campus to the greater San Francisco Indian community. Those selected
to the board would have an overwhelming impact on the program and
the community. The first positions filled were by Eastern Cherokee
citizen Jeannette Henry Costo and Cahuilla citizen Rupert Costo. Both
Jeannette and Rupert Costo were instrumental in the creation of the
American Indian Historical Society. The society was also responsible
for the groundbreaking academic journal *Indian Historian*, which
brought together Indian scholars and scholarship from a diversity of
disciplines.[100]

The third member of the advisory board would forever change the
students' and community's political understanding. Lakota citizen Belva

Cottier, aside from being affiliated with the San Francisco Indian Center, was responsible for the short-lived 1964 takeover of Alcatraz Island.[101] She informed Oakes and the other students that under treaty stipulations from the Fort Laramie Treaty of 1868, the Lakota people could reclaim any surplus land that the government had abandoned. Cottier had worked on the historical and legal research needed for the occupation, and she explained the dramatic details of the failed attempt to secure the island.[102] Oakes listened as the older Cottier explained that the media had ignored their actions and how within a few hours their occupation had ended.

Alcatraz Island had been a federal prison in the midst of San Francisco Bay for many decades until its closing in 1963 and had remained unused ever since. Both the state of California and the federal government sought proposals for what to do with the island. In 1968, Lamar Hunt, the son of

Lakota takeover of Alcatraz Island on March 9, 1964, with Russell Means (far left) and unidentified Lakota occupiers. AP Photo.

a Texas oil millionaire, hoped to develop Alcatraz into an entertainment park; others sought housing developments.[103] But no new proposal ever made it past the drafting board. Soon Richard Oakes and LaNada Means, representing a coalition of community institutions and Native Studies programs at San Francisco State and the University of California at Berkeley, proposed the ultimate response to the failed government experiment of relocation and termination: the occupation of Alcatraz Island.

It was at a local party hosted by Pomo citizen Carmen Christy that Dean Chavers first met Richard Oakes. Several students from Berkeley and San Francisco State met at Christy's house to hang out and enjoy their summer before classes picked up again in the fall. Dean Chavers recalled the party: "So I'm in Carmen Christy's house and I'm talking to some girl. . . . I'm very interested in this girl and this guy [Oakes] is going around trying to line up people to go take over this former prison island in San Francisco Bay. I thought . . . I don't want to hear this. . . . I kept talking to the girl and he just kind of passed me by."[104] Throughout the summer Oakes and Al Miller were attending a course taught at Berkeley. The class was titled "Indian Liberation," and it was taught by Jack Forbes. The students met in an abandoned basement room in a building on the north part of campus. It was in this room that the students from SFSC and UC Berkeley began making plans for Alcatraz.[105] Of the coalition between the two organizations, LaNada Means remembered,

> This was the first and last time in my lifetime that I ever experienced "Indian unity." As Indian students we worked, studied, played together, helped and cared for each other as brothers and sisters. We were tight. We worked with all the Native organizations in the bay area and California. Our emphasis was community/reservation based. . . . Our campus organization held joint meetings regularly with the Native American students at San Francisco State. . . . We became one larger coalition of Native students. We planned and did mostly all our activities together.[106]

Oakes was serious about the idea of Alcatraz, but he soon realized that they needed more time and support to make it work. Little did Chavers, so annoyed by Oakes at that party, know that he, too, would later respond to his call to occupy Alcatraz.

The Red Man's Burden; Private War in Laos; Spain on the Cross; "Malvenido Rockefeller!"; Deserter Underground 75¢

Ramparts

BETTER RED THAN DEAD

February 1970

LaNada Means on the February 1970 cover of *Ramparts*, the leading underground magazine in America, published from 1962 to 1975. *Ramparts* permissions courtesy of Guy Stilson and Greg Stilson.

Throughout June and July of 1969, Richard learned how to juggle several duties when he requested additional funding for NAS from SFSC president S. I. Hayakawa. The funding request, for $470 with additional funding from the Equal Opportunity Programs Office, was meager by today's standards. The proposal sought to fund a total of six staff positions at NAS. Oakes also worked on the hiring committee for faculty, attended weekly meetings for NAS at the Indian center, directed both SCAN and MANY, developed NAS job descriptions and course content, recruited students for the program, and studied, networked, and in his spare time was a father, husband, and friend to many. Oakes seemed to thrive under the pressure as he was also beginning his second semester as a Native American Studies major.

August appeared no different from the previous months as Oakes waited for a reply on their funding request. The funding for all Ethnic Studies programs remained uncertain, which led student leaders to criticize Hayakawa and to threaten SFSC with another campus-wide strike. The student paper, *The Daily Gater*, published an article entitled "Ethnic Studies Flop?" and attacked the Hayakawa administration as a "do nothing administration."[107] Hayakawa also received pressure from David Risling of the California Indian Education Association to promote NAS at San Francisco State. A month earlier Risling had written to Daniel Feder, SFSC's dean of academic planning, specifically highlighting the California State Legislature's decision to require all state colleges to develop an Indian Studies program.[108] Hayakawa was under political pressure to act quickly, yet responsibly, with regard to NAS. Meanwhile Oakes continued to recruit potential students by creating an information packet for new students. Within the packet he introduced SCAN and the NAS program, giving recruits his home number if they needed any assistance. By this time he had also drafted a mission statement for NAS:

> The Department of Native American Studies will offer new
> perspectives, new meanings and a new relationship to both the
> Native American and the peoples of the society in which he
> resides. It will relate to the Native American as an individual, as
> a Native American and as a member of a pluralistic society. The
> philosophy is one of self-help and self-discovery with emphasis
> on the development of a *whole human being.* . . . Native
> American Studies must first reassert the cultural-historical
> reality of the Native American in a society that has long
> demanded his assimilation . . . [the] program will offer progres-
> sive educational perspectives.[109]

Oakes and other students designed course curriculum around a simple philosophy: acquisition of knowledge in the fall and application of knowledge in the spring, a perfect formula for the invasion of Alcatraz.

By the end of the summer Richard and the search committee had hired two new faculty for the NAS Department: Quapaw and Cherokee composer Louis Ballard from the Institute of American Indian Arts (IAIA) in Santa Fe and Standing Rock Lakota anthropologist Beatrice "Bea" Medicine. Guest lectures that first semester featured one of the most famous artists of his day, Luiseño painter Fritz Scholder. Having recently left IAIA, Scholder's recent fame was tied to a series of paintings that highlighted the Indian or "new Indian," in which he had vowed, as an artist, to never paint the Indian. Scholder described the philosophy of the New Indian as a "responsibility not only to his own ancestors and his people, but to all . . . It may be that the most dignified and universal approach to this new role be through the arts."[110] Scholder's character, philosophy, and artistic vision must have cast a large influence over Richard Oakes and other students. More specifically the art of political statements that later graced dozens of buildings and Indigenized signs across Alcatraz Island had mimicked modern artistic forms and symbols of Indian freedom.

Ballard, who helped bring Scholder to campus, was aware of Oakes's strong political ideals and sought to work with him to focus these ideals into a positive message. In a letter to Oakes shortly before accepting his appointment to the program, Ballard wrote, "I have always veered away from political commitment. . . . Our time could be better spent by making a contribution to the arts that would uplift ourselves and our fellow man. . . . And by increasing our knowledge and thereby our power, we could probably gain back our land in a better way."[111] Ballard was able to show that Red Power could be achieved not through the fist but rather through an ability to utilize and use knowledge correctly. In a later interview, Oakes reflected on the reasons for developing Native American Studies:

> They still are not . . . they aren't the answers—for the education.
> The answers . . . the actual material has to be gathered from the
> fields. I am talking about the reservations . . . so that they can be
> incorporated into the school system. So that they can be put into
> a workable curriculum, so that the individual can learn and
> profit. In turn when a person gets his degree he can return to
> the reservation and use this knowledge. It then takes the form
> of useful knowledge which then he can service his people, his or
> her people.[112]

Ballard impressed upon Oakes that education is the most powerful tool for protecting and promoting Native sovereignty. By the end of August, Richard Oakes received the news that his meager budget request had been turned down. He had succeeded, however, in recruiting at least thirty more students and hiring two new faculty for the program. So he eagerly awaited the beginning of a new semester.

Oakes continued to gather political support for NAS when he wrote to Lumbee citizen Helen M. Scheirbeck, the director of education for the American Indian Unit in Washington, D.C., and asked for her involvement with the program. He outlined the numbers of Native American students enrolled in programs throughout the Bay Area: forty at SFSC, forty-eight at San Francisco City College, thirty each at UC Berkeley and Sonoma State, and thirty-two at Cal State Hayward. Beyond symbolizing awareness through a networked coalition of Native students, he remarked that the number of Native students at San Francisco State had seen a 75 percent increase. Throughout the letter he explained the complexities involved in establishing an effective Native American Studies program: "We are the valid factor in shaping our destin[ies] and will accept no substitutes. . . . The picture may change again in a few weeks because the students from our program and Berkeley, have made it their business to see that all the brothers and sisters receive a relevant education, developed by the community, the college, and the students. We consider ourselves the vanguard of Native American reality."[113]

That semester, Oakes enrolled in Louis Kemnitzer's Native American Heritage course. Kemnitzer described Oakes as being "the major thinker and actor in this process" of creating the foundation for NAS.[114] Throughout the course, Oakes was influenced by the works of Standing Rock Lakota intellectual Vine Deloria Jr., author of *Custer Died for Your Sins*; Kiowa writer N. Scott Momaday's *House Made of Dawn* (winner of the Pulitzer Prize in 1969); Stan Steiner's *The New Indians*; and many other works such as Frantz Fanon's *Wretched of the Earth*. More contemporary writers, attempting to expose the complex problems affecting Indian Country, had identified overt and covert systems of oppression embedded within the colonization of America. In September, at Oakes's request, Kemnitzer invited spokesmen from the White Roots of Peace caravan to give a guest lecture in his course. The White Roots of Peace spokespeople included Haudenosaunee leaders Alice Papineau, Franklin Leaf, Tom Porter, Peter Mitten, Steve Boots, Noah Mitchell, and Jerry Gambill. They lectured on the teachings of the Great Peacemaker and the Great Law of Peace that serves as the foundation for the Haudenosaunee Confederacy.[115] Oakes invited the speakers to stay with him and his family.

Al Miller remembered the impact the caravan had on Richard Oakes: "We spent a lot of nights sitting up all night talking with the elders of the White Roots of Peace. Richard . . . told me that he didn't go into the Longhouse and he didn't know much about the religion of the Mohawks, but after . . . [they] left he went through a complete transformation."[116] Inspired by the speakers, Oakes and the other students became more vocal on behalf of NAS.

Mohawk citizen Rarihokwats, also known as Jerry Gambill, was one of the speakers and founders who worked to spread the vision of the White Roots of Peace; he was also the editor of *Akwesasne Notes*, a national Native newspaper.[117] *Akwesasne Notes* was created by Gambill and others to draw support for the 1968 Mohawk occupations over the duty tax.

Gambill and his colleagues stayed for two weeks with Richard and Annie Oakes. Their visit proved somewhat of a logistical nightmare for Annie, as she was overwhelmed in a crowded two-bedroom student house filled with twelve guests, six children, and visitors around the clock. Along the hard tile floors and up to the dark faux-wood paneling of the living room stretched endless numbers of sleeping bags. Still, amidst all the confusion, it was an opportunity for Richard, as he and Gambill as well as others sparked a lasting friendship. Gambill even wrote a few articles for the first issue of *Akwesasne Notes* on Oakes's typewriter. He later described Oakes as "a strong, good humored man, always kidding and laughing and cajoling people into committing themselves deeper in their causes. He was the sort of natural born leader kind, although he himself searched for guidance and direction—he had just become aware of his Indian heritage in a political way as a young adult."[118] Oakes not only became aware of his political heritage during this time, but he shared his message with the world.

ALCATRAZ OCCUPATION AND THE CONSTRUCTION OF AN INDIAN CITY

In the late night hours of November 20, 1969, two boats carefully deposited the occupation force of over eighty men, women, and children onto the desolate Alcatraz Island. Overnight the organization Indians of All Tribes (IAT) set up security posts throughout the island, discouraged the Coast Guard from invading the island, and created a media barrage of press releases from the San Francisco Indian Center. After the devastating loss of the San Francisco Indian Center in a highly suspect fire, the community and student leaders had created the ultimate proposal to transform Alcatraz into an Indian City. The island would host a center for Native American Studies with a traveling university; an American Indian spiritual center to practice Native religion not yet protected by the federal government; an Indian center of ecology to formulate conservatory plans; an Indian training school, complete with a center for traditional arts and crafts; a Native restaurant; and an economic school to study ways to increase employment and standards of living. Finally, their proclamation called for the creation of an American Indian museum to expose the "true" history of Native America.

Contrary to government officials who sought to evict Indians of All Tribes from the island as soon as possible, the IAT was highly organized. It included a mainland office, donated by Blackfeet medical doctor Dorothy Lonewolf Miller. Along with Dean Chavers, the mainland coordinator, Miller started to administer all accounts and bookkeeping and established the IAT bank account.[119] The organization eventually created a newsletter, a radio show called Radio Free Alcatraz, the Big Rock School, a health care system (complete with one doctor and a registered nurse), and a host of other programs. On the island, IAT elected a seven-member Intertribal council: Richard Oakes; Al Miller; Ho-Chunk citizen Ross Harden; Luiseño/Cahuilla citizen Ed Castillo; Inuit citizen Bob Nelford; Luiseño citizen Dennis Turner; and Cherokee citizen Jim Vaughn. The council established the housing and security committee and began a new school. The IAT improvement committee marked dangerous areas, sorted through clothing donations, planted shrubs, chopped wood, and cleared away the trash, debris, vines, and weeds that had accumulated over years of neglect. Everyone on the island was assigned to work on sanitation, daycare, cooking, laundry, supply lines, or repairs. Rules were established that advocated total sobriety and a drug-free environment for all residents. The symbol and Intertribal idea of Alcatraz and Indians of All Tribes to which Bay Area students and community members gave birth became larger and more pronounced.

Soon occupiers attracted the attention of politicians. From California Governor Ronald Reagan to President Richard Nixon, a media frenzy fueled national and international support for the occupiers. Although thousands of Native peoples made pilgrimages to the island and sent in monetary and logistical support, the occupation lasted another nineteen months.[120]

The Native occupation of Alcatraz, beyond securing title to the island, fueled hundreds of similar occupations throughout Indian Country and became a catalyst for the Red Power Movement. In Seattle, Washington, Indians of All Tribes from Alcatraz teamed up with Colville citizen Bernie Whitebear to create United Indians of All Tribes and transform the abandoned Fort Lawton property into the Daybreak Star Center. Pit River Tribe in northern California launched a campaign to restore the lands stolen by Pacific Gas and Electric Corporation. Taos Pueblo regained control over Taos Blue Lake. In 1972, the Trail of Broken Treaties March on Washington took place. Finally, Wounded Knee was occupied in 1973. Ultimately, all have long roots in the IAT liberation of Alcatraz Island. In turn, Red Power as a national movement relied on urban Intertribal institutions and organizations forged out of Indian Cities. It was also a movement that mobilized the entire San Francisco Indian community around a central belief that the path to social justice would ultimately transform Native political relationships with local, municipal, state, Tribal, and federal governments.

This path to social justice and self-determination was rooted in an urban-centered, Intertribal perspective. In many ways Alcatraz and IAT were symbolic of the utopian desires of Native migrants into San Francisco: a microcosm of the ideal Indian City most Indians wanted to live in. Alcatraz emerges not as an abandoned prison in the Indian community but as a sacred space emblematic and redefined as Native self-determination and Red Power. The rippling effect brought together Native peoples from rural, urban, and reservation communities and forged a new Intertribal reality that forever changed federal Indian policy. President Richard Nixon's administration championed former President Lyndon B. Johnson's 1968 call for self-determination when Johnson launched the passage of over twenty-six pieces of legislation that ended the old policies of termination/relocation and solidified a new self-determined commitment to Indian Country.

Emerging from the development of an Indian City was a new Intertribal perspective that altered how Native peoples define themselves and their world. This new awareness affected the local political and organizational structure of groups like Aztlán, a Chicano movement that forged together a uniquely Intertribal perspective to protect and enhance their claim for human and civil rights. The Brown Berets staged an Alcatraz-like takeover of Catalina Island, and the Indians of All Tribes demonstrated in solidarity with the Chicano Moratorium March in East Los Angeles. The Black Panther Party, founded by Huey Newton and Bobby Seale, explored community building through breakfast programs like those launched by the San Francisco Indian Center. The hippie movement's capital of Haight and Ashbury coopted the Intertribal philosophy of urban Indians that defined its cultural style and political movement. In 1970, the national environmental movement sponsored an Earth Day celebration in San Francisco and incorporated Native images to commercialize and authenticate its conservationist agendas. As the federal government shifted money to states and municipal governments for Indian programs, local governments had to reinvent themselves as Indian Cities. The impact of Indian Cities had a profound influence and ultimately reshaped national Indian policies and cities for decades to come.

CHAPTER FOUR

I'm Not Your Indian Anymore

RELYING ON CONNECTIONS he had established throughout the Bay Area's Indian community, in the fall of 1969 Richard Oakes began to work diligently on a plan to take over Alcatraz Island. Oakes's vision for Alcatraz was not born in the solitude of the university; it was the culmination of a long journey from the small St. Regis Reservation in New York to the boulevards of San Francisco. Surrounding his vision was a growing backdrop of civil unrest flooding campuses and cities across America. Richard Oakes began to believe that change was inevitable as the world around him was exploding in protest. Oakes took his message and vision of change to the center of the Indian community in San Francisco. He continued to absorb valuable lessons that he would ultimately need to force progressive change throughout Indian Country.

A "tribal" atmosphere of nonconformity had been appropriated by both hippies and Yippies at the epicenter of the countercultural revolution in San Francisco. Self-determination was not only the cry of the Aquarians; it was also echoed by other organizations, like the Black Panther Party. It represented a fight to take control of one's own destiny, to be the sole determining factor in the political and social infrastructure of one's own community. During the 1960s, the leaders of rebellion were transforming bureaucrats and members of the older establishment into figures of distaste. Many Americans viewed them as puppets of conformity destined to rob a generation of its freedom.

Throughout the 1960s the media flocked to the fires of rebellion and the proponents of this idealistic liberation. Images blanketed television screens with curtains of protest against the war and the Black Panther Party with its idea of Black Power. The Black Panthers called on the consciousness of America to promote justice or to understand why they had the right to decide their own fate. While seeking to take control of their political future, the Black Panther Party also sought to control their cultural image. Members of this movement began to sympathize with more populous movements and with global indigenous efforts for empowerment and liberation from colonial forms of government. Black Panther Party members paralleled aspects of their movement's foundation in third world liberation around a link with Native American history and a common struggle against American repression. This became apparent when members of the party changed their names to resemble famous Indian heroes', such as Elmer "Geronimo" Pratt. Perhaps they believed that appropriating select Native American images of "rebellion" would enable them to establish a symbolic link with Indigenous Nationalism. Huey Newton is best known for his poster image—dressed in black leather and a black beret, seated in a high-back wicker chair, holding a rifle above a pile of shotgun shells in his right hand and an African spear in his left, his right foot forward, as African shields lean upright against the wall alongside other symbols of Africa. The Tribal images purposefully placed in Newton's poster provided the Black Panthers the authenticity needed to appear as a movement rooted in Indigenous or third world struggles. Propaganda played a critical role for the political organization to advertise their powerful ideology to a commercially fed public. Ultimately these "tribal" images of revolution sensitized San Francisco to aspects of self-determination.[1]

During the 1960s, communes were springing up all over the Haight-Ashbury tenements, and art colonies were quickly recruiting members. Richard Oakes and the Native American community found themselves surrounded by the propaganda of the street and the ideals of liberation; they faced the difficult task of deciding what meaning, if any, these countercultural philosophies had in their own lives. Liberation theology was awash throughout the free speech movements, including the Red Guard, the Third World Liberation Front, the Brown Berets, and Students for Democratic Society.[2] Battle lines were being drawn in the hills of San

Francisco, and Native students were searching for answers. The concept of freedom in Oakes's life and actions would be closely allied to these ideas of liberation that the other movements of San Francisco had already embraced.

Back at Akwesasne, the nationalist protests against the St. Lawrence Seaway project were just beginning to take a more self-determined approach. When he heard of the occupation at Cornwall Island on December 18, 1968, Richard Oakes rediscovered a cause that had surrounded him for most of his life. Back at Akwesasne, Mike Mitchell, wearing his St. Regis Mohawk lacrosse jacket, led a caravan of cars to the International Bridge that passes over Cornwall Island. Each driver blocked the bridge, but before they exited their cars some locked their keys in their car, engaged their emergency brakes, or flattened their own tires. Mohawk women, men, and children were soon met by the Cornwall Police Department, soon to be reinforced by Royal Canadian Mounted Police and the Ontario Provincial Police. All were under orders to clear the blockade. Before they arrived at the protest, many of the police had removed their badges to prevent them from being identified by the media.[3]

In the months leading up to the standoff, Mitchell, Ernest Benedict, and others had petitioned Ottawa to honor the provisions of the Jay Treaty, which afforded free passage to Mohawk citizens crossing the border. Secondary to the customs issue, the bridge, like many structures imposed upon Akwesasne, had been built without just compensation. Battling freezing temperatures, the protesters spoke in both Mohawk and English while they handed out eviction notices to the long lines of cars stopped near the protest.

To throw off Canadian law enforcement, they communicated strategy strictly in their Mohawk language. They marched proclaiming to authorities, "You are on Indian Land" and held a banner reading "1794 Treaty." As word traveled throughout the tight-knit community more and more Mohawk people began to arrive at the protest site. With new protesters and a swelling crowd, the Cornwall city police began to make arrests. They pushed against the crowd and tried to solicit any act or offense from the crowd worthy of arrest. Elders shouted in Mohawk, "Don't get mad, don't fight back." Mohawk women took the lead, placing their bodies in front of tow trucks refusing to allow the removal or taking of any more

Akwesasne property. Soon teenagers and others followed their lead, and as everyone swarmed around the tow trucks, arrests escalated, targeting the leadership. Mike Mitchell was arrested, placed in a squad car, and taken offsite for booking in Cornwall.

Those elders and leaders who remained continued to remind the police and their Mohawk relations that this was a nonviolent and peaceful demonstration. Ernest Benedict asked the crowd for their vote to continue. Kahnawà:ke Mohawk activist Kahentinetha Horn reminded everyone that the "whole world is looking at us, right here and now. Are we going to give up . . . or are we going to send out a call to our brothers and sisters all over North America to come and help us?" It was a poignant question for both the moment and the times.[4]

After the Akwesasne band chief arrived, he refused to step out of his car to meet with the protesters and instead asked for a permit to carry a sidearm. The band chief's actions reveal how little power they actually wielded among their own people—as most refused to vote in band elections. As five o'clock drew near, tensions escalated; the police grew impatient and feared the repercussions of an enormous traffic jam once people got off work in Massena or Cornwall. More and more activists protested their arrests by simply refusing to move at all. They were subsequently overpowered by police, as two officers carried each protester to a nearby OPP squad car.

After over forty arrests, Ernie Benedict climbed onto the back of a nearby tow truck and stood clutching a binder of precious legal documents. He addressed everyone in the Mohawk language, and the message quickly calmed the crowd. He reminded everyone there about their original intent and urged them all to leave and reassemble back at the community house on Cornwall Island. Benedict announced for the benefit of the police and Mohawk activists that they needed to seek legal counsel for those protesters who were already arrested. They had to plan their next move as a community. For the sake of unity, his advice was heeded by the crowd. As they started to walk away, one protester suggested in Mohawk that they should arrest the officers. Protected by the international media coverage of their protest and demands, all of the protesters were acquitted by Canadian courts. After numerous sit-ins, marches, and police arrests, the Canadian government lifted the duty tax and tolls for all Mohawk citizens. The border-crossing protests also served as the foundation for a new international Native newspaper, *Akwesasne Notes*. The power of this protest alongside the subsequent 1969 film debut of *You Are on Indian Land* and the publication of *Akwesasne Notes* underscores the power of the media on Richard Oakes's activism.[5]

Beyond the struggle to study at SFSC, Oakes was also engaged in the pursuit to seek new answers to the perplexing issues afflicting Indian Country. Through meetings with NIYC leaders like Mel Thom and Clyde Warrior, alternative classes in the Far "Out" (West) lab, and conversations with representatives of the White Roots of Peace, Native students began to learn more about their complex histories and how their understanding of themselves as Native peoples would be a viable factor in determining a brighter future for Indian Country. They also learned about traditions and ceremonies that stretched back thousands of years. Born out of these meetings was a genuine Intertribal perspective, an awakening that occurred throughout San Francisco's Indian City.

On the streets of the Mission District and during late nights at Gatorville, Richard Oakes began organizing a fight to unify Native peoples. Having watched the recent protests at Cornwall Island and listened to the stories told by Belva Cottier about the 1964 occupation of Alcatraz, Oakes was left with a blueprint for 1969. Five years had passed since the first takeover, and the newly sensitized media were awaiting the next big movement. The stage was set for Oakes and other students to rally around the energy of liberation. The media establishment in San Francisco helped to propel various movements into the spotlight, educating the public about organizations' demands. Without public support, the struggle for liberation would have proven an even more daunting task for Native students.

The streets, campuses, and personal trials of each Native student served as valuable lessons to pave the road to Alcatraz. More importantly, Richard Oakes and other Native students were learning how to work through a bureaucratic system to make their voices heard. A year earlier, LaNada Means had taken over an abandoned bungalow on the Berkeley campus and claimed squatter's rights to secure a center for Native students. Oakes and other students had braved the waters of administration to create a viable Native American Studies department at San Francisco State. These student leaders and their larger Native community possessed a strong ability to negotiate risk and take the necessary action to see their visions through. Only through this type of determination could the takeover of Alcatraz be born.

Because of his commitment to an Alcatraz occupation, Oakes was faced with the real prospect of losing his job, housing, and education or even confronting jail time and separation from his family. Would their children remain in school at the SFSC's Frederic Burk School? As a family, they faced some incredibly difficult choices. The fear that Alcatraz would be a failure was an obvious pressure in Oakes's life, but it was one that he could handle. Sacrifice was not an unfamiliar reality for the former ironworker, nor was it a new experience for many other Native peoples in the Bay Area. Everyday battles for adequate housing, education, a voice in politics, paying the bills, and putting food on the table were a part of many Native households. Alcatraz would not be a failure as long as the preparations included professional legal assistance and the risks were measured; increasingly, failure was not an option.

Legal aid stood at the forefront of the support that Richard Oakes and other Native students deemed necessary to promote their rights to take over the island. Lacking a firm understanding of the law, the students were in dire need of legal representation. Therefore, lawyers would prove integral to the promotion of solidarity for the takeover and ultimately as protection of the ideology of Native self-determination. Oakes sought assistance from the San Francisco Native community to locate effective representation. One lawyer, Aubrey Grossman, was known in many circles as a radical. Grossman was a longtime labor attorney, a supporter of unions and defender of civil rights, and as a result, he had been black-listed during the thirties. He was almost disbarred for his political beliefs, which included sympathy for socialist ideologies. Consequently, Grossman had given up securing a high-powered job and resigned himself to protecting individual liberties. A perfect legal ally for this movement, he soon became a true friend to Oakes and other Native students. Through this relationship, the legal case for Alcatraz had reached the framing stage.[6]

The students also recruited two other lawyers, a Missouri-Otoe and Osage lawyer F. Browning Pipestem, who was a recent graduate of the University of Oklahoma law school and a practicing attorney in Washington, D.C. Pipestem proved to be a critical part of the legal framework for Alcatraz. He possessed a strong background in Indian law, and he used his location to lobby White House staff and Congress to support the occupation. More importantly, Pipestem, a Native lawyer, was trusted and respected by Oakes and the other students. His role in the occupation would be felt much later during the settlement of Alcatraz.[7]

At the time of the occupation, Donald Jelinek was a thirty-five-year-old former Wall Street and civil rights attorney who was working pro bono for Indians of All Tribes. Among Jelinek's jobs was to establish and maintain constant negotiations with the local and national law enforcement and other government agencies. Most importantly, Jelinek also managed part of the financials and donations for the occupation; in a later interview he estimated the occupation's costs totaled approximately three thousand dollars a week in order to sustain IAT on the island. Much of this outlay went to fuel for generators, vehicles, and boats; food and medicine; and bedding, blankets, and clothing.[8]

With the questions of failure out of the way, Oakes and the other organizers were left with a hole in their attempt; they needed support from older residents within the Native community. If Alcatraz were viewed solely as a student movement it might lack credibility; it might be seen as just another student movement. To counter this probability Richard Oakes was forced to make alliances within the older, established leadership of the Indian community. He had been living in the Bay Area since 1968, but he was still a newcomer to San Francisco and the internal politics of its larger Native community. Those intent on the takeover of Alcatraz had to secure representative members of the core leadership in the Native community at large, and they had to be involved in the planning.

Native dances in the Bay Area were becoming increasingly popular during this decade. Historically, these frequent social gatherings had formed the communal fabric for many Native peoples. Powwows brought Native people back to sharing the drum, traditional songs and language, and to movements celebrating tradition. After powwows and long into the evenings, 49s, which consisted of round dance and social songs, could be heard at various beaches. During the early twentieth century, these dances had been outlawed in many Native communities, but now they were returning and experiencing a revival. When Northern and Southern Plains songs filled the air, the Intertribal was born: straight, fancy, grass, traditional, shawl, all worked together. Richard and Annie Oakes attended several dances, exposing their children to the arena and the culture. He found that these gatherings helped him find out what was going on in the community. The dances were a type of Native media center. One contact

Oakes made at these events was Adam Nordwall, a Red Lake Anishinaabe citizen who was a regular at most dances. A short and limber fellow, Nordwall owned his own successful termite extermination business in the Bay Area. During one of these gatherings the two men talked, and plans for Alcatraz soon took a much different turn.

Catastrophe struck the Bay Area in the early hours of October 10, 1969, when a fire ravaged the San Francisco Indian Center. The three-story center had served thirty thousand Native peoples in the Bay Area since 1958.[9] Arson was suspected as the cause of the fire, but no one was ever brought up on charges.[10] The community was devastated, for they had lost a place that provided health care, employment, legal aid, social programs, important documents, and more. For many, the destruction of the center became yet another driving force that accelerated the Native community's claim to Alcatraz. The occupation of the island would not only draw attention to the political needs of the Indian community, it also held the real possibility of replacing the Indian center. A few days after the fire, a makeshift Indian center was created in a rented storefront on 16th Street, not far from the charred remnants of the old center. Although the new center lacked any tables or chairs, it was soon packed with concerned students and community members searching for new alternatives.

October 1969 proved to be a month of major impact on the greater San Francisco Indian community. Jess Sixkiller, a Cherokee citizen and former Chicago police detective, brought American Indians United, a national organization based out of Chicago, to the Bay Area for a conference. From October 24 to 26, participants came together to discuss the state of affairs of urban issues throughout Indian Country. American Indians United brought with them a unique message, that

> cities . . . must recognize and adjust to the needs of Indian
> People. The failures of the cities and in particular, various
> government bureaucracies to recognize and adequately serve
> and include Indians in the power structures continues to
> deprive Indian people of their right to self expression . . .
> Therefore, urban Indians must take it upon themselves to
> develop new methods for gaining access to political and
> economic structures which have bureaucratic control over
> Indian affairs.[11]

This conference and its message pointed to a growing voice of protest within the Indian community of San Francisco. Only a few months earlier, community leaders had organized protests in front of the federal building and vocalized their concerns before the National Council on Indian Opportunity (NCIO). The conference carried with it the potential and the ideology for self-determination.

Securing viable media connections was another obstacle that Oakes worked diligently to solve during the fall semester at SFSU. Nordwall invited Richard and Annie Oakes to a Halloween party held at the home of Tim Findley, a local reporter with the *San Francisco Chronicle*. Richard Oakes had discovered that Adam Nordwall and Tim Findley were close friends. Findley would prove valuable to the efforts of the occupation because he also had connections with the maritime community in San Francisco. When Richard and Annie Oakes arrived, the party was in full swing, with reporters conversing about a multitude of topics as they drank beers and smoked cigarettes. Oakes and Nordwall kept a critical eye on one another as the party wore on. Each was observing how the other handled himself around the media. As the evening continued and conversations on Native topics grew increasingly intense, some reporters began to sense that a story was there to be covered . . . but from where . . . and when? Shortly thereafter, Nordwall, after a brief conversation with Oakes, decided to make an announcement. Standing before a large group of Findley's guests, he announced plans to take over Alcatraz Island on the afternoon of November 9, 1969. Oakes recalled, "One fellow had jumped the gun and was already making plans with local reporters."[12] Stunned by the early date, Oakes was pressured into carrying the news back to the students.

With a fixed date came new problems. The SFSC and Berkeley students had been planning an occupation to coincide with their summer break in 1970, so as not to interfere with their classes. The November date might distract the most important occupation leadership—the students. As soon as word of the November 9 date spread, distrust for Adam Nordwall quickly emerged.[13] Fear dominated conversations in the Indian Psychology course at San Francisco State. Had all of their work and planning been for nothing? Was Nordwall or the older establishment going to help or hinder the occupation? These were serious questions, but they were easily answered when the need for transportation, media, and legal support was brought up.

Unbeknownst to Nordwall, Oakes and other students from Berkeley and San Francisco State had already made an attempt to occupy Alcatraz. Joe Bill, a Hooper Bay Inuit citizen and a student at SFSC, recalled the "first part [or] last part of October. . . . First time we went down there the same night and hired a boat, but he didn't want to go at night and so we cancelled it and went back and had another meeting."[14] This occupation failed to materialize for the very reasons that Oakes was working to recruit Aubrey Grossman, Tim Findley, and others. He was seeking the necessary legal aid and media connections to ensure a successful occupation of the abandoned prison.

During the fall planning for the occupation, Oakes relied heavily on his wife Annie for her support. The love for his wife and their kids served as a positive distraction from the daily struggles of administration, deadlines, organization, and studying. Annie Oakes also had a strong tie to politics in her own community. The Marrufos, Annie's family, were pushing to take a larger role in the Tribal politics at Kashaya Reservation in northern California.[15] Annie was able to bring experienced advice and grounding to Richard, who was still a newcomer to California Indian politics. Like Richard, Annie was under tremendous pressure as she managed to care for six kids, maintain a stable household on a meager budget, and hold their marriage together. These times proved difficult for them, since Richard was often away from home, attending meetings, networking, and organizing. The family of eight had to pack themselves into one vehicle, an older station wagon, which forced Richard to seek alternative transportation. He often hitched rides with friends from San Francisco State or grabbed one of the crowded seats on the city bus to make meetings. At times the finances were tight for the couple, since they were forced to get by on Richard's modest student income and took shelter in their community.

On the morning of November 9, 1969, reporters, having kept their secret, showed up by the dozen to witness the historic moment when the newly formed organization Indians of All Tribes (IAT) planned to take over the island. The crowds grew, there was no boat in sight. The reporters grew restless as singers gathered around the drum to ease the spirit of disinterest settling in among the crowd. When Adam Nordwall arrived, he began making his way to the pier, where the crowd had congregated. Oakes and others hurriedly approached, asked Nordwall about the boat

Richard and Annie Oakes on Alcatraz Island, December 8, 1969, with the iconic lighthouse in the background. AP Photo/*San Francisco Examiner*.

that was supposed to take them to the island. Nordwall started to make a run to the phone booth when he noticed a historic three-mast ship docking at the pier. Meanwhile, Oakes rounded up the restless crowd to read the proclamation for the Indians of All Tribes.[16] The reporters huddled in close to Oakes with microphones and tape recorders. Oakes, who was holding a handful of beads and red cloth, began to read:

> To the Great White Father and All His People: We, the native
> Americans, re-claim the land known as Alcatraz Island in the
> name of all American Indians by right of discovery. We wish
> to be fair and honorable in our dealings with the Caucasian
> inhabitants of this land, and hereby offer the following treaty:
> We will purchase said Alcatraz Island for 24 dollars . . . in glass
> beads and red cloth, a precedent set by the white man's
> purchase of a similar island about 300 years ago.
>
> We know that $24 in trade goods for these sixteen acres is
> more than was paid when Manhattan Island was sold, but we
> know that land values have risen over the years. Our offer of
> $1.24 per acre is greater than the 47 [cents] per acre the white
> men are now paying the California Indians for their land. We
> will give to the inhabitants of this land a portion of that land
> for their own, to be held in trust by the American Indian
> Government—for as long as the sun shall rise and the rivers go
> down to the sea—to be administered by the Bureau of
> Caucasian Affairs (BCA).
>
> We will further guide the inhabitants in the proper way of
> living. We will offer them our religion, our education, our life-
> ways, in order to help them achieve our level of civilization and
> thus raise them and all their white brothers up from their savage
> and unhappy state. We offer this treaty in good faith and wish to
> be fair and honorable in our dealings with all white men.[17]

As Oakes continued to read the proclamation, his crisp voice added life to the words. Those listening observed a transformation in him. Perhaps it came from a new awareness that he was vocalizing their right to determine their own future. No matter how eloquent his reading, Oakes could not distract attention from the urgent need to secure transportation, without which they would be chewed up and dismissed by the press.

Nordwall, dressed in his traditional dance regalia, made his way down the pier, where Ronald Craig, the captain of the *Monte Cristo*, was docking. Craig, who used his Canadian ship for reenactments, was startled to see Nordwall—in full regalia—striding up to his vessel. The captain was already dressed in *his* period clothing, complete with a frilly cravat. Craig agreed only to ferry the occupiers around the island. Nordwall, who knew that Oakes was approaching the end of the proclamation, quickly agreed to Craig's terms. The weary-eyed protesters hurried on board and were soon casting off toward Alcatraz. Craig found the opportune moment to add to the drama. Noticing that the press was eagerly taking pictures of the voyage, he fired a blank round from the ship's cannon. A surge of cheers emerged from the onlookers back on the mainland and among the passengers on the boat.

Just as the boat neared the island, Richard Oakes jumped overboard and swam toward the island. Then Jim Vaughn, Ross Harden, Walter Heads, and Joe Bill followed Oakes's lead and swam toward the island.[18] In a blatant act of self-determination they decided to go where the *Monte Cristo* would not take them. Each of them followed Oakes's lead, diving into the cold waters of the bay, all of them at different distances from Alcatraz. Once on the island, the group made plans to come back that night and "take it over." After fifteen minutes, the group was escorted back to the dock by the media. Reporters seized the moment to dramatize the events of the day. Back at the pier, dripping wet and freezing, Oakes found new hope. He realized that the eventual occupation was just a matter of time. After returning to the mainland, the occupiers went to the Indian center for an impromptu meeting to discuss returning to Alcatraz that same evening.

As 5:00 p.m. approached on sleepy Fisherman's Wharf, a small group of Native peoples met with the captain of the *New Vera II* and his crew, who were busy scrubbing down their fishing boat. LaNada Means strolled over to the small vessel to speak with the captain. Means soon discovered that this particular fisherman was unaware of the earlier attempt to seize Alcatraz. She used this to her advantage, stating that they were in need of transportation to the island to perform a ceremony. Noticing that the captain was growing weary, she offered to pay him three dollars for every person to be ferried. This was an offer he could not refuse—indeed, it must have seemed harmless, a way to earn a quick buck. The small group began to pile into the boat, but then they noticed that Richard Oakes was not there. They waited, but soon the captain put the boat into gear. About that time Means and Earl Livermore spotted Oakes and a group of San Francisco State students running up to the pier. Encouraged by the added number of passengers, the captain reluctantly turned around to pick up Richard Oakes and the others. This now increased the group to twenty-five, a slightly smaller group than had been assembled that afternoon.

They were on their way once again to Alcatraz without the press or the extravagance that the morning attempt had provided. As the night swallowed up the light of the small fishing boat, the passengers huddled together to keep warm and dry. The cool dark air and the spray from the boat chilled their faces. With the captain distracted by the demands of piloting the boat, the organizers began discussing their assault plan. The *New Vera II* made a risky landing as it surged next to the docks. The captain, fearing damage to his vessel, began to tie the boat to the docks. The opportune moment had presented itself, and Richard Oakes and fourteen others made their way onto the docks.[19] Caught off guard, the captain soon took notice of his missing passengers. Fearing that his boat would be confiscated or, worse yet, that a startled guard might be trigger-happy, he threw the craft into reverse, breaking the rope. Eleven of the others, including Earl Livermore and Nordwall, were stranded on the boat as it pulled away, but more importantly, the students had made it onto the island.

While the enormous spotlight of the lighthouse circled the silent bay, the fourteen occupiers began to study the layout of the land. Oakes relates:

> We landed at about six o'clock and hid. I guess the caretaker was
> alerted that we had landed. . . . He, his three patrolmen, and
> their ferocious guard dog came out and tried to find us. There
> were fourteen of us hiding in the grass, and at times they passed
> within inches of us. Even with their dog they couldn't detect us.
> We could see that dog, wagging his tail and barking occasionally.
> I guess he was used to us by then.
>
> They soon gave up the search, and we split up into three
> groups, just to be safe. Some of us slept outside and some in
> the buildings. It was cold that night. The next morning, we did

a lot of exploring, looking for food, wood supplies, places to sleep, and generally getting the lay of the land for the next landing. The place was desolate. It was so run down that it was already beginning to feel like a reservation.[20]

As the morning light crept into the main cellblock through the shattered remnants of windows, they discussed a plan. This was a place where generations of countless prisoners and outcasts had also dreamed of their freedom; now a new generation of Native students began to envision a freedom of their own. Despite having only two loaves of bread and no water, they decided to split up to prevent an easy capture. They prohibited each other from divulging where the other groups were hiding if the authorities captured them. This strategy might just give them the advantage of remaining on the island undiscovered, prolonging the occupation. It was not long before a large press corps, followed by T. E. Hannon, regional director of the General Services Administration (the federal agency in charge of administration for the island), and the Coast Guard arrived on the island.

Interestingly, after a game of cat and mouse, the press was the first to locate Richard Oakes, Ross Harden, and others holed up in the main cellblock. The reporters informed Oakes that the Coast Guard was there to arrest them unless they agreed to leave peacefully. It was a perplexing and tough proposal. If they abandoned the island, it could cause ill feelings among the supporters on the mainland as well as within the group occupying the island. However, an arrest and possible jail time or fines could devastate any future attempt to claim Alcatraz. After weighing the terms and probabilities, Richard Oakes made the decision to fight again another day. Without proper provisions, support, and more people on hand, Oakes, aware of the difficult choice that had to be made, quickly agreed to the terms.

Eventually, Harden and others began the search for the hidden remnants of the occupation force. Many were no doubt confused and dismayed by Oakes's choice to abandon the island. For the sake of solidarity, they emerged from their hiding places. They realized what Richard Oakes was already planning: With a larger population, the settlement of Alcatraz could be sustained. The fourteen occupiers made their way down the main road to the docks, where Hannon and the Coast Guard were waiting. The press following the organizers realized that the students had acquired a keen knowledge of the layout of the island. Once he had arrived at the receiving docks, Oakes, treating the moment like a press conference, began to read the proclamation. Hannon and others listened as Oakes continued to read after the preamble:

> We feel that this so-called Alcatraz Island is more than suitable as an Indian Reservation, as determined by the white man's own standards. By this we mean that this place resembles most Indian reservations, in that:
>
> 1. It is isolated from modern facilities, and without adequate means of transportation.
> 2. It has no fresh running water.
> 3. It has inadequate sanitation facilities.
> 4. There are no oil or mineral rights.
> 5. There is no industry and so unemployment is very great.
> 6. There are no health care facilities.
> 7. The soil is rocky and non-productive and the land does not support game.
> 8. There are no educational facilities.
> 9. The population has always exceeded the land base.
> 10. The population has always been held as prisoners and kept dependent upon others.
>
> Further, it would be fitting and symbolic that ships from all over the world, entering the Golden Gate, would first see Indian land, and thus be reminded of the true history of this nation. This tiny island would be a symbol of the great lands once ruled by free and noble Indians.[21]

The proclamation also called for the creation of several institutions on the island: a center for Native American Studies with a traveling university; an American Indian spiritual center to practice a Native religion not yet protected by the federal government; an Indian center of ecology to formulate conservatory plans; an Indian training school, complete with a center for traditional arts and crafts; a Native restaurant; and an economic school to study ways in which to increase employment and standards of living. Furthermore, the proclamation identified the need for the creation of an American Indian museum to expose the "true" history of Native America. After patiently listening to Oakes read from the proclamation, Hannon offered the settlers a ride back to the mainland. Oakes, wanting the last word, turned toward the reporters and with a characteristic grin announced, "We've proven our point. Beyond that, the next time we come, we're going to come to build. . . . If a one-day occupation by white men on our land years ago established squatter's rights, this should establish our rights here." As the occupiers grabbed their bedrolls and began to climb aboard the Coast Guard cutter, one of the group, succumbing to a humorous impulse, shouted, "You got any food on board?"[22]

A day later, the occupiers learned that their risky attempt was a hit with the local media. Despite all the excitement, hilarity, and drama of the past two days, one objective remained certain: Alcatraz remained a real and obtainable goal. If anything, the first two assaults would be recognized as reconnaissance missions. They now diverted their attention toward obtaining a larger occupation force. New recruits were needed, along with enough provisions to maintain a stable residence. The students could have easily settled for the meager success of the two previous occupation attempts, but it soon became certain they were serious about their claim.

In the next couple of days, Richard Oakes made his way to Los Angeles and the campus of the University of California at Los Angeles. In the sprawling city, a much larger Native student and community base could be recruited for the third invasion. Oakes worked through the night to draft a compelling speech for recruitment. During the fall semester of 1969, Cahuilla/Luiseño professor Edward Castillo was teaching a course on Native American history at UCLA. When he received a notice from Ponca historian Roger Buffalohead that Richard Oakes was going to present a proposal for a protest at San Francisco State, Castillo agreed to have the then-unknown Oakes speak to his students. As Castillo described the moment in Campbell Hall:

> I clearly recall Oakes's speech to our students. He made a positive impression: He was a handsome adult, solidly built. Although he obviously was not a polished public speaker, he delivered his message with simplicity and power. I was delighted to hear that he proposed to lead a coalition of American Indian

students from San Francisco State, UC Berkeley, and UC
Riverside to occupy the abandoned federal prison on Alcatraz
Island . . . He then read the declaration that explained the
reasons for seizing the island. Cleverly, it made truthful comparisons between Alcatraz and Indian reservations (i.e., isolation,
lack of running water, lack of employment) and, better still,
offered to pay the government twenty-four dollars in trinkets for
the land![23]

Afterwards, Richard Oakes spent time with the Native students and
faculty, discussing plans for another assault. These meetings took Oakes
to the Los Angeles Indian Center and local Indian bars to recruit for the
target date—November 20, 1969. Ironically, the students had planned
their new date around Adam Nordwall's departure from San Francisco.
Nordwall would be out of town attending the first conference for the
newly formed National Indian Education Association. The core group of
organizers clearly wanted to control the next attempt for Alcatraz. Oakes
was recharged, returning to San Francisco confident after his successful
recruiting efforts at UCLA.[24]

It must have been difficult for the student leaders to control their
excitement as they resumed their studies at Berkeley and San Francisco
State. Those who attended the regular meetings at the new Indian center
continued to discuss the topic of Alcatraz. The day before D-Day,
November 19, Aubrey Grossman met with organizers to discuss nonviolent strategies of civil disobedience.[25] Meanwhile a large contingency
from UCLA arrived in university vans and parked outside the Indian
center. Ed Castillo remembered the climate of the meeting, which was
anything but nonviolent:

When our group arrived at the Indian Center, a rancorous debate
was under way in a meeting of perhaps two hundred people. A
tall, long haired, non-Indian biker-type (with what appeared to
be an Indian wife) was expressing his apprehension about the
wisdom of the proposed Alcatraz enterprise. Abruptly, someone
jumped up from the audience and punched the biker's lights
out. Apparently, the time for debate had passed. Thereafter, the
discussion turned to logistical questions about our transportation to the island.[26]

As a large group from a diverse range of backgrounds, many brought their own valid opinions. Obviously, uniting them was no easy task. Oakes was now rapidly becoming the catalyst who could solidify or dismantle the movement.

Aside from the intensity of this meeting, life was growing increasingly stressful in the Oakes household. During mid-November, Tim Findley was scheduled to meet with Oakes, as well as Shirley Keith, a Native student from San Francisco State. During the meeting, Oakes seemed to be collapsing from all the planning and frequent meetings. Findley and Keith both took notice of Oakes's drinking habit, which had increased sharply as the three discussed the logistics of the occupation. At this moment, Annie was busy with the kids, patiently waiting in their station wagon for her husband to finish with yet another meeting. As the waiting wore on, Annie naturally became agitated and entered the smoky little bar. Once at the table, her anger reached a boiling point. Perhaps it was seeing Oakes drinking so much, or perhaps it was finding him in a deep conversation with Shirley Keith. It is unclear what triggered her next response. Before anyone could react, Annie Oakes jumped up from the table, grabbed an empty beer bottle, and shattered it against Shirley Keith's mouth. Richard, who was shocked, angry, and most likely embarrassed, quickly got Annie out of the bar. Unfortunately, Shirley was left with a busted lip and a longtime fear of Annie Oakes. Richard's focus on organizing the occupation meant that he was being pulled away from his family. If anything, he had to make sure to include his family more in the future. Oakes had been used to a single life free of commitment and was still stumbling at times to maintain his marital responsibilities. The situation could have been handled without violence, but emotions obviously got the best of Richard and Annie on that occasion.[27]

One positive contact that came from the meeting with Findley was Peter Bowen, who tended bar at the No Name Bar in Sausalito. The bar was infamous as a frequent watering hole for liberal reporters. Coincidentally, he also was the owner of a large boat capable of transporting most of the members of Indians of All Tribes to the former prison. Al Miller made a cautious phone call to ask Peter Bowen for transportation to an undisclosed location in the bay. Bowen quickly understood just what Miller was asking: transportation to Alcatraz. After a pause, Bowen agreed to serve as the taxi for the occupiers, as long as they could wait until 2:00 a.m., when he closed the bar.

Earlier that evening Richard Oakes and the UCLA students went down to the Berkeley Marina. They were in search of a backup boat to take them to Alcatraz. Relying on their previous experience, the students wanted some insurance in case Bowen backed out. Edward Castillo reflected on the long trip across the bay:

> Oakes located the designated boat, but the skipper suddenly
> erupted into an agitated harangue. After a short while, Oakes
> walked back to the caravan of cars to tell us that the "chicken-
> shit coward" now refused to transport us to the island. Oakes
> later explained that the captain feared the Coast Guard had been
> alerted to this new attempt to take over the island, and he
> believed his boat would be confiscated. Fortunately, we had a
> back-up boat and captain at the Sausalito Marina across the bay.
> There followed another trip across the Bay Bridge, through San
> Francisco, and over the Golden Gate Bridge. It was my first sight
> of that famous landmark, and I studied it with a degree of awe.
> The night was clear and cold, with just a hint of fog coming
> through the channel.[28]

Discouraged, the caravan of cars and vans turned around to meet at the No Name Bar. The reporters lingering at the bar had become acutely aware that something newsworthy was about to happen. (Obviously, it was difficult to conceal over eighty Native people with sleeping bags and provisions crammed into a bar that was about to close.) Once Bowen had completed his last chore, he and two others, Bob Teft and Mary Crowley, worked diligently to gather up the occupation force onto two more boats. Oakes soon realized that someone still needed to notify the press. Dean Chavers, a journalism student at Berkeley, was the perfect choice. He and a UCLA student hurried back to the Indian center to write a press release. According to Bowen, the whole thing began with

> a marathon of phoning sessions involving Indian spokesman Al
> Miller and Richard Oakes, crew for the boats, many faceless
> voices all wanting assurance you're for their cause, lawyers who
> promise full legal support should your boat be impounded by
> the Federal authorities, and one lone trusted establishment
> radical reporter. Several drinks and hours later arrangements

seem complete. Crew ready, lawyers reassuring . . . Indians
arriving at Midnight. . . . Silently 30 Indians file down onto the
two floating piers which immediately wallow and sink causing
many a wet moccasin. Crews from both boats report the island
is lit up like a Christmas tree. "They're ready for us." But the
momentum is on.

    Everyone feels they're part of a great movement. . . . Huddled
on the bow, waiting to cast off, three young Indian students
explain the poverty of their reservation years to a crewman.
Miller and Oakes go over their plans for disbursement and
tactics should they encounter resistance. . . . One of the boat
owners stepping from the water barge moored to the dock into
one hell of a splash and a miraculous climb up 15 feet of sheer
steel bulkhead minus his glasses and cap. All this while
provisions are rushed ashore, more proclamations read and
from under one pile of bedding emerges a very small and
sleepy Indian child [Yvonne Oakes]. One of the youngest
invaders ever anywhere.[29]

Even if unwittingly, Yvonne imitated Richard's mythic actions of some
fifteen years earlier, becoming a young stowaway on Bowen's boat.
Yvonne, who was only twelve years old, was just one of many children who
joined the occupation force. The occupiers believed that having their families with them would deter a hostile removal by federal officials, a strategy
borrowed from the civil rights movement. Yvonne, in a spontaneous burst
of energy, had a front seat to witness her community's claim over Alcatraz.

    Security guards on the island were more than aware of the takeover.
Soon enough, after two trips to shuttle the occupation force across the
bay, the island was surrounded by the searchlights of Coast Guard cutters
and helicopters.[30] It must have been quite a spectacle from the slum-
bering shores of the mainland. Amidst all the excitement, the settlers
began to congregate in what had once been the warden's residence. A tiny
fireplace began to put out a small amount of heat from paper cups and
twigs. Richard Oakes, Al Miller, and others gathered around the drum
listening to the singers carry and lift the spirits of the occupation force.
Over the mantel was a black-and-white poster of Chiricahua Apache
leader Geronimo, whose image represented one of the last truly free

Annie and Yvonne Oakes on Alcatraz Island, November 20, 1969. Annie is leading Yvonne with one hand and carrying a poster of Geronimo in her other hand, a poster that was featured in several prominent occupation press photos. This is the first time this photo has been shown to the public. Photo courtesy of the *San Francisco Examiner,* photographer Eddie Murphy. Original photo negative in Kent Blansett Private Collection.

Native leaders in the United States. The dream was now becoming a reality, but soon it was distracted by the birth of a new day.

At sunrise the settlers were abruptly awakened when they heard helicopters landing on the island. Reporters and cameramen exiting the helicopters were greeted by the newly formed IAT security force and began hustling for interviews. Security posts had been set up and maintained throughout the long night to observe Coast Guard actions. An office for the Bureau of Caucasian Affairs (BCA) was formed in the receiving office by the docks. Settlers armed with buckets of red paint began to transform the signs, walls, and brittle concrete structures into political slogans of "Red Power"—phrases of home.[31]

A cooking area was established in the courtyard outside the main cellblock. Wood for heat and cooking was scarce, but soon settlers began collecting scrap lumber and breaking apart wooden pallets for fuel. It was evident to reporters covering the event that the Indians of All Tribes were highly organized, but getting supplies to the island remained a top priority.

The prison had only three working toilets, clean water was scarce, and food was tightly rationed. As word of the occupation and the need for supplies spread, the Coast Guard would have their hands full. Boats ferrying supplies to the island began an assault on the blockade. Overnight, IAT carried out a plan, devised by Richard Oakes, for six supply drops on Alcatraz. Opposite the Golden Gate side of the island, members started throwing Molotov cocktails at the rocks below, distracting the Coast Guard's attention. Another faction used rickety ladders tied together with ropes to descend the steep cliff walls to reach the shore and haul in key supplies. This routine of cat and mouse with the Coast Guard went on until daybreak.

Later that morning, the occupiers were on edge, expecting that the U.S. Marshals Service, the Coast Guard, or someone else would evict them from the island. Luiseño citizen Dennis Turner summed up the mood on the island when he stated, "We won't resist. . . . How will they find us? It's why we are here in the first place—we are the invisible

Richard Oakes on Alcatraz Island, November 20, 1969. This is the first time that this photo has been made available to the public. Photo courtesy of the *San Francisco Examiner*, photographer Eddie Murphy. Original photo negative in Kent Blansett Private Collection.

Americans."[32] As afternoon approached, the waters of the bay filled with boats, largely pleasure cruisers, which confused the blockade on Alcatraz. Under maritime law, motored boats must yield to sail- or wind-powered boats, and the Coast Guard was outnumbered in their effort to maintain the perimeter. Several boats easily slipped past the blockade and brought more supplies and reinforcements to the occupied prison.

While Apache occupier Anthony Garcia and Colville/Lakota nurse Stella Leach organized a much-needed health clinic, Richard Oakes and R. Corbin Houchins, a lawyer for individuals on the island, phoned a message to William Devoranon, regional coordinator of the Office of the Secretary of the Interior in San Francisco:

> To the Government of the United States from Alcatraz Island, Indian Territory. We native peoples of North America have gathered here to claim our traditional and natural right to create a meaningful use for our Great Spirit's land. Therefore, let it be known that our stand for self-determination is on Alcatraz. We invite the United States to acknowledge the justice of our claim. The choice now lies with the leaders of the American Government—to use violence upon us as before to remove us from our Great Spirit's land, or institute a real change in its dealing with the American Indian. We do not fear your threat to charge us with crimes on our land. We and all other oppressed peoples would welcome spectacle of proof before the world of your title by genocide. Nevertheless, we seek peace.[33]

Houchins was able to lend impromptu legal advice to the occupiers. By four o'clock that afternoon, T. E. Hannon, William Devoranon, and Aubrey Grossman made their way out to Alcatraz for an official meeting. Hannon reiterated the federal government's position that the occupiers were trespassers and for their safety should evacuate the island. A compromise was reached as Hannon promised to allow one supply boat to land in the evening with the demand that the occupiers vacate by noon the next day. For their part, IAT gave the government two weeks to surrender Alcatraz. At that time, federal officials were unaware that this takeover would last another nineteen months, despite repeated negotiations. Government officials counted on a lack of organization and media attention to drown out IAT's hopes for a prolonged occupation.

Left to right: an unidentified individual, Thomas Hannon, Ross Harden, Tanya Oakes, and Richard Oakes. Tanya is standing next to her father. Alcatraz Island, November 25, 1969. This is the first time that this photo has been published. Photo courtesy of the *San Francisco Examiner* and Sara Glines, photographer Paul Glines. Original photo negative in Kent Blansett Private Collection.

Contrary to Hannon's expectations, IAT was highly organized. It opened a mainland office, donated by Blackfeet citizen Dorothy Lonewolf Miller, who along with Dean Chavers, mainland coordinator, administered all accounts, took charge of bookkeeping, and established the IAT bank account.[34] On the island, IAT elected a seven-member council of Richard Oakes, Al Miller, Ross Harden, Ed Castillo, Bob Nelford, Dennis Turner, and Jim Vaughn. By unanimous decision Richard Oakes and Dennis Turner were elected as spokespersons for IAT. Clearly, Richard Oakes was emerging as the leader. He had been the catalyst in the movement up to this point: He had led the charge, recruited supporters, run supplies, and handled the media and government superbly.[35] He used his gift of oratory, drawing on a long history of Iroquois orators, to calm the nerves of occupiers: "We have nothing to fear. We are not seeking to destroy the U.S. government. We are not seeking to overthrow the U.S. government. We are seeking to change that which must be changed."[36]

It was critical to the efforts of IAT to keep to a unified message for the press. Without a stable message, different opinions could alter the original motivation. The goals had to remain clear. Having multiple spokespersons would lead to confusion among the public, the government, the press, and throughout Indian Country as well. Although occupiers proposed a law of consensus, the structure and organization did not lack leadership. This leadership was led and sponsored by the citizens of IAT. Oakes maintained a precarious role as part of the leadership core on the island. Only time would demonstrate just how important Oakes's presence would be for maintaining a successful settlement.

While Indians of All Tribes worked to sponsor a clear title to the land, the Nixon administration scrambled to formulate an informed response. The White House received a ticker tape wire that read, "Indians Seize Alcatraz."[37] Nixon aides, quickly realizing the enormity of the situation, postponed any local attempts at removal. Leonard Garment, Nixon's special assistant for minority affairs, quickly appointed Brad Patterson, Garment's assistant in charge of Indian affairs, to represent the White House and to assume control over local law enforcement with regard to Alcatraz. At the time of the takeover, Nixon was drafting his new Indian policy that would eventually usher in the era of self-determination. Nixon was caught in the public crossfire between the antiwar and Black Power movements, and his administration remained sensitive about any additional bad publicity that could derail his policy-making efforts. Eventually, President Nixon gained political favor among some Indians as over the next two decades a remarkable twenty-six pieces of self-determination legislation forever altered the federal government's relationship with Indian Country.[38]

By Sunday, November 23, 1969, a thick fog consumed the tiny island. That afternoon Richard Oakes climbed onto the bed of a faded blue Chevy truck to call a general meeting to order. After updating the community on recent issues, he introduced Joe Brewer to the people on the island. Brewer proposed to IAT that he be allowed to film a documentary on the island. Lifting his right hand and repeating after Oakes, he swore confidentiality before IAT.[39] This action exemplified the tight control exerted by IAT over the media and, more importantly, over their own image.

Life on the island was not without its lack of breaks in between all the press visits, security patrols, and general maintenance. During these times occupiers relieved stress by playing softball and basketball games in the courtyard or catching the Michigan/Ohio State football game on tele-vision. Many of them fished for bay cod or trapped an occasional crab. The down time and activities that consumed these moments not only relieved tension, they also brought a marked feeling of community to the island. The nightlife strengthened the mood, as Oakes later explained:

> We did a lot of singing in those days. I remember the fires at nighttime, the cold of the night, the singing around the camp-fire . . . songs of friendship, the songs of understanding. We did a lot of singing. We sang into the early hours of the morning. . . . A few of us would go off alone and start talking about our expe-riences on the different reservations, about the more advanced problems and finding solutions for them.[40]

It was this type of unity that drove hundreds and thousands to Alcatraz, which soon became a "Mecca of Indian Country." Oakes stated later that this unity had been undreamed of. The occupation called upon a revival of traditional ways, an awakening of Intertribal unity that had not taken place since the Ghost Dance of the late nineteenth century. Solidarity was the key to creating one of the most powerful symbols of the 1960s Red Power movement: "Alcatraz."

Over the next couple of days Oakes challenged Walter Hickel, Secretary of the Interior, to meet with occupiers and officially hand over the title to Alcatraz.[41] In response Hickel agreed to meet with IAT, but he explained that he did not have the authority to grant title. The Coast Guard began to loosen their control over the blockade on the island. Oakes kept up pressure on government officials to force a response: "We want this island," he said. "This is the beginning of our fight for justice and self determination—and Alcatraz. Then Alaska, yes, Alaska is next. There is a dual sense of justice in this country, one for Indians, one for whites. If they're going to continue to treat us in this manner, why not set up dual governments."[42] The occupation quickly turned into a waiting game. The government hoped that the press would lose interest, whereas Richard Oakes and IAT were sponsoring a solid media campaign. Oakes even offered to take the GSA's T. E. Hannon fishing to discuss the occupa-tion.[43] Hickel eventually postponed a visit to the island, citing a pinched nerve in his neck. Oakes made a joke of it: "I just wonder . . . if that nerve happens to be his Indian nerve."[44]

This is the only posed photo from the occupation. It was taken by Art Kane and appeared in the June 2, 1970, issue of *Look Magazine*. The identified occupiers in the front row, left to right, are John Trudell, Tara Trudell, Annie Oakes, Richard Oakes, Stella Leach, Ray Spang, and Ross Harden. Peeking out behind Ray Spang is Joe Morris, and seated behind Richard and Stella Leach is Luwana Quitiquit. Photo © Art Kane courtesy Art Kane Archive.

As Thanksgiving approached, the support for IAT increased; restaurants around San Francisco donated turkeys and other food for what was billed to the press as an "Un-Thanksgiving" dinner. Monetary donations flooded the mailroom at the mainland headquarters. Press from around the world arrived in the Bay Area to cover the takeover. San Francisco Mayor Joseph Alioto, on business in Europe, recalled, "You have no idea how much publicity this has had in Europe. Everywhere I went I was asked about Alcatraz and the Indians. They're using Alcatraz as a means of negotiating their serious and in my opinion justifiable claims. The Indians and the federal government will have to work out their differences . . . between themselves."[45] Ronald Reagan, governor of California, witnessed the overwhelming public support for IAT. So he began pressuring the federal government for more assistance for California's Indian health needs.[46] Native peoples from across the country, both young and old, had begun making "pilgrimages" to Alcatraz. The symbol and idea of

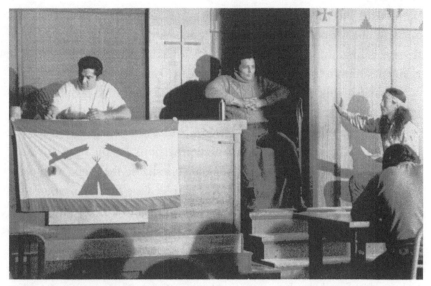

Indians of All Tribes Mock Trial on Alcatraz Island, November 26, 1969, featuring
Shoshone/Paiute citizen Tom Joseph from UCLA serving as judge. Richard Oakes is on
the witness stand being interrogated by Joe Bill. Also shown is the original Indians of All
Tribes flag with the symbol of the occupation, a broken pipe over a lodge. AP Photo.

Alcatraz and Indians of All Tribes that Bay Area students and community
members had given birth to was growing larger and larger.

On November 26, the Indians of All Tribes sponsored a mock trial of
Indians versus the United States government. The organizers utilized a
popular form of 1960s protest through political theater. Richard Oakes
played the defendant, represented by Ed Castillo and Joe Bill and prosecuted by Dennis Turner and LaNada Means before a jury comprised of
thirteen IAT members. Staged in the prison chapel, the judge, embodied
by Tom Joseph, a Native student from UCLA, sat behind the pulpit which
displayed the first IAT flag symbolizing Native Nationalism and unified
claim for title of Alcatraz. The first Alcatraz occupation flag featured two
large stripes of equal dimensions above and below a lighter interior,
which contained a broken sacred pipe suspended over a lodge with an
open door (for many Tribes, the tipi or lodge is represented by a star or
stars and is also a symbol for the Native American Church). The broken
pipe, which followed the contours of the tipi below it, critiqued America's
failed promise to Indigenous peoples. This imagery emerged as one of
the most pervasive symbols from the occupation, as IAT residents often

painted the flag on the backs of their jackets along with their Tribal affili-ation. While the occupiers placed the United States on trial, the theatrical display helped inform the press about Native rights and unified Alcatraz residents behind the ideology of their greater cause.[47]

Thanksgiving Day hosted over three hundred Native peoples on the island, some from as far away as Washington state and Oklahoma. A powwow and huge feast was planned for that afternoon. Cooks on the island worked double time to organize provisions for the large turnout. When the dances began, young hoop dancers shared the arena with older traditional dancers wearing their "war hair."[48] One occupier who made his way onto the island was a young Santee citizen named John Trudell, who lived in Los Angeles. Trudell listened carefully and at great length to Oakes as he talked about the goals, objectives, and history of the occupa-tion. Trudell liked what he heard so much that he returned to Los Angeles to bring his family back to stay on Alcatraz. Grace Thorpe, a Sac and Fox citizen and the daughter of Jim Thorpe, one of the greatest Indian athletes of all time, put her possessions into storage and began making the long trip west from Oklahoma to the former prison. One young occupier summed up what Alcatraz meant when he stated: "On the mainland we were a minority. . . . On Alcatraz we're a majority."[49]

After two weeks on the island, Oakes took breaks between interviews and meetings to spend time repairing the island's crumbling docks and help haul supplies. Whenever he had a free moment, he offered support, ran supply lines, or used knowledge derived from his blue-collar skills for needed repairs across the island. Dressed in a large raincoat, he climbed beneath the docks on a handheld ladder to stabilize loose boards and patch hazardous areas. Richard proved that he was not simply a "pencil pusher"; he was also the muscle behind some of the physical improve-ments on the island. The IAT improvement committee marked dangerous areas, sorted through clothing donations, planted shrubs, chopped wood, and cleared away trash, debris, vines, and weeds accumulated over years of neglect. Plumbers eventually restored forty-five toilets to supplement the three that had been in working order. Electricians rewired parts of the island and brought more power options back to the abandoned prison.

Responding to IAT's penchant for organization, government officials created a task force to construct a proposal for self-determination. The committee pulled representatives from various agency offices in and

Richard Oakes and Anthony Garcia (in a checkered shirt) making dock repairs and improvising with a ladder. "Indian occupiers work on the dock of Alcatraz Island" and "Indian occupiers stand on the dock of Alcatraz Island," Michelle Vignes photograph archive [graphic] BANC PIC 2003.108—NEG, NEG box 62, Roll 1308, frames 15 & 12. © The Regents of the University of California, The Bancroft Library, University of California, Berkeley.

around the Bay Area.[50] On December 2, 1969, Richard Oakes, Dennis Turner, and Aubrey Grossman met with the committee. After the ninety-minute meeting, Oakes emerged with the following review: "We're still going to stay on Alcatraz. Alcatraz offers us the insulation necessary for us to develop intellectually. . . . [We invite] all the Federal people . . . to come to the Rock and talk to the Indians there. . . . [We've] open[ed] the lines of communication. The Federal Government has to respond to the needs of the people."[51] As a reply to Oakes's invitation, T. E. Hannon made a trip out to the island with U.S. attorney Cecil Poole. Oakes greeted both Hannon and Poole with a smile. Clearly, every government official Oakes met had their hands tied, and all were limited by their position or title to create sweeping or effective policy changes. The IAT Council also reached out to their respective communities and home lands. In the process, they created an organization called Confederacy of American Indian Nations (CAIN), which sought to unify delegates and representatives from all Tribes into a larger Confederacy:

> there is a sense of urgency beneath the apparent lassitude [on Alcatraz]. . . . Sitting at a desk in the old Warden's office, he talks about the hope of beginning a new organization, the Confederacy of American Indian Nations [CAIN], to weld Indian groups all over the country into one body capable of taking power away from the white bureaucracy. He acknowledges that the pan-Indian movements which have sprung up before have always been crushed. "But time is running out for us," he says. "We have everything at stake. And if we don't make it now, then we'll get trapped at the bottom of that white world out there, and wind up as some kind of Jack Jones with a social security number and that's all. Not just on Alcatraz, but every place else, the Indian is in his last stand for cultural survival. . . . But the past is not really at issue. What is at stake today," as Richard says, "is cultural survival. Some occupiers have known Indian culture all of their lives; some have been partially assimilated away from it and are now trying to return."[52]

By December 6, 1969, Indians of All Tribes sent an official invitation to Tribal leaders to attend a conference to discuss the Confederacy and to formulate plans for a new cultural center on Alcatraz. This meeting would take place on December 23, at the onset of winter and just two days before Christmas. The date already spelled trouble for the conference. On the same day that these invitations were sent out across Indian Country, Oakes was interviewed by Lynn Ludlow of the *San Francisco Chronicle.* The article, titled "Man in the News," appeared in the Sunday edition of the paper and featured a photo of Oakes standing behind his wife Annie with his arms around her:

> Richard Oakes is Mohawk; his wife Annie is a Pomo, and their five children he says are Pomohawks . . . the family lives on Alcatraz. They symbolize the Indian unity. . . . Mrs. Oakes was sorting donated clothes. Her husband was explaining why the Alcatraz experience means so much to him and other Indians.

... "It's the first time we've gotten all the Indians together—
perhaps we can develop an all-tribe consciousness," he said. . . .
A young man was leaning over the rusty motor of a long dead
government pickup truck. "How's it going?" Oakes asked. . . .
"It's coming along." . . . the island to Oakes represents hope and
liberation, "a living monument to the American Indians, a place
for the living, not the dead." He is reserved, especially with
outsiders. On his sweater, next to an Indian neck ornament, is a
button that says: "We Won't Move." "We might—might—just
wake up the conscience of America. . . . For 400 years, America
has been trying to change us.

"Now let us do it ourselves. . . . It meant giving up a $300 a
week job, in Rhode Island for the subsistence of money offered
by the Educational Opportunity Program. It doesn't really bother
me. . . . I was making money, I wasn't making anything else."
Last week he was informed that the college would cut off his
EOP allowance if he were arrested and convicted.

"What's happening here on Alcatraz is more important. . . .
We're not giving up anything, We're gaining." . . . Oakes avoids
the rhetoric of the radical campus left. . . . "What the Indian
learns, he explained is seldom pertinent to the needs of the
Indian community. He seldom returns to the reservation. So far
our biggest problems are freelance photographers and the
hippies. . . . They stay and eat up our stores, then leave. Then we
have to clean up after them."

A sailboat lined with gawking spectators floated past the
island, and someone aboard shouted the woo . . . woo . . . woo
. . . woo . . . cry. "It's hard to say whether they're friend or foe.
. . . We get quite a bit of harassment from sailboats and cabin
cruisers. But I'll wave at them anyway. . . . We're only young
people concerned about our future. . . . These are the future
leaders of most of these Indian tribes." . . . Then the
Pomohawks came and took him away."[53]

Contrary to the growing publicity and countless demands placed upon
him, Oakes was working to build a home for his family on the island. His

and other people's children were not only getting a big lesson in the civics of IAT, soon they would also be enrolled in classes on the island.

Creek occupier Linda Aranaydo and others organized an alternative school known as the Big Rock School, sponsored by a grant written by Dorothy Lonewolf Miller. Classes were held on the first floor of the Ira Hayes Building. The school focused not just on reading, writing, and mathematics, it also sponsored a curriculum that facilitated the cultural development of students. The pre-school brunch typically consisted of spam and eggs with a television set tuned in to *Sesame Street*.[54] Richard and Annie's kids benefited from a rich learning environment as well as instruction in traditional arts and crafts taught by older residents, for instance Sac and Fox beading from Francis Allen. Instead of being spread throughout the city, the Big Rock School brought all Indian children together. Alcatraz kids were required to attend school every day—to avoid the threat of social workers dividing families; social workers in many American cities were notorious for separating Indian children from their families. Far from the reach of social workers, each child received instruction from Native teachers who had a college degree in English or another related field. Students were able to learn mainstream academics in the setting of their own community. At recess the children made use of broken-down trucks and tractors for jungle gyms. Children enrolled in the school gained experience from residents by having constant exposure to their greater Indigenous community.[55]

Puyallup fishing rights activist Ramona Bennett recalled a particular experience at the Big Rock School involving film actress Candice Bergen. Bergen stayed on the island a couple of days after her latest film, *Soldier Blue*, had wrapped up production. One afternoon, Bergen visited one of the classes at the Big Rock School. Before her arrival, all the children were told that they would meet a beautiful movie star. When Bergen entered the schoolroom of scattered stools and chalkboard, one of the kids plainly asserted, "She's not Indian. . . . She's not that beautiful." Instead of being embarrassed or hurt by the child's reaction, Bergen turned to the teachers and said, "What you're doing is working—especially going against mainstream ideas of beauty."[56] Soon the IAT children became a popular target for many of the press photographers visiting Alcatraz. Both Yvonne and Rocky Oakes were the subjects of many photos. Rocky wore a fur coat overlooking the bay, and Yvonne smiled with a flower in her mouth or posed alongside her siblings for photographs. Most of the photos of children on Alcatraz showed laughter and excitement, an indicator of the quality of life on the island.[57]

Life on the Rock was not without its moments of conflict, few of which made press coverage early in the occupation. Increasingly, Oakes found himself in the center of most of the conflicts, as jealousy began to rise among IAT members. In 1968 the American Indian Movement (AIM) was founded in Minneapolis, Minnesota, to protect the rights of all Native peoples. During the first week of the occupation AIM sent a delegation to San Francisco to learn more about the takeover. Dennis Banks, Leech Lake Anishinaabe; Clyde Bellecourt, White Earth Anishinaabe; George Mitchell, Leech Lake Anishinaabe; and Lehman Brightman made a trip out to Alcatraz.[58] While visiting the island, AIM witnessed the effectiveness and potential of the occupation. It is unclear just how the event transpired, but certain members of AIM's delegation began to assert that the leadership on the island should be handed over to the larger organization. Dean Chavers recalled that Oakes represented the final voice on the matter. Oakes found the AIM representatives by the docks and approached them. According to Chavers, they said to Richard, "'You guys did a good job, you took it over and we'll take it and run it from here.' Richard just says, 'Get the fuck off this Island, I'll kick your ass,' and he meant it! They didn't even blink. They got on the boat and left. . . . Richard was that kind of a guy. He would clean your clock; he was not afraid to fight."[59] Oakes obviously did not make any points with AIM, but he did earn the respect of those who elected to remain silent. In truth, he probably also earned the respect of the AIM members, who witnessed firsthand the determination of the leadership that had founded the Alcatraz occupation. AIM knew what many were just learning, that the leadership on the island would protect their objectives by any means necessary. This would not be the last physical challenge to leadership on the island.

Richard Oakes made plenty of mistakes along the way. For instance he made one serious misjudgment with Frank Chase. Oakes was under fire from many different sources, and the stress of being the lead spokesperson was mounting. Frank Chase, who was dating LaNada Means's sister, caught Oakes on the wrong day. As Chavers told it, "Frank . . . crossed Richard some way one day out at Alcatraz and Richard just mopped the floor with him, beat the crap out of him. He shouldn't have beat that guy up. . . . He was a tough guy. . . . He would not back down from anybody."⁶⁰ Fighting would not be very useful in unifying the membership. For some on the island, this behavior from the leadership was not acceptable. Oakes had to learn to control his emotions, and he would have ample opportunities in the coming months.

One person who helped Oakes learn self-control was Kahnawà:ke Mohawk Peter Blue Cloud. At times Blue Cloud spoke to Richard Oakes in Mohawk to set him at ease. Blue Cloud also worked with several others to organize the first newsletter for Indians of All Tribes, to be released in January. The newsletter featured artwork from IAT children and news from other protests around the country, from Pyramid Lake to the battle over fishing rights in the Pacific Northwest. Printed on paper of different colors, Pueblo activist Robert Free remembered dumpster diving outside the art department at UC Berkeley to collect free paper for use in printing the *IAT Newsletter*. Every newsletter contained a motley assortment of colors throughout each print run.⁶¹

Soon enough, Annie gave Richard Oakes another reason to learn self-discipline. They were going to have another child. Life was not easy for the Oakes family, and Annie was slowly growing despondent about keeping the family on the island. Oakes was a role model for many, and he was just learning about the responsibilities such a position required. Rocky, Annie's oldest son, got into a fight with a group of other children on the island. Apparently, he was being harassed by a few of the other kids because of his dad's leadership. Mimicking Oakes, Rocky rose to the occasion and began to fight with the other boys. Unfortunately, Rocky was not built like Richard, and he received a serious beating from the other kids.⁶² Tensions on the island were not just reserved for the adults; they were now beginning to affect their children as well.

In the meantime, support and donations flooded the mainland headquarters, accruing a three-week total of twelve thousand dollars. IAT received more publicity when Hollywood celebrities like Jonathan Winters, Jane Fonda, Ethel Kennedy, Candice Bergen, and Dick Gregory spoke out about the issue. Merv Griffin filmed part of his show on Alcatraz, and Anthony Quinn made his way out to island too. On December 15, Quinn, on leave from the set of *Nobody Loves a Drunken Indian,* visited the former prison. Some occupiers on the island flocked to get a glimpse of Quinn, while others kept their distance from all the hype. Quinn immediately hit it off with Richard Oakes, inviting him to attend local functions alongside the actor. For the next couple of days Oakes left the island and tried to secure donations or further contacts from the people in Quinn's orbit. It appeared that the actor did not intend to donate much to IAT, and perhaps he was using Oakes and the occupation to promote his next movie. Oakes came away empty-handed and returned to the island. Some even speculated that he was offered a movie contract. Rumors spread as tensions were quickly surfaced about Oakes and his leadership position.[63]

Another celebrity of Indian Country fame, Piapot Cree folk musician Buffy Sainte-Marie, provided crucial support for the occupation. On December 13, 1969, she staged a benefit concert at Stanford University with all proceeds going to Indians of All Tribes. Earlier in the day, Buffy brought her guitar and wonderful charm to residents on the island. Her songs of freedom were welcomed and broke the monotony of the solitary life on the Rock. That very evening, after intense speeches by members of IAT and a riveting performance by Buffy, Richard Oakes walked out on stage and presented a bouquet of flowers to the singer. Throughout the long evening, he chose to remain backstage and behind the scenes, allowing others to share the vision of Alcatraz. Adam Nordwall, master of ceremonies that evening, noticed Oakes on stage and immediately turned the microphone over to him to speak. Caught off guard, he simply thanked the crowd for their generous donations and left the stage. He was not scheduled to speak, but Oakes's presence brought a feeling of authenticity to the festivities that night. He was the most identifiable person from Alcatraz, and although some in the crowd were disappointed that he failed to say more, most were equally eager to call it a night. Oakes was maintaining control, making sure everyone understood that the event was not just about his views. He was encouraging others to make a deeper public commitment to the cause.[64]

Six days later, Oakes spoke at a poetry benefit for Alcatraz hosted by minister Cecil Williams at the Glide Memorial Church located in San Francisco's Tenderloin District. The Glide Memorial Church sponsored a progressive platform that connected multiple communities and populations throughout San Francisco. The poetry reading that evening at the Glide featured several prominent Beat poets, such as Gary Snyder,

Michael McClure, and Joanne Kyger. Starting at 7:00 p.m., Richard Oakes took center stage and gave a riveting speech. His address summarized both the Alcatraz takeover and larger Red Power movement:

> Alcatraz is not an island, it's an idea. It's in the hearts and
> minds of every Indian, whether they [be] young, old, or middle-
> aged. It's the promise of tomorrow, so that the Indians can have
> something. It's a betterment for the Indian people today. The
> idea of Alcatraz is the acquisition of land, and to better the lot of
> American Indians everyplace. The news media picked up
> Alcatraz and made it into a big farce, made it into something of
> which it is today . . . dependent upon the white people. When
> we went out to Alcatraz we thought different. We have a lot of
> different meanings put into it. We wanted to see a cultural
> center. We wanted to see a higher education system, because the
> education system today turns out an Indian, who is not an
> Indian, he is a white man. The white person goes out and finds
> a place in white society, he doesn't find a place in Indian society
> and this is what we want. We want to turn out a product that is
> serviceable to the Indian peoples so that they can develop their
> Indian reservations or rancherias and hopefully get more land.
> We also want to develop an economic system entirely
> independent of the white structure and interdependent upon
> other Indians. The black people have a call for assimilation,
> equality. All along since 1492 we've been fighting this type of
> assimilation, and we continue on fighting this here. This is
> somewhat militant talk but it's feasible, it is entirely feasible
> because Indian people are kind of frustrated. They are fed up
> with this white society—that wants to promise when a
> missionary comes over and says, "hey, come on, we'll make you
> civilized." They are far away from civilization today.
>   The educational system in this country is not a part of this
> country, if it doesn't get in tune with the thinking of the
> American Indian people. It seems to me it's just . . . a part and
> parcel of the European educational complex. That's all it is.
> We're going to promote another type of Alcatraz. I say promote
> because that is the type of words that the non-Indians use too

. . . so they can understand what is going on in this country. But Alcatraz is . . . a catalyst between a past and a present. The implementation of the idea of Alcatraz is at Pit River, the Alaskan Native lands claims case, and a large part of Canada. California land claims case is divided into three parts, it's the Mission Indians, California Indians Incorporated, and the Pit River Tribe. Years ago, you had what you call the Trail of Tears, the Cherokee Indians, they removed the Cherokee Indians from their land base. They moved them a thousand miles, suffering a lot of deaths for the sum of 21 cents per acre. The person of generosity, Jackson and a few others, the president said well let's give the Indians a fair shake. We'll give them 50 cents per acre, so that's what they got . . . but that was many years ago, yet the same thing is happening today, here in California.

The California Indians are receiving from 21 cents an acre to 47 cents per acre. From here to San Jose you can't buy a parcel of land for less than a $1,000 dollars an acre, but look at the importance, look at the feelings Indian people held for this land. It's our contention as American Indians to respect the land for what it is—you can't sell your mother earth. The earth is your mother and to sell it would be to deny your younger generations a part of their heritage, a rich part.

Pit River, for so long, has stated that they do not want the money for the land, they want their lands and who the hell is the rest of this world to tell them, the Indian people that they can't have their land—that they should settle for the 47 cents an acre. What people are going to stand for them, no one. The Indian people have to stand up for their own rights and that's what they are doing at Pit River. Pit River is three-million-four-hundred-thousand acres of land in the state of California. It covers Shasta, most of Shasta County, Lassen, Modoc, and Siskiyou Counties . . . but we are there idealistically to protect not just Pit River but to protect the rest of the Indians throughout the United States. The California Land claims case, Cherokee removal, Trail of Tears, the Six Nation Iroquois Confederacy confinement to lands they have in New York state and elsewhere, the Alaskan Native Land Claims case—now going on are all part of the things we are going to develop in the future. So, that we can become people with land, people with a hope . . . so, all these troubles have boiled down to the Pit River action.

In a few weeks, even a month, we are going to reclaim the whole of the Pit River area. This is the next Alcatraz. We are going to fight to retain this land, to give it back to the Pit River people, as a spark. All three-million-four-hundred-thousand acres—less than that previously occupied by the small white people. Our big targets are the Department of the Interior, two branches of it—the Forestry Service and the Bureau of Land Management—oh, that is nothing. Bing Crosby has a large holding of land and he won't let any Indians go up there and hunt and fish or in other words live. So he's another one of our targets. The special interest groups like Southern Pacific, like PG&E and the rest of them. There is a list of a lot of people on our side. Sierra Club and quite a few small ecology groups. . . . I don't know for what reason they are tearing the country apart, turning it upside down. It almost seems to me that the white people in this country, the non-Indians people, are exploiting the land turning it upside down in the last determined rush to go someplace else. If this is what they are going to do then we have every right to stop them—this is our land—all of it![65]

Back on the island, preparations were made for a larger population scheduled to visit for a conference on December 23, 1969. By late December, winter was in full force across Indian Country, and many people were refusing to travel. The date of the conference had another serious flaw. It was just two days before Christmas. Attendance was expected in the thousands, but only a quarter of that total made the long journey out to Alcatraz.

Also, the media were prohibited from attending the conference. This was a bold move, but a large media presence might have distracted the participants. The meeting was broken down into committees, with Richard as the moderator of finance. The clear focus, because of the dismal showing, was aimed at plans to transform the island into a cultural center and university. Some IAT members and the press criticized the conference as a failure, but this critique was based on attendance and not substance. As plans were debated and drafted, the occupiers became all too aware of the daunting tasks that lay ahead of them to complete the transformation of their vision.

Although IAT chose to ban reporters from the conference, they did manage to create their own media center, called "Radio Free Alcatraz." Al Silbowitz, manager of KPFA-FM, a radio station out of Berkeley, received a grant to sponsor the radio project. Silbowitz worked through the winter chill of the prison to install radio equipment on Alcatraz. Radio Free Alcatraz began broadcasting on December 22, 1969, to an audience with a population in the tens of thousands. The listening audience was not confined to California. Radio Free Alcatraz was also re-broadcast by KPFA's sister station in New York. Behind a clothesline draped with red and orange blankets, John Trudell hosted the radio show, which featured interviews with many of the original occupiers. Richard Oakes was one of many IAT settlers who sat down at the masonite tabletop for an interview with Trudell.[66] During the interview, Oakes spoke about the idea of Alcatraz and the changes needed in Indian education:

IAT press conference on Alcatraz Island, December 24, 1969. Left to right: Richard Oakes, Earl Livermore, Al Miller, and Vine Deloria Jr., who is in the background next to the IAT Christmas tree. Photo courtesy of Getty Images, Bettmann Collection 514678430.

The Bureau of Indian Affairs structure is such . . . that it doesn't serve us. So let's make this one point clear, it does not service the Indian people, it provides a service for the federal government only. . . . You see, the situation is that the whole school system, the BIA school system should be chucked, should be shelved and restructured. But restructured in such a way that the Indian culture is revealed, so that the Indian person going to these schools, if these schools are still in operation, will get the knowledge and the understanding of who he is, what he is, and why he is in that situation; as well as an understanding of the different Indians surrounding him and *get* different Indians in the whole United States and Canada and Alaska. We have a great history, and I think it should be brought forth.[67]

Radio Free Alcatraz became another vehicle in the cause to transform Alcatraz into Indian Country. It provided listeners with an opportunity to become privy to the many conversations dominating the island.

Radio Free Alcatraz broadcast, December 26, 1969, featuring Grace Thorpe and John Trudell with copies of Deloria's *Custer Died for Your Sins* and Edgar Cahn's *Our Brother's Keeper: The Indian in White America*. Displaying books showed the intellectual merits of the movement and provided educational resources for the public. Photo courtesy of Getty Images, Bettmann Collection 660778708.

Back east in Washington, D.C., Browning Pipestem mounted a successful lobbying campaign. Congressmen George E. Brown Jr. and Phillip Burton worked to get a bill through Congress that would grant title of Alcatraz to IAT.[68] In the United Nations, U.S. delegate Shirley Temple Black referenced Alcatraz when she spoke before the U.N. social committee on refugees: "The value of Alcatraz today is symbolic. . . . It represents an anguished cry from impoverished descendants."[69] Other politicians differed in their opinion on Alcatraz. San Francisco representative William Maillard, a Republican, stated, "It doesn't look realistic to me. . . . I'm skeptical that they really want Alcatraz. [They] are using the occupation to dramatize some very real needs they have."[70] T. E. Hannon continued to make frequent trips to the island to investigate conditions and to report back to Brad Patterson in the Nixon White House. At Oakes's request, regional committee members met with occupiers on Alcatraz to hear the demands of residents firsthand.[71] Both Browning and Grossman continued to work diligently on the legal framework for the transfer of title to the island. The holidays were fast approaching, and the settlement was nearing its month-and-a-half anniversary.

On the tiny island, Christmas was approaching quickly. A small scraggly pine tree was decorated to represent the holiday. Children on the island used lids from tin cans and yarn to decorate the thinning tree. Using nail polish, each lid was painted with the names of Tribes or events like the "Trail of Tears" or "Wounded Knee." Some bore the single word "genocide."[72] Every ornament represented the historic sacrifice made by previous generations. Blackfeet occupier Joe Morris was approached by the IAT Council to be Santa Claus for the Christmas party:

> We had a big celebration for Christmas 1969. A lot of Indian
> people came out to the island that day. We had Indian singing,
> Indian music, food, and speeches made by people from different
> tribes. Most of them spoke about their problems and getting the
> shitty end of the stick from the state and federal shafters.
> Speeches were made by Richard Oakes, Earl Livermore, Grace
> Thorpe, Stella Leach, John Foster, and George Woodard. This
> meeting went on for about four hours. . . . We had to elect a
> Santa Claus, and I made a deal with Richard Oakes. We split the
> job, one-half hour a piece with the Santa Claus suit, passing out

the Christmas presents to the kids. All these presents were
donated by the big stores in San Francisco. There were about
fifty presents for the kids. I think Richard turned out to be a
better Santa Claus than I was. He laughed like Santa Claus,
saying "Ho ho ho" and just having a lot of fun.[73]

Contrary to Oakes's tough image, he was more than willing to make
Christmas a special day for the children. Presents were handed out, and
as the evening wound down, Morris helped Richard and Annie put their
kids to bed in their tiny apartment. The door of their residence was tagged
in red paint that simply read "Oakes Place." That night, after all the Oakes
children had fallen fast asleep, Richard, Annie, and Joe Morris stayed up
talking into the wee hours. Richard mentioned that he feared for the
safety of his family and his own life. Annie had been having bad dreams
and had confided to Richard about her dark premonitions: "She was
afraid that someone in our family would be hurt if we stayed on the island.
She felt that it was time to leave. I had been thinking about leaving to
develop the idea of Alcatraz in other places. However, I put her off. I wish
I had listened."[74]

On Christmas Eve, Richard encountered another confrontation back
at the pier on the mainland. While boarding a boat heading toward the
island, Oakes crossed a group of men who had been drinking too much.
In the early days of the occupation, IAT enforced a strict prohibition policy
of no alcohol or drugs on the island. The last public image or stereotype
the occupiers wanted to market was that of the "drunken Indian." It was
important to maintain tight control over their image. According to one
account, when Oakes approached, he "noticed a group of Indians in a
heated argument that was turning into a brawl. A large, striking Indian
was keeping several drunk Indians from joining him in his boat to the
island. He didn't want them there if they were drunk. The drunks finally
gave up and left. [Colin] Wesaw and the others approached the man and
learned he was Richard Oakes. . . . Oakes found out they had come all the
way from Chicago and immediately offered them a ride across the Bay to
Alcatraz. . . . Oakes seemed kind and generous, with a good heart for his
people."[75] Ideas about drinking differed on the island. Some altruistically
believed that they could help those in need and allowed some intoxicated
individuals shelter on Alcatraz. For those seeking an escape from the law,

the former prison offered a sanctuary, if not a hiding place. Caretakers Don Carroll and John Hart complained to Hannon that drug and alcohol abuse were making life increasingly difficult.[76]

Oakes's leadership position on the island was increasingly threatened by the heightened rumors and gossip. The climate and mood changed on Alcatraz as the new year approached. News coverage of the occupation began taking a back seat to the Charles Manson trial, the violence at the Rolling Stones' Altamont Speedway concert, and the growing revolt of the antiwar movement. As more people visited and exited the island, one of the core leadership groups, the college students, began returning to their classes, leaving the island permanently.

New leadership was moving into the former prison with its own objectives for Alcatraz. Pomo citizen Lawana Quitiquit charged Oakes with stealing money from the movement. She handled the sorting of mail that was delivered from the mainland. Lawana recalled that Oakes forbade her to open his mail. Donations were still pouring in to IAT. The table in the mailroom supported stacks of bills, all of which were contributions sent through the mail. Lawana began to suspect that Oakes was pocketing money earmarked for IAT.[77] She possessed no actual proof for this allegation, but her speculation was enough to contribute to the rumor mill and encourage further challenges against Oakes and his family. (It should be noted that it is quite possible that Richard Oakes was making deposits into the IAT bank account and was saving his receipts.)[78] Al Miller remembered the growing opposition toward Oakes:

> . . . [Richard Oakes] was really hot on Indians all over the
> country start'n to do things for themselves. He was a dreamer
> you know . . . that's what his dream was. See there was a lot of
> people that wanted to talk with the press. They wanted to state
> what they thought Alcatraz was about, but Richard was protec-
> tive of it. Because we had given birth to it . . . [Richard] would
> always talk about this being the catalyst for other activities and
> we need to protect it. The more people that we would get on the
> island the more leaders would emerge, people thinking they
> should be the rightful leader. . . . Richard, he was confronta-
> tional. He would get up in front of people if he saw somebody
> being mistreated . . . his face in theirs. . . . His wife Annie would

tell him, "Don't trust everybody because some of these guys are jealous of you, and you should know that" . . . but [Richard] trusted people. He trusted everybody and thought everybody was a good person. Resentment was building up against him.[79]

Oakes realized that the dream of Alcatraz and his own life were in jeopardy. On January 3, 1970, Richard and Annie headed for the mainland to run a few errands. They left behind their now-thirteen-year-old daughter on the island. Yvonne Oakes was old enough to take care of herself in her parents' brief absence and to babysit her younger siblings.

Later that day, Yvonne was playing tag with Ed Willie and another boy in the dining hall. The IAT kitchen staff, who suspected that the children were up to no good, urged them to go play outside. They then ran over to the Ira Hayes Building—the caretakers' building—and started running

Yvonne Oakes on Alcatraz Island, November 20, 1969. Photo courtesy of the *San Francisco Examiner*, photographer Eddie Murphy. Original photo negative in Kent Blansett Private Collection.

up the stairwell. Yvonne headed up first, laughing and carrying on, while racing the two boys to the top of the three flights of stairs. The next thing the two boys heard was Yvonne's scream, just before they saw her fall headfirst down the corridor between the stairs. Yvonne's body lay on the concrete floor, unconscious and bleeding. Stella Leach, a registered nurse on the island, was one of the first on the scene, as her clinic was in the same building. John Hart's son, who was staying in the apartment next to where Yvonne lay unconscious, scrambled to call the Coast Guard.[80]

Yvonne was rushed to the Public Health Service Hospital in San Francisco and was immediately placed in critical condition. As soon as Richard and Annie learned of the news, they rushed to the hospital. It is uncertain just how much they knew about Yvonne's condition before arriving at the hospital. Annie became frightened by the reality of the premonitions she had experienced a week earlier. Richard did his best to comfort her and to study Yvonne's condition. Dr. Roller, chief of professional services, was the surgeon who operated on Yvonne; he explained to Richard and Annie that Yvonne just might pull through, but to what extent she would recover was unknown. Richard asked Dr. Roller if there were any signs that Yvonne's fall had not been an accident. Roller stated that he could not detect any physical signs that would warrant such a claim. Richard and Annie stood helplessly aside and began maintaining a constant vigil outside Yvonne's room.

T. E. Hannon arrived at the hospital around 2:30 p.m. to offer condolences and express his regrets to the family. Soon Annie's family arrived from Kashaya. Her mother and father were also accompanied by Annie's two brothers and her sister. Richard Oakes went down to the hospital cafeteria to get a cup of coffee with a reporter. While he was gone, Annie confided in Hannon, mentioning the jealousy toward Richard on the island and the growing dissension among the members of IAT. She also stated that there was too much drinking and fighting, that "nothing was going right." When Richard arrived back at the waiting room, he told Hannon that he was not interested in discussing Alcatraz; Yvonne was his only concern. Hannon informed Oakes that if he suspected foul play, he would request an official investigation. After a moment, Richard asked Hannon not to forcefully remove IAT from Alcatraz. Hannon asked

Left to right: Annie Oakes, Yvonne Oakes, with short hair, standing with her arms around her little brother Leonard Oakes, and Tanya Oakes, November 25, 1969. Photo courtesy of the *San Francisco Examiner* and Sara Glines, photographer Paul Glines. Original photo negative in Kent Blansett Private Collection.

Richard to visit him at his office in a few days and they would discuss the matter further.[81]

For the next five days Richard and Annie Oakes clung to any hope that Yvonne might pull through her injuries. In an interview on January 4, 1970, Richard Oakes, his voice trailing off, said, "I don't know what I'll do. . . . My wife doesn't want to go back there: I don't know. . . ."[82] The hospital kept Yvonne under constant supervision and promised the sad and worried couple that the hospital would absorb the costs. Friends and family regularly visited the hospital to offer the Oakeses sympathy and assistance. Yvonne's brothers and sisters offered prayers for their sister's speedy recovery. Emotions ran high each day as the family hung onto every word from the doctors and nurses. For the first time in his life, Richard Oakes was absolutely powerless, but he had to remain strong for Annie and the kids.

On January 8, 1970, Yvonne Rose Oakes, having struggled for five days, passed away under the tearful watch of her family. Services were donated by the Daphne Funeral Home, which was flooded by a large group of family and friends who offered the Oakes family their condolences. Richard and Annie sat on a couch inside the funeral home staring in disbelief, the shock apparent in their eyes. Yvonne was laid to rest at her birthplace, at Stewarts Point Rancheria.[83] Richard and Annie Oakes rarely spoke of Yvonne's passing. Richard reflected, "Sorrow couldn't bring her back. We could only take it and deal with it. Even in death she was still within the circle, the circle of life, our universe."[84]

CHAPTER FIVE

Alcatraz Is Not an Island, It's an Idea

RICHARD OAKES WAS THE MOST RECOGNIZABLE FACE of the Alcatraz takeover. As a leader he formed a vast network of associations throughout Indian Country and with the federal government. His central belief that Alcatraz was an idea held vast meaning for many Native organizations and individuals struggling to make sense out of Red Power. Now, through the actions of Oakes and others, the Intertribal foundations of this movement were visibly enacted through the takeover of Alcatraz Island. Oakes understood that the island remained a viable symbol, for it now served as a critical link to inspiring a vast Intertribal network to support Native rights. Such a network held the potential to challenge destructive federal policies and create a powerful coalition. Activists and leaders from the noted fish-ins occurring in and around Seattle, Washington, shared in this same vision. Inspired by Alcatraz and Richard Oakes, Seattle Indian leaders soon established their own Intertribal coalition that linked prominent fish-in leaders, Indians of All Tribes, Seattle's Indian City, and a sympathetic public into one of the most successful takeovers of the Red Power era—Fort Lawton. Oakes played a vital role in the success of the Seattle Indigenous movement as the idea of Alcatraz began to take over Indian Country.

Back in the Bay Area, on January 15, 1970, Oakes had been appointed by BIA area director William Oliver, later the director for American Indian Studies at UCLA, to the San Francisco Regional Council of the National

Richard Oakes meeting with U.S. attorney Cecil Poole (who also negotiated with the 1964 Lakota occupiers) on Alcatraz Island, December 1, 1969. Left to right: Richard Oakes, John Hart (Alcatraz Island caretaker), Anthony Garcia, and Cecil Poole; the remaining four individuals are unidentified. AP Photo/Robert W. Klein.

Council on Indian Opportunity. Oakes was the only participant and occupier of Alcatraz to be selected for this position. That afternoon, Indians of All Tribes (IAT) officially filed their articles of incorporation with the state of California. IAT was now seeking grant money to build their cultural and educational center on Alcatraz, and legal incorporation was crucial. The articles of incorporation listed Richard Oakes as one of the seven council members of IAT. The majority of the by-laws followed typical state guidelines of voting and governance. Instead of the traditional consensus model that IAT had touted in the beginning, the council now was to operate by two-thirds majority. The IAT Council held separate meetings from the general membership and could call a meeting to order with only four members of the council present. Oakes and other initial occupiers began to see that the "traditionalist" ideas of Alcatraz were being transformed.[1] Over the next few years, Oakes would engage in a wide variety of occupations in a concerted grassroots campaign for home rule. Most historians have focused almost exclusively on Oakes's role at Alcatraz, but in reality, Alcatraz was a spark for a much larger movement.

Disappointed in the fighting and dissension on the island, Tim Findley published two scathing reports in the *San Francisco Chronicle*. Findley drew a strong parallel in his comparison of life on the island to the novel *Lord of the Flies,* an association that haunted the remaining months of the Alcatraz occupation.[2] Although dissent and counter-opinions were welcome, Alcatraz residents were now asserting their own opinions through physical violence. It was this strong-armed discord that Oakes and his family could no longer tolerate. After moving from the island, Richard Oakes eventually resigned from the IAT Council.[3] Those in opposition to Oakes's leadership on the island sought to conceal his resignation by postulating that he was voted off the island.[4] After Yvonne's death, he became the scapegoat for the dysfunctional climate that was slowly ripping the movement apart. By leaving the bickering behind, Oakes could, at best, concentrate his talents more effectively on the greater goal—liberation. Alcatraz was the symbol, but Oakes knew that direct action would be the determining factor in the struggle to protect sovereignty. Al Miller recalled the day that Richard Oakes resigned: "I still remember the last conversation. He said, 'Well, you guys . . . do what you can with it. I don't have the heart for it.'"[5] Oakes had sacrificed everything for the Alcatraz cause, and ultimately Yvonne's mysterious death and the power struggles on the island were far too much for the young leader.

He returned to life at San Francisco State and settled back into his residence with Annie and the kids at "Gatorville." There Oakes resumed his coursework and the regimented routine of classes—a far cry from the freedom he had experienced on Alcatraz. He carried with him complicated lessons drawn from IAT and an education he had gained outside the classroom. Oakes continued to work for the Native American Studies Department and raised money for the newly established Yvonne Oakes Memorial Fund. Created in Yvonne's honor, this fund was designed to generate much-needed revenue for the Native American Studies Department, which was still struggling to remain financially afloat.[6] Even though Oakes was no longer affiliated with Indians of All Tribes, he continued to support the original goals of the organization he had helped to create. More importantly, Oakes had established a network of lifelong friends and associates, and he was not forgotten.

Recognized for his talents at organizing, he was recruited by the Pomo at the Six Confederated Round Valley Tribes Reservation in

Richard Oakes receiving a check from an unidentified IAT member for a donation to the Yvonne Oakes Memorial Fund at San Francisco State College. I discovered this photograph in a small white envelope, missing from the original archive index, which had been hidden unnoticed between the cardboard folds of an archive box from the Alcatraz Island Occupation Records. San Francisco History Center, San Francisco Public Library.

northern California. People there were struggling to keep a proposed dam from flooding their homelands. The Army Corps of Engineers proposal sought to relocate the Round Valley residents, sacrificing their nineteen thousand acres of ancestral lands for California's hydroelectric needs. Alongside his work at Round Valley, the Elem Pomo had become increasingly active, winning a key off-reservation fishing rights case and successfully ending the use of a derogatory "Him Konocti" mascot, a twenty-year-old symbol of a Labor Day fair for Lake County. By March of 1970, Oakes was attending meetings with leaders from the community to organize a direct action and media campaign to take over Rattlesnake Island. The idea of Alcatraz was spreading, and Oakes began to lead the second critical phase of the IAT occupation.[7] Ultimately the Elem and Round Valley nations relied on Red Power strategy in their successful pursuit of Tribal land retention and reclamation. Oakes continued to organize with northern California Tribes as well as Indian Cities.

Colville citizen Bernie Whitebear, a former Green Beret with the 101st Airborne Division, had heard Alcatraz's message when he and a delegation from Frank's Landing (including Al Bridges, Hank Adams,

and Ramona Bennett) visited with Oakes and toured Alcatraz several
months before March 1970. Frank's Landing is a six-acre parcel of land
off the banks of the Nisqually River, which feeds into Puget Sound. The
waters supplied by Mount Rainier were protected by Klucket-sah or Billy
Frank Sr., where for over sixty years it served as the epicenter for the
fishing rights struggle. The first documented arrest occurred in 1916
when Billy Frank Sr. was taken into custody for unlawful or out-of-season
salmon harvesting.[8] From the 1930s to the 1960s, state conservation officials backed by private interests launched a campaign to regulate
Indigenous salmon harvesters. By the mid-1960s Frank's Landing came
to represent an international movement to protect treaty rights and
Indigenous resources. By March 1970 Bernie Whitebear, who had come
of age politically during the fishing rights movement at Frank's Landing,
was so overwhelmed by the vision of Indians of All Tribes and Alcatraz
that he founded a similar organization, United Indians of All Tribes
(UIAT). This new Seattle-based organization was first sponsored by the
veterans of the fishing rights struggle as well as Indians of All Tribes. The
roots of this organization did not come about overnight. Both the Indian
City of Seattle and the politically charged northwestern Indian Nations
had cultivated its origins, backed by years of resistance and debate over
reform. For over a hundred years, the Puyallup, Nisqually, Muckleshoot,
and other northwest coast and Columbia River Plateau Tribes had maintained and protected their right to harvest salmon as guaranteed in the
1854 and 1856 treaties.[9] The takeover of Fort Lawton in Seattle relied on a
well-established network and alliance of northwest Native nations along
with support from Seattle's Indian City. Just as the occupation of Alcatraz
is linked to the complex and rich Intertribal history of San Francisco, the
struggle for Fort Lawton must also be historicized in the context of Native
spaces for organizing.

INDIAN CITY SEATTLE

Seattle was forged out of the multiple Native nations that have claimed the
Puget Sound region as their homeland since time immemorial. Puget
Sound provides an outlet for several major rivers carrying rich freshwater
flows that originate from the fortress of mountain ranges that surround
Seattle. Puget Sound, which straddles the international border between
Canada and the United States, contains hundreds of islands. The

surrounding lands and ocean around Puget Sound supported the wealth and power of Indigenous nations and peoples for thousands of years. Several of their economies were organized around the sophisticated potlatch system. The potlatch is a ceremonial, social, political, and economic event that occurs primarily in the winter months as notable families reinforce their kinship and citizenship by redistributing their collective wealth to other Tribal citizens. The potlatch tradition signals a time to impart sacred knowledge, as traditional stories are often reenacted in elaborate staged performances, where each movement and every action solidifies the shared history of the people.[10] Puget Sound is host to sophisticated coastal whaling communities like the Makah, who construct intricately carved and balanced canoe boats that travel hundreds of miles in order to harvest the largest of whales for their community.[11] By the twentieth century many of these powerful Nations, despite American attempts at confinement, assimilation, acculturation, and allotment, remained strong and rooted to their traditional ways. Seattle increasingly had become a suburban hub, linked both economically and culturally to the Duwamish, Nisqually, Muckleshoot, Suquamish, Skokomish, Snohomish, Puyallup, Quinault, Tulalip, and Lummi, among other Native nations. Seattle even derived its name from the famous Duwamish leader Chief Sealth.

From the 1920s to the 1970s, American Indians in Seattle forged their own institutions and organizations. Like San Francisco and Brooklyn, Native peoples during these years increasingly relied on the "Indian City" to defy the political, social, and economic constructs of government-related assimilation and acculturation programs. As previously stated, the mass post-World War II migration from reservations and rural spaces to the city represented one of the greatest per capita internal migrations of a people in the United States. Before the 1970s, the national urban Indian population had grown at a rate that was three-and-a-half times faster than the mainstream population.

In comparison to San Francisco, Seattle's American Indian population was rather low, growing from 1,729 in the 1960s to around 12,000 by the 1970s. At face value, these census figures obscure the true Native Seattle population. U.S. Census officials failed to acknowledge that Seattle's urban Indian community was highly mobile, made up of thousands of Canadian First Nations peoples, and situated in close proximity

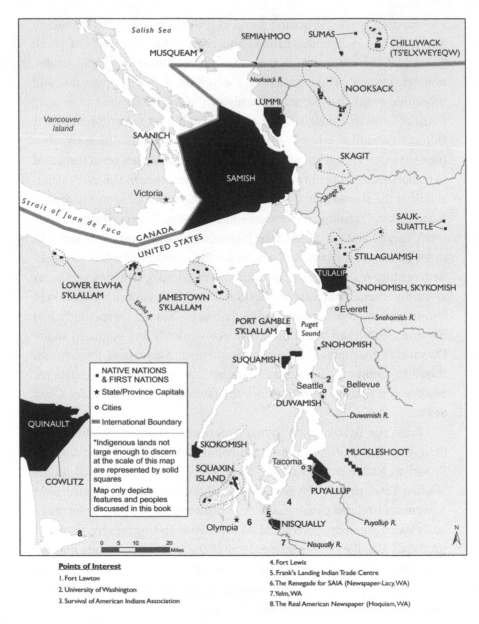

Salish Sea

SEMIAHMOO   SUMAS
MUSQUEAM   CHILLIWACK
                                     (TS'ELXWEYEQW)

Nooksack R.
                          NOOKSACK
LUMMI

Vancouver
Island
SAANICH   SKAGIT

                SAMISH   Skagit R.

Victoria   SAUK-
                                                SUIATTLE
Strait of Juan de Fuca
              CANADA   STILLAGUAMISH
              UNITED STATES
                                          TULALIP
                                          SNOHOMISH, SKYKOMISH
LOWER ELWHA   ○Everett Snohomish R.
S'KLALLAM   JAMESTOWN
             S'KLALLAM
             Elwha R.   SNOHOMISH
             PORT GAMBLE Puget
             S'KLALLAM   Sound
                                          SNOHOMISH
             SUQUAMISH

NATIVE NATIONS   1
& FIRST NATIONS   Seattle 2 Bellevue
★ State/Province Capitals
○ Cities   DUWAMISH
≡ International Boundary   Duwamish R.

*Indigenous lands not
large enough to discern
at the scale of this map   MUCKLESHOOT
are represented by solid   SKOKOMISH
QUINAULT squares
                      SQUAXIN Tacoma ○ 3
Map only depicts   ISLAND
features and peoples   PUYALLUP
COWLITZ   discussed in this book   4
                              5
                   6 NISQUALLY   Puyallup R.
          0 5 10 20   Olympia
                Miles   7   Nisqually R.   N
8

Points of Interest
1. Fort Lawton   4. Fort Lewis
2. University of Washington   5. Frank's Landing Indian Trade Centre
3. Survival of American Indians Association   6. The Renegade for SAIA (Newspaper-Lacy, WA)
                                  7. Yelm, WA
                                  8. The Real American Newspaper (Hoquiam, WA)

Native Nations and Landmarks Surrounding Seattle. Map by Ed Brands.

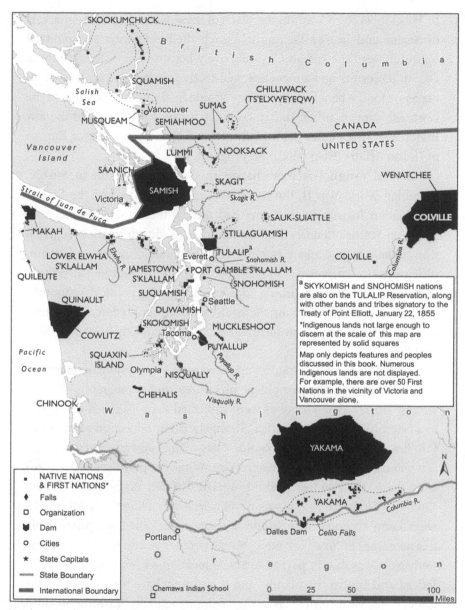

Northwest Indigenous Nations. Map by Ed Brands.

The map includes the following labels and features:

SKOOKUMCHUCK
British Columbia
SQUAMISH
Salish Sea
CHILLIWACK (TS'ELXWEYEQW)
MUSQUEAM
Vancouver
SUMAS
SEMIAHMOO
CANADA
UNITED STATES
Vancouver Island
LUMMI
NOOKSACK
WENATCHEE
SAANICH
SKAGIT
SAMISH
Victoria
Skagit R.
COLVILLE
Strait of Juan de Fuca
SAUK-SUIATTLE
MAKAH
STILLAGUAMISH
Columbia R.
LOWER ELWHA S'KLALLAM
Elwha R.
Everett
TULALIP[a]
Snohomish R.
COLVILLE
QUILEUTE
JAMESTOWN S'KLALLAM
PORT GAMBLE S'KLALLAM
QUINAULT
SUQUAMISH
Seattle
SNOHOMISH
DUWAMISH
SKOKOMISH
Tacoma
MUCKLESHOOT
COWLITZ
PUYALLUP
Pacific Ocean
SQUAXIN ISLAND
Olympia
Puyallup R.
NISQUALLY
CHINOOK
CHEHALIS
Nisqually R.
Washington
YAKAMA
N
YAKAMA
Columbia R.
Portland
Dalles Dam
Celilo Falls
Oregon

[a] SKYKOMISH and SNOHOMISH nations are also on the TULALIP Reservation, along with other bands and tribes signatory to the Treaty of Point Elliott, January 22, 1855

*Indigenous lands not large enough to discern at the scale of this map are represented by solid squares

Map only depicts features and peoples discussed in this book. Numerous Indigenous lands are not displayed. For example, there are over 50 First Nations in the vicinity of Victoria and Vancouver alone.

Legend:
- NATIVE NATIONS & FIRST NATIONS*
- Falls
- Organization
- Dam
- Cities
- State Capitals
- State Boundary
- International Boundary

Chemawa Indian School

0   25   50   100 Miles

to Tribes in western Washington. Each of these Nations used the markets of Seattle and nearby Tacoma to enrich their economic and political opportunities. The Indian City effectively became a vehicle and tool to recruit protesters and supporters, sell treaty salmon, and gain national exposure for the benefit of the Tribes. Seattle held a unique position in the twentieth-century urban Indian complex because it was one of the few major West Coast cities not initially selected by the controversial Bureau of Indian Affairs (BIA) relocation program.[12]

Several external factors shaped this great migration to Seattle, including World War II, the BIA's relocation program, and the federal termination legislation that emerged during the 1950s. Indians who moved to Seattle often faced extraordinary odds: discrimination, segregation, isolation, inadequate public housing, police brutality, and unemployment. In response, Indigenous peoples in Seattle collectively challenged these overwhelming odds by constructing political, economic, and cultural coalitions among themselves. Community centers, organizations, and institutions that formed Seattle's Indian City bolstered these coalitions.

The BIA relocation program operated with a vast system of relocation officers employed with pamphlets, brochures, and photographs of "real" success stories. Often families were subjected to propaganda that spoke to a better life in urban America. Strangely, many relocation officers had families and individuals pose beside a large white government car—their last photo before leaving the reservation. While the promises and dreams were there, the realities of the program differed vastly across Indian Country.[13] However, Seattle was never selected as a target city. Of course, we can only speculate why Seattle appeared to lack the appropriate qualities necessary to "lose" or "melt" Native peoples within its urban milieu. Perhaps it was due in part to Seattle's location—it was surrounded by federal and Indian trust land—and it also may have been linked to the hotly contested historical issue over fishing rights in Washington state. The closing of Celilo Falls, the ancient fishing site of the Columbia River, in the mid-1950s captured national headlines. The construction of the Dalles Dam drowned the famous falls and eradicated over 450 fishing stations and permanently disrupted an ancient salmon harvesting area.[14]

While few Native peoples in Seattle avoided the auspices of the federal policy of relocation, most encountered the classic challenges met by relocatees, and their community activists met each challenge head on by politicizing and advertising this new Indian City. Seattle also served a largely migratory Native labor force, attracting roughly 60 percent of the city's migratory labor from local Tribes. Furthermore, Indian City leaders maintained a strong resistance against the forces of local segregation and discrimination. The growth of Indian Cities in Brooklyn, San Francisco, and Seattle represented another challenge to the federal Indian policies of relocation and termination.[15]

Ultimately, Native peoples in Seattle challenged municipal, state, and federal policies and, in so doing, also developed an Intertribal network for which Intertribalism emerged as a viable cultural and political strategy. The Seattle Indian community, like its counterpart in San Francisco, formed institutions, chartered organizations, infiltrated college campuses, established business networks, politicized and thereby Indigenized Seattle. By operating through their own community institutions and organizations, Seattle's Native populations effectively challenged colonial constructs to transform and reclaim their city, and like the Indian Cities of Brooklyn and San Francisco, they relied upon coalition politics.

Between 1900 and 1930, Seattle's Native population experienced a rapid increase due to the corporate canning and logging industries. These industries provided seasonal labor, which meant that a majority of Seattle's Indian population remained largely migratory, moving between Seattle and the reservations, similar to Brooklyn and Akwesasne. Initially the Indian Bureau tried to force Native layoffs at the canneries to promote farming on the reservations. However, the Office of Indian Affairs plan reflected a dearth of knowledge about Puget Sound and its primary industries. Soon enough, Indian Affairs would ease up on its enforcement of government-backed labor discrimination in Seattle. By 1920, the Indigenous migration into Seattle increased by 31.8 percent, and the new industrial boom altered Seattle's skyline and enlarged its opportunities.

Energized by the new politicization and nationalism of the Society of American Indians (SAI), formed in 1911, Native peoples increasingly began to press for greater freedom in the economy by arguing for land reform and the protection of treaty fishing rights. Inspired by SAI, in 1914 Native leaders like Snohomish citizen Thomas Bishop, who grew up near Seattle, helped found the Northwestern Federation of American

Indians (NFAI), a membership organized by Tribal affiliation. The sole function of NFAI was to press for treaty rights and hold the state and federal government accountable for the protection of these rights.[16]

Like the Brooklyn neighborhood where Richard Oakes was employed in ironwork, large numbers of American Indians in Seattle joined labor unions to protect their wages in the logging and canning trades. The largest concentration of Native peoples resided in downtown Seattle and along the waterfront, where they lived in low-rent or transient boarding houses. By the 1920s and 1930s, following a heightened sense of nativist sentiments and the economic depression, national unions began to oust and bully out their Native membership, and labor increasingly became a closed shop catering exclusively to Anglo-American unions.[17]

Throughout the 1920s and into the 1940s, the Northwest Federation of American Indians rallied behind the goal of protecting their fishing and treaty rights. Another major Intertribal organization that held meetings throughout Washington state was the Northwest Indian Congress (NIC). In order to attract tourist dollars to the host city, the NIC sponsored the annual Northwest Festival of American Indians, a three-day festival with a fundraising ball, parade, and powwow competition. At a 1926 event in Everett, Washington, thirty miles north of Seattle, the organization observed strict rules about settling Tribal boundary lines and claim allocations despite the parade-like atmosphere. Ironically, the title for a *Seattle Times* article that appeared in 1926 declared "City becomes Indian Village." Over three thousand Native peoples gathered in Everett for the festival, representing over twenty-one Nations from Washington, Oregon, and Idaho. The event capitalized on local tourism and boosterism, but more dramatically, it exposed local politicians and Seattle lawyers to key Tribal political issues, including fishing and treaty rights.[18]

Beyond politics, Indigenous Seattle was also undergoing sociocultural changes, as illustrated by newspaper stories of Native women with bobbed hair, also known as the "Native flapper." This new generation of "modern" Indian women revealed to Seattle that they loved Hollywood actor Ronald Colman just as much as the next young woman. Native flappers in Seattle defied convention, as they publicly claimed an identity unchained from stereotypes or assimilation discourse. Progressive Indians could maintain their heritage even while sporting bobbed hair, embracing modernity, and Indigenizing their world. Everything changed when the stock market crashed in 1929. Shortly thereafter, Seattle businesses began to lay off workers. Growing economic fears and sympathy with eugenic movements led white employers to target both Indian and Filipino laborers for layoffs. A fortunate few urban Indians opted to return to their Tribes to find jobs, while others began the tedious process of applying for any government-sponsored employment through the Indian New Deal, such as the Indian Civilian Conservation Corps. Despite the mass layoffs, Seattle's Native community remained steady at three thousand people, representing roughly 1 percent of the total population.

In addition to a harsh economic climate, discrimination in Seattle was also quite overt, with many downtown business windows displaying "No Indians Allowed" signs. A select few American Indian couples owned their own homes during the Great Depression. Another small group of Native home owners consisted mainly of Indian women who had married white men. Access to capital or loans in Seattle was regulated on the basis of race and gender. Unlike Native men or women in general, white men faced little discrimination in securing home loans or credit. When a Native woman married a white man, sometimes the woman emerged as an Indian rights leader who openly challenged segregation within Seattle neighborhoods and businesses. Still, the majority of the American Indian population in Seattle faced outright segregation, which had forced so many to settle in restrictive areas like the haunts of Pioneer Square and Skid Road districts.[19]

The major push/pull factor for Native migrants moving into Seattle occurred during and after World War II, when more than forty thousand Native men and women secured employment in the West Coast defense industries. With increased federal expenditures for new shipyards and hangars came thousands of new jobs and training in the wartime factories. Haida citizen Adeline Garcia commented, "I came to the big city to go to work and save our country and get an education." Garcia worked in the shipyards as a welder and later reapplied her skills for work at Boeing. Native laborers, by their large presence alone, would help to desegregate the wartime industries in many western cities. For the first time, hundreds of American Indians gained new skills and economic independence. Approximately 44,500 Native men and women also enlisted in the armed forces.

Despite this unprecedented support for the war effort, many Native
laborers were laid off at the end of the war to provide jobs for returning
troops, as previously mentioned, "[b]y 1950 the unemployment rate for
urban Indians had reached fifteen percent nearly three times that of
whites." Opportunity vanished as quickly as it had come, for many Indian
wartime laborers, as most faced the grim prospect of sudden employment
loss. Like their counterparts during the 1920s, those who could afford it
returned to their home communities, while those who lacked travel funds
sought affordable housing, semi-skilled jobs, and continued to advocate
for better employment and living conditions in Seattle.[20]

Many Native veterans who returned to Puget Sound after the war
began to embrace traditional ways, including the sacred act of harvesting
salmon. Despite losing their home to a fire, fourteen-year-old Billy Frank
Jr. experienced his first arrest for salmon fishing in 1945. Between jobs
Frank worked as a non-union laborer in nearby Olympia, Washington,
the state capital, and as a salmon harvester on his family's allotment lands
at Frank's Landing. This initial arrest sparked a thirty-year war that eventually drafted Richard Oakes for his leadership abilities, to help defend
the rights of Northwest Tribes (as clearly spelled out in their 1854 Treaty of
Medicine Creek). In the acclaimed book *Uncommon Controversy*, the
importance of fishing for Native peoples is straightforward:

> Fish, particularly salmon, still are an integral part of Indian life.
> . . . They still represent meanings and relationships so old and
> tenacious that even Indians who no longer fish will fight to
> preserve the accustomed rights in the rivers and streams with
> which they are traditionally connected. Fishing is the heritage of
> hundreds of years of use and development. It is a stronghold of
> the Indian person's sense of identity as an Indian. It is a
> remaining avenue of close relationship with the natural world.
> And in this modern world, it is at the heart of his cry for recogni-
> tion and respect.[21]

In 1952, Billy Frank Jr.'s draft number called him to serve in the Korean
War. He enlisted in the Marines and served as an MP (military police);
after the war's end a year later, he returned to Frank's Landing. Upon his
return home, Frank witnessed the struggle for fishing rights intensify at
the height of the termination era. Tensions especially escalated after 1953

with the passage of Public Law 280, which provided select states—including Washington—legal jurisprudence over criminal and civil matters that had formerly been under Tribal jurisdiction. The state of Washington eagerly sought to exploit the loose script of PL 280 for their own financial advantage. Hunting and fishing rights procured through federal treaty provisions had, however, been excluded from the reaches of state jurisdiction.[22]

In 1957, the state of Washington drafted its own legal interpretation of Public Law 280 to include the regulation of hunting and fishing rights. This same year, Washington's Supreme Court decision *State v. Satiacum* arrived at a deadlocked decision. The court's opinion reversed charges against the defendants and reaffirmed the rights of Puyallup citizens to fish on their lands as guaranteed by the Medicine Creek Treaty of 1855. Although the decision was not a total victory for the state or the Tribes, it signaled an extended courtroom and legal battle to protect treaty fishing rights for Native peoples in Washington state.[23]

The debate over Celilo Falls and the growing legal pursuit to protect fishing rights were also occurring during the height of the anticommunist hysteria known as McCarthyism and the federal Indian policy called termination. House Concurrent Resolution 108, more commonly known as the Termination Act, passed in 1953, and it also affected the Native migrants who moved to cities. Termination policy devastated many Native communities, overturning the protection of Tribal land held under trust, negating treaty rights, and threatening entire ways of life for thousands of Indians. As a direct consequence of termination legislation, over 1,362,155 acres of Indian land were legislatively transferred from Tribal ownership to the control of the federal government. This legislative land grab was second only to the Dawes Act of 1887, which had sponsored the loss of over 90 million acres of Tribal lands. Statistics on the number of Indians who moved into the city as a result of termination legislation are lacking. By 1954, the Intertribal Council of Western Washington Indians brought both federally recognized and non-recognized nations together in a joint effort to battle against termination policy. Fortunately, most Tribes in Washington escaped the devastation that had befallen so many other Native nations.[24]

The state's closest brush with termination occurred on the Colville Nation of north-central Washington. The Colville, a multi-Tribal reservation, came under severe pressure from both federal and internal sources to support termination through a Tribal referendum, but fortunately, Colville had voted collectively against voluntary termination. This policy placed a stranglehold over several non–federally recognized Tribes as well. Under the threat of this legislation, Tribes had to work twice as hard to protect their treaty rights and press their case to earn federal trust status for their respective citizens.[25]

Countering this wave of destructive federal policies in the 1950s, Native activists and organizations throughout Seattle constructed the first Indian-controlled and Indian-managed Indian centers in the United States. As one of the founding institutions of the Indian City, the center remains by far one of the most important. The Seattle Indian Center was similar to the San Francisco Indian Center in the Mission District that Richard Oakes's family had frequented. The center, like an Indigenized Hull House, extended social services to urban Indians, ran a trade/craft shop to sponsor local Native artists, introduced youth programs, held annual powwows, oversaw job placement and assistance, hosted food and clothing banks, and provided legal assistance, health care referrals, and meeting space for local Native organizations.

The Indian center in Seattle was created through the progressive efforts of the American Indian Women's Service League founded in 1958. Its first president was a Makah woman, Pearl Warren, who became the most outspoken advocate for a Seattle Indian Center. Warren selected the First Avenue location for the Indian center, just north of Pioneer Square, a location where there were many Seattle Native peoples. Some of Seattle's Indian leaders envisioned a greater Indian center that would require financial support and would be located outside the "Red Ghetto" of Pioneer Square. In 1967, Warren became even more vocal about this dream: "We feel the city should give us back some land . . . and we won't settle for any old haphazard deal. We want an Indian-style longhouse—a place with a meeting room, craft workshop and display center." This push for a new Indian center constructed from a culturally relevant architecture foreshadowed the growth of Native Nationalist movements in and around Seattle during the late 1960s.[26]

Another facet of support for the Indian City appears in the printed record. For years Native peoples in Washington state published their own newsletters and newspapers. Between 1922 and 1924, *The Real Americans*

The American Indian Women's Service League, 1960. Left to right: Martha John, Lona Lyness, Hazel Duarte, Dorothy Lombard, Ella Aquino, and Pearl Warren. Photographed by Harvey Davis, Photo courtesy of the *Seattle Post-Intelligencer* Collection, Museum of History & Industry, Seattle; all rights reserved, 1986.5.30279.

was published in western Washington. The newspaper, although short-lived, focused on national as well as local Indian news. By the late 1950s and early 1960s, two of the most popular Seattle Indian publications appeared under the titles *Northwest Indian News* and *Indian Center News*. Stories covered local events, community happenings, historical information, and news about national political issues ranging from termination policy to fishing rights. Together, these publications created a vital link among Native populations and were critical aids for collectively organizing the larger Intertribal Native community. These media outlets also served the larger goals of the Indian center, to inform and unite Indian City Seattle.[27]

Several Indian cultural organizations arranged a number of activities for the Indian community, which provided a recreational outlet, including baseball, basketball, and dance clubs that hosted local powwows. The Seattle Indian Center and the Northwest Intertribal Club sponsored powwows that occurred at least once a month and fostered Intertribal awareness. Powwows also provided another source of income for many

Indians in the city, since traders sold traditional crafts to the general public and Indian business owners used sponsorship of these cultural activities to advertise. Like the United Indian Development Association in San Francisco, Seattle's American Indian Professionals Association also provided fellowship and assistance to Indian business owners throughout greater Seattle. This organization enabled Indian doctors and lawyers to fraternize and to establish occupational relationships. Indian businesses ranged from Indian bars to Haida-owned Walt's Barber Shop, located on Pike Street in downtown Seattle.[28]

Similar to Brooklyn and San Francisco, another critical and controversial institution of the Indian City appeared in the form of the Indian bar. Indian Skid Road (not "Skid Row") contained a handful of "bow and arrow joints"; most of these bars were a product of anti-Indian discrimination during the 1950s. Seattle Indian bars often served as both entry points for newcomers to the Indian City and as the first stops on the road to urban survival for many Native peoples. Historian Coll Thrush identified the Britannia Tavern in Skid Road as the local Indian bar that served Alaskan, First Nations, and American Indians. Partly owned by a Native woman who was known by locals as "Mom," the atmosphere of the Britannia promoted increased socialization in the larger Native community. The Indian bar was also a place to find housing, to secure an address for employment, and to converse in multiple Indigenous languages, which made it easier for languages to be shared and retained. Thrush also argues that Indian bars offered more than just a social component. They served as a place where people offered tips on jobs, services through the Indian center, housing opportunities, and health services. Political organizers within Native Seattle often took advantage of Indian bars for lobbying purposes. At one Indian tavern Bernie Whitebear announced his commitment toward becoming a dedicated Seattle Indian activist.[29]

While this description provides a very positive outlook on Indian bars, another deeper issue remained. Indian bars sometimes fostered a perilous social setting and encouraged the habitual dependency of some of their clients. As in the Mission District of San Francisco, police typically patrolled the bars of Indian Skid Road. Law enforcement often relied on racial profiling and stereotypes, which played a role in the disproportionally higher arrest rates for Native peoples.[30] These arrests inflicted their own damage to families and the economy. Arrests led to higher

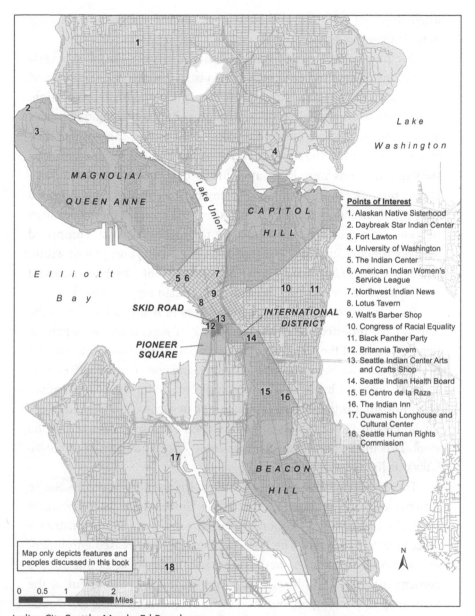

Points of Interest
1. Alaskan Native Sisterhood
2. Daybreak Star Indian Center
3. Fort Lawton
4. University of Washington
5. The Indian Center
6. American Indian Women's
   Service League
7. Northwest Indian News
8. Lotus Tavern
9. Walt's Barber Shop
10. Congress of Racial Equality
11. Black Panther Party
12. Britannia Tavern
13. Seattle Indian Center Arts
    and Crafts Shop
14. Seattle Indian Health Board
15. El Centro de la Raza
16. The Indian Inn
17. Duwamish Longhouse and
    Cultural Center
18. Seattle Human Rights
    Commission

Lake Washington

Elliott Bay

MAGNOLIA/ QUEEN ANNE

Lake Union

CAPITOL HILL

INTERNATIONAL DISTRICT

SKID ROAD

PIONEER SQUARE

BEACON HILL

Map only depicts features and
peoples discussed in this book

0   0.5   1   2
                        Miles

N

Indian City Seattle. Map by Ed Brands.

unemployment rates and weakened the economic and political solvency of the Indian City.

The physical spaces of Seattle's Indian City were linked to several institutions like the Indian center, Indian bars, Indian organizations and businesses; the neighborhood itself became the fourth institution. Despite the widespread Indian population scattered throughout greater Seattle, Pioneer Square and Indian Skid Road proved the primary residential core for the Indian City. Much of the housing in this area was substandard, rents were high, and slumlords exploited Native tenants. Due to prejudice and low income, many families in this neighborhood were highly mobile, and this increased mobility within the community necessitated a growing dependence on the institutions that comprised Seattle's Indian City.[31] Successful political organizing and protest within Seattle's Indian City, just like the Indian Cities of San Francisco and Brooklyn, relied on knowing the American Indian neighborhood.

Founded in 1969, the Seattle Indian Health Board, so central to the Indian City, reflected the cumulative work of several Indian organizations. The goal of the board was to establish a medical facility to provide health services for Native peoples in Seattle, and one of its executive directors was Bernie Whitebear. The looming obstacle for the Seattle Indian Health Board was to find a land base for the new clinic. Sponsored by the Public Health Hospital, the clinic was open only three days out of the week. This made it rather difficult for emergency situations, and accessibility was limited.[32]

The last institution within Seattle's Indian City was the Native American Studies program created at the University of Washington. In 1968, the Black Student Union organized a sit-in at the administrative offices for the university. The BSU had demanded increased enrollment for all minority students as well as the creation of a viable Ethnic Studies department. Native students had a long history of enrollment at the University of Washington, but even active recruitment in the late 1960s only increased the Native student population from twenty-five to a hundred students. The American Indian Studies program, like that of San Francisco State, shared similar goals, but one particular objective linked the program with the Indian City. The objective promoted student participation in American Indian community development. This core component sought to partner students with local Indian agencies to conduct research and develop programs for Seattle. Out of the core program, University of Washington students would forge a coalition to foster political support for fishing rights and ultimately the Fort Lawton takeover.[33]

FORT LAWTON OCCUPATION AND THE CONSTRUCTION
OF AN INDIAN CITY

The roots and ideology behind the Fort Lawton takeover originated in two other events: the fish-ins of the mid-1960s and the Alcatraz takeover in November 1969. For decades, Puyallup and Nisqually collectively fought to protect their right to harvest salmon from state and game officials who cut nets, confiscated boats, and arrested hundreds of Native citizens for invoking their basic treaty rights. By 1964, iconic Hollywood figures attracted the national press when celebrity voices stepped in to offer support at the fish-ins. Soon, Marlon Brando was arrested near Franks Landing; Cree folk singer Buffy Sainte-Marie lent her soulful voice and joined the struggle; and, eventually, comedian Dick Gregory served time in jail and created his own hunger strike to bring national attention to treaty and fishing rights.

Each of these acts was supported by an organization called Survival of American Indians Association (SAIA), which was founded in January of 1964 by Tulalip citizen Janet McCloud, Puyallup Don Matheson, and Al Bridges, who was of Puyallup, Nisqually, and Duwamish descent. This organization attracted a key new member in Fort Peck Assiniboine Hank Adams. Adams had spent his early years on the Quinault Reservation along the Washington coast, and he later had joined the leadership ranks of the National Indian Youth Council. By 1964, Adams had dropped out of the University of Washington after two years to join the SAIA and the fishing rights cause full time. The fish-ins, as Janet McCloud labeled them, began early in 1964 and attracted the press, who witnessed Native peoples being arrested for exercising their most basic treaty right. When Hank Adams joined SAIA, after a successful NIYC support protest/fish-in in March of 1964, he skillfully relied on a similar coalition formula using media pressure, legal counsel, and physical and financial support from Seattle's Indian City. After nearly a decade of fierce challenges, on February 12, 1974, federal judge George Hugo Boldt in *U.S. v. Washington* issued a landmark ruling in favor of the Tribes and the fish-in movement to protect their treaty right to harvest salmon.

Many of the lead organizers for the takeover of Fort Lawton emerged from this fishing rights struggle. Bernie Whitebear (who had fished in protest with Bob Satiacum well before the fish-ins) often ran supplies for the fishing rights movement. By the time the idea to take over Fort Lawton came into being, Whitebear, Adams, and others were seasoned protest veterans. Obviously, in its most simple terms, land reclamation, treaty rights, and self-determination became the core objectives and definition of Red Power politics.[34]

Hundreds of miles away on November 20, 1969, another coalition of Native activists in San Francisco Bay was laying siege to Alcatraz Island. Overnight, IAT, led by activist Richard Oakes, took over the island. Over the course of the next few months, fish-in leaders like Bridges, Adams, and Whitebear made pilgrimages to this new "Indian Land." Adams was the new executive director of SAIA, while Whitebear was an important link between Seattle's Indian City and the activists involved with the fishing rights struggle. Richard and Annie Oakes had both supported the fishing rights movement by providing room and board to Ramona Bennett, a Puyallup who often sold treaty salmon for SAIA, at a dollar a

Ramona Bennett, Iah-huh-bate-soot, Hank Adams, and Anita Collins (Wind River Shoshone) at a press conference in Washington, D.C., for the Trail of Broken Treaties occupation of the Bureau of Indian Affairs building, November 15, 1972. Photo courtesy of Getty Images, Bettmann Collection 517263488.

pound, from the back of an ice-packed U-Haul trailer. During the day Bennett sold treaty salmon at Black Panther rallies throughout the Bay Area. Ramona recalls staying up late at the Oakeses' SFSC apartment talking about Native rights. Both Adams and Bennett remembered Richard Oakes as a visionary and a leader who saw beyond the localized struggle when he asserted, "Alcatraz is not an island, but an idea." That idea was that through organized direct action, Native peoples and Tribes could control and determine their own destinies. Oakes's simple and powerful vision inspired thousands of Native peoples across Indian Country. In Seattle, Bernie Whitebear was enthralled and energized by IAT and Richard Oakes. Soon the two and others started coordinating Seattle's response to Alcatraz—the takeover of Fort Lawton.[35]

Whitebear was so inspired by IAT that he and other northwestern Natives formed their own Seattle-based organization, United Indians of All Tribes (UIAT). Whitebear, along with Bennett and Satiacum (both of whom were leaders in the fish-ins) created UIAT as an answer to Seattle's pressing need for a new cultural center. Bennett, a member of SAIA, had ample contacts in Seattle, and she was an alumna of Seattle Community College and the American Indian Women's Service League. A brilliant organizer, Bennett understood that Native success with fishing rights also hinged on Native success in Seattle. For many in SAIA, a takeover of Fort Lawton, like Alcatraz, could secure critical media attention for fishing rights.

Two years after the Seattle World's Fair, which constructed the iconic Space Needle that towers over the heart of the city, Defense Secretary Robert S. McNamara announced in 1964 that Fort Lawton, a military base in north Seattle, would close in six years. The 1,103-acre site initially founded in 1900 was named after General Henry W. Lawton, whose major exploit was having "captured" the legendary Chiricahua Apache war leader Geronimo. By April of 1964, the City of Seattle created a committee to investigate the transfer of the legal title to the base. At first, Republican Mayor James Braman considered utilizing the lands for either a community college or park, but the cost of the sale from the federal government remained an unknown factor. As previously mentioned, in 1967, Pearl Warren, president of the American Indian Women's Service League, began pressuring the mayor's office to support the building of a new Indian center in Seattle. The following year, anticipating future development costs, Seattle residents voted in favor of a municipal bond measure that allocated $3 million towards Fort Lawton lands. Backed by the Seattle referendum, newly elected mayor Wesley Uhlman appealed to Senator Henry M. Jackson to sponsor and pass the Federal Lands for Park and Recreational Purposes Act in 1969, a law that allowed the federal government to sell surplus property back to states or municipal governments at a reduced cost. Mayor Uhlman formed the Fort Lawton Park Citizens' Advisory Committee to hire park planners and to create a large recreational park for city residents.[36]

Fort Lawton's coastal location and large open acreage made the military base prime open space land for neighborhood associations and property owners eager to increase the worth of their homes with the creation of a large public park. The city began entertaining proposals from the community as to the future of the site. A host of organizations from the local Magnolia Club (a prominent neighborhood association that borders Fort Lawton) to the Sierra Club formed a committee during the mid-1960s to decide the fate of Fort Lawton. Their ultimate plan envisioned the creation of additional park land for local residents of Magnolia members and property owners. Contrary to Seattle organizers, Whitebear and Bennett understood the potential of the site, and they began a concerted campaign to achieve their goals. They teamed up with members of IAT from Alcatraz to secure Fort Lawton for the Native community of Seattle. By February 1970, council members representing Kinatechitapi, an Indian and Alaskan Native service organization, along with members from IAT met with Mayor Uhlman and Senator Jackson at Fort Lawton. While there, Native leaders discussed acquiring the military base for use by the Seattle Native community. IAT liberator and Pueblo citizen John Vigil witnessed Uhlman and Jackson completely dodge their proposal and intentions by referring their representatives to submit a request to the Department of the Interior. So, they selected March 8, 1970, as the first date in a long series of staged occupations to win the title to Fort Lawton.[37]

Well before the first takeover, Bernie Whitebear received numerous offers of support from many national Native organizations, from the West Coast (San Francisco–based United Native Americans) to the East Coast (*Akwesasne Notes*). Their efforts to secure Fort Lawton also caught the attention of actress and activist Jane Fonda, who was eager to participate in the siege. Fonda appeared in over eighteen Hollywood films including *Cat Ballou* (1965) and *Barbarella* (1968). By 1969, her brother Peter Fonda was equally famous for his iconic countercultural role as a free-spirited biker in the film *Easy Rider*. Fonda lent her celebrity to support Native political issues, women's rights, the Black Panthers, and the antiwar movement, but her activism had the result of jeopardizing her recent nomination for an Academy Award for the film, *They Shoot Horses, Don't They?* (1969). While in Tacoma, Washington, Hank Adams and Janet McCloud introduced Jane Fonda to members of an American Indian GI resistance group, whose members wore red berets and advocated against both the draft and the war. They took her to a meeting of the American Serviceman's Union at Shelter Half—a Tacoma coffee shop used for regular meetings of the GI advocacy group. As she listened to veterans' opposition to the Vietnam War, Grace Thorpe, who had helped coordinate Fonda's visit to Alcatraz a week earlier, drove up from Alcatraz to Frank's Landing.[38]

Thorpe planned to meet up with Janet McCloud. When she finally arrived, Thorpe saw the famous actress sitting in the McClouds' kitchen. While the three visited, McCloud explained the latest in a series of campaigns for protecting fishing rights. A long war was being waged in the courtroom, and further protests sought to protect the traditional fishing and treaty rights of northwestern Tribes. Fonda told Thorpe that she was on her way up to Seattle to aid UIAT in their struggle for Fort Lawton. The next morning the popular actress and Grace Thorpe departed Frank's Landing for Seattle. Fonda insisted on driving alone and was soon out of sight, barreling down the road. Although the two had briefly discussed the planned occupation, Thorpe was concerned that Fonda did not know where she was going.[39]

On Sunday, March 8, 1970, UIAT met at the Kinatechitapi Center on South Empire Way and led a caravan of cars to make their first attempt. The key organizers looked around but still saw no sign of Fonda. As organizers scaled the fences surrounding the base as a diversionary tactic, Thorpe and thirty others scaled the high cliffs, carting camping gear, food, and other supplies. Their occupation force liberated the military fort from its western shore. Several more protesters clamored through local neighborhoods and scaled fences next to the base. Ramona Bennett remembered the thoughtfulness of a young Turtle Mountain Anishinaabe activist named Leonard Peltier, who helped everyone safely over the fences. Additional organizers were arrested when they tried to establish an impromptu settlement and a large tipi inside the military base.[40]

Shortly after organizing their makeshift settlement, forty military police (MPs) arrived in full riot gear, and Bob Satiacum began to read the UIAT proclamation. Sid Mills, seeking a peaceful truce, approached the sergeant in command, who without hesitation shoved the fishing rights activist out of his way. For Mills, a decorated Vietnam veteran, the act must have triggered something. With a single blow, he dropped the sergeant. Within seconds the peaceful encampment was swarming with MPs. Mills was quickly overpowered by them, wrestled to the ground, and handcuffed. As the MPs approached UIAT members, they each practiced civil disobedience, sitting on the ground and refusing to physically stand or walk on their own volition. Grace Thorpe, a World War II veteran, sat on the ground next to a first-aid kit, teasing the troops about how many of them it would take to lift and carry her plus-sized body to the stockade. Of the few photographs that remain, one captured fishing rights activist Valerie Bridges as she was wrestled to the ground and forced into a squad car by four soldiers. Another picture published in the *Seattle Post-Intelligencer* revealed two MPs carrying a mother and her frightened child to the nearby trucks.[41]

Once inside the yellow-framed prison structure, Richard Simmons, a reporter for *The Seattle Times,* described the scene as absolute chaos. After the soldiers noticed the reporters, they quickly relocated the women and children to a less visible cell near the back of the prison, well out of sight. After hiding the prisoners from the journalists, all reporters were forced to leave the stockade. Other prisoners watched as MPs repeatedly slammed Bernie Whitebear's face into a wall while he was waiting to be processed. The military personnel at the base had dealt with several antiwar demonstrations at the fort, and their compassion for protesters quickly disappeared. After several hours of being detained, UIAT members demanded water, and they received a bucket of water for each cell.[42]

Outside of the remaining twelve members of UIAT's holding cell, around fifteen MPs assembled before the door, anticipating a fight or perhaps worse. Mills quickly swallowed his fear. As the entrance to their holding cell opened and the troops began to walk into the cell, Mills went for the biggest soldier. Despite getting a few punches in, he was quickly knocked to the floor, his neck pinned against the wall as a soldier kicked him repeatedly in his midsection. Mills caught a brief glimpse of Leonard Peltier, who had managed to overpower his assailant only to get hit from behind. Struggling to break free of his distracted assailant, Mills proceeded to push the soldier off Peltier and started to clamber back into the brawl. Then the sergeant who had had an altercation with Mills earlier in the day spotted Mills again. He lifted his nightstick and ordered the rest of the MPs to get that "son-of-a-bitch." That evening, Mills learned that he had dislocated his shoulder, as had Whitebear. The next thing they knew, some guards threw a broom and dustpan into the cell and called them all dirty pigs. The soldiers threatened them all with another beating if they failed to clean up their cell. With one arm, Mills clenched the broom and tried to sweep, as he lacked the strength to move mattresses. After over six hours of being detained, they issued the remaining prisoners their expulsion orders and released them at the front gate.[43]

Every UIAT member who was detained had been photographed, fingerprinted, and received expulsion papers before being officially released from the stockades. Sources estimate that between 70 and 120 activists had laid siege to the base. A few protesters arrived late to the occupation—such overwhelming numbers forced the military to call in extra help from Fort Lewis and Seattle police. Fearful of bad press, the military ordered all the reporters to hand over any film or photos taken during the siege. Only a few photos made it to the papers.

After being released, many of the occupiers looked around, asking where all the reporters had gone. The next day they received their answer, when they saw the newspaper headlines: "Fonda Arrested." Apparently, Jane Fonda arrived late in the takeover and received her expulsion papers from Fort Lawton. Afterwards, she and a few Native GIs drove eighty miles down to Fort Lewis, where she was promptly arrested and detained for over three hours. The press coverage of Fonda's arrest was beneficial to advertising the cause internationally, but her arrest also shifted public attention away from Fort Lawton.[44]

Later that evening Jane Fonda appeared at a press table with John Vigil, Bernie Whitebear, Bob Satiacum, Raymond McCloud, Sid Mills, and Gary Bray, an IAT activist from Colville. They held the press conference at the newly built thirty-nine-story Fifth Avenue Washington Plaza Hotel. Reporters snapped photos of Whitebear and Mills, who each wore

Fort Lawton Occupation Press Conference, March 10, 1970. Seated left to right: John Vigil, Bernie Whitebear, Jane Fonda, Sid Mills. Standing in the background left to right: Robert Satiacum; Raymond McCloud, a Nisqually citizen; and Gary Bray. Both Bernie Whitebear and Sid Mills are wearing arm slings. AP Photo/Barry Sweet.

slings documenting their dislocated shoulders. Sid Mills, seated behind Fonda, presented a face swollen from all the fighting. Together, UIAT and Fonda invoked the same legal rights as had been used in the Alcatraz takeover. Their leadership pulled from treaty rights and made a careful note that Fort Lawton remained Duwamish territory (a non–federally recognized Nation).

On Monday morning, over ninety protesters gathered in front of the U.S. Court House in downtown Seattle and marched with signs that read, "Give Us Back Our Land," "Custer Wore Arrow Shirts," and "You Are on Indian Land Ft. Lawton." As they walked single file in a circle with hand-drawn signs, in the center a drum and a couple of singers echoed honor songs off the walls of justice. Gary Bray, wearing a faded denim jacket that read "Alcatraz Security," helped connect and draw attention to both movements. One of the UIAT leaders, Bob Satiacum, informed a group of reporters that they were at the Court House to protest the mistreatment of occupiers by police forces at Fort Lawton. Some marchers wore sunglasses in traditional regalia, others wore suits or work uniforms. Together they represented a formidable display of unity and diversity from Seattle's Indian City. By late afternoon, marchers moved their protest over to Fort Lawton.[45]

Throughout the next few weeks, UIAT maintained a twenty-four-hour-a-day settlement at the main gates to Fort Lawton. Ramona Bennett secured a large tarp donated by a local trucker which served as a large canopy for a lean-to shelter. Bob Satiacum helped set up two tipis on either side of the front gates. Soon thereafter coffee and food supplies were delivered and then refilled to support a twenty-four-hour protest vigil. Hank Adams had experienced some success with similar strategies during the Poor People's Campaign, when Native and Chicano activists came together on May 29, 1968, to become the first group to actually stage a protest on the steps and entrance to the U.S. Supreme Court. Adams had also relied on a similar direct-action approach when blocking the doors to the Washington press corps—one reporter, a young Sam Donaldson, actually got stuck between the entry doors, sandwiched among the other protesters. In anticipation of future occupations, the military made preparations; the fort command ordered barbed wire installed around the fort's perimeters. In frequent phone conversations, Sid Mills had been keeping Richard Oakes, still in San Francisco, informed about their progress and the details of their next major action in Seattle.[46]

A few days before March 15, 1970, Oakes made the long car ride up from San Francisco to Frank's Landing. Hank Adams remembered driving him over to the Shelter House so that he could meet with local American Indian GIs. On their car trip up to Seattle, Adams recalled that he was startled and surprised by an observation Oakes made about the movement. Oakes, riding in the passenger side of the car, had for some time watched the scenery as they drove by tall smoke stacks, factories, electrical lines, and ships. Taking it all in, the scenery must have reminded Oakes of the gritty industrial sections of Brooklyn where he had grown up. Then he asked Adams what he knew about the process of deindustrialization. It was the first time Adams had ever heard the term *deindustrialization*. Before this conversation, Adams had never given too much thought to any process for land reclamation and ecological restoration as integral to the larger Native rights movement. In this moment, Adams

Left: The Fort Lawton takeover featured on the front page of *Akwesasne Notes*, vol. 2, no. 1 (April 1970). Grace Thorpe and Col. Stuart J. Palos are depicted. Right: A Pit River story on the front page of *Akwesasne Notes*, vol. 2, no. 4 (July/August 1970). Shown are a map of Pit River lands, Grace Thorpe, and a little girl crying as authorities arrest thirty-four people on charges of trespass for their part in a takeover of a PG&E campground near Big Bend, California. Photo courtesy of Rarihokwats (Jerry Gambill).

quickly realized that Oakes represented a key figure and voice in transforming the rhetoric, ideology, and philosophy of Red Power.[47]

On Sunday at 3 a.m. Richard Oakes and ninety other members of UIAT assembled at a rendezvous point in downtown Seattle. A veteran and leader of the Alcatraz takeovers, Oakes must have been transported back to the three attempts it had taken IAT to secure the former island prison in the bay. His presence, along with other IAT members, offered newcomers a sense of unity, authenticity, and direction.[48]

At five o'clock, several reporters joined the occupiers before they headed out in three successive waves of car caravans in an effort not to draw the attention of local authorities. Instead of an approach by boat, for this occupation Oakes traveled comfortably in a car in the still and calm of an early morning. Each caravan traveled to the southern end of the military base before quietly parking in residential neighborhoods. After exiting their cars, large searchlights could be seen slowly circulating throughout the entire military base. It was a windy night as Richard Oakes and others moved along the western shoreline of Shilshole Bay beneath the dim light of a crescent moon and stars. Many of the occupiers were wrapped in blankets for warmth. They moved quietly, carrying bedrolls, provisions, and supplies. As they neared a residential area the people moved undetected between walls and over fences as residential wind chimes concealed their every step.[49]

Finally, they made it up the steep incline and next to a three-hundred-foot ridge overlooking the glistening waves of Puget Sound. Quickly, organizers assembled and lifted the foundational lodge poles before a large canvas cover was secured around the lodge. For organizers it was a significant gesture: to highlight a Native architectural form and a universally recognized symbol of Indigeneity. Raising the lodge demonstrated a long-term commitment and claim as the original title holders to Fort Lawton. Oakes gathered in with everyone drawing heat from a campfire that sparked against a blackened sky. After forty-five minutes of freedom, the occupation force was spotted by a patrol jeep. Singers began to lift their voices, which provided strength and resolve to all the protesters—some danced while others remained still, gathering their wits for what was about to play out. It was not long before a military force of fifty soldiers arrived in full riot gear and started to march toward the encampment of men, women, and children. The protesters acted as a unified body, as everyone simultaneously sat on the ground. Together they invoked their right to civil disobedience. In a repeat of a few days ago, soldiers grabbed and lifted the limp bodies of the protesters, who were carried and then loaded onto the backs of two Army transport trucks.[50]

The tiny brig at the fort began to overflow with prisoners, and soon they ran out of space as occupiers pushed against the bars of the small 12-by-4-foot cells. One witness stated, "As they stood and sat in the crowded brig of the abandoned post, Oakes used his gift for oratory to encourage and inspire the activists."[51] His voice conveyed a unique form of confidence, that of a leader who clearly understood the emotion, time, patience, and sacrifice it required for activists to lead a liberation movement. The crowded military brig fell to silence when he spoke. Oakes had been a negotiator all of his life, moving between gangs and police, ironworkers and foremen, students and administrators, protesters and politicians; for him, this situation was all too familiar. Tensions escalated as the occupiers pushed officers back to the booking hall, where they witnessed the physical abuse of fellow protesters. One witness saw a woman being inappropriately handled by disgruntled officers. The crowded brig grew loud in protest over the brutality they had collectively witnessed. Outside the brig, officers tauntingly jammed their fists into the air and mockingly displayed the victory sign with their hands. By midday, representatives from the Seattle Human Rights Commission had arrived at the base in order to observe and report any prisoner abuse.[52]

After over six hours locked in the stockade, the prisoners were finally released. Many of the occupiers received trespass offenses for failing to observe their previous expulsion orders. Soldiers rotated dropping prisoners off at one of two main gates. Documentary filmmaker Carol Burns, who would release her fishing rights documentary *As Long as the Rivers Run* a year later, had her cameras rolling and captured Richard Oakes's release from the stockade on film. As he departed the military jeep escort, Oakes began a walk toward freedom. On the other side of the gate cheers rang out from a large crowd of protesters and spectators. Suzette (Bridges) Mills counted this as her favorite memory of Oakes:

> He was a dynamic person, tall and handsome. . . . You cleared a path for him. He was not loud; he was very calm, and things he said about the struggle all fell into place. He was a great leader; he was down to earth. He tried to see and understand what you were really trying to say and he put a lot of thought into where we wanted to go. I was proud of Richard when everyone came out of Fort Lawton. These guys went to jail; the energy behind it was exciting . . . especially the amount of people it took to haul him into that jail. I am proud of that unity, we needed to have that for [our] people.

After his release from the stockade, Oakes traveled back to San Francisco in order to participate in further liberation and reclamation movements occurring throughout northern California.[53]

Those arrested in the first attempt were scheduled to go to trial April 2, 1970, on charges of trespassing for having ignored their previous expulsion orders. Instead of attending their trials, several UIAT leaders joined forces with more supporters at their "Resurrection City" encampment located just outside both entrances to the fort. Security, noticing that a large group was massing at the gate, dispatched soldiers to survey the situation. The occupiers informed the soldiers that they would be packing up and asked for their assistance. While the soldiers anxiously began breaking down tents and lodges, the occupiers slowly moved toward the now-opened main entrance. Whitebear began to read the UIAT proclamation authored by Hank Adams: "We, the Native Americans, in our independent sovereign rights and rights of alliance, herewith claim the land known as Fort Lawton . . . by the acknowledged right of discovery. In the name of all Indians, therefore, we claim this land before the international community for all our Indian nations. We know this claim is just and proper, that this land is, in perpetuity, rightfully ours!"[54] As Whitebear finished reading the proclamation he came to the final passage, which contained the signal phrase, "in the name of Indian sovereignty," and everyone made a sudden dash for the open fort gates, running at full stride, as soldiers busy dismantling the encampment looked on in disbelief. Dropping tent poles and tables, the soldiers scrambled to pursue, racing forward as the protesters fanned out in multiple directions across the base. One MP from the 382nd Military Police Battalion reported to his commanding officer about the siege, "It's impossible to stop them. Wow! Now I know how Custer felt." This strategy of spreading out in the base prevented the use of tear gas and allowed some protesters to go undetected, thereby prolonging the occupation. The short and wiry Colonel Stuart Palos, who was in charge of Fort Lawton, was in shock at being an "April fool" in the press and quickly turned to frustration. While being chauffeured around the base in a military jeep, Palos commented that he had "never seen such deception in all his life."[55]

Right before Whitebear gave the signal to storm the gates, Ramona Bennett pulled up and parked her car alongside the front gates to the base. The next thing she knew, a group of occupiers waved to her as they climbed on top of her car and jumped from her car's roof over the main fence. After being captured and released, Bennett discovered that the roof of her car had been caved in from the weight of all the protesters. This car was like her second home, as she made frequent trips between Seattle and San Francisco to sell treaty salmon for Frank's Landing. During the April 2, 1970, occupation, one of the canisters of tear gas fired by the soldiers got lodged in the underside of her car. Afterwards, every time she hit a bump, some more tear gas would seep through her floorboards. Another tear gas canister sparked a fire at an older building on the base. Colonel Palos blamed the unarmed protesters for the incident and denied any culpability by the army for using tear gas. In all, about eighty people joined in the effort to seize Fort Lawton on April 2, 1970, only to wind up again in the hands of angry MPs.[56]

Despite the taunts of soldiers and the arrest of some of the supporters, the April 2 UIAT takeover had won a decisive victory. Ultimately, after a long fight, Fort Lawton was turned over to UIAT, who through the use of Model Cities funds would found the Daybreak Star Center on the controversial site. The occupations and the press attention unified the Seattle populace into a concerted campaign supporting UIAT's claim to Fort Lawton. Bernie Whitebear and others began drafting plans to convert the retired base into a cultural and ecological center.[57]

Several days before the third attempt on Fort Lawton, on March 23, Richard Oakes, having just returned from Seattle, led a takeover of the Bureau of Indian Affairs office in Alameda, California. He and twelve other protesters were arrested in their attempt to seize control of the regional government agency (their protest followed the March 14 takeover of a BIA office in Denver, Colorado, over job discrimination). The arrests in Alameda occurred after days of staged sit-ins at the BIA offices had produced little in the way of results. While their protest specifically highlighted job discrimination, their demands spoke to a greater question of self-determination. Native people lacked any positions of authority within regional BIA offices. That afternoon, fifty people picketed outside the BIA office in protest. After marching for several hours, thirty protesters entered the BIA building and secured a meeting with local director Donald H. Spaugy. Twelve members, including Richard Oakes, elected to stay in the building after closing hours.[58]

The police arrived in the evening to arrest the members of the occupation force. After the liberators were booked on a minor charge of failure to leave a closed public building, a press conference was held at the police station. Standing before the press in his San Francisco State College sweatshirt, Oakes demanded the removal of Interior Secretary Walter Hickel, Commissioner of Indian Affairs Louis Bruce, and area director Donald Spaugy. More importantly, he called for Native suffrage,

The BIA takeover in Alameda, California, March 23, 1970. Here, Richard Oakes, wearing his San Francisco State College sweatshirt, and twelve unidentified supporters surrender to local authorities. All occupiers were charged with trespass for staging a sit-in at a government office. Photo courtesy of Getty Images, Bettmann Collection 640119060.

demanding that new appointments require a majority vote from all Native peoples. The occupiers' demands included preferential hiring for American Indians within the BIA; termination of BIA area offices; an interagency review board to investigate Indian employment; the separation of the BIA from the Interior Department as a standalone governmental agency; tuition assistance for Native college students; and full restoration of legal status and benefits for all off-reservation Native peoples. Afterwards, Oakes was released on probation, with his arraignment set for June 12, 1970. Months later, the BIA's Alameda office, in an effort to subdue growing protests, replaced Spaugy and appointed its first Indigenous director, Lakota citizen Al Trimble. Oakes, despite great odds and adversity, was beginning to see new outcomes for Red Power.[59]

This Intertribal coalition consisting of United Indians of All Tribes along with Indians of All Tribes, Alcatraz, and Indian City Seattle sought to create an environmental preserve and ecology center, educational and cultural centers, an Indian museum, and a halfway house for Native migrants coming to Seattle. After three failed attempts to claim the fort by right of discovery, countless arrests, physical confrontations with the military police, picket lines in front of the courthouse, a twenty-four-hour occupation settlement outside the fort, and a concerted letter-writing campaign to state senators and Seattle Mayor Wes Uhlman, UIAT ultimately won the war for a new cultural center. In November 1971, Mayor Wes Uhlman presented a proposal that would provide UIAT with over $600,000 in Model Cities money to construct the Daybreak Star Center. The countless occupations and press attention unified the Seattle Indigenous populace, who joined in a concerted campaign supporting UIAT's claim to Fort Lawton.

The legacy of this movement has yet to be fully measured. Whitebear secured Pearl Warren's great dream of establishing a land base and constructing a new Longhouse for Seattle's Indian community. In turn, Red Power as a national movement increasingly relied on urban Intertribal institutions and organizations forged out of Indian Cities like those in Brooklyn, San Francisco, and Seattle. Fort Lawton, like Alcatraz, was also a movement that mobilized the entire Seattle Indian community around a central belief, that the path to social and political justice would ultimately transform Indigenous relationships with local, municipal, state, Tribal, and federal governments.

This path to social justice and self-determination was rooted in an urban-centered Intertribal perspective. In many ways, Fort Lawton and United Indians of All Tribes mirrored the growing desires of Native migrants and Native nations in and around Seattle; each was a central ingredient toward creating a viable Indian City. The Daybreak Star Center, like Alcatraz, emerged not as an abandoned piece of property or an open-spaced park but as a sacred space emblematic of Native Nationalism and Red Power. The rippling effect brought together Native peoples from rural, urban, and reservation communities and forged a new Intertribal reality and awareness. Upon his release from the BIA takeover in Alameda, Richard Oakes began to work with the Pit River Nation in northern California for land reclamation. Fort Lawton, like Alcatraz, relied on a nonviolent and media-driven Intertribal movement. The strategies Oakes and others created with Alcatraz steadily gained legitimacy throughout Indian Country. This newfound fame and strategy, while successful in Seattle, would meet violent opposition from law enforcement and corporations at Pit River. For Richard Oakes, now the iconic face of Red Power, the next few years became a constant struggle just to stay alive.

CHAPTER SIX

You Are on Indian Land

PIT RIVER AND LAND RECLAMATION

OAKES HAD FOUND NEW INSPIRATION during these months, and he was elated when Annie gave birth on April 10, 1970, to their daughter Nuwhakawee—Little Fawn.[1] After leaving Seattle, Richard Oakes returned to San Francisco a proud new father, stimulated by the potential of Alcatraz, Fort Lawton, and the Alameda BIA takeovers. The idea of self-determination had to be applied outside the urban context to protect Native sovereignty. Oakes sought to merge the sheer numbers, resources, and contacts from within the Indian City into an Intertribal coalition that could lend further support to Pit River. In part, this coalition held the real potential to strengthen the political resolve and objectives sought by Pit River leaders, who often stood outnumbered against larger forces. The idea of Alcatraz was not compromised when Oakes resigned from Indians of All Tribes. Moreover, Alcatraz had become a catalyst for grassroots occupations spreading throughout Indian Country: from Ellis Island and Pyramid Lake to Denver and Akwesasne, Mohawk organizers reclaimed Stanley and Loon Islands. In this explosive climate, Pit River citizen Mickey Gemmill offered Oakes the opportunity to bring liberation theory to the tiny Pit River Rancheria in northern California. Gemmill, a fellow student at San Francisco State and a psychology major, was recently appointed Tribal Chairman at Pit River. Only twenty-five years old, Gemmill had catapulted to the top leadership position in his Tribe.

Shown here at an abandoned missile base in El Cerrito, California, taken over by Indians of All Tribes, are Mickey Gemmill, seated on the floor in the center, alongside five unidentified individuals, on June 15, 1971. The giant map on the wall details occupations on Pit River Nation lands. Beneath Lassen National Park it reads "26 Freedom Fighters," and beneath PG&E Campground, "34 Arrests." Photo courtesy of Getty Images, Bettmann Collection 640900794.

Pit River has a long and rich history rooted in protection of their land rights. By 1970, Pit River had around 530 residents. The small Nation survived the onslaught of the Spanish Mission period and the genocide campaigns of gold miners and the U.S. military during the nineteenth century. In 1853, the state of California negotiated a treaty with eighteen different Nations and Tribes, some collectively known as Pomo. The treaty outlined the settlement of land claims and eventually led to the formation of rancherias. However, the treaty process excluded representatives of Pit River Nation. Consequentially, Pit River had never agreed to a settlement or treaty to cede any portion of their 3.5 million acres of ancestral homelands—roughly the same size as the state of Connecticut. The traditional land base for the Tribe is located within four sacred landmarks: Mt. Lassen and Mt. Shasta to the north and Goose Lake and Eagle Lake in the south. The territory contains a rich geologic history with lush and thick forests in the center, ancient lava flows in the north, and dozens of lakes and rivers elsewhere. The Pomo had survived on the abundance of salmon

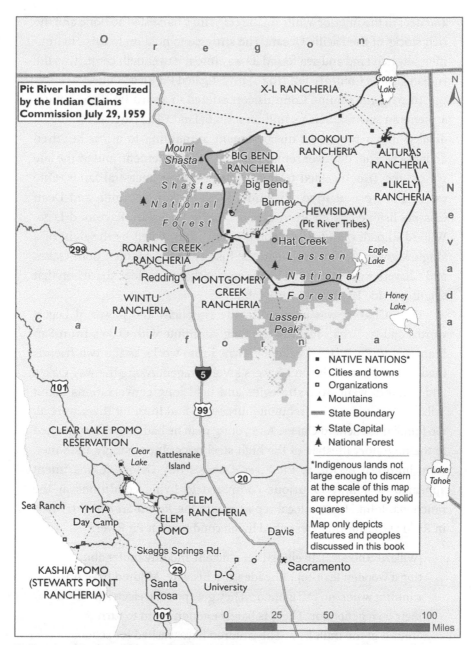

Pit River Land Reclamation. Map by Ed Brands.

and deer in the interior, while on the coast they harvested abalone and the rich stocks of the Pacific Ocean. The struggle to hold on to this environmentally rich land and sea found its way into the twentieth century, as the Indian Claims Commission (1946) investigated Pit River's title.[2]

In 1959 the Claims Commission offered to award Pit River a mere 47 cents an acre for their 3.5 million acres of land.[3] The payment would be divided into a per capita disbursement amounting to a few hundred dollars a person. Pit River refused to accept the settlement, and by the late 1960s, the Tribe decided to fight to regain their ancestral lands. One evening in April of 1970, Richard Oakes, Mickey Gemmill, and Dean Chavers listened as Pit River elders Charlie Buckskin, Raymond Lego, Willard Rhoades, and Ross Montgomery, illuminated by the light of a single kerosene lamp, explained the history of the conflict. Both Oakes and Chavers were enthralled by the stories that each elder shared on that evening inside Raymond Lego's cabin.

Dean Chavers was inspired by the simplicity and power of Lego's words, and he began making the long commute with Oakes from San Francisco to Pit River. Weekends turned into weeks as the two friends made the six-hour drive in Chavers's Volkswagen. Along the way Oakes and Chavers went over strategies and held long conversations about Tribal sovereignty.[4] The frequent journeys to and from Pit River were all too familiar to Richard Oakes. As a young man he had grown accustomed to the migratory lifestyle of the high steel trade. Increasingly, both men were humbled by life at Pit River. Oakes's tiny Gatorville apartment appeared strikingly luxurious compared to living conditions at the rancheria. John Hurst, a local reporter with the *Record-Searchlight*, based in Redding, California, described living conditions at Pit River:

> [Willard Rhoades] dwelling is an ancient and tiny trailer abutting a wooden lean-to[.] Rhoades and his wife, Mildred have no running water, no refrigerator. They get sporadic electricity from their own generator. There is barely enough room to turn around in the trailer. . . . The children have washed for school outside in the cold morning air. There is no running water in Lego's cabin. The children studied their school lessons by kerosene lamp the night before. There is no electricity in Lego's cabin. Of the 530 Pit River Indians . . . not more than one or two

families have running water or plumbing in their homes. Many families have no electricity . . . two telephones in the entire [Tribe]. Families live as a rule in makeshift cabins, with as many as eight, 10 or 12 people crowded into two, three or four tiny rooms.[5]

Contrary to the harshness of life for many residents at Pit River, several wealthy corporations and the federal government claimed thousands of acres of their ancestral lands. Pacific Gas and Electric Company (PG&E) maintained six dams and some 52,000 acres to appease California's growing need for power; the Los Angeles Times-Mirror Corporation and Hearst Publishing both operated successful timber camps (96,000 acres combined); Southern Pacific Railroad maintained 38,000 acres; Pacific Telephone and Telegraph, 18,000 acres; Kimberly-Clark, some 80,000 acres; and various smaller corporations and ranches consumed 100,000 acres. The federal government, through the National Parks and other venues, held the remaining acreage.[6] Richard Oakes knew that the battle against these national conglomerates and the federal government would require the legal talents of Aubrey Grossman. Pit River appointed the gregarious Grossman to head their legal counsel, and he willingly volunteered his legal expertise to the Tribe.

Oakes began hosting community meetings and organizing sessions to formulate a decisive attack to regain Pit River lands. The media and courtroom would play a crucial role in advertising and protecting the claim. Richard Oakes organized his contacts, inviting local press to participate in the meetings. Without the press, the isolated rancheria faced potential obscurity by an apathetic public and corporate muscle. A successful campaign, as Oakes understood it, also depended on his ability to recruit large numbers of Native peoples and allies. The foundation of the support rested on the shoulders of Pit River residents, Aubrey Grossman, the media, local Native college students, and Indians of All Tribes. Galvanizing such a force depended on direct action during the summer months to allow Native students a larger role in the numerous occupations.

By mid-May 1970, a second occupation was well underway at the Round Valley Rancheria, located 180 miles north of San Francisco. At the same time, Oakes was working with the Elem Pomo at the Sulphur Bank

Rancheria to coordinate the liberation of Rattlesnake Island. Since time immemorial, the Elem have resided and maintained lands along the shores and tiny islands of Clear Lake in northern California. Clear Lake has a horrifying past, in particular the acts of genocide committed on Pomo peoples in the wake of American territorial expansion. On May 15, 1850, the north shores of the lake became red with blood, as over two hundred Pomo men, women, and children were slaughtered by the U.S. military in what is known as the Bloody Island Massacre.[7] Officially organized nearly a hundred years later, in 1949, the fifty-two-acre rancheria struggled to survive next door to a hazardous 417-foot hole that was being utilized for the large-scale extraction of mercury. The small rancheria finally received electricity in 1969 and running water and a sewage system a year later. The government constructed their homes and roads from tailings at the abandoned mercury mine, which shut down in the late 1950s.[8]

For centuries, Elem remained active in protecting their lifeways and sovereign rights. One year prior to meeting Richard Oakes, Elem leader Dewey Barnes won a decisive courtroom battle to secure off-reservation fishing rights after he was arrested for fishing without a state license at Rattlesnake Island.[9] One month later, in April of 1970, the Elem won their lawsuit and public protest against Lake County Fair's use of Him Konocti, a derogatory Indian mascot that advertised the annual festival.[10] The effort to liberate Rattlesnake Island represented a test case to encourage solidarity and support for Pit River land reclamations. Rattlesnake Island or "Mu-dóne," located off the eastern shore of Clear Lake, five hundred feet from the rancheria, is a sacred site and an ancestral burial ground that the Elem Pomo maintained for over six thousand years. In 1877, Governor William Irwin of California claimed patent on the island and sold its title to several wealthy San Francisco residents. This fraudulent sale occurred in direct violation of the Indian Trade and Intercourse Acts, which proclaimed that title to Indigenous treaty lands could only be extinguished by an act of Congress.[11] Protection of the island was heightened when the Elem learned that the Boise-Cascade Lumber Company, based in Idaho, had plans to subdivide the island for use as a vacation resort. Construction on the island ensured that ancestral graves would be desecrated or even destroyed outright. On May 1, 1970, a large force of Elem Pomo and representatives from Indians of All Tribes made their stand on the island. The occupiers erected tents and shelters and began running supplies to the one-mile-long Rattlesnake Island. Representatives from the Boise-Cascade Company quickly made their way to the island. Realizing that their economic venture to produce a resort on a burial ground might be a hard sell, the company entered into negotiations with the Elem.[12]

Oakes and others at Pit River realized that the Rattlesnake Island victory gave them the momentum needed to reclaim their lands. In 1964, Pit River citizens protested against the destruction of a building on Pit River land by staging a thirty-day standoff with local authorities. Pit River, in tandem with Indians of All Tribes, proposed staging a series of occupations at Lassen National Forest and on PG&E lands. Grossman was counting on the local authorities. He expected them to evict the liberators, but more importantly, he hoped that the occupiers would be charged with trespassing. The burden of proof would then rest with the federal government and the corporations. They would be forced to prove that Pit River, in spite of the Claims Commission ruling, did not have original title to the lands. The courtroom was the prime battleground for Pit River to assert their claim. Pit River had also made a public appeal to PG&E clients to pay their bills directly through the Tribe and guaranteed the fulfillment of any and all services. In addition to collecting customer payments, the land liberations were scheduled to start on June 5, 1970.[13]

Tari Reim, a reporter for the British underground newspaper *Friends*, arrived at the Pit River Tribal headquarters, located at Hat Creek in northern California. As Reim steered his car into the large parking lot, a big sign outside the headquarters read "Pit River Indians Welcome Indians of All Tribes."[14] Pit River was nearing the end of an official Council meeting. Making his way across the parking lot, Reim noticed the Asp, a converted school bus covered bumper-to-bumper in acid inspired psychedelic murals. Propped up against the bus was Wavy Gravy, a familiar personality from the previous year's Woodstock Music festival. Formerly known as Hugh Romney, Wavy Gravy led a carnival of pranksters who were impossible to miss at any gathering. Decked out in his characteristic stars-and-stripes garb, Wavy Gravy pointed his Donald Duck water pistol at the approaching reporter and shot him three times—a playful greeting. Wavy Gravy often branded his extended family or commune as an "Army of Clowns." In a Native construct, clowns manage an important contrary life as they mimic outrageous human traits or behaviors. Indigenous communities depend on these keepers of the contrary as a way to maintain social, political, intellectual, and spiritual balance. Wavy Gravy became a quick ally for the cause after he heard Richard Oakes speak at a political rally, and he remembered Oakes's call for "back-up from friendly freaks or anyone else who wanted to help." His family at the Hog Farm represented an important ally for Pit River, for the Hog Farmers had fed and peacefully overseen security for the estimated five hundred thousand people who attended the Woodstock Music Festival in Bethel, New York.[15] Such experiences and resources were instrumental for the Pit River cause. Wavy Gravy's idea of clowns was deeply imbedded in a 1960s countercultural awareness—that lending support to Native occupations countered mainstream society's view of Native peoples and issues. Off in the distance Tari could see a group of Native peoples hanging outside an edifice passing sodas and chips back and forth while kids chased each other. Wavy Gravy informed him that an official Pit River Council meeting was taking place inside the large community building. Curious and eager for a story about a Native revolution, the reporter quickly strolled over to the building and peeked through one of the outside windows.[16]

Inside he saw what appeared to be a meeting veering out of control, everyone talking to the person next to them. This went on for a little while, and then a woman elder stood up and began to sing. All of the conversation and commotion stopped. As her powerful voice rang through the auditorium, the attendees, devoted to their traditions, perceived these actions as illustrating proper respect and dedication. Then, one by one, every Pit River citizen joined his or her voice in unison until everyone shared one voice—balance was restored and conversations remained on point. Moving away from the window, Tari walked back over to the Army of Clowns as he inquired to learn more about the revolution. One of the long-haired Hog Farmers spoke up: "We're going to Lassen National Park."[17]

Looking around the parking lot, Tari spotted a recognizable face of the movement: Richard Oakes. After he approached Oakes, he asked him about the next strategy for Pit River. "Well, there are two plans," he said, "We want to go to PG&E land, but the Pit River Indian Council has been planning to take over Lassen National Park for a long time. So that's what we're going to do." Oakes smiled as he walked over toward a small group of IAT members. Someone announced, "WE'RE OFF!" as everyone exited the council meeting and entered their vehicles.[18]

Tari hitched a ride on the Asp, as vehicles streamed out of the parking lot and onto the highway. After sunset the caravan of Pit River residents, supporters, and Oakes drove south on Highway 89 to Lassen National Forest. Under a blanket of stars, cars and trucks packed with men, women, and children slowly made their way to the park. Nobody knew what to expect; anticipation ran high; a rush of excitement highlighted the conversations. As the caravan of over a hundred liberators approached the entrance to the park, they could make out the glow of several headlights in the distance, and then, as the cars slowed down, those leading the procession came across four police cars parked in a V-like formation, blocking the entire highway. Word of the occupation had leaked. The long line of vehicles came to an abrupt stop, and people began exiting their cars to get a closer look: Why had they stopped? At the roadblock, seven law enforcement officers greeted the caravan. Four uniformed, two in suits, and a police captain were armed with riot sticks, mace, and shotguns. Upon seeing a big crowd gather near the roadblock, the officers nervously announced that the park was closed for road construction. A film crew traveling with the liberators shined a floodlight on a dark outcropping of trees near the park's entrance. Their searchlights unveiled an incredible police presence, a combined force numbering into the hundreds of Forest Service Rangers and Shasta County Sheriff's deputies mingled with U.S. Marshals in riot gear.[19] An army of men stood ready to attack if the roadblock somehow failed to stop the caravan. Fearing that violence would postpone any attempt at a trespass charge, Raymond Lego faced the caravan and said, "All right, we'll leave." In disbelief and shock, everyone looked to Richard Oakes, who calmly announced, "Okay. . . . Everybody back in the cars. . . . PG&E Camp."[20]

It appeared too easy a victory for law enforcement as the caravan turned their cars around and disappeared into the night. Driving their packed station wagon, Richard told Annie that they were on their way to Big Bend, California. Pacific Gas and Electric maintained a vacant campground for corporate guests and company picnics. Pit River decided to make their stand at the campground. Richard and Annie's son "Little" Joseph was asleep in the back seat. He had slept through the spectacle at the park's entrance. John Hurst, a local reporter covering the story, found irony in Joseph's ability to sleep throughout the ordeal. Hurst realized that despite his own anxious response, this was nothing new for the three-year-old. Only three months earlier Joseph had lived at one of America's most feared prisons, Alcatraz.[21]

As the caravan made their way along winding roads to Big Bend, Shasta County Sheriff John Balma sent two deputies to tail the large motorcade. Some members of the caravan noticed the new additions and broke away from the train of cars to create a distraction. Some locals feared retaliation by Sheriff Balma and local police, but many more were inclined to be decoys. Arriving late that evening, Richard Oakes and others found the quaint cabins at the campground deserted. The cabins, which were complete with all the modern conveniences, must have seemed a luxurious retreat for Pit River residents. Each cabin had running water, electricity, air conditioning, and appliances—a stark realization to Pit River citizens and activists of the extent to which PG&E corporation had profited from their lands.

Around a bonfire, Raymond Lego assembled the large group, now reduced to around eighty men, women, and children. Pausing as he glanced at the cabins and then at the people who had come together, he began to speak. Determination was evident in Lego's voice as he read their proclamation with a commanding posture: "Don't feel you're a stranger here. This is your land. This is my land. This is Indian Country. My ancestors lived here. The Great Spirit planted them here. Just like he did the oak trees and water. Feel welcome. Let your spirit be free."[22] Along with Lego's words, Oakes and Gemmill highlighted the Pit River call for liberation. Singers gathered around the drum, and victory songs filled the night air. Occupiers organized into groups to discuss their strategy and to insure a unified stance when officials arrived to evict them. First, a sheriff's officer arrived to survey the camp, and then a representative from PG&E visited to explain that their occupation "inconvenienced some of our executives who planned to stay here this weekend." Oakes responded in kind: "Our people have been inconvenienced by you guys for hundreds of years. We plan to relax and enjoy." To Richard and Annie Oakes, the climate that evening must have reminded them of the many nights spent on Alcatraz.[23]

By morning the settlers made full use of the PG&E campground and its "luxurious" amenities. Annie took the children to the swimming pool, while the afternoon sun strolled among the pines. Cooks began preparing breakfast and lunch; anticipation grew as the hours passed. It was not long before they could hear a large motorcade of twenty-eight cars approaching the campground. The liberation force came together near the entrance to witness the spectacle. Sheriff Balma emerged from his patrol car, followed by eighty-five deputies dressed in riot gear. Richard Oakes stood beside Raymond Lego as Sheriff Balma approached them. Lego politely asked the sheriff to leave their property unless he could produce a document proving that PG&E owned the land. Balma smiled and ordered the camp cleared; everyone was to be charged with trespassing. Thirty-five occupiers, including Richard and Annie Oakes, willingly assisted officers with their arrest, trying hard not to crack a smile as they were escorted to squad cars. The rest of the liberators avoided arrest by agreeing to vacate the campsite. A small victory had been won, for the burden of proof for clear title to the land rested with PG&E. It was now up to Aubrey Grossman and the courts.[24]

After a long afternoon of swimming and watching the police arrest his parents, "Little" Joseph fell asleep again on the lap of reporter John Hurst. Richard and Annie, wearing handcuffs, were on their way to being booked and processed in Redding, a fifty-mile trip. Later that evening, a good friend of the couple arrived at the county jail—Buffy Sainte-Marie. Only thirty-five men and women had been arrested as Buffy strolled into the crowded jail. Cheers went up from the prisoners as they instantly recognized the popular Native folk singer. While Buffy Sainte-Marie spoke words of encouragement to the prisoners, the deputies grew irritated, informing the singer that she would be arrested if she continued to talk with the prisoners. Buffy turned to the deputy, smiled, and began to sing to her friends behind bars. She had driven from Los Angeles to Redding, and after an impromptu concert, she posted bail for many of the prisoners, including Richard and Annie.[25]

Later that evening, everyone arrested by the Sheriff's Office was released from jail. When they returned to the Pit River headquarters, they were greeted with smiles and hugs from the other liberators. Pit River headquarters came to life as they enjoyed a feast prepared by the Hog Farmers. Buffy Sainte-Marie greeted the people and later sang Cree songs by the flicker of a campfire. Making their way toward the psychedelic bus, Richard and Annie were finally reunited with their children. They had returned victorious, but this represented only the first of many future battles.[26]

At the arraignment the next day, Aubrey Grossman presented his clients' defense argument before Shasta County Judge Billy C. Covert. The locally elected judge did not possess a law degree, but he had served in law enforcement. Grossman presented a polished argument to the court, urging the judge to prosecute PG&E for trespass and dismiss all charges against his clients. Grossman cited the Claims Commission ruling of 1959, which upheld Pit River's historic deed to the land, and maintained that this was indeed an unconstitutional false arrest. PG&E lawyers grew anxious while Shasta County deputies stood nervously in the courtroom, now realizing why the occupiers welcomed the trespass charge.[27]

The lawyers representing PG&E immediately considered dropping charges to prevent further debate on the issue of title. Afterwards, as Grossman conveyed the legal situation to his clients, he discussed probable outcomes and defense strategies. Meanwhile, another group of occupiers and reporters were again laying siege to the campground at Big Bend. Like the thirty-five settlers the previous day, they also hoped to be arrested for trespass in order to prevent PG&E from dropping charges. Richard and Annie left the arraignment to spend time with their children. It had been a long couple of days for the family.

On the afternoon of Monday, June 8, 1970, the small band of reporters and Pit River holdouts waited for arrest at the campgrounds. To pass the time, they staged a football game, Pit River versus the journalists. The climate appeared joyful in light of pending arrests. After the game a journalist asked the occupiers to pose for photos documenting the takeover. A drizzling rain began to fall on the campground. One by one, patrol cars raced into the campgrounds, sliding to a halt as officers exited their vehicles and spread throughout the camp. A force of sixty officers, complete with helmets and riot sticks, located only ten occupiers. Reporters rushed to get photos of the arrests and to interview Sheriff Balma, who was irritated by the paltry numbers in the camp. Balma questioned the tiny group as to the whereabouts of any more holdouts. Fortunately, those arrested were charged with trespass and taken to Redding for booking.[28] The charge of trespass required proof that PG&E and not Pit River had maintained original title to the land; Balma failed to get the message from the court before making the arrests.

News of the arrests spread fast, and Richard Oakes rallied another force to reoccupy the vacant camp. Before leaving, Balma assigned two deputies to stay behind and had all cabin doors bolted shut to prevent entry. Balma was becoming acutely aware of Pit River's strategy, since PG&E officials made it known that no more arrests were to be made on trespass grounds. At about a half-hour before midnight, Richard Oakes led a caravan of cars and trucks through the drizzling rain into the PG&E camp.[29] The parade of cars surrounded a row of cabins while two deputies turned their spotlights on the group. The standoff was underway as Oakes shouted commands to fellow drivers to turn on their high beams. He wondered what it would take to get arrested. Reporters with the caravan likened the event to a complex game of checkers. Waiting patiently for any response, one of the patrol cars darted out to flank the perimeter. Oakes quickly responded, "Get your car on the road and block 'em." Still no arrests. . . . What to do? Richard Oakes then told the drivers to try and enter the cabins; again, the deputies sat motionless, assured that the cabins were bolted shut. Finally Oakes opened up their perimeter and allowed one of the deputies to pull forward in his prowler. Standing in the rain, soaked and confused, Oakes asked the deputy what it was going to take:

> "I don't know. You tell me," the officer said, "We just might do
> something if anyone enters a cabin." It was all very friendly.
> Oakes explained the Indians' position. "But it's already in court.
> What are you going to gain by getting more people arrested?"
> the officer asked. "Think of the public that's paying for these
> courtroom and enforcement expenses," he added. "The
> taxpayers will get mad at PG&E, not us," another Indian
> predicted. "No, the public will get sick of the Indians," the
> deputy replied. "Your move," said Oakes—grinning. The patrol
> car left. "Now it's our move," Oakes told the Indians . . . [with]
> no arrests the group decided to call it a day. Oakes pronounced
> the final benediction: "The game is being called on account of
> the rain."[30]

Obviously, Oakes understood that it was going to take more drastic measures to solicit an arrest. Pit River leaders decided to elevate their strategy to "guerrilla" tactics to encourage a response. On the morning of

Tuesday, June 9, 1970, yet another occupation force made their way back into the PG&E camp. Meanwhile, in Redding, Judge Covert listened to arguments in the arraignment proceedings for forty-four occupiers charged with trespass. Richard and Annie attended the arraignment and listened patiently as Grossman presented their case. Grossman demonstrated that the court did not have the jurisdiction to prosecute his clients, who represented a federally recognized Nation. Again he cited the Claims Commission's ruling of 1959 as a reference to Pit River's legal right to occupy the lands in question. Grossman continued to urge that Judge Covert arrest PG&E officials on trespass and to dismiss charges against his clients. Fearing possible political suicide, the judge declined to prosecute PG&E officials.[31]

While proceedings in court continued, the occupation at Big Bend escalated. Trees were cut to barricade the entrance to the camp to prevent an easy eviction. Sheriff Balma arrived shortly with a force of eighteen to arrest four men and three women. After the sheriff entered, a barricade was quickly erected, as freshly cut trees fell over the road. As if he had a crystal ball, Balma somehow produced a bulldozer and quickly removed the fallen trees. He arrested the protesters, not on trespass charges but rather for destroying private property.[32]

After the arraignment Richard Oakes and Mickey Gemmill elected to occupy Lassen National Forest for a second time. Another caravan was organized, and as occupiers converged on the park, they held the element of surprise. This occasion produced no roadblocks as they freely drove through the entrance. Around thirty men, women, and children huddled together by a large bonfire. As evening wore on, "49" songs were heard throughout the camp. Leaders talked in detail about the events of the previous few days. Word spread quickly to the camp that Forest Service Rangers were congregating at the entrance and were planning an assault. Gemmill feared that under the protection of darkness the police assault potentially could take an ill-fated turn. He quickly organized everyone and made plans for a daring escape. Near the entrance the caravan was cornered and forced to pull over. Park Superintendent Richard Boyer walked nervously, with a flashlight in hand, as he frantically searched for Gemmill, but he had eluded Boyer's sting and was now on his way out of the park. Frustrated, Boyer arrested twenty-two supporters, not for trespass but for leaving a fire unattended and unlawful assembly.[33]

On June 10, Oakes and Gemmill met with Raymond Lego in his weathered cabin back at Pit River to discuss the courtroom battle. The kerosene lamp burned into the night as they debated their next move. At the arraignment hearing the day before, Gemmill was offended by Judge Covert's reluctance to prosecute PG&E. If the court would not prosecute, then Pit River would have to prosecute the conglomerate. They decided that Mickey Gemmill, Richard Oakes, Charlie Buckskin, and Raymond Lego would make a citizens' arrest on PG&E President Shermer Sibley in San Francisco.³⁴ The leaders were still reeling with anger over another event earlier that day. In an effort to discredit Gemmill, PG&E officials had flown in Ike Leaf, the former Tribal Chairman for Pit River. At a press conference, the elderly Leaf claimed that Mickey Gemmill was not the "official" Tribal Chairman for Pit River and that he was the "true" chairman. As the real chairman, Leaf renounced Pit River's claim on PG&E property. The press conference, open only to reporters, was not only sponsored by PG&E but was also held at Shasta County Sheriff's Offices. Gemmill and others at Pit River were irritated by PG&E's lavish attempt to discredit their leadership and governance. By morning they were on the road to San Francisco, eager to assert their sovereignty and to arrest the PG&E president.³⁵

On June 11, 1970, after enduring numerous takeovers, the PG&E press conference, and Judge Covert's reluctance to prosecute the corporation, the four leaders pulled into San Francisco. Richard Oakes had contacted Grace Thorpe, who arranged for a press conference that afternoon at Dorothy Lonewolf Miller's office on California Street. The speakers made eloquent statements reflecting on the history of the Pit River movement. As the leaders spoke, they brought forth a symbolism founded in Red Power politics, something reporters were accustomed to hearing from Richard Oakes. At the end of the press conference, Thorpe hailed a cab and the five were off to PG&E headquarters, racing through the hilly boulevards of San Francisco to Market Street.

As the taxi pulled up to the headquarters the four men emerged from the cab, where they were soon joined by a crowd of reporters. Thorpe hurried to pay for their cab as the small group entered the building. She walked through the main entrance and immediately saw that the leaders were already at the elevators surrounded by security. Trying to appear inconspicuous, Thorpe ducked into a nearby stairwell and began searching for the president's office. Security informed the four leaders that they would only allow one of the men to meet with an official representative of the company. They selected Gemmill, the Tribal Chairman, to carry out the arrest. Head of PG&E Security James Neel escorted Gemmill and a drove of reporters to the corporate secretary's office.[36]

Once Gemmill reached the office, PG&E employees stood outside their own offices to get a glimpse of all the excitement. The hulky James Neel opened the door for Gemmill but blocked reporters from entering. Gemmill presented his charges for an arrest to the corporate secretary, who appeared shocked by all the attention. Neel informed Gemmill that PG&E Security would not permit any of the employees to leave the office with him. Gemmill would need a warrant and police support before Neel would honor such a request. The Tribal Chairman promised further occupations and legal actions if the company continued to deny Pit River's title.[37]

Despite their failure to arrest the PG&E president, they succeeded in advertising their legal case to the press. Meanwhile, unsuccessful in her search, Grace Thorpe returned to the lobby just in time to catch up with the others. Together again, the five made their way back to the office on California Street. When they arrived at the office they began discussing future strategies and assessed the events earlier that day. Grace noticed that Richard had poured himself a full glass of whisky and was quickly downing it. Worn out with their efforts, Thorpe, Lego, and Charlie Buckskin called it a day and left the office. Richard Oakes and Mickey Gemmill decided to continue their conversation at Warren's Bar.[38]

At Warren's, Richard and Mickey met up with Arnold Gemmill (Mickey's brother) and Akwesasne Mohawk Louis Mitchell. Louis was a close friend of Richard's and was staying at his family's Gatorville apartment. The bar was packed with people as the four shared stories and drinks. As a former employee, Oakes was comfortable at Warren's. He had frequently recruited for Alcatraz and SFSC at the bar. By evening, he was unaware of who else was in the bar. While Richard talked to some old friends, he heard his name being called out. He turned around just as a pool cue smashed against his skull, sending him crashing to the floor. The assailant struck again, delivering another punishing blow to the right side of Richard's head. As he lay lifeless on the floor, the perpetrator quickly fled the scene. Louis Mitchell, Mickey, and Arnold Gemmill found Oakes unconscious. They assumed that the alcohol had taken an ill effect and that the experienced fighter was just knocked out. The three worked hard to get Oakes back to his apartment.[39]

Hoping not to frighten Annie, Mitchell told her that Oakes had been in a fight and was drunk; he just needed to sleep it off. By this point, Annie was not happy with Richard's drinking. Mitchell helped get him to their bedroom. Then, exhausted, he went to the couch in the living room and passed out. By morning Annie tried to wake her husband up, but he failed to respond. Frantic, she woke up Mitchell and demanded to know exactly what had happened to Richard. She noticed that he had been bleeding from his nose and that the right side of his head was bruised and swollen.[40] The children became frightened as Annie phoned the police and paramedics. An ambulance arrived and rushed their father to the hospital.[41]

When Richard Oakes arrived at the San Francisco General Hospital, reporters had to be pushed out of the way as they scrambled to snap photographs of the beaten leader. Doctors informed Annie that Richard's injuries were severe. He was suffering from a skull fracture and a blood clot to the brain and required immediate surgery.[42] They could not assure her that he would make it through the six-hour surgery. Annie was devastated but had to remain strong; she knew that her husband was a fighter. Police began to question her and Louis Mitchell about the events surrounding Oakes's injuries. Oakes made it through the surgery but afterward faced a long struggle as he lay in a coma in the intensive care unit, his head wrapped in bandages. Annie offered prayers for her husband's recovery.

The days ahead proved a testament to the bond that existed between Annie and Richard Oakes. Annie maintained a constant vigil by his bedside as hundreds of friends, supporters, and members of the community came to the couple's aid. On July 17, detectives arrested Tommy Pritchard, a twenty-eight-year-old Samoan, on assault charges with the intent to commit murder. Apparently, two months earlier Oakes and Pritchard had been in a brawl at Warren's, and Richard had broken Pritchard's nose. On the evening of the assault, Pritchard had been secretly waiting for Oakes to return to the bar to exact his revenge. The San Francisco police feared a race war would ensue after news of the arrest reached both communities. To deter such an outcome, the department issued a press statement that the fight was between two individuals and not two communities. Cops in the Mission District worked overtime and increased their forces to prohibit any further retaliation.[43]

The San Francisco Indian community was stunned by the news. The Indian center rallied, creating a fund to assist Annie and the children with food, financial support, and even a blood drive for Richard Oakes. Indians of All Tribes on Alcatraz also offered their assistance and support to the family.[44] Financial difficulties took a back seat, however, as Annie weighed the possibility of losing her husband. Reluctantly, she agreed to a rare interview with reporters. Wearing sunglasses and seated on a bench outside the hospital, Annie recalled the events of the past few months:

> "I don't think I'm the only one going through all the tragedy. . . . I think every Indian suffers. . . . Since the death of my daughter . . . we have never talked about the island." Mrs. Oakes still contends that her daughter didn't fall. She believes foul play was involved. "They hated us," she said, meaning the other Indians occupying Alcatraz. . . . "I told Richard the day before that we should pack up and take the children and leave. I knew something would happen—and it did. . . . I didn't like it at first," she said, talking about the leadership role her husband took. . . . "But Richard saw a cause. He always knew he could help his people. I didn't want to stop him. . . . I never knew anyone who cares for the Indian people like Richard does. . . . You know we went through a lot. . . . I wish the Indians would stop and think what all this means . . . ." . . . the family was supposed to leave for Sonoma County to visit Mrs. Oakes mother. From there they were scheduled to be back in Shasta County for a big . . . [meeting] on the next strategy [at] Pit River. . . . "We have never talked about the important part of it. . . . He mostly kept everything to himself, unless there was a meeting or something."[45]

Both the San Francisco *Chronicle* and *Examiner* followed Oakes's condition closely with daily reports to update the community on any improvements. As the days turned into weeks, Oakes remained in a coma, and his body shook from a 106-degree fever. With every little movement of Richard's body, Annie continued to hold out hope that he would wake. The doctors treating Oakes had done all that they could do; they too could only observe.

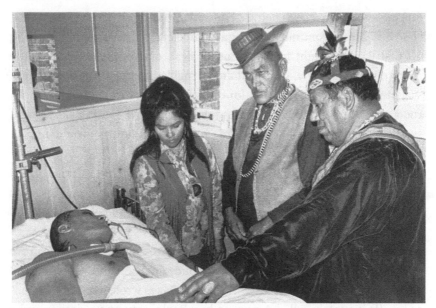

Richard Oakes at the San Francisco General Hospital, June 25, 1970, with (left to right), Annie Oakes, Peter Mitten, and Mad Bear Anderson. Photo courtesy of Getty Images, Bettmann Collection 640119160.

On June 24, 1970, having learned of Richard's condition, medicine person Mad Bear Anderson from Tuscarora, along with Cayuga healer Peter Mitten, made their way into Oakes's hospital room. Hospital staff and doctors agreed to allow the two healers to work with Oakes. At this point, doctors were open to anything that might assist in Oakes's recovery. Standing at Richard's bedside, Mad Bear held onto Oakes's hand, becoming misty-eyed as he remembered the young man who was so eager to assist Longhouse leaders.[46] Mitten, wearing a tilted cowboy hat, and Mad Bear retreated to a private room, away from curious doctors to mix the medicine. Doctors and nurses watched as Mitten added a teaspoon of the liquid medicine to Oakes's feeding tube. Five minutes later a red spot appeared on Richard Oakes's chest just above his heart and began to spread. After an hour his body became relaxed and his temperature started to drop; the baffled doctors could only scratch their heads. The medicine had a dramatic effect. In a couple of days, Oakes was able to wiggle his toes and yawn on command.[47]

As Richard Oakes struggled to hang onto life, he was haunted by a recurring dream. He saw a human body laid out in front of him, broken into pieces. The body was being devoured by hundreds of maggots. As the "horrific" dream continued, the figure pulled itself back together, shaking off that which sought to consume its flesh or spirit. The body of the person, now complete, trembled and struggled to rise from the ground. Walking toward Richard, this lone figure stopped and said, "I am an Indian."[48] Struggling for his life and enduring his dreams, Oakes's fight symbolized the idea that freedom for Indian Country would not be without physical harm.

A few days later, Richard Oakes, while he may have suffered from paralysis over the left side of his body, was awake, scribbling messages with his right hand to Annie on a notebook. Their son Rocky Oakes stood at the doorway watching as his hero fought to execute the simplest of movements. His head was shaved, and he bore a large scar rising from his ear to the top of his head. Richard noticed his son and with his hand shaking, motioned for him to come closer. Oakes wrote a note to "Anna," as he affectionately called Annie, to buy Rocky some new clothes and a baseball bat. Rocky smiled when his mom read the note, reassured that his dad could overcome his injuries.[49]

By August, Oakes had become restless. He had been confined to a hospital for almost two months. Back in June, Bruce Oakes made a long trip to San Francisco to visit with his cousin and was overcome when he entered the brightly lit hospital room. Bruce stayed by Richard's side constantly, having arrived only a few days after Oakes was admitted to the hospital. With Bruce's assistance, *Chronicle* reporter Mary Crawford interviewed Richard Oakes about the statement President Nixon had made to Congress on July 8, 1970, calling for a new era of self-determination. In typical eloquence and symbolism, Oakes challenged Nixon to follow through:

> The policy is discouraging. It is one step toward dust, without much to do about anything. The spirit of today's movement has instilled pride and dignity to every individual with Indian blood. Yet we find an absence of what was a culture, what was a heritage . . . a denial of the very language that ma[d]e [us] . . . so proud. This cannot be tolerated. . . . The past and present policies have castrated the American Indian.[50]

Despite his injuries, Oakes was claiming to the media and to Indian Country that he was still as potent of a political force as ever. In the meantime, Oakes was eager to launch plans for his Native American Traveling College. He was moved to the Moffitt Hospital at the University of San Francisco, where he went through intense physical therapy to learn to walk again and to regain his speech and the movement on his left side. While he was in the hospital, a gentleman from Florida who was familiar with Oakes's project to found a traveling college donated a bus to the cause. Reenergized by the stranger's generosity, he informed Annie that they would travel soon.

On August 19, 1970, Oakes checked himself out of the hospital, against the doctors' advice, to make arrangements for the traveling college. Seated in the couple's Gatorville apartment, Oakes told Tim Findley about his plans:

> I'll be learning everything I can. . . . I hope to record and document what I learn and bring it back to teach a real American history. . . . I don't know yet what the basic factor of "Indianness" is. . . . I know we're finished with symbols. Now we're looking for positive creative solutions together. We've had enough of coming out with more [word] problems. We will go and learn wherever we can, and maybe the result will be that we will return with not just one bus, but with a caravan—an army—of Indian people to reclaim their history and their land with new pride. . . . It is an era, Oakes concluded, of meaningful slogans— "white is right, black is beautiful. I plan to add one more— Indians are permanent."[51]

On September 22, the Oakes family and three other people pulled out of San Francisco State College and embarked on their journey. With only three hundred dollars for gas and food, the college's survival was dependent on Oakes's continuing good health and the kindness of the road. Ultimately, these factors led to the attempt getting cut short as Oakes became plagued with severe headaches and was stranded with a bus in need of numerous repairs. Oakes was seeking to build a college that was an institution rooted in the "experiences" of Indian Country. His ideas would soon turn into a different direction.[52]

It had been almost five years since Oakes had been home to St. Regis. As he was recovering from his surgery, Richard and Annie recalled a letter that Akwesasne leaders had sent to them at Alcatraz in which they had asked for Oakes to return. By the fall of 1970, the couple packed up their station wagon and said their goodbyes to family and friends and left California. Along the way the children stared out of the windows at the changing landscape while they listened to Richard reminisce about his childhood in Brooklyn and Akwesasne.

Once they arrived at St. Regis, Richard Oakes met up with Jerry Gambill and other members of the White Roots of Peace. The organization asked him to join the Longhouse movement and help spread the message of the Great Peacemaker. In the midst of his community he was able to share his visions with a larger audience of young people. Jerry Gambill remembered the times fondly: "Anne . . . bravely managed to care for the family in our crowded vehicle. Richard had a strong craving for ice cream, and our tiny refrigerator worked overtime keeping him in supply."[53] Oakes's involvement with the White Roots of Peace was crucial. His life served as a testament to the very nature of the Great Law of Peace and Iroquois tradition.

During their stay, Oakes was able to receive medical care in Canada, and he made frequent trips to Montreal in order to receive treatment. On one occasion, Gambill was traveling with the Oakes family when Richard Oakes gunned the station wagon past a Cornwall Island checkpoint. Oakes remained keenly aware of his sovereign rights, and he refused to compromise his actions. He defended his right to free passage and that of others at Akwesasne to cross the border freely without interference.

After several weeks, Annie and the children felt the pull of home, Kashaya. They missed their family and friends, and Richard Oakes promised they would return. At Akwesasne he had applied for housing, only to find a long wait as well as growing debt from a life on the road. Due to his physical condition, he was unable to return to a career in ironwork. Gambill hated to see Oakes leave after such a short stay, but he supplied the couple with a list of contacts for their trip home.

Pit River recruited Oakes to return and assist the Tribe in further demonstrations. Despite Oakes's absence, Pit River continued to wage a fierce courtroom battle when they called together an organizational meeting in Santa Rosa, California, to plan new actions. At the meeting Oakes learned of previous occupations: the takeover of a PG&E dam, the placement of the Pit River flag atop Mt. Lassen, and progress on their $5

YOU ARE ON INDIAN LAND 223

billion damage suit against corporations on Pit River lands.⁵⁴ During the gathering they decided to occupy PG&E lands in Burney, California. The location was much closer to the court in Redding, helping to curb the mounting travel expenses. By late October, Pit River rented a Quonset hut to construct a dwelling or shelter on the land.

Locals would later refer to the events that transpired on October 27, 1970, as the "Battle of the Four Corners." Seventy men, women, and children began the day with meetings in the Quonset hut. That afternoon the children played in the surrounding glades. Oakes talked with Raymond Lego and Mickey Gemmill, while Annie helped prepare a late breakfast for the settlement. The occupation site, located at the junction of Highway 299E and 89, turned silent at 10:40 that morning. A huge force of seventy sheriff deputies, Forest Service Rangers, and federal officials stopped at the encampment, parking along Highway 89. Nervously, Chairman Mickey Gemmill made his way over to where the officers had gathered for a parlay with Sheriff John Balma and District Attorney Ronald Baker. While listening to their demands, Gemmill cautiously took note of the huge force, armed with shotguns, riot gear, mace, and clubs. The situation was tense as Balma explained that they were there to evict the settlers and to tear down the Quonset hut. After hearing both Baker and Balma out, Gemmill peered over his shoulder to confirm the determination and commitment apparent in his companions' countless faces. Without hesitation, he informed Balma that they were not going to abandon their property.

Mickey Gemmill returned to the encampment; the occupiers knew they were in for a fight. The large company of officers began marching slowly toward the camp. Pit River citizen Ross Montgomery grabbed a chainsaw and made his way to a nearby tree as others followed, picking up two-by-fours and sticks. Just as Montgomery began to pull the ripcord, deputies moved in fast, bringing the large framed man to his knees. Peter Blue Cloud remembered, "Then all hell broke loose, as the armed 'protectors of the law' waded into our people, spraying mace, and breaking heads, swinging clubs and striking even those who already lay unconscious. One of the men, beaten and clubbed unconscious, was an elder of the Pit River Tribe, a cripple. Women had to push through the police to be sure he wasn't killed."⁵⁵ John Hurst, covering the event for the *Record-Searchlight*, was stunned:

Mace filled the crisp air. Women with tears rolling down their
cheeks from Mace and anger cursed the officers as Indians were
beaten to the ground and dragged to waiting squad cars. Gordon
Montgomery, an elderly and crippled Pit River Indian, was
clubbed into semi-consciousness. . . . Women had to push their
way past officers to minister to his head wounds. . . . As the officers and workers advanced, women and children moved into
the hut and a line of young men stood at the doorway. "You're
not wanted here," said Erik Mattila to the officers as he stood
shoulder-to-shoulder with Pit River Indian Darryl Wilson and
other young men. . . . Mattila went down as a riot stick cracked
across his head. Blood gushed down the side of his face. Men
and women were handcuffed and dragged to squad cars as
forest workmen slammed away the corrugated metal walls of
the hut with hammers and crowbars, and then shoved the entire
frame of the structure to the ground.[56]

Oakes emerged from the battle uninjured. He was able to muster enough
strength to stand unarmed against the onslaught of lawmen.[57] Annie and
the children raced out of the Quonset hut to protect Richard and to make
sure that he was not brutally attacked. Wearing black sunglasses, dressed
in a dark suit and tie, the district attorney, Robert Baker, observed the
chaos with a slight grin. Only five of the occupiers were arrested for the
serious charges of assaulting a federal officer and resisting arrest; most,
ironically, faced obstruction charges.[58] Meanwhile, Baker made sure that
nobody arrested by Balma was charged with trespass.

Outraged, Aubrey Grossman quickly filed another lawsuit against
Balma and Baker for brutality and excessive use of force. Annie persuaded
Richard to move to Kashaya, fearing further violence and retaliation by
local police. The occupations had taken a dramatic and violent turn. The
Pit River community regrouped. They sought new action but allowed
time to pass in an effort to cool frustrations. Reluctantly, organizers realized they had been fortunate. Despite the violence exerted by law enforcement that horrific day, no one had been critically injured or, worse
yet, killed.

One month later, Richard Oakes organized two more occupations.
On November 3, 1970, a dozen activists raided an abandoned CIA

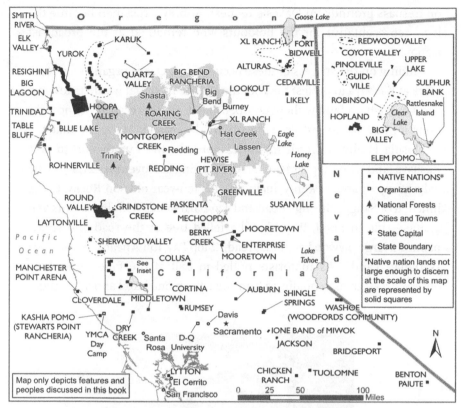

Northern California Native Nations and Landmarks. Map by Ed Brands.

listening post in Forestville, California, near Santa Rosa. One critical member of the four-day occupation was Kashaya Maru, or Dreamer, Essie Parish, a leader in the Bole-Maru religion, a movement with roots in the Ghost Dance movement of the 1870s. At the Stewarts Point Rancheria, Essie Parrish taught children Kashaya language, ceremony, and culture. Her acknowledgment and approval of liberation theology lent further authenticity to the cause. The occupation ended with the arrest of five activists on trespass charges, but ultimately title to the land was handed over to the Pomo. The institution created on the 125-acre site was the Ya Ka Ama American Indian Education Center. The next day, just twenty miles from Kashaya, protesters moved in on a former monitor station of the Foreign Broadcast Information Service at Healdsburg, California. Sonoma County deputies arrived at the station, arresting four of them on trespass grounds. At Oakes's request, Aubrey Grossman became the legal representative for the holdouts who remained at the broadcast station.[59]

Riding on the success of these occupations, Oakes organized a road-block at Kashaya to protest the widening of the road that would take three acres of Kashaya land without compensation. Oakes recalled the occupations he had witnessed growing up at Akwesasne. He knew that the California Highway Department did not have the jurisdiction to take Kashaya land without payment. On the evening of November 21, 1970, he led a group of about twenty, including his ten-year-old son Rocky, to the junction of Skaggs Springs Road and Tin Barn Road. With flashlights and a single rifle in hand, they placed a felled tree in the road and spray-painted a large plywood sign that read, "Stop Pay Toll Ahead—$1.00 This Is Indian Land." As motorists pulled to halt at the fallen tree, they observed a large man holding a hunting rifle in one hand and a flashlight

Richard Oakes in wheelchair several months after his release from the hospital. The swelling from his surgery is still visible on his face. Photo courtesy of Stephen K. Lehmer/www.stephenlehmer.com.

in the other. Don Richardson, a rancher, was stopped at the makeshift tollbooth. Richardson recalled that "Oakes politely explained the purpose of the tolls, I said I wouldn't object to paying and he gave me a receipt."[60] Later, a California Highway Patrol officer arrived on the scene, and Oakes greeted the him with a smile and said, "What took you so long? You can never find an officer when you need one."[61] Oakes was immediately arrested for armed robbery and related felony charges; his bail was set at $6,125. He was later released from jail when he agreed to pay back his toll fees, but he still faced another charge, that of blocking a public roadway. His trial was scheduled for September 1971.[62]

After waiting only three days, Oakes organized a second roadblock at the same location. Two of Annie's cousins, Jon and Thorn Marrufo, accompanied Oakes and twenty more protesters to the road. Most who passed through the roadblock willingly paid the one-dollar toll and received a firsthand lesson in Tribal sovereignty from Richard Oakes. Larry Castillani lacked any sympathy as he entered the roadblock. Exiting his car, he explained to Oakes that he simply did not have the dollar to pay. While the two talked, one overzealous supporter slashed Castillani's rear tires. Embarrassed, Richard Oakes quickly helped Castillani change his tire and located another spare for the nervous father. Just as they were changing the second tire, the highway patrol arrived and promptly arrested Oakes a second time.[63]

Aubrey Grossman once again came to Oakes's legal aid, arguing that the trooper was outside his jurisdiction and that Oakes's intentions were to protect Kashaya land. The occupations were covered by the local press as well as the *San Francisco Examiner* and were later featured in *Akwesasne Notes*. Richard Oakes was proving that he was still a key player in the political processes of defending the tenets of Tribal sovereignty. However, not everyone at Kashaya appreciated Oakes's efforts. Chief James Allen scheduled a meeting with the leader and related that the Kashaya Council were concerned that Oakes was committing the Tribe too deeply in a political stand they simply could not afford. Oakes listened as Allen cautiously told him that he was violating Tribal law. He explained further that if the council asked him, he would have no choice but to have Oakes removed from the forty-acre rancheria.[64]

By December Richard Oakes was now well known among the sheriff's officers in the tri-county area (covering Sonoma, Shasta, and Lake counties) and faced another attack on his ability to remain an organizing presence at Kashaya. In a strange twist of events, the Sonoma County Sheriff's Office issued a warrant for the arrest of ten-year-old Rocky Oakes. The Castillanis believed that Rocky was responsible for the tire slashing incident of November 25. Richard and Annie refused to turn their young son over to authorities. The couple knew that the warrant was a billboard for local law enforcement eager to retaliate against Richard's increasing activism. As soon as the incident passed, Rocky avoided arrest because of press coverage of the event. The public was outraged that the Sheriff's Office was seeking to jail a ten-year-old boy based solely on the testimony of Castillani's nine-year-old daughter.[65]

On December 20, Richard Oakes's manifesto was printed in the *San Francisco Examiner*, and he threatened more blockades. Oakes was convinced that if Kashaya and Pit River were to become truly sovereign Nations, then they must become self-sufficient and develop an economic infrastructure that could lead to freedom from federal funds. Concurrently, he called for the creation of a security force responsive to the needs of the community and Tribal laws, an end to the current Indian foster care program, and the construction of a community center that placed grandparents with grandchildren. Instead of separating the generations, Oakes felt, they should be brought together; only then would tradition and pride be imparted. The manifesto also sought to reestablish ancient trade routes by forming an economic confederacy of Indian Nations. Oakes demonstrated that through greenhouse farming and domestication of local deer herds, Tribes could then trade for wool from the Navajo or cattle from the Lakota. Developing these traditional commodities might help to alleviate unemployment and economic dependency. Although many of his proposals were far ahead of their time, Oakes was not shy in his pursuit of liberation.[66]

By New Year's Day of 1971, Richard Oakes had been involved in countless occupations, from Seattle to Round Valley; he had fought to overcome an otherwise debilitating injury; and he was now able to walk again. He forged a new era for self-determination through the call for sovereignty and land reclamation. Although Oakes had dropped out of his program at San Francisco State, his education continued. He battled severe headaches and double vision to organize mass movements throughout California.

On January 29, 1971, eight months after he was beaten at Warren's, Oakes went into surgery again. Doctors inserted a metal plate into his skull, hoping that this might ease the agonizing pressures of his headaches.[67] Before the surgery, Oakes learned the shocking news that Hank Adams had been shot at Frank's Landing in Washington. Late one evening on January 19, 1971, two men had approached Adams, who was there to prevent the theft of fishing equipment. One of them rammed a shotgun into Adams's stomach and pulled the trigger. Fortunately Adams, although he was bleeding profusely, was able to call for help and survived the attempt on his life. The two men were never found, and the local authorities, who opposed Adams's politics, proposed that the leader had shot himself in an attempt to gain press attention.[68] Furious, the tiny Washington Native community erupted in protest at the accusation. Eight months earlier, Valerie Bridges, the nineteen-year-old daughter of Frank's Landing fishing rights activist Al Bridges, had died in a suspicious drowning on the Nisqually River. The blind justice exuded by local authorities in Adams's case had allowed the two assailants to escape, and no one was ever brought up on charges for the crime. News of these attacks troubled Richard and Annie, who remembered both Bridges and Adams from their visit at Alcatraz and their travels to Fort Lawton.

By mid-February of 1971, Richard and Annie Oakes solicited help from Mike Knight and the Mendo–Lake Pomo Tribal Council to challenge Mendocino County Sheriffs with racial bias and physical abuse of three of Annie's brothers: Robert, Harold, and Dale Marrufo. The men were charged with attempted murder in the shooting of Eugene Leighton outside the Gualala Hotel. The shooting victim was a Point Arena resident, who remained in fair condition at a Santa Rosa hospital after having sustained two gunshot wounds from a .30–30 Winchester rifle in his arm and side. The Sheriff's Office denied Richard Oakes visitation rights, masking the physical abuse that the Marrufos received while in custody. In an effort to protect Annie's brothers, Oakes threatened to stage a sit-in at the Sheriff's Office. On Thursday, February 18, 1971, at their preliminary hearing, Richard Oakes wore a sock cap and dark sweater and sat outside the courtroom discussing the case with public defender Richard Peterson. A photographer, Robert Curry for the *Ukiah Daily Journal*, snapped a photo of their conversation. Judge Hale McCowen Jr. held Curry in contempt of court for violating a court order against any photography inside or in the corridor during the trial. Obviously, the judge was worried about the local media transforming his court into a circus. All three brothers were held in prison for eight months until October of 1971, when Harold Marrufo pled guilty to having fired the rifle that had injured Leighton.[69]

Organizers back at Pit River, continuing to maintain legal pressure, challenged PG&E and other corporate claims to Tribal land. The ongoing resistance movement at Pit River relied heavily on the unified support of Tribal citizens. Pit River citizens openly defied any formal acceptance of the federal government's final offer of 47 cents an acre for their home-lands. Oakes remained in constant contact with the Pit River leadership. Over the next few years, the movement at Pit River slowly began to buckle under the pressure of federal officials, who intensified their lobbying efforts to secure a settlement offered by the Indian Claims Commission. Oakes's return to California was important, as he was widely known for his strategy, leadership, and organizing talents. Making their home at Kashaya, Oakes was next called upon to organize for the Elem Pomo.

CHAPTER SEVEN

Freedom

THROUGHOUT THE NEXT TWO YEARS, Native activists and leaders fervently defended Red Power objectives against a destructive wave of anti-Indian national sentiment. Despite all the "success" that emerged from the Alcatraz takeover, it triggered an intense backlash from a radical extremist element that gradually rose in direct opposition to Red Power. The 1972 Trail of Broken Treaties March on Washington, D.C., and the 1973 occupation of Wounded Knee, South Dakota, would catapult the American Indian Movement into international spheres of recognition as it emerged as the exclusive and mythic icon and vanguard of Red Power. Many members of IAT, including Richard Oakes and his family, continued to fight for greater Native rights and simply to earn a living. The events that unfolded from 1971 through 1973 forever altered the Oakes family and our present understandings about Red Power. Most poignantly, the historical events that transpired raise key questions about the foundations of American justice, democracy, citizenship, and freedom.

On Saturday night, May 1, 1971, Oakes and twenty others liberated an unoccupied Army radio transmitter base near Middleton, California. The former Army receiving station had sat vacant since 1958. The Elem Pomo hoped to transform the 640-acre site into a Tribally controlled cultural and spiritual center, thereby increasing their land base. Lake County Sheriff's deputies arrived on Sunday and posted a twenty-four-hour roadblock on all roads entering and leaving the site. After a two-day standoff, supplies grew thin; Annie and the children needed food and other provisions. Whether a product of poor planning or a part of their strategy, the occupation force had packed only two days' worth of provisions. Elem Tribal citizen Rose Barnes was arrested on Sunday when she tried to deliver much-needed food and medical supplies to the occupiers. Reportedly, the sheriff's deputies allowed only one loaf of bread into the former Army post. Complicating matters further, the deputies had set up an armed barricade, blocking with chains the single entrance to the former Army post.[1]

Fearing a possible invasion, or worse, a violent encounter with deputies, Oakes decided that he would make the trip into nearby Middletown, California, to secure more supplies. He was quickly surrounded by sheriff's deputies and forced to exit his vehicle. Deputies then moved in fast, evicting the rest of the holdouts. Richard Oakes was charged with trespass and unlawful entry of a government facility. He was convicted by an all-white jury, sentenced to ten days in jail, and fined 125 dollars.[2] Despite the short duration of the takeover outside Clear Lake, the occupiers continued to garner more press attention for Indian land claims in northern California. Oakes's strategy was critical, for it relied on three major objectives: changing public opinion, depleting law enforcement, and straining court resources.

This strategy continued to be central to the liberation theology behind the Pit River land claims. Only two days later, Judge William Gallagher refused Pit River's challenge to move the trial of thirty-five defendants arrested during the Burney occupation to the Superior Court. While Judge Gallagher rejected their appeal, he also informed the Pit River legal defense team to automatically appeal if found guilty of trespass in the lower court. In an article that appeared in the local *Record-Searchlight*, Aubrey Grossman, attorney for Pit River, reinforced Pit River's core media strategy when he claimed that the court's decision would make it "incredibly tough on the taxpayers of Shasta County" and estimated the public cost of upwards of fifty thousand dollars for the trial.[3] It was a risky public relations move, as local opinion could easily shift for or against the Pit River objectives.

Only ten days later, the Pit River defense team received notice that twelve more defendants were to stand trial on October 5 for charges of assault on federal officers during the Battle of Four Corners. Throughout the rest of May the trials appeared frequently in local newspaper head-lines.[4] Building on the momentum of the failed army center takeover, a new occupation target slowly emerged, uniting both Wintu and Pit River nationalists.

The Wintu Tribe of northern California was historically located adja-cent to the Pit River Nation, between the snowy peaks of Mount Shasta and the Cascade Mountains. Originally comprised of nine bands, by the early 1970s only three bands of Wintu remained: the Nor-El Muk Nation, Winnemem Wintu, and the Wintu Tribe of Northern California. In 1851, the Wintu entered into treaty negotiations with the U.S. government. The provisions of their treaty, which was never ratified, exchanged all Wintu traditional lands for a tiny twenty-five-square-mile reservation in northern California. By 1941, the Tribe shared a fate similar to that of the Akwesasne encounter with the St. Lawrence Seaway, when their allotted lands were reclaimed under the Central Valley Project's Indian Lands Acquisition Act for hydroelectric development. It was a history all too familiar for Richard Oakes and local Pit River activists, a shared history that cultivated the seeds for new occupation strategies.[5]

After a short stint in jail, Richard Oakes was reunited with Pit River and Wintu leaders who sought to occupy the former Toyon Job Corps Center near Redding, California. In May of 1969, the sixty-one-acre site had been stripped of funding by the Nixon administration and had been placed under the custodial care of the Bureau of Indian Affairs. Officials in the Bureau of Indian Affairs made preliminary plans to turn the camp over to the Inter-Tribal Council of California, founded in 1965 on the Susanville Reservation. Soon the Inter-Tribal Council, in a show of soli-darity, revoked their claim to Toyon.[6]

The camp itself was rather large and contained over forty cabins, complete with electricity, indoor plumbing, manicured lawns, and other modern conveniences. Coincidentally, during the 1940s, the former Job Corps campground had also served as housing for the many construction workers contracted to build Shasta Dam, a federal project that confiscated and destroyed hundreds of acres of traditional Wintu lands. A dozen or more activists faced little resistance when their caravan pulled into the Toyon campground. Maintenance men making repairs on the cabins thought the group had rented the camp and willingly offered the occupation force a tour of the facilities. After the tour they gave the occupiers keys to all the cabins and other buildings located on the property. Wintu leader Chris Ryan declared, "This land is now occupied by the Wintu Nation and Indians of all tribes. . . . We are occupying this land for all free Indians." Ryan's words referenced the ideology and philosophy of the initial Alcatraz occupation. For the Wintu leaders involved in reclamation, it must have seemed like their lucky day; if only previous liberations had gone so smoothly.[7]

Instead of a large show of force by local law enforcement, occupation leaders met with Sacramento BIA officials, Deputy District Attorney William Lund, and the director of the Shasta County Community Action Project (CAP) behind closed doors. The official policy handed down from the BIA headquarters in Washington to local officials was to cease all negotiations and evict the occupation force on the legal grounds of trespass. Local authorities, however, refused to carry out their orders from Washington. At a stalemate, the liberators next attended a meeting at William Emmal's office at the Shasta County Legal Aid Society to negotiate their terms. During the meeting Toyon liberators also met with Wes Barker, acting area director for the BIA, and their organizing took a positive turn. The liberation force received ninety days to present a proposal and to secure funding for Toyon. Additionally, they had to maintain a permanent residence at Toyon, while adhering to the required upkeep and maintenance for the facility. Richard Oakes was stunned: what was the catch? As it turned out, there was no hidden agenda; they had proven title to the site. At the end of the meeting Pit River elder Mildred Rhoades approached Wes Barker and extended her hand: "I never thought I'd be shaking the hand of a BIA man."[8] The rapid victory in securing Toyon as Indian land justified and created a kind of retroactive precedence for previous Pit River occupations. A possible legal victory in the courts seemed all the more plausible.[9]

By June the assault trial from the Burney occupation was well underway, and the Pit River legal defense team had organized activists to carry signs and picket the trial. Beneath the somber structure of the Sacramento Court House, the picketers, including Oakes, distributed leaflets to passersby. The leaflets, which were simply, yet provocatively, entitled, "The Pit River Story: A Century of Genocide," prompted Municipal Court Judge Michael Virga, an appointee of Governor Ronald Reagan, to threaten a mistrial based on the fear that the leaflets might influence a juror. Upon learning of Virga's intent, the picketers immediately discarded all leaflets, and the picket lines continued marching outside the court-room. Aubrey Grossman began to present his defense, which consisted of the Pit River's historical and legal title over the lands that PG&E Corporation presumed to also have title and control. Carefully and quite deliberately, Grossman directed his opening remarks toward Shermer Sibley, president of PG&E Corporation, who sat in the court pews awaiting his summons to testify before the court. Richard Oakes approached, with confidence, the area where Sibley was sitting with his legal counsel. Oakes held two cardboard signs from the picket line in his hands as he neared the president of PG&E Corporation.[10] While Sibley's legal counsel peered back as if interested in the message, Sibley avoided any confrontation and promptly left his seat. Reporters gathered in the courtroom seized on this opportune moment as the camera bulbs flashed. Through this single action, Richard Oakes brought the Pit River struggle before the president of a powerful corporation. Symbolically, Oakes's gesture and response echoed the greater struggle. Most importantly, the trial had brought together both the head of PG&E Corporation and the Pit River cause under the same roof. Clearly, PG&E would not be able to ignore the Pit River cause, hoping that in time the Pit River claim might somehow just disap-pear. The photo also captured the emotion and power behind the Pit River struggle, and the caption that appeared in the *Redding Record-Searchlight* read, "Sibley decides to move as Richard Oakes approaches."[11]

Once Sibley took the stand, his memory and knowledge of PG&E's resources seemed insufficient at best, especially when he asserted that he was unaware that PG&E had legal title to the land. Grossman, who saw an opportunity, continued to press Sibley with further questions. Sibley admitted to not knowing the worth of PG&E facilities in the Redding area. Sibley went on to add that he had not ordered the arrest of Pit River activ-ists the previous June. Grossman possibly feared that Sibley had been coached by his legal counsel all too well, for the continued plea of igno-rance left very little room for Sibley to incriminate himself or PG&E. Using the tactic he had learned during his days as a lawyer for labor inter-ests, Aubrey Grossman asked Sibley if he felt that Pit River had a "good moral claim." This line of questioning elicited an immediate objection from District Attorney Robert Baker. Judge Virga sustained the objection and proclaimed that the trial was not about Sibley's mental state. Once Sibley made his final remarks on the stand, Grossman called in Pit River elder and Tribal Councilman Raymond Lego to testify. It is unclear if Shermer Sibley stayed to listen to any further courtroom proceedings. Lego's testimony, however, established the oral tradition and Tribal claim over their lands in the official court record and also before the jurors.[12]

Beyond the courtroom and trial, tensions began to escalate between the District Attorney's Office and Pit River. The very next day, District Attorney Robert Baker notified the Pit River Tribal Council that they would be charged with criminal trespass if anyone decided to follow through on a Tribal warning issued to logging companies. In the letter, Baker employed stern prose: "any actions of trespass and business inter-ference as threatened in your letters . . . would be prosecuted by this office to the fullest extent of the law." When he was interviewed by reporters about land titles, Baker stated, "Well, just from general knowledge of the area . . . I've gone through the assessor maps," and he proceeded to denounce Pit River's claim as well as his firm intent to back corporate interest in the assault case. Inside the courtroom, the D.A. attempted to sway public and juror opinion against the Pit River claim. While cross-examining Raymond Lego, Baker attempted to lure Lego into admitting on the stand that the Tribe's intentions were to evict private home owners and corporations from Pit River lands. Lego, the Tribal elder, was both quiet and then shrewd when he replied, "I don't know of any case where a white man came to us in friendship and was rejected." Eventually Baker continued the same style of questioning when he examined Grace Thorpe and defendants Andy James and Daryl Wilson. Thorpe's wry and infec-tious wit cut Baker short in mid-question: "I am convinced that the Pit River people have no intention of trying to take people's private property, if that's what you're getting at." Daryl Wilson brought silence to the court-room when he testified about the loss of his own mother and brother who had been killed on a bridge by a logging truck: "Why is it so necessary to have a bridge . . . And why was it so necessary to have a logging truck?" With each new testimonial Pit River defendants were out to win the hearts and minds of the court and the greater public.[13]

A few days later Pit River attorney Aubrey Grossman was juggling three separate federal trials against PG&E, D.A. Baker, and Shasta County Sheriff John Balma. Running between trials, Judge Virga granted Aubrey

Grossman time to recess and reschedule the trial. When the trial resumed a few days later, the last defendant to take the stand was a young Shoshone activist, Colleen Evening Thunder. Evening Thunder was already a veteran of the Alcatraz and Pit River occupations. The twenty-five-year-old summed up why she put herself on the line for the Pit River cause: "Our hearts are in the land. Without the land we are nothing." The jury and public were witnessing a crash course in modern Indian history and self-determination. Grossman used his closing statement to offer hope, invoking the great American mythos. Tactfully recalling his initial conversation with Pit River leaders, Grossman referenced the moment they asked him to be their legal defense: "I'll guarantee the legal results if you get your story to the people. Because I believe in them. You may not believe in them because of the way you've been treated by whites. But I believe in the people. If I didn't believe in the American people I don't know what I'd believe in." His closing statement together with Colleen Evening Thunder's powerful testimony, offered much for the jury to debate.[14]

On June 11, 1971, the second day of deliberations for the jury, a crowd of supporters, including defendants Richard and Annie Oakes, gathered in the hallways of the courthouse awaiting any news from the jury. Unfortunately, a different type of news reached the crowd. Supporters learned that the nineteen-month occupation of Alcatraz had come to an abrupt end as U.S. Marshals moved onto the island with shotguns. Only fifteen people were on the island when the government decided to reclaim Alcatraz. Reporters on the scene at the courthouse rushed to interview Annie Oakes. Shocked and deeply saddened by the news, she left the hallway. It was all too much. Alcatraz was the first place where Annie had felt freedom, and it was the last place where she had seen her daughter Yvonne alive. Richard Oakes, obviously reeling with emotions after hearing the news, was separated from Annie and swarmed by a host of journalists eager to hear his immediate thoughts. He took a while to gather his words and feelings before he proclaimed, "Alcatraz is not an island. It's an idea." He went on to label the federal move as "a sissy victory," comparing the U.S. government's action at Alcatraz to its actions in Vietnam: "the pressure's been on them to do something in Vietnam. And the only way they could do something was turn it around and use it on Indian people." Pointedly and prophetically, Oakes referenced the

Alcatraz occupation as the "door to our future. . . . It will not be closed. We're taking it back." Although the reporters seemed to place literal meaning onto Oakes's statement, in reality his words symbolized that Red Power as a movement could not be confined to one island or one occupation. Rather, the "idea" of Alcatraz was spreading, and this idea was about to politically transform both America and Native nations.[15]

It was a foreshadowing statement by Oakes. Just a few days later, joint liberations occurred in both Chicago, Illinois, and El Cerrito, California. Led by Anishinaabe citizen Michael Chosa, a Chicago Indian community activist, many of the occupiers identified themselves as "Alcatraz Indians." The new residents in what was dubbed the "Chicago Indian Village" were survivors and urban refugees left over from the failed Bureau of Indian Affairs relocation program, which had sought to transplant hundreds of American Indians into various Chicago districts. Initially formed in 1970, the Chicago Indian Village had advocated for lands near Wrigley Field, home of the beloved Chicago Cubs, a major landmark that would surely secure ample press attention. The liberations, shifting to additional sites,

A press photo of Richard Oakes on Alcatraz Island, November 28, 1969, when he made a public request to negotiate directly with either Secretary of the Interior Walter Hickel or President Richard Nixon for proper title to the island. Photo courtesy of Getty Images, Bettmann Collection 640119072.

continued for over a year and a half, with Indian Village residents frequently moving first to a downtown Chicago church, then a county park, then the federal surplus lands of Argonne National Laboratory, and finally to Camp Seager. After the Chicago Housing Authority and the federal Department of Housing and Urban Development reached an agreement, they promised the leaders new housing and land. Like Alcatraz, each occupation, from Chicago to El Cerrito, was about land reclamation that targeted federal surplus property—for instance, an abandoned Nike missile site in California became the new "Indian land" for former Alcatraz residents.[16]

In El Cerrito, California, the occupiers were the evicted remnants of Indians of All Tribes who had been forcibly removed from Alcatraz. It appeared that American Indians across the country were carrying forth the "idea" of Alcatraz. In New York City the police arrested a group of six activists for having spray-painted "Return Alcatraz" underneath a statue of former President Theodore Roosevelt located outside the American Museum of Natural History.[17]

Just as the trial for the "New York Six" was about to open, California Judge Virga called the jury into the courtroom and proceeded to inform the jurors that in his legal opinion PG&E held clear title to the land in question. Virga's move to sway the jury, for which there was slender precedent, if any, shocked the Pit River defendants and their attorney Aubrey Grossman. The jury took no less than twenty-four hours before announcing their final verdict. Contrary to Judge Virga's opinion, the jury found that the defendants arrested on the contested lands were not guilty of trespass. All the defendants arrested on June 6, 1970, were acquitted. (However, the jury also ruled that just seven of the defendants from the June 8 and 9 arrests—only those who had entered the cabins—were guilty.) The cheer that went up throughout the courtroom made its way out into the crowded hallways, where Pit River supporters had gathered to hear the jury's decision. After the trial, a few of the jurors asked some of the defendants for their autographs. One of the jurors remarked, "We're proud of the Indians." Clearly, the defendants and Grossman had won over the hearts and minds of the jurors. It was a much-needed victory, and for Richard and Annie Oakes it proved a double victory. The jury's verdict meant they had avoided having to separate their family. Joy and relief must have consumed their immediate thoughts.[18]

Continuing their legal strategy, the Pit River Nation filed a civil suit against PG&E Corporation shortly after the verdict was announced in the courtroom. The civil suit intended to force PG&E to return fifty-three thousand acres of land to the Tribe. In addition, the suit requested that all profits procured by the corporation be reinvested in the Tribe. Pit River leaders added that this civil suit was the first of many to come. Since every corporation operating on Pit River lands faced litigation, this strategy aimed to drive court costs up for the corporation while securing further exposure in the media. Grossman and Pit River leadership understood that their fight must be unrelenting if they wanted to secure their desired results. District Attorney Robert Baker, interviewed after the trial, dismissed the jury's verdict as pure sympathy and claimed it was outside the law. Baker also told reporters that he would continue to prosecute any Native person who trespassed on PG&E property.[19]

On June 17, 1971, over one hundred sheriff's deputies moved in with riot gear to arrest more than eighty-five occupiers at the Nike site in El Cerrito, California. Richard Oakes and his family received the news at their new residence at Toyon. Since they had gained official title to the center, Oakes and others worked diligently on a proposal to turn the facility into an educational and cultural center for local Tribes. On June 18, Richard returned to his cabin after a long day of meetings and facility repairs. Late that Friday evening he awoke, having heard someone struggling to open their front door. Alerted by the noise, both Richard and Annie quickly went to open the door, but when Richard opened it he was immediately struck over the head. He collapsed to his knees, gripped by pain and adrenaline, as both he and Annie struggled to fend off the intruder. The assailant, who was never identified, made off into the night. Hearing Oakes call out, Annie quickly ran to her husband's aid, helping him to their car. She gathered up the kids, who had been frightened out of their sleep, and piled everyone into their car. She rushed Richard to the nearest hospital. Because of his previous injuries, doctors immediately placed Oakes under critical observation for the next two days. Annie called the Shasta County Sheriff's Office to file a burglary and assault charge. Richard had been blindsided and failed to get a close look at the assailant. No arrests were made, and considering Oakes's history with the Shasta County Sheriff's Office, this was not exactly shocking news to the young couple. The attack itself came as no surprise. Clearly someone wanted to send a stern message to Oakes, hitting him where they knew it would hurt, at his home.[20]

Fearing for their family's safety, the Oakeses returned to Akwesasne. Ironically, in an interview conducted with the *Watertown Daily Times,* a newspaper in upstate New York, on October 15, 1970, Annie Oakes mentioned that "this had been the third attack [in relation to the Warren's Bar incident] on Oakes' life since he started his fight against the large corporations in the west to regain land which belonged to the Indian people." Clearly, this recent attack was all that they could take. Arriving in Richard's community, they began where they had left off and continued to work with the White Roots of Peace caravan. Once again, Richard began to look for employment and housing at Akwesasne. The family of eight found shelter with friends and relatives, living out of suitcases and sleeping bags. Beyond their immediate financial crisis, Oakes never stopped organizing and recruiting as he attended community and Longhouse meetings. Newly elected Tadodaho Leon Shenandoah, took a quick liking to the brawny Oakes. Many an evening the two leaders stayed awake sharing stories and ideas about liberation and sovereignty.[21]

Oakes often returned to Indian bars at Akwesasne to converse and debate with other Mohawks. These times were much different for Richard because he had sworn off drinking since the attack the previous year at Warren's.[22] Back at home, Richard was known as "Ranoies," his Mohawk name, meaning "A Big Man." He was learning to speak the Mohawk language and was increasingly becoming an active member of his community. He was surrounded by the support and guidance of the Longhouse, but for the family of eight it was in many ways tragic that they had to start all over again.

In late August of 1971, a few months after they returned to Akwesasne, Richard and others were asked by traditional leaders at Onondaga to participate in a demonstration. The New York Highway Department proposed the widening of Highway 81 in order to add a third lane for trucking that would pass through the Onondaga Reservation south of Syracuse. The proposed construction confiscated additional Onondaga lands for an acceleration lane, but without any compensation from the state. Construction was about to start when Onondaga leaders sent out a call for support to all Haudenosaunee Nations. Richard Oakes and other Mohawks drove all night to assist in the protest. Over a hundred

Haudenosaunee converged on Highway 81, and soon they began to barricade the road from eager construction crews. Using their bodies as barriers, they sat on the highway blocking traffic for miles and halting all construction on the road. When local authorities arrived on the scene, Tadodaho Leon Shenandoah stood up and said, "the United States ends here."[23]

Tensions escalated further when New York state troopers tried to serve an injunction against the demonstrators. The state troopers knew they were outnumbered and in questionable jurisdiction. Onondaga leader William Lazore presented a proclamation to the authorities: "These people are trespassing . . . and we demand their removal. Under existing treaties, you are required to remove any unauthorized persons from our territory." Following long discussions with Onondaga leaders over strategy, the protesters agreed to leave the area, which prevented any arrests. For the next few weeks protesters continued to barricade and block the highway, even tearing out survey stakes. Their actions gained popular support from rock icons John Lennon and Yoko Ono, who visited Onondaga to advertise their ongoing public support for Native rights. After much legal negotiation, the Onondaga Nation won their battle with the state. Construction resumed, but the crews added only a shoulder to the highway. Oakes was reminded of the roadblock back at Kashaya and the legality of trespass laws in northern California; in this situation he had witnessed positive results that derived from direct action. The Iroquois Council of Chiefs eventually negotiated a six-point agreement with Governor Nelson Rockefeller over construction along Highway 81.[24]

Richard Oakes established many friendships while at Akwesasne, but life proved increasingly difficult for the Oakes family as he and Annie were still seeking employment. As a Kashaya Pomo, Annie Oakes found employment options more limited. Her husband had accrued years of experience in ironwork and direct action and had attended Syracuse and San Francisco State College, but, much to his misfortune, he had never finished his degree. With his physical condition weakened from the attack at Warren's Bar, ironwork was out of the question. His options were narrow, if not altogether nonexistent. In near-desperation, Oakes published a letter in *Akwesasne Notes* seeking a job and shelter for his family. As much as Richard loved being at home, the family had to relocate if they were to survive. Saying goodbye was never easy for Richard Oakes;

Richard and Joseph Oakes on Alcatraz Island,
November 25, 1969. AP Photo/Sal Veder.

he often called his friend Jerry Gambill, editor of *Akwesasne Notes,* to talk
out the latest issues. The drive back to Kashaya was not without complications. Shortly after leaving St. Regis, their station wagon broke down. After
Richard and Annie were able to scrape together enough money for repairs
and gas, they drove across the continent to Annie's homeland.

By February of 1972, news of Lakota citizen Raymond Yellow
Thunder's public lynching had spread across Indian Country. Yellow
Thunder's badly beaten body was found in his pickup truck, which sat for
days, unnoticed, in a used car lot in Gordon, Nebraska. The tiny town of
Gordon, located just across the state line from South Dakota and the Pine
Ridge Reservation, had long been a notorious border town. In its neighbor
city, Alliance, Nebraska, Native peoples could shop only in certain stores.
Indian children were also often sent to segregated classrooms at public
schools. This region, despite influencing the monumental works of writer
Mari Sandoz, earned an ominous reputation for extreme exploitation,
racism, and violence toward Native peoples. For years the town of Gordon
profited from liquor sales to Pine Ridge residents, who drove to Gordon

because it was illegal to purchase alcohol on the reservation. Those arrested for drunk and disorderly conduct worked off their sentences doing free labor for the community. Just about every reservation community across America is complemented by the existence of border towns. Often these communities thrived from the business of exclusion—that is, providing exploitable goods and services not found on the reservation.[25]

Yellow Thunder, an Oglala cowboy and military veteran, had been kidnapped, beaten, stripped naked, thrown into a car trunk, and made to dance naked before other veterans at the American Legion Hall. Afterwards, the beating and kidnapping continued, to the point that he was lucky to find refuge at the local jail. The next day, on a cold February morning, after his "release" from jail, seated in the cab of his pickup truck, Yellow Thunder died from his injuries. The attorney charged Yellow Thunder's murderers with manslaughter and false imprisonment; the defendants' attorney stated that the death was a practical joke that had gone wrong. The entire incident was enough to send an organized caravan consisting of Raymond Yellow Thunder's family, local Pine Ridge residents, and the American Indian Movement into Gordon, Nebraska. After a successful economic boycott and protests in Gordon, the city responded by creating a human rights commission; for its part, the state ordered an official investigation into the death of Raymond Yellow Thunder. Robert Warrior and Paul Chaat Smith, who summarized these events in their book *Like A Hurricane*, wrote that "Raymond Yellow Thunder's story reached out to every Indian person who could see in him not just another Indian drunk, but a brother, a father, an uncle, or a cousin." Just about everyone in Indian Country was affected by the news of Yellow Thunder's lynching. It is not known just how Richard Oakes responded to this news, but as Warrior and Smith concluded, Yellow Thunder's death struck a solid chord of indignation and protest with all Native peoples.[26]

Over the course of the next six months, Richard Oakes worked diligently on a book manuscript while putting in hours at a greenhouse farm at Kashaya. He also began to construct a new home for Annie and the kids, and he continued to lend his support to other occupations. Annie remained happiest at home with her garden; she was also gratified to have the kids back in school. The family now was much larger since they joined Annie's cousins and immediate family for frequent gatherings. Almost two years had gone by since Richard had sat with reporter Tim Findley in their Gatorville apartment at SFSC: "A lot of people say I would be justified in leaving it all now; after all it's been a hell of a year. But I think the law of averages says I have to get a positive response out of nature sometime, and this time I think I'll find it." Oakes was still seeking to make a difference as he continued to press for Native political and economic independence and, ultimately, freedom.[27]

In August, Oakes and his family were excited by the news that long-time friend Mad Bear Anderson and other Iroquois leaders were scheduled to make an appearance in Big Bend, California. The North American Indian Unity Caravan, led by Mad Bear, hosted the two-day affair to draw continued public support for Indian rights. The event, which combined prayer, dances, and speeches, was also about condolence and healing. Pit River Tribal Council Chairman Ross Montgomery sponsored the caravan to encourage further Tribal unity at Pit River.[28] Throughout the month of August, Richard Oakes continued to lend tactical and physical support to the Pit River occupation at Big Bend. He made frequent trips back and forth from Kashaya to Big Bend. On September 9, 1972, he attended a meeting with the California Indian Land Claims Commission in Sacramento, California. At this meeting the Pit River Tribe continued to resist the Claims Commission settlement offer of forty-seven cents an acre. Oakes, one of the keynote speakers, got up to address the audience. Ronald Anthony Hodge remembered that "Oakes got up to make a speech, walked up front to the stage, but tripped and nearly fell in taking the first step up to the stage. . . . It embarrassed him . . . and he spoke from the floor without going to the stage. . . . He couldn't elevate his body." Hodge also remembered Oakes walking with a prominent limp, as he struggled to overcome the lingering effects of paralysis.[29]

By mid-September 1972, construction crews resumed work on the widening of Skaggs Springs Road, which Oakes had protested two years earlier. Richard Oakes was hosting two teenagers, Billy Lazore and Lloyd Thompson, who traveled from St. Regis to stay with the leader. On September 14, Oakes left the house with Billy Lazore and Little Fawn to find Rocky, who had not come home for dinner. When he approached the Gualala YMCA camp, he let Billy out to see if he could find him on foot. Later, after Oakes returned to the camp, he saw Billy and twenty-three-year-old camp employee Robert Myers, arguing in the YMCA parking lot. Myers was holding a rifle. Alarmed, Oakes quickly went over to see if everything was all right. He discovered that the two were arguing over Indian hunting rights versus non-Native property rights. Oakes began debating Myers. Soon the argument became more and more heated as the three men stood in the parking lot. Around this time, thirty-four-year-old Michael Oliver Morgan came storming over from his house, where his family had been entertaining friends. Taking the rifle from Myers, he pointed the gun above Oakes's head and fired a shot.[30] Stunned, Billy pulled a knife in self-defense. Oakes quickly took the knife away from Lazore and turned his back to Morgan, who was still aiming the rifle at Oakes's back. According to four eyewitnesses, when the deputy sheriff arrived, he told Morgan, "Why did you shoot over his head? Why didn't you shoot him? I have an M16 in the car that eats up Indians."[31] Morgan pressed further, asking the deputy if a "white man" could get away with killing Oakes.[32] The deputy merely nodded his head, suggesting to Morgan that the law would be on his side.

The morning after the incident, Frank Greer, a visitor to the YMCA camp, which was located ten minutes from the Pomo Reservation, over-heard Michael Morgan threaten Oakes's life. Greer, who had gone on a hunting trip with Morgan, recalled that he had "heard Morgan remark during a conversation on hunting, that it was 'open season on coons, foxes, and Indians' . . . Disturbed . . . [I] . . . pressed further and heard Morgan say that Oakes was a troublemaker, and that the country would be better off without him; that he was half-crazy from being hit over the head with a pool cue and that he might be better off dead."[33] Later that same day, September 15, Richard and Annie Oakes, with their six children, drove back to the YMCA camp to smooth things over with Morgan. Unfortunately, the situation again ended in an argument, and once more Morgan went back to his house for a gun. Oakes and his family left while the disgruntled Morgan was searching his house for a weapon.[34]

Just four days later, another strange event occurred. Billy Lazore and twenty-year-old Lloyd Thompson from Akwesasne, who was staying with Oakes, went to the YMCA to get some horses. Again Michael Morgan appeared. He began chasing Lazore and Thomson, who, he thought, were there to steal horses. Armed with a 9mm handgun and carbine rifle, Morgan and his friend Tom Neville jumped into Neville's car to chase down the two young men, as Neville later recalled:[35]

He [Morgan] found Billy who was trying to hitch a ride on the
county road, forced him into the car at pistol point. . . .
Thompson escaped by sliding down a 60-foot embankment to a
riverbed. . . . Spotting Thompson, Morgan fired. He [Morgan]
said he fired into the air to frighten Thompson into staying
down in the riverbed and to keep him from returning to the
reservation for help before the sheriff came for Billy.[36]

Billy had been missing overnight, and Thompson finally told Richard
Oakes what had happened. A day later Oakes dropped Thompson off at
the ravine to locate his lost hunting rifle. Apparently, Oakes had sent the
two young men to get horses so they could go hunting, which is why
Thompson was carrying his hunting rifle.[37] Oakes, who was wearing a
brown shirt, proceeded down Skaggs Spring Road on foot to find out
exactly what had taken place the previous afternoon.[38] At about 3:45 p.m.,
Forestry Captain Harold A. Rose drove past Richard Oakes on Skaggs
Springs Road; he was approximately one and a half miles out from the
YMCA camp. Oakes waved at Rose as he passed by in his truck. He
continued walking toward the camp.[39] At 4:30 p.m., Morgan had just
finished working at the corral and was walking, armed with a loaded
Walther P38 9mm handgun, along the YMCA camp road to his home.[40]
Soon Oakes and Morgan crossed paths at the intersection of the two
roads. When they were twenty feet from each other, Morgan claimed,
Oakes jumped from behind a redwood tree, confronted Morgan, who
dropped his farrier tools and began to back away when Oakes lunged for
him, moving so fast that he failed to notice if Oakes was armed. Morgan
drew his gun, aimed, and fired a single shot that penetrated Oakes's
heart, killing him instantly.[41] Forty-five minutes later, the deputy sheriff
arrived. Oakes was pronounced dead on the scene; he was lying on his
back when law enforcement arrived at the crime scene.

Less than two hours later, Annie Oakes and a friend were driving
back home to Kashaya from a trip to the grocery store. Nearing the
crime scene, Annie slowed down the car; a large crowd had gathered near
the entrance to the YMCA camp. A blanket was all that covered Richard
Oakes's lifeless body on the road. As she passed, she moved her eyes
back and forth from the road and then back to the scene, looking for
clues as to what had happened. Just as the car had cleared the crowd, her

friend who was riding on the passenger side announced, "No. It's Richard. I can tell by his boots." Recalling Richard's cherished pair of cowboy boots, Annie slammed on the brakes; she rushed to exit the car and quickly ran to the lifeless body on the road. She knelt down and removed the blanket. She refused to believe it. She had to see her husband's face. She reached out tenderly to touch Richard's arm; his body was still warm, but he was gone. Time stood still as Annie tried to pull herself together and asked officers at the scene for information. The deputies informed her that they had apprehended the man who killed Richard Oakes, and that was all that they would tell her. Annie, in horror, watched as a hearse from the county coroner's office arrived to transport her beloved husband's body to the mortuary. Annie asked that she be allowed to follow the hearse but was quickly left behind, attempting to turn her car around in the middle of the road. Her "knight in shining armor" was gone.[42]

Shock waves swept across Indian Country as Native peoples struggled to deal with the overwhelming loss as well as to learn the circumstances of Richard Oakes's death. The loss and grief was particularly difficult for Richard Oakes's father, Arthur Oakes, who was living back at Akwesasne in Rooseveltown, New York. Several days after he learned the tragic news, Arthur Oakes let Annie know that he would like Richard's body returned to New York for burial. Perhaps in his anger and sadness, it was a way for the elder Oakes to have closure, or maybe he simply wanted to say a final goodbye. Whatever Arthur Oakes's initial reasons were, he changed his mind and decided to support Annie's wishes.[43]

Upon learning of Richard Oakes's assassination, Hank Adams and Ramona Bennett carpooled together from Puyallup to Kashaya. Along the way, they both tried to sort out their emotions and figure out what had happened to their friend. Once they crossed the state line into Oregon, Adams stopped at a local gas station and placed a call to Kashaya, hoping to learn the latest information. When Adams returned to the car, Bennett, who was carrying her newborn child on her lap, asked for the news. Adams in disbelief, informed her that Morgan's charges had been dropped from first-degree murder to involuntary manslaughter. Outraged and heartbroken, they continued pressing on down the road toward Kashaya.[44]

On September 26, 1972, Richard Oakes's coffin was carried from the Kashaya Roundhouse and loaded on an old flatbed construction truck.

Multiple pallbearers carried him to his final resting place beside his daughter Yvonne on the Kashaya Pomo Reservation. Hundreds of people gathered from all over Indian Country, including many whose lives he had touched or changed, to pay tribute and their final respects to the assassinated leader, activist, brother, and family man.[45]

After he learned of Richard Oakes's assassination, fishing rights activist Hank Adams released the following press statement, which would be reprinted in several national newspapers: "Richard Oakes' presence beyond Alcatraz and his influence upon many Indian people shall continue to live within the body and soul of Indian experience. Born to the American soil, and responding strongly to his peoples' struggle and suffering upon it, the living spirit of Richard Oakes could not die nor cease to be remembered upon American land."[46] Shortly after attending the funeral, Adams and Bennett took the long journey back to northwest Washington. Adams, having survived a near-fatal attack of his own, searched for an action that might demonstrate the extreme loss, anger, betrayal, and injustice that surrounded Oakes's assassination. He relied

Relatives and friends gather outside the Oakeses' house at Kashaya after Richard Oakes's funeral. Leonard Oakes (Richard's brother) and Annie Oakes converse with Ross Montgomery as Dewey Barnes stands in the doorway. Photographed by Stephen Shames. Photo courtesy of Polaris Images 01297465.

on his extensive national connections and began to contact other national organizations. Soon Adams brought together the American Indian Movement (Minnesota), Indians of All Tribes, and Survival of American Indians Association (Seattle) to plan a dramatic course of action. Fueled by the news of Richard Oakes's assassination, leaders of eight national Indian organizations from both the United States and Canada agreed to meet and determine a new course of collective action.[47] Gathering on September 30 in Denver, Colorado, Adams and the leaders of these groups met at the New Albany Hotel, where they began to organize the "Trail of Broken Treaties" march on Washington, D.C., scheduled for November 3 through 9, 1972. Scholar Vine Deloria Jr. stated, "Plans called for the caravan to begin on the West Coast, pick up Indians as it traveled east, and arrive in Washington, D.C., during the final week of the 1972 presidential campaign. The idea was to build up both tension and publicity as the caravan proceeded across the nation, and to present a list of demands to both Presidential candidates in the week before the election."[48] On October 6, 1972, three auto caravans started the trek to Washington, D.C., from Seattle, San Francisco, and Los Angeles. The three caravans converged in Minneapolis, Minnesota, where leaders drafted a proclamation, entitled simply *The Twenty Points*. This document became a new call for reform of constitutional treaty-making authority, a new treaty commission, the resubmission of nonratified treaties, land reform, repeal of termination acts, the abolition of the BIA, the creation of a new office of Federal Indian Relations and Community Reconstruction, and protection of religious freedom, just to name a few. After the caravan arrived in Washington, D.C., the officials blocked participants from holding any meetings with President Nixon or any of the presidential candidates. This led to the takeover of the Bureau of Indian Affairs building for what ended up being a six-day occupation. Demonstrators occupied BIA area offices across the country in Everett, Spokane, Seattle, San Francisco, San Diego, Missoula, Pine Ridge, Phoenix, and Omaha. Clearly, the initial objective was to stage a nonviolent sit-in to highlight the twenty points proclamation.[49]

By the end of the siege, Nixon's administration brokered a deal with the caravan leadership that provided immunity from prosecution and over $66,000 dollars in cash to cover travel expenses to move the caravan safely out of Washington. The caravan leaders chose legal protection and

Left to right: Bernie Whitebear, Hank Adams, Russell Means, Sid Mills, and Robert Free. The image originally appeared in the article "Indian Leaders Discuss Caravan" in the October 7, 1972, issue of *The Seattle Times*. These leaders were to spearhead the three separate caravans originating on the West Coast as they made their way to Washington, D.C., on the Trail of Broken Treaties. Photographer Jerry Gay, *The Seattle Times*, used with permission, copyright 1972.

financial assistance to return home and to fight another day. In the end, most of those involved considered the takeover and caravan a success. The media attention alone was explosive. It was the first time since the War of 1812 that a federal building in Washington had been taken over. The national media outlets turned AIM leaders into iconic images; one memorable image showed Russell Means carrying a painting of Richard Nixon as a shield. Encouraged by the Nixon administration and the BIA, reporters began to document and photograph the broken ruins of the BIA building. Tribal leaders were also urged by the Bureau of Indian Affairs and the Nixon White House to pay witness and tour the premises. Many of the leaders noticed that some of the graffiti was freshly painted, perhaps in a smear campaign to discredit the intentions of the caravan. Other Tribal leaders proudly scoured the painted walls for signs that their Nation was represented.[50] Due to fears of invasion, confrontation, and violent eviction, the caravan had used machines, file cabinets, furniture— indeed, anything not tied down—to barricade doors, windows, and entrances. The result looked as if a riot had occurred in the heart of the capital. Vine Deloria Jr. later compared the destruction of the BIA to the Watts riots. Rather than an urban crisis, the physical destruction and dismantling of the BIA building stood as metaphor for injustice that was bound up in years of failed and destructive federal policies.

On the flip side, one of the major negative effects that emanated from the BIA occupation was the lengthy delay of aid for education, housing, and health services that many Native nations needed. Additionally, it took months if not years for the BIA to recover from the loss of documents as well as the voluminous contracts, machinery, and paperwork that flooded the agency and created a bureaucratic nightmare. As a means of protection, the occupation confiscated thousands of documents to expose corruption in the agency. Unfortunately, some of these documents involved undecided claims and federal recognition cases. The occupation leadership grew more divided as they became increasingly alienated from representatives of Native nations and the U.S. government. This wedge would later be exploited by corrupt Tribal leaders to discredit these national organizations and question their tactics. Finally, the occupation solidified the "militant Indian" stereotype, an image that would haunt many Native organizations for years to come. The caravan founded in Richard Oakes's honor almost came to a violent conclusion. Was this standoff to be the sole legacy of Oakes's politics? It is unknown whether this "militant Indian" image and label affected the prosecution of Richard Oakes's assassin, Michael Oliver Morgan.

While the Trail of Broken Treaties caravan to Washington was happening, an arraignment hearing was scheduled for Morgan, to take place on October 12, 1972. A crowd of over fifty Native peoples and supporters, including Annie Oakes and her children, gathered outside the tiny courtroom in Santa Rosa. Fearful of a potential riot, the local Sheriff's Office kept a tactical squad nearby but out of sight. The heavy security and the threat of a mistrial prevented anyone from protesting the proceedings. There was too much at stake.[51]

Two days later, Frank Owen Greer provided the courtroom with startling testimony. He had been staying with a close friend, Robert Myers, who worked at the YMCA camp. Greer stated that five days before the shooting, he and Morgan had a conversation about hunting in which Morgan had stated that there was an "open season all year long on coons, foxes and Indians," adding that the Indians were not "problems" until Oakes had come along and that Oakes was a "troublemaker." He also called Oakes "half-crazy" and said that "he'd be better off dead." On cross examination, Defense Attorney Richard Pawson tried to discredit the witness. He asked Greer if he was an antiwar activist and if he had been arrested at antiwar demonstrations in San Francisco. Pawson hoped to show that Greer's liberal ties meant that he was sympathetic to Oakes. As the hearing pressed forward, Detective Sergeant Irwin "Butch" Carlstedt entered Morgan's three-page official statement into the court record. Morgan's original statement said that Oakes had jumped out of a clump of redwoods and startled Morgan. Then Oakes questioned Morgan about the arrest of young Billy Lazore, after which Oakes stated, "Deputies can't help you now. I'm going to kill you." Oakes crouched down as if to pull a knife and he told Oakes to stay away, but Oakes jumped at him so fast that he could not tell if Oakes had a weapon or not, so he fired one shot, which dropped Oakes to his knees before he fell backwards onto the road.

The pathologist Dr. Albert Keller testified as to how Richard Oakes died and explained that the bullet was found at an angle twenty-three feet away from Oakes's body. The defense showed color photos of the death scene including those taken of Oakes's body. The experience had to have been horrifying for Annie Oakes to observe. The final witness that day was James Douglas Thompson, a seventeen-year-old who had had a summer job in the camp, under Morgan's direction. Pawson asked Thompson about the altercation on September 15 at Morgan's house. Thompson stated that Oakes had called Morgan a "white nigger." Pawson continued to press the young man and asked if Richard Oakes had ever said, "I'm going to smash your head in"; it was as if Defense Attorney Pawson was putting words into the witness's mouth. Yet District Attorney Edward Krug, a recent law school graduate, posted no objection. The hearing was held to determine if there was sufficient evidence for Judge Frank Passalacqua to hold a trial for Morgan on the charge of involuntary manslaughter.[52]

That same day, the Oakland chapter of the American Indian Movement announced that they would host a memorial powwow in Richard Oakes's honor at the Ya-Ka-Ama lands in Santa Rosa, which Richard Oakes had helped reclaim. In their press release the organization declared that within the previous ten months three Indians had died at the hands of whites. Ironically, in every case in Humboldt, Tuolumne, and Sonoma counties, the assailant was only charged with involuntary manslaughter and not murder. The protest, scheduled for October 28–30, also was intended to gain national exposure for the deaths of Hoopa citizen Michael "Bunky" Ferris, Yurok citizen William Smith, Laguna Pueblo citizen Albert Serracino, Raymond Yellow Thunder, Papago citizen Phillip Oelaya, Omaha-Ponca citizen Luther Little Voice, and Onondaga citizen Leroy Shenandoah. The local AIM chapter, with support from Kashaya leaders like Essie Parrish, had hoped to bring more press attention to the trial of Michael Morgan. The rally gathered at Juilliard Park in Santa Rosa, California, under a large poster image of Oakes and police escort. Annie Oakes spoke at the rally and stated that her husband was trying to make Indians "free." A striking assertion: what does freedom mean in Indian Country? Can Native peoples ever be free? Without justice, Indigenous peoples can never experience true freedom or citizenship in America. Her words struck to the very core of Richard Oakes's lifelong fight.[53]

On October 16, after five and a half hours of witness testimony, Judge Passalacqua ordered Morgan to stand trial for involuntary manslaughter and denied the charge of second-degree murder. The final defendants included Billy Lazore, who had been held at gunpoint by Morgan. He was also arrested and faced criminal charges for allegedly stealing horses. Lazore contradicted a signed statement that Oakes had ordered the young men to steal the horses. On the stand and under oath, Lazore clarified that it was not Richard Oakes's idea but that Oakes had mentioned the need for horses and guns to establish a camp. Lazore had been granted immunity by the District Attorney's office for his testimony, as Defense Attorney Richard Pawson made very clear to the court.

The final defense witness was Robert Meyers, who was also at the September 14 altercation between Morgan and Oakes in which Morgan fired a shot above Oakes's head. Meyers stated, "Mr. Oakes said he would burn us out and he would be back to get us." He countered his friend Frank Greer's testimony, asserting that he thought Morgan's "open season" comment was a joke, like that used against Polish or Italians—"a pun that in my own mind was in bad taste." Meyers also identified himself as a good friend of Morgan's, which confirmed Greer's testimony of Morgan's violent comment that Oakes was "better off dead." In an odd twist, Richard Pawson called Ann Marie Lopoca to testify as a Native woman who happened to be a friend of the Morgans. On the stand she confirmed that Michael Morgan was her son's godfather. It seemed as though the defense attorney was desperately trying to prove that Morgan was not a racist because he was friends with one Indian woman.[54]

It appeared that the defense attorney and Morgan's own testimony formed a generic script that had been copied from some bad western movie. The Indian assailant had jumped out from a tree with a knife because he wanted to "burn us out." Even the words Morgan and others ascribed to Oakes appeared scripted and biased at best. Absent from these accounts was the important fact that Richard Oakes was physically limited in how fast he could move. Yet, apparently he jumped, lunged, and "moved so fast" as to warrant Morgan's quick self-defense. For centuries Americans had been drowned in popular stereotypes and misinformation about Native peoples derived from literature, dime novels, wild west shows, movies, television, mascots, and a host of other sources. Popular knowledge about Red Power was now confined to media coverage about the recent BIA takeover in Washington, D.C., an image that often showcased the government as being held hostage by "militant Indians." It is unknown how these and other stereotypes about Native peoples and activists may have influenced Judge Passalacqua's ruling. In the end, Morgan remained free on his original $10,000 bond.

By November 1, District Attorney Ed Krug added a second charge of voluntary manslaughter. Krug's logic was that it doubled Morgan's chances of being found guilty. At the arraignment Morgan was charged with involuntary and voluntary manslaughter, and his trial was set for February 21, 1973.[55] After hearing the charges and attending many of the hearings, Aubrey Grossman was furious: "The shooting could be the cause . . . to demonstrate whether Indians are fair game for the white man in California."[56]

By November 2, 1972, Grossman began working with Annie Oakes on a legal suit against the Sea Ranch development, or Oceanic Properties Incorporated. The suit claimed ten miles of coastline property as Pomo land. Sea Ranch had been in the news because private property owners feared that Sea Ranch was developing a Coney Island–style theme park next to their properties. The exclusive community of Sea Ranch was located north of Kashaya in Sonoma County.[57] For years, Sea Ranch refused to allow traditional Kashaya fishing and abalone hunts on its "private" beaches. After filing the lawsuit, Annie declared, "When they killed Richard Oakes they did not kill the idea to which he devoted his life." The lawsuit managed to accrue more press attention and ultimately was used for exposure of the Morgan trial.

Between the lawsuit and the trial, Annie Oakes would now have to find balance as a widowed mother of six children. Politically astute Annie had learned from Alcatraz and the subsequent takeovers. In her lawsuit she understood the importance of public support and publically vowed not to remove any individual property owners. The *San Francisco Examiner* secured a brief interview with the widowed Annie Oakes: "I have never been very political or much of an activist. . . . That is why it is important for me to file this suit, to show white men that when they killed Richard, they did not kill the idea to which he sacrificed his life. The idea is even stronger because of his death."[58] In a Santa Rosa *Press Democrat* article, both Annie Oakes and Aubrey Grossman asserted that Richard Oakes's death was "related to his position as an Indian leader seeking to reclaim Indian lands."[59] Considering that the District Attorney's Office lacked training in federal Indian law, the Sea Ranch press exposure was a way for Annie Oakes and Grossman to keep press attention on the trial. If all eyes were watching, public outrage and pressure might force a guilty verdict.

Seven men and five women were selected by the defense and prosecution for the jury to determine if Michael Oliver Morgan was guilty of manslaughter, not murder. Annie watched with disdain as the jury was selected. Not one Native person was selected for jury duty. At five foot nine and slightly balding, Morgan appeared at the trial. He was clean-shaven, dressed in a button down oxford shirt, a tan jacket, and dress slacks; he kept his eyes on Richard Pawson, as Pawson gave an opening statement to the jury. In a courtroom trial, first impressions are priceless, a fact that Morgan had to exploit by not appearing to be a killer. Pawson urged the jury to view Morgan as "presumed innocent," despite his arrest, and to believe that the shooting was the result of a "sudden quarrel or heat of passion." District Attorney Edward Krug asked for a delay in his opening remarks. He was unprepared, having thought the jury selection would have taken longer for such an important trial. Pawson objected, but he was overruled by Superior Court Judge John Moskowitz.[60]

The next day District Attorney Edward Krug made his opening statement. He charged that Morgan had a motive for killing Richard Oakes, which was "racial bias and prejudice." Krug reiterated the fact that the voluntary manslaughter charge is defined as a "specific intent" to commit a criminal act. Under this definition Krug revealed to the court that before the fatal shooting, Morgan had inquired of the sheriff as to how someone might justify the murder of Richard Oakes. After Krug's forty-five-minute opening statement, Pawson quickly rose to his feet to declare a mistrial, a swift tactic to strike doubt in the jury's mind. In a bid to establish reasonable doubt, Pawson further objected to Oakes being referred to as a "political activist in Indian rights."

Despite having his objections overruled, Pawson began his opening statement before the court. He listed the witnesses that Krug would call to the stand and began to discredit their statements; he changed the phrasing of quotes attributed to Morgan, including "open season all year long on coons, foxes and Indians"; he also used Oakes's activism as support for his violent nature. Coincidentally, the occupation of Wounded Knee by the Oglala Sioux Civil Rights Organization and American Indian Movement was making national headlines. Television and newspapers began blanket coverage as the U.S. Army moved two armored patrol carriers toward Wounded Knee, the site of the 1890 massacre of three hundred Lakota men, women, and children by the Seventh Calvary. The *Press Democrat* even ran the headline "Wounded Knee, S.D. 300 Armed Indians Seize Town, Hold 10 Hostages," as their lead story. Clearly, Pawson could capitalize on the "militant Indian" stereotype.[61]

The first witness was Dr. Albert Richard Keller, the pathologist who performed the autopsy on Richard Oakes. Keller testified that while Oakes had suffered previous damage to the right side of his brain, he was not suffering from atrophy or non-use of his muscles. Dr. Keller used life-sized mannequins to illustrate the angle that the bullet entered Oakes's body, which clearly indicated that Morgan was standing on higher ground or that the six-foot-tall Richard Oakes was bent forward. Dr. Keller's testimony was extremely damaging, and Pawson would exploit the testimony to prove that Oakes lunged toward Morgan and that he was physically capable of such a quick move. The next witness that day was Ernest Ohlson Jr., who was the last person to see Richard Oakes alive. He had driven down Skagg Springs Road about 4:00 p.m. when he saw Oakes not walking, but jogging, toward the camp. Oakes thumbed a ride and Ohlson proceeded a short distance down the road and dropped Oakes off. As Oakes exited the car he said, "Thank you, sir." When Ohlson returned after 5:00 p.m. on his way to work in Healdsburg, he saw a body covered by a blanket and two men walking away. He continued to drive on, not knowing that was Richard.[62]

The next day the trial endured objection after objection from Defense Attorney Richard Pawson. District Attorney Krug called to the stand two witnesses, Harold A. Rose, the forestry captain, and Judy Hagel, the sheriff's dispatcher. Krug tried to ask Rose about a previous conversation he had had with Oakes to reveal that Oakes had meant no ill will toward Morgan. Judge Moskowitz sided with the defense, and the testimony was not allowed. A reading of the original dispatch record phoned in by Robert Myer was also blocked by Judge Moskowitz after an objection from Pawson. Krug was being hard pressed to make his case. At every turn Pawson relied on stereotypes to supplement doubt. When Robert Vollmer testified as a technician for the sheriff's department, he used drawings and photographs to demonstrate the distances separating Morgan, Oakes, and the redwood tree. Vollmer also was asked about the location of a yellow beaded medicine bag that Oakes was wearing under his shirt. Pawson tried to imply that the pouch may have contained drugs, using anything to discredit Oakes. Interestingly, Vollmer testified that it was unclear as to the cause of matted grass near the redwood tree in question, but that Oakes was found to have traces of metal, specifically steel, on the base of his index finger. Since Oakes was unarmed, Vollmer was unclear about how to interpret these findings. Had Richard Oakes tried to grab Morgan's gun? Rather than speculate or face another objection, Krug left the testimony to resonate with the jury.[63]

All the while the Wounded Knee occupation continued to make national headlines as gunfire was exchanged daily. On the third day of the trial, Detective Sergeant Irwin "Butch" Carlstedt read the three-page signed statement he took from Morgan on the day of the shooting. He added that when he arrived on the scene he examined the grass behind the redwood, and it was matted as if someone had walked over the grass. The murder weapon, a Walther P38 9mm semi-automatic handgun, was also entered into the court as evidence.[64] The state ballistics expert, Harry Johnson, claimed that Morgan was at least "three feet or further away" from Oakes when the fatal shot was fired. Johnson mentioned that the bullet hole in Oakes's chest was larger than the exit wound on his back but confirmed that Oakes was shot in the chest, not in the back, as some had speculated. The district attorney failed to point out that, in a previous encounter with Morgan, Oakes had turned his back on Morgan, who was pointing a gun at him. Annie Oakes bore witness to the entire proceedings, every day reliving the nightmare of that tragic day.[65]

On March 2, 1973, the fourth day of the trial, Robert Myers, who had perjured his testimony during the hearings, took the stand. Myers testified that "he ran from the camp corrals to Skagg Springs Road, a distance of almost 400 feet, when he heard 'angry, loud voices.' . . . As he approached the county road . . . he saw Morgan . . . standing facing the road, his legs spread apart and with both hands extended in front of him, holding a gun. . . . Just before he heard the report of a gunshot . . . he 'thought' he saw a brown 'blur' coming from a clump of bushes to the left of Morgan." While on the stand Myers admitted that the testimony he provided during the hearing was less than truthful. He had concealed the truth about the time between the argument he heard and the time he arrived to witness the shooting. Myers also told the court that Morgan had asked Myers, in his testimony, to shorten the amount of time to reinforce the heat-of-the-moment argument. In his testimony Myers continued to recall the events of September 14 and 15. Myers's statements resembled his hearing testimony except for a conversation between Frank Greer and Morgan that he recalled at the trial. During breakfast Greer pressed Morgan for information on hunting seasons in California; and Morgan smilingly replied that "there's open season on coons and Indians." Myers recalled that Greer was in absolute shock and that Morgan had labeled Oakes as a "troublemaker," stating that he was "better off dead." Robert Myers's testimony revealed two key points—Morgan was a racist who thought that Oakes would be "better off dead." Clearly Myers's testimony provided further evidence that Morgan was asking witnesses to conceal the truth and that Morgan was well aware of Richard Oakes's politics and reputation as a Native rights advocate and leader.[66]

The next day national attention focused on New Mexico, where Kiva Club president Larry Casuse and Robert Nakaidinae, both Diné students from the University of New Mexico had kidnapped Gallup mayor Emmett Garcia at gunpoint. After an intense escape in which the mayor jumped through a plate glass window while he was shot in the back with a shotgun, local police unleashed a flurry of gunfire on the sporting goods store in which the incident was taking place. In the end, Larry Casuse, the vibrant student leader at UNM, was killed in the gun battle, and Robert

Nakaidinae was taken prisoner. Casuse had tried to lead a student campaign to prevent the appointment of the mayor to the Board of Regents at UNM. The mayor was known by local Navajo in the border town of Gallup for exploiting Native liquor sales. The kidnapping attracted national press attention; the local *Press Democrat* followed suit and ran the headline: "New Mexico Mayor Indians in Kidnap." As all Indian activists must be the same, public support and opinion in the Morgan trial had ample conjecture to label Oakes as just another "militant Indian."[67]

In a stunning move, District Attorney Krug put Annie Oakes on the stand to offer testimony about her husband's physical condition prior to the shooting. She mentioned that Richard Oakes suffered from double vision and an inability to walk properly. In June of 1972 her husband also underwent unsuccessful eye surgery at the University of California Medical Center in San Francisco. Annie also conveyed to the jury and court that Richard Oakes suffered from incredible physical pain on his left side, which would make it impossible for him to lift any heavy object before he was murdered. Simply put, his physical condition was such that he was not able to act as an aggressor. Continuing in a controlled line of questioning, Krug asked her about her husband's medicine bag. She remembered that the spiritual necklace was broken when she received it from the coroner; Krug's inference from this was that the bullet, upon hitting the beaded strand, expanded, causing the entry hole of the bullet to be much larger than the exit hole.

It must have taken every ounce of energy for Annie to sit across from her husband's killer. After she stepped down from the stand, Krug called Mrs. Phyllis McMillan, a cook at the YMCA camp, to testify. Mrs. McMillan, who was a witness to the September 14 altercation involving Billy Lazore, Richard Oakes, Robert Myers, and Michael Morgan, said that Richard was not in possession of a knife when Morgan aimed the rifle at Oakes. Krug then rested his case against Morgan.[68]

Defense Attorney Richard Pawson put Michael Morgan on the stand. On March 7, 1973, Morgan provided his thirty minutes of testimony about how the events of September 14 and 15 unfolded. Morgan stated that he first met Richard at a Christmas party on the Kashaya Reservation in 1971. The next time he saw him was on September 14, when Morgan pulled a rifle on him. Morgan nervously answered Pawson's question as reporters noted how Morgan's complexion shifted dramatically between pale and

Michael Oliver Morgan and Defense Attorney
Richard Pawson walking into the courtroom for the
trial. The photo appeared in the February 22, 1973,
issue of *The Press Democrat*, published out of Santa
Rosa, California. Photo courtesy of *The Press
Democrat*.

flush.[69] Morgan's story had changed very little from his original testimony, and Pawson then relied on secondary witnesses such as Bony
Saludes, a *Press Democrat* reporter covering the trial who remembered
Richard Oakes from the Kashaya roadblock in 1970. The reporter
confirmed that Oakes had a unique way of walking, a limp; he walked
"slow, deliberately," said Saludes, a description that clearly attacked the
credibility of Morgan's story.[70]

   Just one day later, for a second time, Morgan took the stand to recount
what had happened the day he shot Richard Oakes. On the stand Morgan
changed his testimony considerably from his original statement. He
claimed that Oakes had not jumped from behind the redwood tree but
that he first saw Oakes walking toward him with his hands to his sides.
He countered Robert Myers's testimony that he stood in a fixed firing
stance. Morgan stated that Oakes crouched down and then lunged

forward, taking two to three steps toward Morgan before he fired the gun and Oakes fell to his knees. Krug challenged Morgan's testimony when he pointed out that his story was not consistent with the position of Oakes's body at the scene. Morgan then changed his mind, instead claiming that Richard Oakes had "squatted" before he fell backwards. As the questioning continued, Morgan relayed how in one motion he drew the gun from his waistband with his right hand, cocked it with his left, aimed and fired the fatal shot in self-defense. The timing of his court-room statement drastically conflicted with his original testimony, as Krug pointed out to the jury. Morgan denied the racial slurs and said that someone else had made those comments about the open season "and I agreed with him." Morgan also refuted previous witness testimony when he stated that his exact words were: "Some Indians are real trouble makers, like Richard Oakes. . . . This country is better off without people like that." Morgan's closing statement revealed that he shot Richard Oakes "out of fear for my life."[71]

By March 10, Judge Moskowitz had dismissed the involuntary manslaughter charge and informed the jury they would decide only the more serious charge of voluntary manslaughter. The judge agreed with Defense Attorney Richard Pawson that there was little evidence for a conviction on involuntary manslaughter. Krug opposed the ruling, stating that the judge's decision was meant to influence the jury. Judge Moskowitz imposed tight restrictions on Krug's rebuttal witnesses, at times sending the jury out of the courtroom. Deputy Sheriff David M. Carver was the first on the scene during the September 14 incident, when Morgan had supposedly asked if he could go free for killing Oakes. Carver, possibly fearful of a civil suit or of being implicated with Morgan, claimed that he could not remember the conversation. Carver claimed that he had told Morgan that he had the right to protect himself. Interestingly, the deputy sheriff mentioned that Oakes did not wave a knife at Morgan. Annie Oakes was called to the stand to confirm that her husband spent Christmas Eve on Alcatraz in 1970 and in New York the following year. Morgan's credibility and testimony were at issue, but because Judge Moskowitz had thrown out the involuntary charge he ruled that some testimonies were inadmissible. Krug also called Ronald Anthony Hodge from California Indian Legal Services to testify about Oakes's physical condition at the time of the shooting. Pawson quickly challenged the testimony and claimed that Hodge was biased because he had represented the Oakes family in the past.[72]

As the jury began deliberations on March 13, a group of picketers began to march in front of the courthouse. Rocky Oakes was photographed holding a sign that read "Morgan killed my Daddy!!! Murdered!!!" while other banners asked, "Is there open season on Indians?" Soon the crowd dispersed under threat of arrest for jury tampering. In his closing statement Krug announced, "Oakes was not looking for a fight. . . . Oakes had no knife or gun. . . . He only took with him his spoken word and he carries that in his heart. . . . That is all Richard Oakes had—his spoken word. That was his weapon. . . . The angle of shot . . . was proof that Oakes was not facing Morgan but that his left side was closest to the defendant . . . a damn good shot for a man in fear for his life." Pawson referred to Krug's prosecution as good storytelling, and he continued to discredit Krug's lead witnesses.[73]

The jury appeared deadlocked during three days of deliberations. Finally, at 3:35 p.m. on the third day, the jury gave their verdict to Judge Lincoln F. Mahan, a substitute for the absent Judge Moskowitz. Silence gripped the courtroom as Morgan scanned the faces of the jury for any positive signs. Annie Oakes waited with anticipation, standing near the back of the courtroom, unable to sit down. The judge handed the decision to Katheryn Plover, the court clerk, to announce. The verdict "not guilty" fell upon the courtroom like a lead weight. No one moved until Nancy Morgan, the wife of Michael Morgan, started to cry. Morgan himself sat motionless, possibly stunned by the verdict. Annie ran up to District Attorney Krug and crying in disbelief called out, "This is white man's justice . . . this isn't justice he murdered my husband!" Judge Mahan ordered officers to take Annie Oakes into custody, and she was quickly escorted out of the courtroom. On the judge's orders, the officer released Oakes as soon as they were outside the courtroom. In her anger Annie continued to vocalize her pain, "Indians are free to kill! That's all you want . . . ." She was quickly comforted by supporters and escorted out of the building. Annie continued talking with reporters: "In a case like this if an Indian had shot a white man, do you think they would have come out with the same verdict? . . . I'm not bitter, I'm hurt. . . . [Richard] wouldn't hurt anybody. . . . His fight was with the government . . . not the ranchers or private property owners. He thought if he was killed, it would be a federal agent who would kill him." She felt wronged by Krug because he had prevented her from revealing the real reason why Richard Oakes was on the road. She stated that her husband had scheduled a meeting with attorney James King. Oakes was researching the YMCA land titles to see if the property was on Kashaya lands.[74]

The prosecution pointed out that Oakes suffered from debilitating injuries, well known to Morgan, and that his claim of attack was highly unlikely. They similarly argued that if the 230-pound, six-foot Oakes had lunged for Morgan, he should have fallen forward from the single shot, rather than backward. Moreover, Oakes was unarmed. Given Oakes's impaired physical condition, Morgan could have easily escaped any assault. Most importantly, the act of carrying a loaded weapon should have been rendered or interpreted by a just court as premeditated murder. Additionally, District Attorney John Hawkes suggested that the "investigation overlooked evidence" showing that Morgan "had developed a reputation in the community indicating strong feelings of prejudice against Indians," according to CILS (California Indian Legal Services) attorneys. They also point out that failure to charge first-degree murder is part of a northern California pattern in which there have been three killings of Indians by whites in the previous nine months—all with charges which they call "inadequate."[75] Despite all of the many loopholes and Morgan's shaky testimony, he was set free.

CONCLUSION

AT PIT RIVER, MORE OCCUPATIONS continued despite Richard Oakes's assassination. Pacific Gas & Electric and other multinational corporations feared that they might lose the battle as Pit River lawsuits reached higher and more liberal courts. Coincidentally, a rumor spread through the Pit River Nation to the effect that members could cash their Claims Commission Settlement checks and that this action would not deter current lawsuits. The BIA supported the rumor, and that assurance pressured many Pit River residents to cash their Claims Settlement checks. In a scandalous move, the federal government argued that the outright acceptance of these payments was a vote in favor of settlement. Pit River members, through corruption and trickery, may have found that the political rug had been pulled out from beneath their feet, but they were not about to give in to questionable tactics.[1]

On May 26, 1973, the title to Toyon Job Corps Center, which Richard Oakes had fought to acquire, was officially granted to the Pit River Nation. After relentless battles with the federal government and surrounding corporations, the Pit River Nation found itself crippled by debt. The high cost of maintaining legal pressure and direct action campaigns had taken its toll on the Tribe. When Tribal Chairman Mickey Gemmill accepted the title to Toyon, he had to reassess Pit River's future. Eventually Gemmill made a controversial decision to end further action against the government and the corporations. The bold declaration split the Tribe into council supporters and holdouts. The opposing faction, led by Raymond Lego, continued to occupy lands claimed by PG&E. They also added Kimberley-Clark lands near Big Bend, California, to their agenda. Lego maintained a permanent residence on these lands and continued legal pressure on these companies until his untimely death in 1980.[2] Mickey Gemmill resumed his service to Pit River, remained a board member on the International Indian Treaty Council, and aided in the promotion of the Indian Child Welfare Act of 1978. He also remained a steady promoter for protection of Native sacred sites until his unfortunate passing in 2006.

Perhaps the most dramatic legacy of Richard Oakes lay with the Trail of Broken Treaties. But more importantly, his life served as a model for Red Power from his early childhood until his assassination. Oakes's involvement was rooted in Mohawk Nationalism, which planted the intellectual seeds for Red Power. As a prominent member of the first class of Indian students at UC Berkeley and San Francisco State College in 1969, Oakes and other Native students promoted the advent of Native American Studies. Oakes also proved prominent in the move to occupy Alcatraz, in the effort to organize land claims for Pit River and Clear Lake, in the Fort Lawton takeover, and in the training of new leaders in White Roots of Peace. He helped establish the first wave of organizational leadership for the Red Power movement of the 1960s and 1970s. Oakes's life cannot be identified solely with the occupation of Alcatraz, even though it was one of the major events in his brief but powerful career. The trial of Richard Oakes's assassin, Michael Oliver Morgan, in many ways symbolized a larger trial and conflict underway in Indian Country, a struggle for freedom. From a young age and throughout his life, Richard Oakes struggled to ignite a generation that would maintain the independent and sovereign status of Native nations.

The legacy of Richard Oakes is also found in the twenty-six pieces of self-determination legislation that have led to a Nation-to-Nation status as official federal Indian policy. While President Nixon repealed termination in 1970, his administration supported and passed groundbreaking legislation such as the Indian Financing Act of 1974 and the Indian Self-Determination and Educational Assistance Act (1975), leading to the American Indian Religious Freedom Act (1978), to name just a few. As Nixon was establishing his presidency to be the "Indian Presidency," Taos Pueblo regained Blue Lake (1970). By 1978 the Menominee Nation, through a concerted Red Power campaign employed by Tribal leader Ada Deer, had reversed the termination status of the Menominee. By President William Jefferson Clinton's administration some thirty years later, Native peoples were proclaimed to enjoy a Nation-to-Nation status with the federal government and Ada Deer became the Commissioner of Indian Affairs. It is impossible to provide Oakes with sole credit for all of this change, but without Richard Oakes's leadership one would not want to speculate how much worse off Native nations throughout the United States would be today.

Native American Studies departments and programs have continued to prosper and grow; today there are approximately seventy-nine such programs in the United States and over thirty in Canada. About twenty of these programs award master's and doctoral degrees. Native student enrollment at major universities and Tribal colleges continues to accelerate as students learn their Native languages, histories, dances, and lifeways and study Indian law. As a major institution of the Indian City, American Indian Studies departments continue to add diversity, complexity, and Intertribal populations in major Indian Cities. Sizable numbers of Native peoples continue to reside or commute to Indian Cities.[3]

The once-vibrant Mohawk City of Oakes's youth was transformed by new highways and faster speed limits, which have drastically reduced the commute from Brooklyn to Akwesasne and Kahnawà:ke. Despite a depopulated Brooklyn, Mohawks remain one of the prominent populations in the ironworking trade in New York. Iroquois leaders continue to push for recognition in the United Nations, and recently the 2010 Iroquois Nationals lacrosse team exerted media and political pressure on the U.S. State Department to protect their treaty-based right to travel internationally with Haudenosaunee passports. The International Bridge, the Seaway Project, and the reclamation of treaty lands remain a part of the constant struggle at Kahnawà:ke and Akwesasne. The 1990 Oka Crisis at Kanesatake Reserve, in which members of the Mohawk Warrior Society took up arms against the Provincial Police and the Canadian military, was another legacy of Red Power. In the crisis at Oka, Mohawk citizens protected Native lands from a large company that sought to expand its golf course onto reservation land. Years later the president of the Wisconsin Oneida Nation protested a screening of director James Fortier's Alcatraz Is Not an Island at Syracuse University. The Tribal Chairman argued that Richard Oakes was a member of the Warriors and represented values antithetical to the Longhouse and traditional Haudenosaunee teachings. The plethora of misinformation and the lack of a historical biography of Richard Oakes prevents young Akwesasne and Kahnawà:ke, in addition to other young Native peoples, from knowing of Oakes's struggle and leadership.

Richard Oakes's memory continues into the present day. In October of 1996, Akwesasne Mohawk Tom Sullivan opened the doors of the Richard Oakes American Indian Center in Syracuse, New York. The center supported job training and educational programs for low-income residents throughout Syracuse. Sullivan reflected on Oakes legacy: "Oakes['s] dream was for Indians from all over to build an educational and cultural center. Twenty-five years later those ideas are coming back to communities, and some are becoming real . . ."[4]

Richard Oakes with Ross Harden on Alcatraz Island, November 25, 1969. This is the first publication of this photo. Photo courtesy of the *San Francisco Examiner* and Sara Glines, photographer Paul Glines. Original photo negative in Kent Blansett Private Collection.

On March 22, 2001, San Francisco State University dedicated their new multicultural center in memory of Richard Oakes during a grand convocation that lasted several days. At the ceremony, the university honored members of the leader's family and invited them to speak publicly about Richard Oakes. Dr. LaNada War Jack (Means) and Mickey Gemmill reunited their voices to remember their friend and companion. Near the closing of the festivities, traditional dancers gathered close to the drum, dancing with the memory of Richard Oakes. Honor songs once again reclaimed the campus of San Francisco State University. Students and community members collectively witnessed the continuation of Richard Oakes's journey—a journey to freedom.[5]

During the last several years many of the veterans from this era of protest have begun to pass away. Every passing takes with it historical knowledge and stories that can expand our historical understanding of Red Power. Mickey Gemmill, who had worked at the Pit River Nation, died in 2006. Two years later environmental activist Grace Thorpe, the daughter of the famous athlete Jim Thorpe, passed away. Before she joined the Alcatraz occupation, she had served patriotically in World War II in the Women's Army Corps under Douglas MacArthur in Japan. In 2010 Indian Country and the Cherokee Nation lost Beloved Woman and former Principal Chief Wilma Mankiller, who was profoundly influenced by Alcatraz. Countless stories are lost as an entire generation of Red Power veterans are called home.

In 2009, the city of San Francisco witnessed the fortieth anniversary of the Alcatraz takeover. Celebrations and talks commemorating the anniversary took place across the city at San Francisco State University, UC Berkeley, and Alcatraz Island. Annie Oakes looked on as Mayor Gavin Newsom proclaimed November 20 Richard Oakes Day for the entire city of San Francisco. Almost one year later, on August 1, 2010, Annie Oakes, after a long battle with cancer, passed into the spirit world. After forty years, she was reunited with her husband Richard, her daughter Yvonne, and her son Rocky, who was struck and killed by a car as he walked across Route 101 in California in 1977. Despite all the trauma and loss she had experienced, Annie had maintained a quiet life in Santa Rosa, California. She had enjoyed gardening and reading, and she often talked about her late husband. Her son Leonard remembered when his mother received the mayor's proclamation as a joyous event, knowing that Richard Oakes had finally been recognized. On August 9, 2010, Annie was laid to rest next to Richard Oakes.[6]

I made my first journey to San Francisco during the summer of 2001, supported by a research grant from the University of New Mexico. My tiny hotel room was located just a stone's throw from Fisherman's Wharf, from which Alcatraz Island is visible. I alternated between visits to the San Francisco Public Library and San Francisco State University. The day had finally come: I was going to Alcatraz. I boarded a large boat, with hundreds of other tourists, surrounded by the sounds of sea lions and seagulls. As the ferry pulled away from the pier, the winds picked up and we bounced along the choppy bay waters. Standing near the bow, looking down at the water below, I tried to picture Oakes's swim some thirty years earlier.

Pulling up to the island, I smiled, having noticed the welcome sign. The paint, now a little faded, was still crimson. The sign read "Indians Welcome . . . Indian Land." I then realized the irony of the sign. It was the first welcome sign I had ever seen in this country for Native peoples. Walking between the cellblocks and other old structures, I could envision the haunts that Richard Oakes and other occupiers called home. I looked around with other tourists, wondering if the strangers surrounding me shared the same feeling of excitement. Most seemed preoccupied with their headsets that recounted the former prison days, when America's toughest criminals lived on the island. I laughed when I realized that I was there for a similar reason, when America's toughest Indians had reclaimed the island. As the evening grew dark and children on the tour fell asleep in their parents' arms, I sat on an empty railing staring back at the city lights on the mainland. I was reassured that Richard Oakes's memory continues to live on, that Alcatraz had become a sacred space, a memorial to Red Power. On the boat ride back to the mainland, I felt proud even as the island faded from my sight. The occupation of Alcatraz had been a success. Today the island is a living monument and museum to Oakes and to "Indians of All Tribes." The vision of Indians of All Tribes and the idea of Alcatraz continue to inspire future Native leaders and Indian policy.

NOTES

INTRODUCTION

Parts of this chapter and subsequent chapters are republished with permission of ABC-CLIO Inc.: Kent Blansett, "A Journey to Freedom: Richard Oakes, American Indian Activism, and the Occupation of Alcatraz," in *American Indians in American History, 1870–2001: A Companion Reader*, ed. Sterling Evans, 2002; permission conveyed through Copyright Clearance Center, Inc.

1. Richard Oakes, "Alcatraz Is Not an Island," *Ramparts* (Dec. 1972), 38, *Ramparts* permissions courtesy of Guy Stilson and Greg Stilson; interview with Joe Bill (Hooper Bay Eskimo) by Dennis Stanford, transcript, Feb. 5, 1970, Doris Duke Oral History Project, Center for Southwest Research, University of New Mexico, Albuquerque, tape no. 458, side 1, 11.

2. Throughout the book I capitalize the terms *Nation, Tribe, Indigenous, Intertribal,* and *Native* (lowercase *n* is used for other usages of the word *native*), as all of these terms are proper nouns relating to a specific region, peoples, and place. The lowercase or common noun forms of *indigenous, nation,* and *tribe* are used only in reference to global indigenous concepts. One exception to the rule is when two terms meet, as in *Native peoples* or *Native nations,* as it is redundant to capitalize both terms. My scholarship does not attempt to speak for all Indigenous peoples, and I utilize capitalization as a tool to highlight the unique sovereignty of Native nations and recognize the global construct and rhetoric of Indigenous discourse. I also avoid the plural form of *Mohawk* or other Nations (this national term is already plural, as it defines an entire Nation and all its citizens). Instead, I elect to use the terms *Mohawk peoples* or *Mohawk citizens* to demonstrate rhetorical sovereignty, balance, and inclusivity. Finally, I employ the terms *Indigenous peoples* or *Native peoples* or *Mohawk peoples* in a deliberate effort to honor the diversity of status, recognition, enrollment, descendants, genders, sexualities, bands, clans, societies, and multicultural citizenry that comprise various forms of Indigenous citizenship. When possible, I use Mohawk terms and their translations to describe Mohawk governance and lifeways and prefer the term *Haudenosaunee* over *Iroquois* when in reference to the Longhouse or Six

Nations (Mohawk, Cayuga, Onondaga, Oneida, Seneca, and Tuscarora). For example, I use the term *Kahnawà:ke* over *Caughnawaga* or *Kahnawake* to refer to another closely related Mohawk Reserve located east of Akwesasne. I also elect to use the more recognizable term *Mohawk* throughout the book over the term *Kanien'kehá:ka*.

3. My definition and use of *Native Nationalism* is pulled from an ongoing academic conversation about the term and its meaning in American Indian history. The following is a brief historiographical account of the debate and the evolution of its definition. In the 2006 book *American Indian Literary Nationalism*, Native literary scholars offered the following non-exclusionary definition of *Native Nationalism* as including "sovereignty, culture, self-determination, experience, and history, that is central to understanding the relationship between the creative expression of Native American literature and the social and historical realities that such expression embodies." Jace Weaver, Craig S. Womack, and Robert Warrior, *American Indian Literary Nationalism* (Albuquerque: University of New Mexico Press, 2006), xv. Anthropologist Benedict Anderson defined *nation* as "an imagined political community—and imagined as both inherently limited and sovereign." Anderson, *Imagined Communities: Reflections of the Origins and Spread of Nationalism* (London: Verso, 2016), 6. In the 2014 book *Red Skin, White Masks* Glen Coulthard endorsed Taiaiake Alfred and Leanne Simpson's call for an "Indigenous Resurgence," in which Native nations would move beyond the politics of recognition from a colonial state; rather, we should *"enact or practice* our political commitments to Indigenous national and women's liberation in the cultural form and content of our struggle itself." Coulthard, *Red Skin, White Masks: Rejecting the Colonial Politics of Recognition* (Minneapolis: University of Minnesota Press, 2014), 159. Also from 2014, Kahnawà:ke scholar Audra Simpson's *Mohawk Interruptus* wrestles with the concept of Native Nationalism and the politics of recognition: "nationalism issues from the question of state authority and legitimacy . . . literature on nationalism has difficulty viewing Indigeneity as possibly nationalist. . . . Rather, Indigeneity is imagined as something entrapped within the analytics of 'minoritization,' a statistical model for the apprehension of (now) racialized populations 'within' nation-states. . . . Nationalism expresses a particular form of collective identity that embeds desire for sovereignty and justice." Simpson, *Mohawk Interruptus: Political Life across the Borders of Settler States* (Durham, NC: Duke University Press, 2014), 17–18. Native Nationalism as a key historical term has undergone many transformations in its tug of war with the colonial nation-state and Red Power, which advocated for greater independence. Future historical studies might attempt to investigate these transformative periods of Native Nationalism, as I suspect these periods will differ greatly among every Indigenous nation and produce a rich and valuable historical subfield.

4. Indigenous sovereignty lies outside the constructs of nation-state or colonial recognition. Indigenous sovereignty is older than America and is bound to a

continuous record of laws, governance, structure, sacred geography, language, and practices of autonomy and confederation that predate colonization. Indigenous sovereignty is timeless, and its expression is not bound strictly to governing or political structures but also occurs in story, art, architecture, labor, song, dance, war, and the historical actions/lifeways of its peoples or citizens.

5. Red Power as a historical subfield of American Indian history has a rich historiography. The foundational texts start with literary journalist Stan Steiner's *The New Indians* (New York: Harper & Row, 1968), the first contemporary study to try to unravel the complexities of Red Power politics. In 1968, Steiner's singular narrative drew popular press attention to the fish-ins of the Pacific Northwest and the young activists of the National Indian Youth Council; it also documented the struggles of several urban Indian communities. In 1976, Stan Steiner dedicated his book *Vanishing White Man* (New York: Harper & Row, 1976) to Richard Oakes. Clearly, Oakes's life had influenced Steiner's evaluation of Red Power in the mid-1970s. A year later, Standing Rock Lakota scholar Vine Deloria Jr. published *Custer Died for Your Sins: An Indian Manifesto* (New York: Macmillan, 1969) and First Nations Cree author Harold Cardinal published *The Unjust Society* (Edmonton: M.G. Hurtig Ltd., 1969). Both Deloria and Cardinal highlighted the transnational scope of Red Power as a major North American Indigenous movement. Beyond geopolitical borders between Canada and the United States, Indigenous authors Deloria and Cardinal issued a call for a reawakening of Indian culture and politics and reforms at the Tribal and federal level. Vine Deloria Jr. continued to record and critique the progress of Red Power through an immense collection of works: *We Talk, You Listen* (1970), *Of Utmost Good Faith* (1971), *God is Red* (1973), to name just a few. Complementing Deloria's epic and voluminous work on Red Power, historian Alvin M. Josephy in 1971 published *Red Power*, which was mainly a reprinting of primary documents that held the popular philosophical and ideological core of Red Power politics. Later, Josephy's *Now That the Buffalo's Gone* (1982) offered yet another rich historical study that documented the struggle from Pyramid Lake in the Great Basin to the fish-ins in the Pacific Northwest.

6. "In 1969, eighty members of AIM, chanting 'Red Power,' snatched control of Alcatraz Island," Gary A. Donaldson, *The Making of Modern America: The Nation from 1945 to the Present* (Lanham, MD: Rowman and Littlefield Publishers, Inc., 2009), 178; "In November 1969, a small group of activists from the American Indian Movement (AIM) occupied Alcatraz Island," William H. Chafe, Harvard Sitkoff, and Beth Bailey, *A History of Our Time: Reading on Postwar America* (New York: Oxford University Press, 2008), 159; "Important AIM actions have included the 1969 takeover of Alcatraz Island," Barry M. Pritzker, *A Native American Encyclopedia: History, Culture, and Peoples* (New York: Oxford University Press, 2000), 412; "In 1969 AIM organizers joined local Indian activists in occupying San Francisco Bay's Alcatraz

Island," Robert V. Hine and John Mack Faragher, *The American West: A New Interpretive History* (New Haven: Yale University Press, 2000), 539; "more militant members of AIM dramatized their dissatisfaction by seizing the abandoned federal prison on Alcatraz Island," James West Davidson, Brian DeLay, Christine Leigh Heyrman, Mark H. Lytle, and Michael B. Stoff, *Nation of Nations: A Narrative History of the American Republic Volume II: Since 1865* (Boston: McGraw-Hill Higher Education, 2008), 904; "The occupation of Alcatraz by American Indian Movement activists and others in 1969," Coll Thrush, *Native Seattle: Histories from the Crossing-Over Place* (Seattle: University of Washington Press, 2007), 170; "The mission of AIM was to force the dominant U.S. culture to listen and to act on Indian rights, and the organization felt that only militant action, which would attract media coverage, could effectively communicate their message. Among their first actions was the seizure and occupation of Alcatraz in San Francisco Bay," Mark O. Sutton, *An Introduction to Native North America*, 3rd ed. (Boston: Pearson Education, 2008), 370. These examples are a mere sample of the scholarship that has stripped proper credit for the Alcatraz takeover away from Indians of All Tribes (IAT) and falsely apportioned credit to the American Indian Movement. This major error and militant label continues to be repeated by prominent American historians and Indigenous studies scholars.

7. D'Arcy McNickle, *Native American Tribalism: Indian Survivals and Renewals* (New York: Oxford University Press, 1973), 170.

8. See Gerald R. Alfred, *Heeding the Voices of Our Ancestors: Kahnawake Mohawk Politics and the Rise of Native Nationalism* (Toronto: Oxford University Press, 1995), 6–24. *Native Nationalism* is defined differently from the former term *ethno-nationalism*. *Ethno-nationalism* is typically used to describe political movements like the early twentieth-century movement associated by Marcus Garvey's call for Black Nationalism (implies lacking sovereignty or an independent nation/territory). Thus, *ethno-nationalism* as a term misrepresents Native political history and is incredibly problematic for two primary reasons: the terminology assumes an ethnic status and racial identity for American Indians, and it ignores the preexistence of Indigenous sovereignty. Late nineteenth-century assimilationist efforts sponsored by both federal policy and "friends of the Indian" organizations were often rooted in the hysteria of eugenics rhetoric, which strove to "racialize" or impose a singular "American Indian" race on all Indigenous peoples. Former efforts to "kill the Indian and save the man" served an ulterior purpose, namely to destroy Tribal citizenship, sovereignty, and culture and dismantle all Indigenous rights.

9. Definition and historiography are necessary for any historical study that attempts to identify the complicated origins of Red Power and Native self-determination. The genesis of Red Power is not exclusive to any one individual or organization; rather, as a movement, it was a shared experience with multifaceted origins that emerged in the early 1960s. As a political ideal, Red Power is often confused as a synonym for the self-determination and

nationalism of the early twentieth century. Self-determination was born out of the World War I idealism of Woodrow Wilson, who advocated for a League of Nations, as spelled out in his Fourteen Points doctrine. In the fifth of his Fourteen Points, Wilson urged the world powers to promote self-determination and to divest themselves of their colonial states and territories. Self-determination under Wilson's plan (excluding the United States) called for the gradual right of self-governance and sovereignty for all nations currently under the boot heel of a foreign imperial power. A controversial notion, self-determination sparked a rise in nationalism throughout the world as well as the return of Indigenous politics and culture and the subsequent overthrow of a colonial or foreign power. Beyond the original "Fourteen Points" document are several articles that attempt to define self-determination and nationalism. In 1957, Marshall E. Dimock examined the "New Freedom" that Wilson referred to in his humanitarian goal to promote anticolonialism, concluding that this goal dismantled the acceptance of the League of Nations by Congress. Marshall E. Dimock, "Woodrow Wilson as Legislative Leader," *Journal of Politics* 19:1 (Feb. 1957), 9. See also Craig Calhoun, "Nationalism and Ethnicity," *Annual Review of Sociology* 19 (1993), 213; and Ernst E. Haas, "The Attempt to Terminate Colonialism: Acceptance of the United Nations Trusteeship System," *International Organization* 7:1 (Feb. 1953), 2.

10. Rupert Costo and Jeannette Henry Costo, *Indian Voices: The First Convocation of American Indian Scholars* (San Francisco: Indian Historian Press, 1970), 299–307. Red Power emerged out of Native Nationalism and by the 1960s had distinguished itself as an Intertribal movement that employed nonviolent direct action to promote Indian self-determination (Indian control and autonomy over Indian institutions, policies, lands, and jurisdictions). Deeply tied to global movements in decolonization, nation and community rebuilding, liberation theology, and cultural revitalization; Red Power called for land reclamation and restoration of treaty lands and an assertion of Indigenous human rights/sovereignty; it was an Intertribal movement born out of but not entirely separate from Native Nationalism. Richard Oakes and other activists of the Red Power era studied and employed liberation theology as central to their fight for Indigenous land reclamation.

11. Like racialization, Americanization as a process also functioned as another process of twentieth-century American colonization. In essence, Americanization promoted the assimilation and acculturation of vast numbers of noncitizen populations and relied on various state and national institutions to aid in transformation of the immigrant "other" into American citizens. Such systems were meant to strip an individual of their "foreign" citizenship in order to replace it with a new, American identity and citizenship. Since its inception, American citizenship valued one core principle to deny immigrants and Indigenous peoples all allegiances to a separate foreign or domestic power and eradicate the potential of rival nations to form within the nation. The strict regulation of American citizenship served as a national defense strategy to thwart any internal insurrections and limit "other"

populations from gaining access to power in American political institutions. The preservation of U.S. sovereignty depended on covert and overt systems of colonization. Colonization enabled America to absorb millions of immigrant individuals and hundreds of sovereign Native nations. The ethnic-Americanization process emerged as another powerful tool to de-Tribalize Indigenous nations and eradicate their rights to dual citizenship or self-governance. The passage of the 1887 Dawes Severalty Act imposed a Reconstruction-era brand of *colonial citizenship,* a closed and racialized citizenship, on Native peoples. Imposing closed citizenship on Indigenous peoples served several ulterior purposes: to destroy Indigenous governing systems and prevent rival nations from gaining power within America. The battle to contain Indigenous citizenship resulted from a fear of competing demographics (or, potentially, citizenships). As a structured system, American colonization actively sought to strip Native peoples of their independent citizenship and to replace that citizenship with a racialized third-class citizenship that was completely dependent on the federal government or colonial state. Ultimately these systems failed to eradicate Indigenous citizenship, but their devastating effects have lingered into the twenty-first century. See also Joanne Barker, *Native Acts: Law, Recognition, and Cultural Authenticity* (Durham, NC: Duke University Press, 2011); and David Roediger and Elizabeth D. Esch, *The Production of Difference: Race and the Management of Labor in U.S. History* (New York: Oxford University Press, 2012).

12. Currently, all urban histories, like Tribal histories, tend to focus exclusively on one major city like Chicago, Los Angeles, or Seattle. *A Journey to Freedom* represents the first comparative urban history to explore three major cities through the lens of biography. My concept of Indian Cities builds upon the scholarship of Reyna K. Ramirez's *Native Hubs: Culture, Community, and Belonging in Silicon Valley and Beyond* (Durham, NC: Duke University Press, 2007).

1. AKWESASNE, KAHNAWÀ:KE, AND "LITTLE CAUGHNAWAGA"

1. State of California, County of Sonoma, *Certification of Vital Record for Thomas Richard Oakes,* prepared by Bernice A. Peterson, Recorder, Sonoma County, California, May 15, 2001.
2. North American Indian Travelling College, *Tewaarathon (Lacrosse): Akwesasne's Story of Our National Game* (Cornwall Island, Ontario: North American Indian Travelling College, 1978), 59.
3. For the purpose of simplification I will use *Akwesasne* to refer collectively to both the Canadian and U.S. sides of the Nation. The Haudenosaunee Confederacy or Longhouse is made up of six nations: the Oneida, Seneca, Tuscarora, Onondaga, Cayuga, and Mohawk Nations. For a more detailed assessment of the formation of the Confederacy, see Daniel K. Richter, *The Ordeal of the Longhouse: The Peoples of the Iroquois League in the Era of European Colonization* (Chapel Hill: University of North Carolina Press, 1992), 1–284; and Barbara Barnes, ed., *Traditional Teachings* (Cornwall Island, Ontario: North American Indian Travelling College, 1984), 1–101.

4. "Caughnawaga was the Anglicized version of 'Kahnawake' used prior to 1892, when the community switched to the Mohawk spelling and pronunciation," Stephanie Phillips, "The Kahnawake Mohawks and the St. Lawrence Seaway" (Master's Thesis, McGill University, 2000), 4. See also Matthew Noah Turchow, "The Mohawks of Brooklyn: A History of the Caughnawaga Community," Senior Honors Essay, Yale University, Brooklyn Public Library Special Collection, 1983.

5. Jack A. Frisch, "Tribalism among the St. Regis Mohawks: A Search for Self-Identity," *Anthropologica* 12:2 (1970), 209–210.

6. Jack A. Frisch, "The Abanakis among the St. Regis Mohawks," *The Indian Historian* 4:1 (Spring 1971), 27–29. "Among them were members of all the tribes in the Iroquois Confederacy. . . . There were also a few Hurons, Eries, and Ottawas who had been captured and adopted by the Iroquois and had been living with them in the longhouse villages. Mohawks greatly predominated." Joseph Mitchell, "The Mohawks in High Steel," in *Apologies to the Iroquois*, ed. Edmund Wilson (New York: Vintage Books, 1960), 11.

7. Canada is host to several other Mohawk Reserve populations: Tyendinaga or Kenhtè:ke, Ontario (named after the controversial Mohawk leader, Joseph Brandt), Oka or Kanehsatà:ke, Ganienkeh Territory in upper New York, and Six Nations, Ontario (located next to Lake Erie).

8. Thomas A. Britten, *American Indians in World War I: At War and at Home* (Albuquerque: University of New Mexico Press, 1997), 69. See also Susan Applegate Krouse, *North American Indians in the Great War* (Lincoln: University of Nebraska Press, 2007); and Micheal L. Tate, "From Scout to Doughboy: The National Debate over Integrating American Indians into the Military," *Western Historical Quarterly* 17:4 (Oct. 1986), 417–437. For a more general history of World War I, see Martin Gilbert, *The First World War: A Complete History* (New York: Henry Holt, 1994).

9. "Carlisle alone contributed 205 servicemen," Russel Lawrence Barsh, "American Indians in the Great War," *Ethnohistory* 38:3 (Summer 1991), 278–279.

10. Johnny Beauvais, "Lacrosse We Remember," *The Eastern Door* 1:19 (Nov. 6, 1992), 8. *The Eastern Door* was the Tribal newspaper for Kahnawà:ke Reserve and accessed through the Kanien'kehá:ka Onkwawén:na Raotitióhkwa Language and Cultural Center.

11. The number of American Indians who served in Canadian regiments is unknown because Canada and the Indian Affairs Branch failed to develop a process to track numbers on this minority population of enlistments. "press reports indicated that hundreds of Native Americans from the United States enlisted in the Canadian army between 1915 and 1917." Britten, *American Indians in World War I*, 60.

12. Jennings C. Wise, *The Red Man in the New World Drama*, ed. Vine Deloria Jr. (New York: Macmillan, 1971), 320.

13. Barsh, "American Indians in the Great War," 288. On the foundations of SAI, see Chadwick Allen and Beth H. Piatote, ed., "The Society of American Indians and Its Legacies," *American Indian Quarterly* (Special Edition), 37:3 (Summer 2013).

14. Hazel Hertzberg, *The Search for an American Indian Identity: Modern Pan-Indian Movements* (Syracuse: Syracuse University Press, 1971), 175. While my own work refutes parts of Hertzberg's original thesis and use of the term *Pan-Indian*, her book created new inroads into the study of SAI and early twentieth-century Native history. On the Society of American Indians, see Peter Iverson, *Carlos Montezuma and the Changing World of American Indians* (Albuquerque: University of New Mexico Press, 1982); Jane Hafen, "Gertrude Simmons Bonnin: For the Indian Cause," in *Sifters: Native American Women's Lives*, ed. Theda Perdue (New York: Oxford University Press, 2001), 127–140; Zitkala-Sa, *Dreams and Thunder: Stories, Poems, and The Sun Dance Opera*, ed. P. Jane Hafen (Lincoln: University of Nebraska Press, 2001); David Martinez, *Dakota Philosopher: Charles Eastman and American Indian Thought* (St. Paul: Minnesota Historical Society Press, 2009); Raymond Wilson, *Ohiyesa: Charles Eastman, Santee Sioux* (Urbana and Champagne: University of Illinois Press, 1983); and Joy Porter, *To Be Indian: The Life of Iroquois-Seneca Arthur Caswell Parker* (Norman: University of Oklahoma Press, 2001).

15. Johnny Beauvais, "Lacrosse We Remember," *The Eastern Door* 1:19 (Nov. 6, 1992), 8.

16. Hertzberg, *Search for an American Indian Identity*, 168. Coincidentally, the Iroquois soldiers had received their bonuses before the rest of America. This payout added fuel to the fire, as the campaign for the Bonus Army March on Washington, D.C., intensified during the Great Depression.

17. Before becoming the commissioner, Collier gained notoriety by headlining the campaign in New Mexico against the Bursum Bill. After defeating the Bursum Bill, he served as the executive secretary for the American Indian Defense Association until he was nominated to be the commissioner. On Collier, see Frederick E. Hoxie and Peter Iverson, *Indians in American History: An Introduction* (Wheeling: Harlan Davidson, Inc., 1998), 177–197.

18. The Indian Reorganization Act is divided into four separate parts, outlining provisions for self-government, education, lands, and development of corporation bylaws, as well as a later, deleted portion that dealt with Tribal jurisdiction or Tribal courts. Title One sanctioned that a Tribe could organize as a self-government under a constitution approved by the Secretary of the Interior and create a corporation to apply for loans under a credit fund for economic opportunity. Title Two, influenced by the Meriam Report of 1928, pushed for a transfer from boarding schools to day schools, appropriations for scholarships and loans for higher education, and funding to revive cultural traditions in arts and crafts. Title Three abolished provisions under the Dawes Act for allotment, returned lands "not allotted" back to the Tribe, and sponsored conservation plans on existing lands—such as forestry units. The final provision, Title Four, later omitted from the bill, called for the establishment of a Tribal court system and Tribal jurisdiction over Tribal lands. The Dawes Act was devastating to Native nations. The accumulated land lost after the Dawes Act was 86 million acres out of a total of 138 million acres. The Dawes

Act had also created a checkerboard effect on reservations in which lands that fell out of inheritance were sold off to white speculators, farmers, and ranchers—further eroding the land base. Even though the Dawes Act was repealed by the IRA, the damage it caused for Native peoples was tremendous. On the Dawes Act, see Angie Debo, *A History of the Indian of the United States* (Norman: University of Oklahoma Press, 1970), 299–315; Fredrick E. Hoxie, *A Final Promise: The Campaign to Assimilate the Indians, 1880–1920* (Lincoln: University of Nebraska Press, 2001); and Emily Greenwald, *Reconfiguring the Reservation: The Nez Perces, Jicarilla Apaches, and the Dawes Act* (Albuquerque: University of New Mexico Press, 2002).

19. North American Indian Travelling College, *Tewaarathon (Lacrosse): Akwesasne's Story of Our National Game*, 70.

20. David H. Getches, Charles F. Wilkinson, and Robert A. Williams Jr., *Cases and Materials on Federal Indian Law*, 5th ed. (St. Paul: West Publishing Co., 2005), 953. See also Robert N. Clinton, Nell Jessup Newton, and Monroe E. Price, *American Indian Law: Cases and Materials*, 3rd ed. (Charlottesville: Michie, 1991), 1222–1223. On the Indian Act of 1876's effects on gender roles and identity at Kahnawà:ke, see Audra Simpson, "To the Reserve and Back Again: Kahnawake Mohawk Narratives of Self, Home, and Nation," PhD dissertation, McGill University, 2003; *Mohawk Interruptus: Political Life across the Borders of Settler States* (Durham, NC: Duke University Press, 2014); and Gerald F. Reid, " 'To Renew Our Fire': Political Activism, Nationalism, and Identity in Three Rotinonhsionni Communities," in *Tribal Worlds: Critical Studies in American Indian Nation Building*, ed. Brian Hosmer and Larry Nesper (Albany: State University of New York Press, 2013), 37–64. The Indian Act would not be amended until 1951, which ended Provincial authority to end treaty rights, and again in 1985, to repeal disenfranchisement of Native women. The Indian Act continues to be an influential and important legal document over First Nations policy in Canada. Interestingly, in the 1960s Native activists tried to repeal the Indian Act, but their efforts failed, largely due to fears that a repeal of the Indian Act might instead promote a policy of termination for Canadian First Nations.

21. Oakes, "Alcatraz Is Not an Island," 35.

22. Jerry Gambill, "How Democracy Came to St. Regis . . .," *Akwesasne Notes* 3:6 (Late Summer 1971), 23.

23. Ibid., 23; Anonymous, "Jake Ice and Jake Fire," *Indian Time* (April-June 1999), 9; and Darren Bonaparte, "Saiowisakeron: The Jake Ice Story," *Wampum Chronicles*, available at www.wampumchronicles.com/saiowisak-eron.html, accessed April 12, 2014. The names of the traditional Life Chiefs who were arrested in 1899 were, Thomas Sand, Louis Thomas, Jacob Fire [brother to Jake Ice], Louis David, John Skin, John Nine Angus, John Angus Louis, Joseph Martin, Angus Papineau, Mitchell Bova, Peter Day, Louis Terrance, Mitchell Oak, John Beck, and William Mussell. I prefer to employ the term *Colonial Agent* rather than the term *Indian Agent*, as it is important for understanding the Indigenous perspective—rather than the Canadian

government's official term. The Colonial Agent's main goal was to enforce Provincial policy over Native governance and sovereignty.

24. See also Frisch, "Abanakis among the St. Regis Mohawks," 207–219.

25. "in 1971, only a small percentage of people at Akwesasne participate in the elective system, and yet it is the only group recognized by the Government of Canada. At the Longhouse, hereditary chiefs still counsel for the Mohawk people, both in the U.S., and in Canada. . . . Neither the United States nor Canada will acknowledge that they exist." Gambill, "How Democracy Came," 23.

26. In 1802, the band council or elective chiefs (Mohawk women were prohibited from voting) was started by the New York Legislature to secure Mohawk lands. Initially the only power of the band council involved drafting policies for the improvement of land as they deemed necessary. In contrast, the traditional government is made up of nine Longhouse Chiefs nominated by Clan Mothers. Aren Akweks, *History of the St. Regis Akwesasne Mohawks* (Malone, Quebec: Lanctot Printing Shop, 1948), 18–19, Akwesasne Library and Cultural Center, "Ray Fadden Material" vertical file, Hogansburg, New York.

27. "The main reason offered for the failure to exercise the franchise is that by voting in the white man's elections, the Indian acknowledges that he is either a Canadian or an American; this would be contrary to the idea that the Iroquois, including the Mohawks, are a sovereign people. Another reason offered is that the franchise is the first step towards taxation." Frisch, "Abanakis among the St. Regis Mohawks," 217.

28. Laurence M. Hauptman, *The Iroquois and the New Deal* (Syracuse: Syracuse University Press, 1981), 68–69. On the Indian Reorganization Act, see also Clayton R. Koppes, "From New Deal to Termination: Liberalism and Indian Policy, 1933–1953," *Pacific Historical Review* 46:4 (1977); D'Arcy McNickle, "The Indian New Deal as Mirror of the Future," in *Political Organization of Native North Americans*, ed. Ernest L. Schusky (Washington, DC: University Press of America, 1980); Graham D. Taylor, *The New Deal and American Indian Tribalism: The Administration of the Indian Reorganization Act, 1934–45* (Lincoln: University of Nebraska Press, 1980); Vine Deloria Jr. and Clifford Lytle, *The Nations Within: The Past and Future of American Indian Sovereignty* (New York: Pantheon, 1984); and Akim D. Rinehardt, *Ruling Pine Ridge: Oglala Lakota Politics from the IRA to Wounded Knee* (Lubbock: Texas Tech University Press, 2007).

29. On F.D.R. and the New Deal reform, William E. Leuchtenburg, *Franklin D. Roosevelt and the New Deal, 1932–1940* (New York: Harper and Row, 1963); Alan Brinkley, *The End of Reform: New Deal Liberalism in Recession and War* (New York: Vintage Books, 1996); and Jason Scott Smith, *Building New Deal Liberalism: The Political Economy of Public Works, 1933–1956* (Cambridge: Cambridge University Press, 2009).

30. The 1930 U.S. Census has an eleven-year-old Arthur Oakes living under the household of Richard and Margaret Oakes in Buffalo (Districts 251–352), Erie, New York, "United States Census, 1930," index and images, Family Search,

Arthur Oakes in household of Richard Oakes, Buffalo (Districts 251–353), Erie, New York, available at https://familysearch.org/pal:/MM9.1.1/X7ZS-FR7, accessed 2 May 2012. Arthur had ten other siblings: Anna May Oakes (b. 1893), Ross Stanley Oakes (1904), Katherine Oakes (Sawati) (1907), Charlotte E. Oakes (Morey) (1912), Frances H. Oakes (1913), Bernie Oakes (1915), Mabel Marie Oakes (1917), Dorothy E. Oakes (Lazore) (1922), Alex H. Oakes (1926), and Harold T. Oakes (1927). Interestingly, Margaret Oakes was born on the U.S. side of Akwesasne, whereas Richard Soriowaue Oakes had been born on the Canadian side. This is important because all the Oakes children were recognized as U.S. citizens through their mother's U.S. birth. Arthur Richard Oakes's obituary stated a birth year of 1920, which is consistent with other family records. Available at www.findagrave.com, accessed online on Jan. 3, 2015. and also accessed online on January 3, 2015, www.obitsforlife.com obituary for Alex H. Oakes, Arthur Oakes's brother, who died on July 10, 2008.

31. Anonymous, "Golden Years of Lacrosse Revisited," *Indian Time* 15:25 (July 11, 1997), 22.

32. The 1930 U.S. Census places Irene Foote, age ten, as a boarder at the Sisters of Mercy Indian Girls' Industrial School, which housed only fifty students. See also Frederick J. Seaver, *History of Bombay, New York: Historical Sketches of Franklin County and Its Several Towns* (Albany: J.B. Lyon Company, 1918).

33. Anonymous, "William Foote Obituary," *Indian Time* 18:1 (Jan.-March 2000), n.p.; and Thomas Patrick Sullivan, "Standing Up for the Seventh Generation," available at www.earth-treaty.com/ts_foote.html, accessed February 14, 2014.

34. Ibid.; United States Bureau of the Census, *United States Census, 1930,* Arthur Oakes and Irene Foote found through ancestry.com, accessed April 16, 2014. On the Residential School in Spanish, Ontario, see Basil H. Johnston, *Indian School Days* (Norman: University of Oklahoma Press, 1989); and J. R. Miller, *Shingwauk's Vision: A History of Native Residential Schools* (Toronto: University of Toronto Press, 2009), 240.

35. Johnny Beauvais, "Memories of the Wharf Days," *The Eastern Door* 1:3 (Feb. 14, 1992), 2.

36. "the CCC-ID at its peak employed a total of 130 enrollees in revolving shifts, or nearly one-fourth of the total work force." Hauptman, *Iroquois and the New Deal,* 120–122. Unfortunately, two major incidents led to the closing of the factory in the late 1960s: plastics soon replaced wood for a lighter alternative, and a fire destroyed the factory. See Donald M. Fisher, *Lacrosse: A History of the Game* (Baltimore: Johns Hopkins University Press, 2002), 256–258; "By the late 1960s Akwesasne Mohawk stickmakers were crafting 72,000 sticks annually . . . satisfying 97 percent of the world's demand." Thomas Vennum, *Lacrosse Legends of the First Americans* (Baltimore: Johns Hopkins University Press, 2007); Thomas Vennum, *American Indian Lacrosse: Little Brother of War* (Washington, DC: Smithsonian Institution Press, 1994), 286; and Philip P. Arnold, *The Gift of Sports: Indigenous Ceremonial Dimensions of the Games We*

Love (San Diego: Cognella Academic Publishing, 2012). The 1930 U.S. census for St. Regis reported 1,219 residents and a quarter of the population is approximately 300 individuals. Leon Truesdell, U.S. Bureau of the Census, *Fifteenth Census of the United States: 1930: The Indian Population of the United States and Alaska* (Washington, DC: United States Government Printing Office, 1937), 42.

37. "The English language is spoken by 95% of the community. About 60% of the population speak the Mohawk language." Cheryl A. Metoyer, "Perceptions of the Mohawk Elementary Students of Library Services," provided by the National Indian Education Association Library Project As Conducted on the Akwesasne (St. Regis) Mohawk Reservation, dissertation, Indiana University, 1976, 4. "Oakes is the son of Art Oakes of St. Regis and Albany, and the late Mrs. Oakes. He attended Salmon River Central Schools and was a steel worker when he left his job to enter San Francisco State College." Eleanor Dumas, "Richard Oakes Renews Cause in East: Saved by Medicine Men," *Watertown Daily Times* (Oct. 15, 1970), 12.

38. Akwesasne Counselor Organization, *The Record, Laws, and History of the Akwesasne Mohawk Counselor Organization* (Hogansburg, NY: n.d.), 4. Copy in possession of author, the latest date that appears in the publication is 1947. The forty-six-page booklet outlines the curriculum for the program and includes numerous photos of its members. Unfortunately, few of the photos are labeled with members' names. It is not known if Richard Oakes's father or other relatives directly participated in the ACMO. On Fadden's role in the organization, see Jerry Gambill, ed., " 'No Man Could Do More,' " *Akwesasne Notes* 3:4 (Late Spring 1971), 22.

39. On the AMCO and the NYA, see Hauptman, *Iroquois and the New Deal*, 122–127.

40. "The New York Times covered this story under a banner entitled: '60 Indians in Brooklyn Barred from W.P.A.: Canadian Iroquois Not Aliens, Not Citizens.' The Times initiated in this story that if the Kahnawake ironworkers became United States citizens, they would then qualify for work. . . . Four days later, on May 20, the Times on its editorial page supported the Kahnawake's position." David Blanchard, "High Steel! The Kahnawake Mohawk and the High Construction Trade," *Journal of Ethnic Studies* 11:2 (Summer 1983), 51.

41. Bruce Katzer, "The Caughnawaga Mohawks: The Other Side of Ironwork," *Journal of Ethnic Studies* 15:4 (Winter 1988), 41. See also Mitchell, "Mohawks in High Steel," 13–17.

42. Anonymous, "Bridge Falls Drowning 80," *New York Times* (Aug. 30, 1907), 1. "A cantilever structure or object that projects into space, supported at one end, unsupported at the other. Applied to bridges, the advantage of a cantilever is that it allows engineers to build inward over the river from each shore, meeting in the middle to form the span, and to do this without any support from below." Jim Rasenberger, *High Steel: The Daring Men Who Built the World's Greatest Skyline* (New York: Harper Collins Publishers, 2004), 143–144.

43. Blanchard, "High Steel!" 48–49. See also three documentary films: Dan Owen, dir., "High Steel," 1965, National Film Board of Canada; Alanis Obomsawin, dir., "Spudwrench: Kahnawake Man," 1997; and the recent documentary by Kahnawà:ke filmmaker Reaghan Tarbell, entitled *To Brooklyn and Back: A Mohawk Journey* (2008).

44. On the constructs of this movement, see Alexandra Minna Stern, *Eugenic Nation: Faults and Frontiers of Better Breeding in Modern America* (Berkeley: University of California Press, 2005). On immigration and illegal aliens, see Mae M. Ngai, *Impossible Subjects: Illegal Aliens and the Making of Modern America* (Princeton: Princeton University Press, 2004); Jason De León, *The Land of Open Graves: Living and Dying on the Migrant Trail* (Berkeley: University of California Press, 2015); and John Bodnar, *The Transplanted: A History of Immigrants in Urban America* (Bloomington: Indiana University Press, 1985).

45. On Diabo's arrest and case, see Gerald Reid, "Illegal Alien? The Immigration Case of Mohawk Ironworker Paul K. Diabo," *Proceedings of the American Philosophical Society* 151:1 (March 2007), 63; and Clinton Rickard, *Fighting Tuscarora: The Autobiography of Chief Clinton Rickard* (Syracuse: Syracuse University Press, 1994), 76–77.

46. "The provision of the treaty invoked was that granting the Indians living along the Canadian border the right to hunt and fish on both sides of the line or to establish homes anywhere in North America without interference of either of the signing Governments." Anonymous, "Old Treaty Saves Indians," *New York Times* (July 8, 1926), 5. See also Associated Press, "Fight Indian's Exclusion: Six Nations Will Test Application of Law to Canadian Iroquois," *New York Times* (Dec. 29, 1926), 25; Associated Press, no title, *New York Times* (Jan. 23, 1927), W18; Canadian Press, "Indians Meet in Canada: Tribal Gathering to Discuss Border Question and Cayuga Claims," *New York Times* (Oct. 30, 1928), 28; and Johnny Beauvais, "Show Time Act II," *The Eastern Door* 1:13 (1992), 8.

47. Matthew Noah Tuchow, *The Mohawks of Brooklyn: A History of the Caughnawaga Community* (New Haven: Yale University Senior Thesis, 1983, 12). Accessed at the Brooklyn Public Library.

48. Blanchard, "High Steel!" 50–51. See also Rasenberger, *High Steel*, 158.

49. Gay Talese, *The Bridge* (New York: Walker and Company, 2003), 106; Morris Freilich, "Scientific Possibilities in Iroquoian Studies: An Example of Mohawks Past and Present," *Anthropologica* 5:2 (1963), 175; and Tarbell, *To Brooklyn and Back*. "For over one hundred years Mohawk ironworkers have helped shape Manhattan's skyline, the twin towers, the Chrysler Building, the Empire State." National Public Radio, "All Things Considered" (July 1, 2002), available at www.npr.org/templates/story/story.php?storyID=3048030; "Cities Service Building, . . . Daily News Building, the Chanin Building, the City Bank Farmers Trust Building, . . . the Bayonne Bridge, the Passaic River Bridge, . . . the Little Hell Gate Bridge, . . . the Marine Parkway Bridge, . . . the West Side Highway, . . . London Terrace, and Knickerbocker Village." Mitchell, "Mohawks in High Steel," 20–23.

50. "In 1952, the average Mohawk steelworker made $3.25 an hour, worked eight hour day, and took a half-hour lunch. His salary was therefore, $130 a week or $6,760 a year, a sizeable salary in 1952 when the median salary in the United States was only $4,070." Tuchow, *Mohawks of Brooklyn*, 40.

51. Rick Hill, "Skywalkers: The Legacy of Mohawk Ironworkers," *Turtle Quarterly* 1:4 (n.d.), 2–4. "Most of the Indians putting up the Kauffman steel are from the Indian reservation near Montreal. They don't think there's much truth to the legend that they're better on high-steel because they're more sure-footed than whites." Meyer Berger, "Indians Go Home to Squaws Near Montreal after Each Week's Work on Building Here," *New York Times* (May 4, 1955), 31.

52. NPR. "All Things Considered" (July 1, 2002).

53. "The New York Research Council of the College of the City of New York undertook a study of Mohawks in Brooklyn a few months ago. The council established that the steelworkers had their first big colony within New York City at Astoria, Queens. They started drifting toward lower Brooklyn around thirty-five years ago." Meyer Berger, "Dodgers, by Leaving, Probably Saved Colony of Mohawks, Skilled on High Steel Jobs," *New York Times* (Nov. 4, 1957), 22. "The earliest settler in Brooklyn in my sample arrived in 1916, but I learned of one family that settled there as early as 1910." Katzer, "Caughnawaga Mohawks," 44.

54. Jon Ciner, "Downtown Brooklyn Home for Montreal Mohawks, City Bound for the Building Trades," *The Phoenix Magazine* (Aug. 5, 1976), 9, 12.

55. Randy Kennedy, "Mohawk Memories: An Indian Community Flourished and Faded in a Section of Brooklyn," *New York Times* (Dec. 26, 1996), 33. "There are between 600 and 800 Indians around Red Hook in Brooklyn, most of them Mohawks who work on bridges and on skyscraper construction." Meyer Berger, "Redskin Colony of the Big City, Fifty Strong, Making Last Stand to Save Its Culture," *New York Times* (May 18, 1956), 26. In another *New York Times* article, Berger places the population at 800 in 1957. Whereas Joseph Mitchell in "Mohawks in High Steel" placed the population around 1949 at 400 individuals. Mitchell, "Mohawks in High Steel," 3. "By 1950, at least 400 Mohawks lived in Brooklyn; as many as 800 were there by the end of the decade. Apartment buildings filled up with Mohawk families." Rasenberger, *High Steel*, 159.

56. Laurie Johnston, "Indians Here Get U.S. Funds to Help Them in Urban Life," *New York Times* (Aug. 30, 1974), 31. In recent years, the Mohawk population has steadily declined as new highways cut the commute to Akwesasne or Kahnawà:ke down to approximately five hours.

57. "When spring comes they send their families back to Caughnawaga and to St. Regis and see them only on week-ends," ibid., 22.

58. Mitchell, "The Mohawks in High Steel," 25.

59. Peter Duffy, "Remembering Mohawk Ironworkers' Urban Haven," *New York Times* (July 18, 1999), CY8.

60. Tuchow, *Mohawks of Brooklyn*, 12.

61. Gay Talese, *The Bridge* (New York: Walker & Co., 2003), 104.

62. "By the time they leave the school, it is fair to say, all children in Kahnawà:ke have visited Ray Fadden's 'Six Nations Museum' in the Adirondacks. One of Fadden's lectures is on the various headwear of the Six Nations. At the end of this lesson he asks the children what the modern day gostowa of the Mohawk is. He then takes out an ironworker's hardhat and announces: 'This is the new symbol of the Mohawk warrior.'" Blanchard, "High Steel!" 60. See also Rasenberger, *High Steel*, 159.

63. Tuchow, *Mohawks of Brooklyn*, 28. Interview with Elizabeth Lazore and Karl Cook (April 27, 2012), VFW Hogansburg, Akwesasne (notes in possession of author).

64. Anonymous. "Mohawk Indian Is Slain: Knifed to Death During Brawl in Brooklyn Cafeteria," *New York Times* (Jan. 26, 1946), 15. In my research this was the only reported incident that appeared in *The New York Times*, which suggests that this was a rare case. Use of this article demonstrates that Indian bars were not always a positive force within Indian Cities.

65. Mitchell, "The Mohawks in High Steel," 29–30.

66. Kennedy, "Mohawk Memories," 29, 33. "Mohawk was spoken constantly in Brooklyn, on the job, and at social gatherings but most parents chose not to pass the language on to their children. In a sense Mohawk became known as the secret language, used when parents didn't want their children to know what they were talking about." Tarbell, *To Brooklyn and Back*. Anonymous, "Boro Pastor Visits Mohawks in Canada: B'klyn's Practically a Suburb of Modern Indian Reservation," *Brooklyn Daily Eagle* (Aug. 11, 1953), 4; Esther Coster, "Boro Mohawks Conduct Services At Cuyler Presbyterian Church," *Brooklyn Daily Eagle* (Nov. 2, 1939), 5; and Anonymous, "Mohawk Indians Dance, Sing for Old Brooklynites Society," *Brooklyn Daily Eagle* (Feb. 2, 1940), 26.

67. Wilson, 4.

68. Ibid., 25.

69. "Ironworkers would come and . . . you just made room for them you would double up the girls . . . and give them a room . . . ironically it was the grand-mother that actually brought the family to New York, after her husband was injured on the job in the 1920s, she had to support her family. She bought a boarding house in downtown Brooklyn and opened it up to Mohawk iron-workers." Tarbell, *To Brooklyn and Back*. "Myrtle Bush . . . grew up in the State Street area, and her grandmother ran a boarding house on Gold Street near Albee Square," "There were a large number of boarding houses, inexpensive hotels and furnished apartments in the area. . . . At first, the workers would leave their families at the reservation and stay here when there was work. They would go back to the reservation during the summer. But New York becomes unbeatable for Iron work, and eventually, families began to stay here during the year." Ciner, "Downtown Brooklyn Home," *The Phoenix Magazine* (Aug. 5, 1976), 9, 12.

70. "The work reached its pinnacle with the production of 'whimsies,' which have been sold at Niagara Falls since before 1880. For years, the Native people of

the area have produced and sold embossed beadwork as a way to supplement their income, and whimsies have always been a popular product. These small pieces of beadwork are fashioned into change purses, pincushions, wall pockets, women's purses with both drawstring and metal-frame European closures." David Dean, *Beading in the Native American Tradition* (Loveland, CO: Interweave Press, 2002), 101.

71. Tuchow, *Mohawks of Brooklyn*, 33.

72. Jacob Riis, *How the Other Half Lives* (New York: Dover Publications, Inc., 1971), 18. Mountain Eagle might have been his stage name, as several Mohawk performers worked for the Wild West and Medicine Show circuits around the world. See also Linda Scarangella McNenly, *Native Performers in Wild West Shows: From Buffalo Bill to Euro Disney* (Norman: University of Oklahoma Press, 2012), 100–139.

73. Jean Katharine Wagner, *An Examination and Description of Acculturation of Selected Individual American Indian Women in an Urban Area*, PhD dissertation, New York University, 1972, 158.

74. Anonymous, "Manhattan Powwow Attracts Hopis and Hobbyists," *New York Times* (March 25, 1968), 34; and Muriel Fischer, "Brooklyn Melting Pot for American Indian, Too," *New York Times* (June 18, 1972), 85. The American Indian Community House is the current Indian center in New York, which was founded in 1969. The Indian center is instrumental in providing cultural resources for Native peoples throughout New York. It also contributes services in the form of job placement, housing assistance, health care, and education.

75. Anonymous, "Indians Dance in Park," *New York Times* (Sept. 25, 1960), 76.

76. Anonymous, "Manhattan Powwow," 34.

77. Judy Klemesrud, "The American Indian: Part of City, and Yet . . .," *New York Times* (Sept. 18, 1968), 34; Tony Reichhardt, "Native New York," *National Museum of the American Indian* 7:3 (Fall 2006), 13–21.

78. Kennedy, "Mohawk Memories," 33.

2. THE EMERGENCE OF A LEADER

Epigraph 1: Oakes, "Alcatraz Is Not an Island," 35.

Epigraph 2: Richard Drinnon, *Keeper of Concentration Camps: Dillon S. Myer and American Racism* (Berkeley: University of California Press, 1987), 239–240. Statement Against the 1966 Omnibus Bill, from Earl Old Person, Chairman of the Blackfeet Tribe, Montana. For excerpts of Earl Old Person's speech, see Vine Deloria Jr., ed., *Of Utmost Good Faith* (San Francisco: Straight Arrow Books, 1971), 219–221.

1. Associated Press, "Chiefs of Iroquois Tribes Vote to Join War: Call on Six Nations Fight Against the Axis," *New York Times* (June 13, 1942), 17. See also Laurence M. Hauptman, *The Iroquois Struggle for Survival: World War II to Red Power* (Syracuse, NY: Syracuse University Press, 1986), 6.

2. "Their struggle, they said, is to maintain their identity as members of the Iroquois Indian Confederacy, which they hold to be an independent, unconquered nation, subject to its own lawmakers and not to Congress." Associated

Press, "Indians in Court Seek Rights of Free Nations; Insist U.S. Has No Power to Draft Youth," *New York Times* (Oct. 21, 1941), 25. "Clinton Rickard wrote to President Roosevelt, "Canada, unlike the United States, kept its treaty with the Six Nations by not requiring any of the members to register or to be subject to compulsory military service. . . . in 1941 the Iroquois in Canada were notified that they would have to register for conscription, but when they called their treaties to the attention of Canadian authorities, the ruling was reversed." Alison Bernstein, *American Indians and World War II: Toward a New Era in Indian Affairs* (Norman: University of Oklahoma Press, 1991), 30.

3. Edmund Wilson, *Apologies to the Iroquois*, 91.
4. Anonymous, "Indian War Bonnet Awarded to Stalin: Mohawk Chief Presents Gift at Ceremony in Brooklyn for 1941's 'Greatest Warrior,'" *New York Times* (Feb. 21, 1942), 21.
5. "By 1943 at least 12,000 women had left the reservations to work in factories and in the nurses corps. Native American women worked as riveters, inspectors, sheet metalworkers and machinists." Jeré Bishop Franco, *Crossing the Pond: The Native American Effort in World War II* (Denton: University of North Texas Press, 1999), 83.
6. D'Arcy McNickle and Harold E. Fey, *Indians and Other Americans: Two Ways of Life Meet* (New York: Harper & Brothers, 1959), 149. "Indian Bureau officials estimated that 24,521 American Indians, exclusive of officers, had served, and another 20,000 off-reservation Indians had also enlisted. The combined total figure of 44,500 comprised more than ten percent of the Native American population of approximately 400,000." Franco, *Crossing the Pond*, 62.
7. The 4,000 number is relatively low, mainly due to inconsistencies in Canadian Indian Affairs Bureau policy and records. For only First Nations people under the Indian Act were counted in conscription. This would exclude large numbers of Métis and other First Nations people not recognized as holding Indian status. See also R. Scott Sheffield, *The Red Man's on the Warpath: The Image of the "Indian" and the Second World War* (Vancouver: University of British Columbia Press, 2004); and Grace Poulin, *Invisible Women: WWII Aboriginal Servicewomen in Canada*, Master's thesis, Trent University, 2006.
8. Judith Bellafaire, "Native American Women Veterans," Women in Military Service For America Foundation, Inc., available at www.womensmemorial. org/Education/NAHM.html, accessed Oct. 11, 2015.
9. U.S. Census, *Sixteenth Census of the United States*, Department of Commerce—Bureau of the Census (Washington, DC, 1940), available at www.1940censusarchives.gov, accessed June 22, 2015. Census enumerated on April 15 & 16, 1940. E.D., no. 45–43, Sheet No. 2B. Anonymous, "Another Fiver Rounder Added to Garden Card," *The Citizen-Advertiser* (Nov. 18, 1938), 10; Anonymous, "Joe Kinch Loses to Art Oaks," *Ogdensburg Journal* (March 7, 1939), 6; Anonymous, "Brenno Wins Auburn Bout," *Ogdensburg-Advance* (March 7, 1939), 8. A boxing round lasts three minutes, with a one-minute break between rounds.

10. Anonymous, "Another Fiver Rounder Added to Garden Card," *The Citizen-Advertiser* (Nov. 18, 1938), 10; Anonymous, "Throop Boxer Gets Good Spot," *The Citizen-Advertiser* (March 3, 1939), 10; Anonymous, "Brenno and Oaks to Headline VFW Fistic Show Tonight," *Ogdensburg Journal* (March 9, 1939), 3; Anonymous, "Brenno and Oakes are Headliners of Fine Card at City Hall Auditorium," *Ogdensburg-Advance* (March 9, 1939), 2; Anonymous, "Brenno Kayo's Art Oaks," *Ogdensburg Journal* (March 10, 1939), 6; Anonymous, "Brenno and Elias Won by Knockouts in Bouts at City Hall Last Night," *Ogdensburg-Advance* (March 10, 1939), 9; Frank Mason, "Punch Party," *Ogdensburg Journal* (March 29, 1939), 3.

11. Anonymous, "Brenno Is Confident of Victory," *Ogdensburg-Advance* (March 29, 1939), 8; Anonymous, "Brenno and Oakes Head Vets' Card: Return Match Between Frankie Brenno and Oakes Headlines Vets' Program," *Ogdensburg-Advance* (March 30, 1939), 8.

12. Anonymous, "Oakes Wins Over Brenno in Dull Bout, Donalski Scores Techinal [*sic*] Knockout," *Ogdensburg-Advance* (March 31, 1939), 8. Anonymous, "O'Neil Decisively Whips Rosen, Evening Their E.J. Ring Series," *Binghamton Press* (March 24, 1939), 32; Jack Bell, "Stands Patter," *Ogdensburg-Advance* (April 1, 1939), 8; and Jack Bell, "Stands Patter," *Ogdensburg-Advance* (April 9, 1939), 8.

13. Anonymous, "Onondaga Indians Arrange Ring Card," *Syracuse Herald-Journal* (June 28, 1940), 29. In February of 1940, Arthur won a fight over Pete Deguilo in Watertown, New York. Anonymous, "Local Boys Win in Watertown," *Ogdensburg Journal* (Feb. 29, 1940), 6.

14. Anonymous, "Reverend Michael Jacobs 1902–1988," *Indian Time* (Sept. 22, 1988), 2. Interestingly, Arthur's uncle Mitchell Oakes had also played on the famed Cornwall Island Indians lacrosse team with Irene's father. It is highly probable that this is how Arthur and Irene first met, at a box lacrosse match or practice. Anonymous, "Golden Years of Lacrosse Revisited Saturday, July 2, 1932 Cornwall Island vs. Cornwall Nationals," *Indian Time* (July 11, 1997), 22; and Anonymous, "Fast Lacrosse Tilt for Thursday Night," *Ogdensburg-Advance* (Nov. 10, 1936), 9.

15. U.S. Census. *Sixteenth Census of the United States,* No. 45–43; Sheet No. 2B. In the biography, I kept the source of Irene Oakes's prior residency to 1939 as her sister-in-law recorded it for the census but failed to locate a city or town of Colborne, Ontario—it is quite possible that the name of the town was misspelled or shortened in the original document. The closest match is Port Colborne off of Lake Erie—this is the strongest lead.

16. Ibid. "About 1930 a powdered milk plant was added. The skim milk was made into powdered milk and the cream went to N.Y. City." Anonymous, "The Town of Lisbon, St. Lawrence County," available at http://townoflisbonny.org/content/History, accessed May 1, 2015.

17. U.S. Census, *Sixteenth Census of the United States,* No. 45–43; Sheet No. 2B. Audrey Shenandoah, "Everything Has to Be in Balance," in *Indian Roots of American Democracy,* ed. Jose Barreiro (Ithaca, NY: Akwe:kon Press, 1992),

36–38; Harold F. Dorn, "Changes in Infant and Child Mortality Rates," *Annals of the American Academy of Political and Social Science* (Nov. 1940), 34.

18. Donaldson Funeral Home, "Alex H. Oakes Sr. Obituary" (July 10, 2008), available at www.obitsforlife.com/obituary/472031/Oakes-Sr-Alex.php, accessed Jan. 3, 2015.

19. Anonymous, "Alex H. Oakes, Sr." *Indian Time* (July 17, 2008), available at www.indiantime.net/story/2008/07/17/obituaries/alex-h-oakes-sr/0417201216346687209.html, accessed July 17, 2015; "American Legion Hogansburg All War Veterans" Folder, Akwesasne Library and Cultural Center, New York State Military Museum and Veterans Research Center, Hogansburg, New York, available at https://dmna.ny.gov/historic/reghist/wwii/wwii_HonorList/Honorlist_O.htm; Anonymous, "Mohawk Code Talkers Honored in Washington, DC," Saint Regis Mohawk Tribe, available at www.srmt-nsn.gov/news/detail/mohawk_code_talkers_honored_in_washington_dc, accessed July 7, 2015; Anonymous, "Thomas H. Oakes," *Indian Time* (May 15, 1998), 2; and Anonymous, "OCS and Navy Enlistees in March Contingent," *Chateaugay Record* (April 9, 1945), 8. On Alex Oakes's mission, see Stephen E. Ambrose, *Band of Brothers: E Company, 506th Regiment, 101st Airborne from Normandy to Hitler's Eagle Nest* (New York: Simon & Schuster, 1992). It is possible that Arthur Oakes deciphered and relayed Mohawk code while serving in the Navy.

20. Anonymous, "Fatality Driver Held Blameless: Two Reservation Residents Killed Walking in Street," *The Post-Standard* (Feb. 15, 1946), 17; Michael Adams, *The Best War Ever: America and World War II* (Baltimore: Johns Hopkins University Press, 1994), 123, 132; Eliza K. Pavalko and Glen H. Elder Jr., "World War II and Divorce: A Life-Course Perspective," *American Journal of Sociology* 95:5 (March 1990), 1213–1234; James T. Sparrow, *Warfare State: World War II Americans and the Age of Big Government* (New York: Oxford University Press, 2011), 115–116.

21. Leonard Oakes interview; New York Telephone Company, *Brooklyn Telephone Directory*, Brooklyn Public Library, Brooklyn White Pages Damaged (1961–62), Microfilm #32 "Oakes, Irene A 219 14 HY 9–1322." While at the Brooklyn Public Library I examined the Brooklyn phone book records from 1962 through 1969 and found the same address "219 14th HY-9–1322" consistently listed for Irene Oakes in the Brooklyn white pages—this address was also confirmed in my interview with Leonard Oakes. See also Kenneth Jackson and John Manbeck, *The Neighborhoods of Brooklyn* (New Haven: Yale University Press, 1998), 165–171.

22. Bess Furman, "Campaign Pushed to 'Free' Indians," *New York Times* (July 22, 1947), 46; Hauptman, *Iroquois Struggle for Survival*, 48.

23. Anonymous, "Jim Thorpe Is Dead on West Coast at 64," *New York Times* (March 29, 1953), 1. Public Law 280 also "passed in 1953. . . . Congress took the unprecedented step of passing general legislation extending state civil and criminal jurisdiction into Indian country. . . . Since HCR 108 was a statement of policy only, individual acts were needed to implement the policy in regard

to specific tribes. . . . This means that approximately 109 tribes and bands were terminated. A minimum of 1,362,155 acres and 11,466 individuals were affected." Getches, Wilkinson, and Williams, *Cases and Materials*, 204–205. Under the Fair Deal policy Truman appointed as director of Indian affairs Dillon S. Myer, a former administrator of the War Relocation Authority who launched administrative efforts to terminate Tribal governments. On Myer, see Richard Drinnon, *Keeper of Concentration Camps: Dillon S. Myer and American Racism* (Berkeley: University of California Press, 1987).

24. On the termination era and its policies, see Donald Fixico, *Termination and Relocation: Federal Indian Policy, 1945–1960* (Albuquerque: University of New Mexico Press, 1986). See also Kenneth R. Philp, *Termination Revisited: American Indians on the Trail to Self-Determination, 1933–1953* (Lincoln: University of Nebraska Press, 1999); and McNickle and Fey, *Indians and Other Americans*, 120–200.

25. Stephen Cornell, *The Return of the Native: American Indian Political Resurgence* (New York: Oxford University Press, 1988), 121. "euphemisms used by Congress to describe termination: it was purportedly a program to 'free' Indians from federal supervision and to eliminate 'restrictions deemed discriminatory' against Indians. In fact, termination did little to promote 'freedom' or to root out 'discrimination.'" Getches, Wilkinson, and Williams, *Cases and Materials*, 205–206.

26. Clayton R. Koppes, "From New Deal to Termination: Liberalism and Indian Policy, 1933–1953," *Pacific Historical Review* 46:4 (1977), 544.

27. Phillips, "Kahnawake Mohawks," 3.

28. Hauptman, *Iroquois Struggle for Survival*, 133.

29. Phillips, "Kahnawake Mohawks," 15. See also Michael L. Lawson, *Dammed Indians Revisited: The Continuing History of the Pick-Sloan Plan and the Missouri River Sioux* (Pierre: South Dakota State Historical Society Press, 2009); and Lawrence Marc Hauptman, *In the Shadow of Kinzua: The Seneca Nation of Indians since World War II* (Syracuse: Syracuse University Press, 2014).

30. Getches, Wilkinson, and Williams, *Cases and Materials*, 953.

31. Anonymous, "Indians Set Back," *New York Times* (Feb. 25, 1959), 23. See also Wilson, *Apologies to the Iroquois*, 108–110.

32. "He went into the Navy when he was sixteen and remained there till he was twenty-one. He drove a landing craft in the Pacific war in the Seventh Amphibious Fleet; was at Saipan and Okinawa; and he later served in Korea. He applied, he says, after the war, for a loan under the GI Bill of Rights, but discovered that this was impossible because he lived on reservation property. Up to the time of the war with the Power Authority, he spent every winter in the Merchant Marine." Wilson, *Apologies to the Iroquois*, 163.

33. Ibid., 272.

34. Associated Press, "Mission in Capital Dropped by Indians," *New York Times* (March 21, 1959), 14. See also Associated Press, "100 Indian Raiders Move in on Capital," *New York Times* (March 19, 1959), 35; and Associated Press,

"Indians Besiege the White House Over 'Injustices,'" *New York Times* (March 20, 1959), 16.

35. Phillips, "Kahnawake Mohawks," 1–3; Christine Greaf, "Mohawk Council of Akwesasne Settles St. Lawrence River Claim with Ontario Power Generation," *News From Indian Country* (July 21, 2008), n.p., available at www.indiancountrynews.com/index.php/news/ politcs-business/4071-mohawk-council-of-akwesasne-settles-st-lawrence-river-claim-with-ontario-power-generation.

36. Winona LaDuke, *All Our Relations: Native Struggles for Land and Life* (Cambridge: South End Press, 1999), 10–23; and Kallen M. Martin, "Akwesasne Environments, 1999," *Native Americas: Akwe:kon's Journal of Indigenous Issues* 16:1 (Spring 1999), 24–27.

37. On Robert Moses, see Hillary Ballon and Kenneth T. Jackson, eds., *Robert Moses and the Modern City: The Transformation of New York* (New York: Queens Museum of Art, 2007); and Robert A. Caro, *The Power Broker: Robert Moses and the Fall of New York* (New York: Vintage Books, 1974).

38. Allen Drury, "Tuscarora Cites Bar to Land Sale," *New York Times* (Nov. 27, 1958), 36.

39. Anonymous, "Tuscaroras Win New State Offer," *New York Times* (Jan. 25, 1959), 35.

40. Wilson, *Apologies to the Iroquois*, 138–162.

41. Alicia McCutcheon, "Wikwemikong Sisters Tell Stories of Abuse, Loneliness while at St. Joseph's Girls' Residential School, Spanish," *The Expositor* (May 18, 2011), n.p., available at www.manitoulin.ca/2011/05/18/wikimong-sisters-tell-stories-of-abuse-lonliness-while-at-st-josephs-girls-residential-school-spanish/, accessed Sept. 7, 2015.

42. Leonard Oakes interview (April 27, 2012).

43. Ibid.

44. Leonard Oakes interview (July 21, 2012); Elliot Willensky, *When Brooklyn Was the World 1920–1957* (New York: Harmony Books, 1986), 173–187; and Anonymous, "Time Ch. Program," *Brooklyn Daily Eagle* (Dec. 1, 1954), 27.

45. Thomas Patrick Sullivan, "Standing Up for the Seventh Generation," 1–4, available at www.earth-treaty.com/ts_foote.html, accessed Feb. 14, 2014; and Anonymous, "William Foote," *Indian Time* 18:1 (Jan-Mar 2000), 2.

46. Leonard Oakes interview (April 28, 2012),

47. Leonard Oakes interview (April 28, 2012); and Anonymous, "Bernice M. Papineau Obituary" *Indian Time* 27:34 (Aug. 27, 2009).

48. Leonard Oakes interview.

49. "Mad Bear Anderson told me later how Richard had sneaked onto the bus taking the Iroquois leaders to Washington when he was only 12." Dean Chavers, "Around the Campfire: The Leader of Alcatraz," *Indian Country Today* 16:10 (Sept. 9, 1996), A5.

50. By May of 1954 in *Brown v. Board of Education* the U.S. Supreme Court ruled that segregation in public schools was unconstitutional. Shortly thereafter schools at St. Regis would begin busing students to local schools in outlying

communities as a part of desegregation. This decision would lead to the
"closing of all but three of New York's Indian schools by 1965." Hauptman,
Iroquois Struggle for Survival, 14.

51. "Standing Arrow . . . insisted that 'more than 2,000 Indians from reservations in Quebec, at Caughnawaga, Oka, and St. Regis, their life changed by
the St. Lawrence Seaway,' were considering his call to resettle their original
homeland in the Mohawk Valley. Citing the Treaty of Fort Stanwix of 1784, the
Mohawks claimed a fifteen-square mile territory and insisted that the New
York State treaty of 1789 that ceded land [to the state] was invalid because the
state had no legal right to enter negotiations with the Mohawks after the
formal adoption of the United States Constitution in 1788." Ibid., 149. See
also Michael James, "Memo to Washington: The Mohawk Indians Are on the
Warpath Again," *New York Times* (Aug 17, 1957), 17; and Wilson, *Apologies to
the Iroquois*, 39–57.

52. Anonymous, "Mohawks Quit Camp," *New York Times* (March 22, 1958), 37.

53. Troy Johnson, *The Occupation of Alcatraz Island: Indian Self-Determination and
the Rise of Indian Activism* (Urbana and Chicago: University of Illinois Press,
1996), 102. "Fidel Castro of Cuba invited Six Nations and Miccosukee delegates to visit Cuba, which they did in July 1958." Troy Johnson, Joane Nagel,
and Duane Champagne, eds., *American Indian Activism: Alcatraz to the
Longest Walk* (Urbana and Chicago: University of Illinois Press, 1997), 131.

54. Oakes, "Alcatraz Is Not an Island," 35.

55. Leonard Oakes interview (April 27, 2012).

56. Ibid.

57. Ibid. On ironworkers in the 1970s, see David Grant Noble, "Mohawk
Steelworkers of Manhattan," *Four Winds: The International Forum for Native
American Art, Literature, and History* 2:4 (Spring 1982), 32–39.

58. Karl Koch III and Richard Firstman, *Men of Steel: The Story of the Family that
Built the World Trade Center* (New York: Three Rivers Press, 2002), 117.

59. Dean Chavers, interviewed by author (August 15, 2001), Albuquerque,
New Mexico, tape recording, tape 1, side 1, 8. Interview in author's
possession.

60. Joseph Mitchell, "Mohawks in High Steel," 16–17; Robert L. Conly and B.
Anthony Stewart, "Mohawks Scrape the Sky," *National Geographic Magazine*
102:1 (July 1952), 133–143; David Weitzman, *Skywalkers: Mohawk Ironworkers
Build the City* (New York: Flash Point, 2010), 32; Bobby Jock, "Mohawks in
High Steel" (unpublished paper), n.d., 3; "Ironworkers" vertical file,
Akwesasne Library at the Akwesasne Cultural Center, Hogansburg, New
York, accessed July 20, 2012. Jock, a former ironworker stated the number in
a typical riveting gang consisted of four ironworkers. He also mentioned that
one of the first major training jobs for Mohawks occurred when the
Dominion Bridge Company constructed the Soo Bridge connecting Sault Ste.
Marie, Ontario, with Sault Ste. Marie, Michigan.

61. Dean Chavers interview. See also Lawrence Elliott, "Daredevils Who Follow
the High Steel," *Reader's Digest* (April 1959), 148; "Ironworkers" vertical file.

62. "he had troubles as a youth in New York City when as a gang member he had frequent brushes with the law." Anonymous, "Killer of Indian Is Arraigned," *San Francisco Examiner* (Sept. 21, 1972), 16.

63. On the history of gangs in New York, see Timothy J. Gilfoyle, *A Pickpocket's Tale: The Underworld of Nineteenth Century New York* (New York: W.W. Norton, 2006); and Luc Sante, *Low Life: Lures and Snares of Old New York* (New York: Farrar, Straus, and Giroux, 1991).

64. Wendell Pritchett, *Brownsville, Brooklyn: Blacks, Jews, and the Changing Face of the Ghetto* (Chicago: University of Chicago Press, 2002), 114–115, 154–155, 206.

65. FBI file; and Leonard Oakes interview.

66. U.S. Department of Justice. Federal Bureau of Investigations. FOIA request. *File on Thomas Richard Oakes.* Prepared August 28, 2001, Arrest record. Washington, D.C., 14. Leonard Oakes Interview (July 22, 2012) and (April 27, 2012) and Dave Mitchell interview (April 27, 2012).

67. Elizabeth Lazore and Carl Cook interviews (April 27, 2012), Hogansburg, Akwesasne VFW; Dave Mitchell interview (April 28, 2012), Bear's Den, Hogansburg, Akwesasne. The frequency of these trips are evidenced by several speeding infractions, stops for improper exhaust systems, and disorderly conduct. Anonymous, "Dec. 8—Richard Oakes. Hogansburg, fined $10, inadequate exhaust system," *Tribune Press* (Dec. 27, 1967), page 1, section 2.

68. Leonard Oakes interview (April 27, 2012); Anonymous, "Hogansburg Man Impaled on Pole When Hit by Car," *Massena Observer* (May 28, 1963), 1; Anonymous, "Man Killed in Car Crash, Is Thrown in Air, Impaled on Spike," *Ogdensburg-Advance* (June 2, 1963), 29; Anonymous, "Hogansburg Man Killed When Impaled on Spike in Sunday Morning Crash," *Ogdensburg Journal* (May 27, 1963), 9; and Anonymous, "Struck by Car, Man is Impaled on Pole Spike at Hogansburg," *Fort Covington Sun* (May 30, 1963), 1.

69. Leonard Oakes interview (April 27, 2012); Anonymous, "Hogansburg Man Impaled on Pole When Hit by Car," *Massena Observer* (May 28, 1963), 1; Anonymous, "Man Killed in Car Crash, Is Thrown in Air, Impaled on Spike," *Ogdensburg-Advance* (June 2, 1963), 29; Anonymous, "Hogansburg Man Killed When Impaled on Spike in Sunday Morning Crash," *Ogdensburg Journal* (May 27, 1963), 9; and Anonymous, "Struck by Car, Man is Impaled on Pole Spike at Hogansburg," *Fort Covington Sun* (May 30, 1963), 1.

70. Leonard Oakes and Dave Mitchell interviews (April 27, 2012).

71. Anonymous, "Rites Held Monday at St. Regis Church for Richard Oakes, 84," *Fort Covington Sun* (Sept. 19, 1963), 4; Anonymous, "Mrs. Oakes Dies in Cornwall," *Massena Observer* (March 3, 1964), 9; Anonymous, "Mrs. Margaret Oakes of St. Regis, Que. Dies: In Hospital a Month," *Fort Covington Sun* (March 12, 1964), n.p.

72. Henry Hampton and Steve Fayer, *Voices of Freedom: An Oral History of the Civil Rights Movement from the 1950s through the 1980s* (New York: Bantam Books, 1991), 288–290.

73. Daniel M. Cobb, *Native Activism in Cold War America: The Struggle for Sovereignty* (Lawrence: University Press of Kansas, 2008), 30–57. See also Alvin M. Josephy Jr., *Red Power: The American Indians' Fight for Freedom* (Lincoln: University of Nebraska Press, 1971), 37–40; and Paul R. McKenzie Jones, *Clyde Warrior: Tradition, Community, and Red Power* (Norman: University of Oklahoma Press, 2015), 41–70.

74. By 1964, NIYC supported direct action and the fish-in movement initiated by Northwest Coast Tribes in Washington State.

75. "This appearance was an outgrowth of the National Congress of American Indians' meeting in Denver. The then Executive Director of this national Indian organization apparently sanctioned the use of 'Red Power' in these terms: 'to run the reservations'; 'to participate in American life on our terms'; 'to withdraw from everything if the tribes so wished'; and claimed that 'treaties give rights.' . . . Most importantly, this media presentation coalesced Indian sentiment to include these wants—'self-government,' 'not asking the bureaucrats.' . . . In short, the dominant theme centered upon self-determination by native enclaves." Rupert Costo, ed., *Indian Voices: The First Convocation of American Indian Scholars* (San Francisco: Indian Historian Press, 1970), 300.

76. "the number of American Indians who served in Vietnam was approximately 42,000, it is nevertheless exceptionally high. During the Vietnam War the total Indian population of the United States was less than one million persons. American Indians thus made up nearly 1.4 percent of all the troops sent to Southeast Asia, while Indians in general never constituted more than 0.6 percent of the total population. . . . Approximately one out of four eligible Native Americans served in military forces in Vietnam, compared to one out of twelve in the general American population." Tom Holm, *Strong Hearts Wounded Souls: Native American Veterans of the Vietnam War* (Austin: University of Texas Press, 1996), 123.

77. Leonard Oakes interview; and Oakes, "Alcatraz Is Not an Island," 38.

78. Leonard Oakes interview.

79. Ibid.

3. BETTER RED THAN DEAD

Portions of this chapter were originally published in a chapter entitled "San Francisco, Red Power, and the Emergence of an 'Indian City,'" which appeared in Kathleen A. Brosnan and Amy L. Scott, eds., *City Dreams and Country Schemes: Community and Identity in the American West* (Reno: University of Nevada Press, 2011), 261–283; copyright © 2011 by the University of Nevada Press.
Epigraph: Wilma Mankiller and Michael Wallis, *Mankiller: A Chief and Her People* (New York: St. Martin's Press, 1993), 73. Wilma Mankiller was the first woman to be elected as the Principal Chief of the Western Cherokee Nation (1985–1995). Her autobiography documents her family's struggle in the 1960s for economic opportunity within the relocation program in San Francisco.

1. Oakes, "Alcatraz Is Not an Island," 35.

2. Very few studies have been devoted to Native San Francisco. Joan Ablon wrote
two articles in 1964 and 1971, and Ann Metcalf wrote one in 1980. These
works lack a cohesive structure in which to understand the internal workings
of the Indian City. I use the term *Intertribal* rather than the dated term *pan-
Indian* because it implies that Native peoples do not relinquish their Tribal
identities in the process of claiming an American Indian identity. The loose
association inherent with the term *pan-Indian* negates the unique process of
reinvention that originates within an urban Indian community and a shared
acceptance of an Intertribal reality. An Intertribal treatment of Indian City
also relies on a transnational focus that attempts to understand the
complexities of members from more than one hundred different and distinct
Tribal Nations who converged in San Francisco. I use the term *Intertribal* over
Supratribal because *Intertribal* originates from the Native community and
identifies both federally and state-recognized and non-recognized Indigenous
peoples. As a process of historical study *Intertribalism* in definition and
application uncovers the roots of Indian Cities and their political relationship
to the constructs of Native Nationalism and Red Power. Native peoples do not
willingly give up their Tribal (political, national, social, and cultural)
connections to become American Indian. Rather, these Tribal connections are
protected and reinforced in Intertribal spaces and places that can promote a
uniquely diverse acceptance of an overall American Indian identity for the
promotion of Tribal political gains. One can trace the scholarly debates over
these terms in the following sources: Hazel W. Hertzberg's *The Search for an
American Indian Identity* was a seminal book for the 1970s and explored what
she termed as the modern "Pan-Indian" movement. Her definition of this
term: "Not until the Progressive Era, however, did a number of organized
movements arise, national in scope, based firmly on a common Indian
interest and identity as distinct from tribal interests and identities, and
stressing Indian accommodation to the dominant society." Hertzberg's
definition of *pan-Indian* stressed that Native peoples dismiss or diminish their
Tribal heritage for a new identity as American Indians. Vine Deloria Jr.
automatically dismissed Hertzberg's use of the term in his provocative review
entitled "The Rise and Fall of the First Indian Movement," *The Historian* 33:4
(Aug. 1971), 663. Deloria stated, "The author herself freely admits that
Indians do not use this phrase [pan-Indian], most abhor it. . . . The mere use
of Pan-Indian, originating as it does within anthropological circles, makes the
past seem more past then it really is. In fact it makes that particular past the
province of scholars and not Indians . . . [it] only perpetuates the tension
already existing between scholars and Indians." Despite Deloria's review, *pan-
Indian* and its definition has persisted and remained entrenched within
scholarship about Native peoples. In his work *The Return of the Native:
American Indian Political Resurgence*, sociologist Steven Cornell expands upon
the work of famed anthropologist Nancy O. Lurie by pressing the application
of what she termed "supratribal." Cornell defines *supratribalism* in a footnote
on page 243 as "a generalized Indian identity and to the tendency on the part

of Indians in certain situations to organize or act on the basis of that identity as opposed to particular tribal identities." Unfortunately, Cornell only reinvents the wheel, and imposes a new term, but with the same hidden principles as its progenitor *pan-Indian*. He pulled the term from Nancy O. Lurie who broke its application into four distinct levels: (1) the nationalist or supratribal/pan-Indian, (2) inter-tribal or pan-Indian, (3) tribal or reservation, and (4) real Indians or "full-bloods," in S. Levine and N. O. Lurie, eds., *The American Indian Today* (Baltimore: Pelican Books, 1970), 314. Clearly, Lurie was more interested in racializing Indian identity into separate political and biological forms of colonized "authenticity." Scholarly acceptance of these terms (*supratribalism* and *pan-Indian*) therefore denies a key element from Native Nationalism—Intertribalism. Beyond two-world theory, or racialized binaries of Indian versus settler worlds, Intertribalism dismisses these former terms and debates. Intertribalism as a theoretical model strives to uncover complexity and to showcase the sophistication of the twentieth-century Indigenous experience as more than simply a choice or navigation between two worlds.

3. Arthur Margon, "Indians and Immigrants: A Comparison of Groups New to the City," *Journal of Ethnic Studies* 4:4 (Winter 1977), 18.

4. Joseph G. Jorgensen, "Indians and the Metropolis," *The American Indian in Urban Society*, ed. Jack O. Waddell and O. Michael Watson (Boston: Little, Brown and Company, 1971), 83; and Donald Fixico, *The Urban Indian Experience in America* (Albuquerque: University of New Mexico Press, 2000), 73. For the urban figure I used the average between ten Indian Cities: Oklahoma City, Los Angeles, Chicago, Minneapolis, Buffalo, Albuquerque, Seattle, San Francisco, New York, and San Diego.

5. M. Annette Jaimes, ed., *The State of Native America* (Boston: South End Press, 1992), 245.

6. Ibid., 82–83; and Tim Peck, *The International Timber Trade* (Cambridge: Woodhead Publishing Limited, 2001), 208–212.

7. On the relocation program, see Fixico, *Termination and Relocation*.

8. "military life provided a steady job, money, status, and a taste of the white world to previously isolated and unassimilated Indians." "Fewer than five hundred of the more than three thousand Indians who decided to live in San Francisco and Los Angeles found steady employment. Even as the economy moved close to full employment, Indians were, for the most part, unskilled or semiskilled laborers, and among the first to be laid off as the job market increasingly required better skilled workers. . . . Neither the reservation nor the urban environment seemed capable of fulfilling the expectations created by their wartime participation in the larger society." Bernstein, *American Indians and World War II*, 60, 150. See also Jere' Bishop Franco, *Crossing the Pond: The Native American Effort in World War II* (Denton: University of North Texas Press, 1999); and R. Scott Sheffield, *The Red Man's on the Warpath: The Image of the "Indian" and the Second World War* (Vancouver: UBC Press, 2004). A rare publication entitled *Indians in the War* includes demographics

from the spring of 1945, "21,767 Indians in the Army, 1,910 in the Navy, 121 in the Coast Guard, and 723 in the Marines." Absent are figures on officers and Native women who also served in various branches of the military. While this number is half what Bernstein quotes, we can assume that her numbers take into account the entire war. Office of Indian Affairs, *Indians in the War* (Lawrence: Haskell Printing Department, 1945), 1, Akwesasne Library and Cultural Center, Vertical Files, Hogansburg, New York (accessed July 20, 2012).

9. Joan Ablon, "Relocated American Indians in the San Francisco Bay Area: Social Interactions and Indian Identity," *Human Organization* 23 (Winter 1964), 297. "In 1940 the number of Indians dwelling in cities was less than five percent of the entire Indian population. By 1950, that figure had quadrupled to nearly twenty percent." Bernstein, *American Indians and World War II*, 86.

10. "Estimates place the number of Indian women working in war industries in 1943 at 12,000 or slightly more than one fourth of the total population that had left the reservations for war related work." Bernstein, *American Indians and World War II*, 73. "The War Manpower Commission offered women free training in light defense jobs that could eventually pay as much as $120 a month." James B. LaGrand, *Indian Metropolis: Native Americans in Chicago, 1945–1975* (Urbana and Chicago: University of Illinois Press, 2002), 36; see also Nicholas G. Rosenthal, "Repositioning Indianness: Native American Organizations in Portland, Oregon, 1959–1975," *Pacific Historical Review* 71:3 (Aug. 2002), 419. Rosenthal estimates that in Portland alone, "warships created 140,000 jobs and brought 260,000 new people to the city." In his book *Reimaging Indian Country*, Rosenthal estimates that 25,000 Native peoples served in the armed forces and 40,000 American Indians served in wartime industries. Nicolas G. Rosenthal, *Reimagining Indian Country: Native American Migration and Identity in Twentieth-Century Los Angeles* (Chapel Hill: University of North Carolina Press, 2012), 25–30.

11. Larry Burt, "Roots of the Native American Urban Experience: Relocation Policy in the 1950s," *American Indian Quarterly* 10:2 (Spring 1986), 86. In the 1930s, few records were kept that can track how many Native peoples actually relocated to California during the Dust Bowl crisis. It is highly probable that thousands of American Indians joined with other "Okies" in their trek west to California.

12. Alison R. Bernstein, *American Indians and World War II: Toward a New Era in Indian Affairs* (Norman: University of Oklahoma Press, 1991), 150.

13. Japanese Americans were relocated from San Francisco during the war out of fear of the American public of spying or sabotage. Yet many of these families had been in San Francisco for several generations. Both their business and homes were sold and their communities interned in camps administered by the Department of Interior. During the relocation program administrators actively sought to spread the Indian population into diverse areas to accelerate forces of assimilation. This is more than likely a reason why the return rates

were so high for relocatees at the inception of the program. See Brian Masaru Hayashi, *Democratizing the Enemy: The Japanese American Internment* (Princeton: Princeton University Press, 2004).

14. In 1966 a race riot erupted along the streets of Hunter's Point in protest of the police shooting of a black teenager who allegedly stole a car. The riot lasted a total of five days with cases of looting and arson, although no one was fatally wounded. Many of the white businesses throughout the city began leaving ethnic neighborhoods and disrupted the tax base, employment, and subsequently led to further ghettoization. This affected the large Native populations in the Mission District; the riot also influenced the formation of the Oakland-based Black Panther Party in 1966. See Arthur E. Hippler, *Hunter's Point: A Black Ghetto* (New York: Basic Books, 1974).

15. Mankiller and Wallis, *Mankiller*, 108–110.

16. "Prohibition of discrimination in redevelopment proposals, in public housing, as well as in employment, became policy slowly, and in the case of public housing only after extensive litigation." William Issel, "Liberalism and Urban Policy in San Francisco from the 1930s to the 1960s," *Western Historical Quarterly* 22:4 (Nov. 1991), 440.

17. "The Outing Program was expanded from the Carlisle School to all of the other federal Indian schools. . . . During World War II the BIA revived the Outing Program concept, using it as a wartime recruitment agency to send Indians to off-reservation work, railroad track repair, ammunition depot labor, farmwork, and domestic service. . . . In 1955 the BIA began a program called American Indian Voluntary Relocation. . . . The intent from the first Outing Programs was to permanently disperse Indians so that there would not be any Indian communities. American Indian identity would cease to exist. Human obstacles to the transfer of reservation land and natural resources would be permanently removed." William Willard, "Outing, Relocation, and Employment Assistance: The Impact of Federal Indian Population Dispersal Programs in the Bay Area," *Wicazo Sa Review* 12:1 (Spring 1997), 30. It is also important to note that during the war Indigenous peoples throughout California started a mass migration to cities to help in the wartime industries. For instance, at Ukiah Valley, by 1941, "more than a third of . . . Indian women between the ages of fifteen and thirty had worked for some time in the Bay Area . . . and Indian women . . . left Ukiah to 'escape the restrictions of their activities in Ukiah, secure better employment opportunities and improve their social and economic positions.'" Most new arrivals found shelter and work assignments as domestics through the Oakland YWCA. Victoria D. Patterson, "Indian Life in the City: A Glimpse of the Urban Experience of Pomo Women in the 1930s," *California History* 71:3 (Fall 1992), 405–408.

18. The six centers were Chicago, Cleveland, Dallas, Denver, Los Angeles, and San Francisco. Alan L. Sorkin, *The Urban American Indian* (Lexington: Lexington Books, 1978), 27; Peter Collier, "The Red Man's Burden," *Ramparts* (Feb. 1970), 30.

19. Collier, "Better Red Than Dead," 30. LaNada Means was interviewed by Peter Collier for this article. Eventually LaNada would be the primary Native student organizer on the Berkeley campus and was later a co-coordinator with Richard Oakes of the Alcatraz takeover in 1969.
20. Sorkin, *Urban American Indian*, 33. By 1959 the BIA had ceased keeping statistics on its relocation program to avoid criticism. Therefore, little data exists except from Native organizations and the Census Bureau. Joan Ablon suggests that the return rate was as high as 75 percent in the early years. Ablon, "Relocated American Indians," 297.
21. Susan Lobo, *Urban Voices: The Bay Area American Indian Community* (Tucson: University of Arizona Press, 2002), 38; Anonymous, *The Warpath* (Spring 1970), 7, miscellaneous boxes, Murray Wax Papers, Newberry Library, Chicago, Illinois.
22. FBI file, p. 32.
23. Ibid.; Leonard Oakes interviews; and Oakes, "Alcatraz Is Not an Island," 38.
24. Richard Oakes, "Native American Studies," "Ethnic Studies-NAS, 1969" folder, 2, Hayakawa Papers, San Francisco State University Archives, San Francisco, California.
25. Ablon, "Relocated American Indians," 297.
26. Sorkin, *Urban American Indian*, 10, 25.
27. Tribes throughout California have a long and rich history of organizing and creating Intertribal coalitions. Several prominent organizations, from the Mission Indian Federation of 1919 to the 1926 California Indian Brotherhood and a host of others, have championed the cause for greater freedoms and rights.
28. On termination, see Fixico, *Termination and Relocation;* Richard Drinnon, *Keeper of Concentration Camps: Dillon S. Myer and American Racism* (Berkeley: University of California Press, 1987); and Kenneth R. Philip, *Termination Revisited: American Indians on the Trail to Self-Determination, 1933–1953* (Lincoln: University of Nebraska Press, 1999).
29. Al Gedicks, *The New Resource Wars: Native and Environmental Struggles against Multinational Corporations* (Boston: South End Press, 1993), 41. "Overall, geologists report that twenty-five to forty percent of America's uranium, one-third of its coal, and approximately five percent of its oil and gas are on Indian reservations in the West." Donald L. Fixico, *The Invasion of Indian Country in the Twentieth Century: American Capitalism and Tribal Natural Resources* (Niwot: University Press of Colorado, 1998), 143.
30. This is a possible explanation for why the government pushed to relocate Navajos and offered free train passage and jobs on the Santa Fe Railroad to members of Laguna Pueblo. Boxcar towns were established in cities along the railroad lines and specifically in Richmond, California, just south of San Francisco. Kurt M. Peters, "Continuing Identity: Laguna Pueblo Railroaders in Richmond, California," in *American Indians and the Urban Experience*, ed. Susan Lobo and Kurt Peters (Walnut Creek, CA: Altamira Press, 2001), 117–126; see also Myla Vicenti Carpio, *Indigenous Albuquerque* (Lubbock: Texas Tech University Press, 2011).

31. Prentice Mooney, "Indian Country Is a Frontier Again," *Nation's Business* (Sept. 1969), 76–78. By 1974, *Nation's Business* ran another story by BIA Assistant Secretary Marvin L. Franklin entitled "Payrolls: An Answer to the Indian Militants," which showcased how industry could quell protests for Indian rights. Franklin, "Payrolls an Answer to the Indian Militants," *Nation's Business* (June 1974), 54–58. "The BIA made it easy for Indians to remove their land allotments from trust status immediately after leaving reservations. This further eroded the Indian land base since non-Indians were usually better able to purchase fee patented land . . . the problem of Indian and non-Indian land as it became so intermingled that it was impossible for Native Americans to muster blocks of reservation land for tribal enterprises . . . leaving an unbalanced population of those least able to make a tribe economically viable." Burt, "Roots of the Native American Urban Experience," 92.

32. "the city's transformation lay in post–World War II efforts by planners and developers to transform a quaint West Coast port into an international corporate center of commerce, finance, and administration . . . a consequence, blue collar activities in the manufacturing and wholesale trades have declined steadily since World War II, while retail, finance, insurance, real estate, transportation, utilities, and tourism have generally expanded." Little did Native relocatees to San Francisco realize that city planners were redefining the work force, and that the job market for blue-collar labor was quickly disappearing. Brian J. Godfrey, "Urban Development and Redevelopment in San Francisco," *Geographical Review* 87:3 (July 1997), 316.

33. On redlining in the Mission District, see Ocean Howell, *Making the Mission: Planning and Ethnicity in San Francisco* (Chicago: University of Chicago Press, 2015), 149–180.

34. Chris Carlsson, ed., *Ten Years That Shook the City: San Francisco 1968–1978* (San Francisco: City Lights Foundation Books, 2011), 46; Fredrick M. Wirt, *Power in the City: Decision Making in San Francisco* (Los Angeles: University of California Press, 1974), 245. For further information on Samoan and Native interactions, see Joan Ablon, "Retention of Cultural Values and Differential Urban Adaptation: Samoans and American Indians in a West Coast City," *Social Forces* (1971), 385–393. See also Christopher Lowen Agee, *The Streets of San Francisco: Policing and the Creation of a Cosmopolitan Liberal Politics, 1950–1972* (Chicago: University of Chicago Press, 2014), 5–6.

35. The Mission Rebels received federal Community Action Program funding as an urban interethnic youth-serving agency. LaNada Boyer, "Reflections of Alcatraz," in *Native American Voices: A Reader,* ed. Susan Lobo and Steve Talbot (Upper Saddle River, NJ: Prentice-Hall, 2001), 507–508. On the Mission District, see Mike Miller, *A Community Organizers Tale: People and Power in San Francisco* (Berkeley: Heyday Books, 2009), 43; and Marjorie Heins, *Strictly Ghetto Property: The Story of Los Siete de la Raza* (Berkeley: Ramparts Press, 1972), 18–20.

36. Mankiller and Wallis, *Mankiller,* 154–155.

37. League of United Latin American Citizens, *Nuestra Misión de San Francisco*, 1:3 (July-Aug. 1969). "Mission Coalition (San Francisco)," box 4, file 28, Al Miller Papers, San Francisco Public Library, San Francisco, California. The Nuestra Misión has possible connection back to famed Cuban intellectual José Martí, whose 1892 essay "Nuestra America" feared American expansion and proposed an autochthonous revolution of continental unity throughout Latin America—linking Latin America to its exceptional Indigenous history and roots might reverse or hinder the process of Americanization.

38. Armando Navarro, *La Raza Unida Party: A Chicano Challenge to the U.S. Two-Party Dictatorship* (Philadelphia: Temple University Press, 2000), 135. See also Ernesto B. Vigil, *The Crusade for Justice: Chicano Militancy and the Government's War on Dissent* (Madison: University of Wisconsin Press, 1999); and Ernesto Chávez, *My People First! Nationalism, Identity, and Insurgency in the Chicano Movement in Los Angeles, 1966–1978* (Berkeley: University of California Press, 2002).

39. Carlsson, ed., *Ten Years*, 33.

40. Mike Miller, *A Community Organizers Tale: People and Power in San Francisco* (Berkeley: Heyday Books, 2009), 42–43. One of the first temporary offices that arose after the San Francisco Indian Center burned down in October of 1969 was located at the Mission Area Community Action Board managed by the MCO on 3189 16th Street. Carlsson, ed., *Ten Years*, 48–60, 158. Model Cities funds were derived from Lyndon B. Johnson's War on Poverty programs, which sponsored the passage of the Demonstration Cities and Metropolitan Development Act in 1966 to direct government funds to encourage community improvements and developments—each major metropolitan mayor had access to these funds. The five-year funding plan was also meant to diminish the prospects of widespread urban unrest and riots.

41. On the Third World Liberation Front and the Red Guards, see Karen Umemoto, "'On Strike!': San Francisco State College Strike, 1968–1969: The Role of Asian American Students," and Daryl J. Maeda, "Black Panthers, Red Guards, and Chinamen: Constructing Asian American Identity through Performing Blackness, 1969–1972," in *Contemporary Asian America: A Multidisciplinary Reader*, ed. Min Zhou and J. V. Gatewood (New York: New York University Press, 2007). See also Carlsson, ed., *Ten Years*, 32–33.

42. Carlsson, ed., *Ten Years*, 39.

43. Marjorie Heins, *Strictly Ghetto Property: The Story of Los Siete de la Raza* (Berkeley: Ramparts Press, 1972), 50–60.

44. Ablon, "Relocated American Indians," 297; Ann Metcalf, "Indians in the San Francisco Bay Area" (Chicago: Newberry Library, 1980), 90. Proceedings of the Third Annual Conference on Problems and Issues Concerning American Indians Today.

45. Chavers interview.

46. "After living with Richard Oakes for five years." Anonymous, "Anne Oakes' Emotions," *Press Democrat* (March 17, 1973), 1. This quote is the best evidence to conclude that Richard and Annie Oakes were possibly married in 1968.

This is also the same year that Richard Oakes moved from New York to San Francisco. More evidence is found in Police Court records published in the *Tribune-Press* out of Gouverneur, New York. "Dec. 8—Richard Oakes, Hogansburg, fined $10. Inadequate exhaust system." Oakes got pulled over between Hogansburg and Syracuse, New York, and in the process left us a document that suggests he arrived in San Francisco in 1968. Anonymous, "Police Courts," *Tribune-Press* (Dec. 27, 1967), 2:1. Before May 24, 1968, the *Newport Daily News* reported a fight at an "Island Park cafe" and a "fine of $15.00" to a "Thomas Richard Oakes." Anonymous, "Tipsy Driver Fined $200; Failing to Yield Costs $25," *Newport Daily News* (May 24, 1968), 2. The arrest record that appears in his FBI file and various newspaper accounts all suggest that Oakes left New York for San Francisco during the summer of 1968. His next arrest occurred in San Francisco on September 14, 1968. In my interviews with Leonard Oakes, he mentioned that Richard had made a trip back to Brooklyn and Akwesasne before he left for California. Leonard Marrufo, 1940 United States Federal Census, Redwood, Sonoma, California, Roll T627_350, p. 4A; Enumeration District 49–36, U.S. Census Bureau, available ancestry.com, accessed July 7, 2015. Anonymous, "Anna Oakes Obituary," *Press Democrat* (Aug. 4, 2010), n.p. A note on the spelling of Annie Oakes's name: While Anne was her legal name, most close associates, family, and friends called her Annie.

47. Russell Means and Marvin J. Wolf, *Where White Men Fear to Tread* (New York: St. Martin's Press, 1995), 96.

48. "we congregated in a nearby bar called Warren's. It was owned by a family of Klamath Indians from northern California. By talking to those people, I found out about an Eisenhower administration program known as termination." Means and Wolf, *Where White Men Fear to Tread*, 96.

49. Dean Chavers interview, tape 1, side 1, 8, interview in author's possession.

50. Johnson, *Occupation of Alcatraz Island*, 25.

51. Gary F. Jensen, Joseph H. Stauss, and V. William Harris, "Crime, Delinquency, and the American Indian," *Human Organization* 36:3 (Fall 1977), 252.

52. Ibid., 253.

53. Oakes, "Alcatraz Is Not an Island," 36. Oakes's personal account of the take-over was published shortly after his assassination on September 20, 1972. It is the only known autobiography of the leader.

54. FBI file, pp. 15, 20, 32.

55. On the rivalry between Samoans and Native people, see Joan Ablon, "Retention of Cultural Values and Differential Urban Adaptation: Samoans and American Indians in a West Coast City," *Social Forces* 49:3 (1971), 385–393.

56. Dean Chavers interview.

57. "The American Indian Council of the Bay Area is a cross-tribal political group working for the general betterment of relocatees. The Council has tradition-ally sponsored the Annual Indian Day Picnic, and in recent years come into

national notice by their widely publicized criticisms of the Relocation programs." Ablon, "Retention of Cultural Values," 299.

58. Mankiller and Wallis, *Mankiller,* 111.

59. Mary Lee Johns interview.

60. Ann Metcalf, "Indians in the San Francisco Bay Area," *Urban Indians* (Chicago: Newberry Library, 1980), 97. Proceedings of the Third Annual Conference on Problems and Issues Concerning American Indians Today.

61. Delores Smith, ed., *The American Indian* (1969), 1–11 (original copy in possession of author). This was the official newsletter for the San Francisco Indian Center, it listed Earl Livermore as the director for the Indian center and Don Patterson as president of the Executive Board. The center located at 3053 16th Street with weekday hours from 9:00 a.m. to 8:30 p.m., Saturdays it was open from 9:00 a.m. to 1:00 p.m., and it closed on Sundays. Center facilities included a ballroom for powwows and dances, snack bar, kitchen, meeting rooms, pool, and sewing facilities. The newsletter was printed monthly but contained no official date.

62. Ibid., 97. See also Ablon, "Retention of Cultural Values," 299.

63. Despite the passage of the American Indian Religious Freedom Act of 1978, Native American Church members were harassed by law enforcement officials, who viewed peyote as a narcotic rather than a religious sacrament. "Roadmen" is the proper name for spiritual leaders within the Native American Church.

64. Further research is needed on Native church service within the San Francisco area; secondary literature on this is lacking, and its treatment by scholars is vague at best.

65. Alan Sorkin, Shirley Fiske, and John Price, who have done useful work on urban Indian migration, account for only three levels of institutional infrastructure in the creation of an Indian City: Indian bars, Indian centers, and organizations. However, during the late 1960s, other agencies must be included. The rise of Indian-owned business, Native American Studies, and Indian neighborhoods are also important factors in the makeup of an Indian City. On powwow culture, see Clyde Ellis, *A Dancing People: Powwow Culture on the Southern Plains* (Lawrence: University Press of Kansas, 2003); for an urban perspective Joan Weibel-Orlando, *Indian Country, L.A.: Maintaining Ethnic Community in Complex Society* (Urbana and Chicago: University of Illinois Press, 1999), 132–152.

66. Sorkin, *Urban American Indian,* 115.

67. On Indians in the marketplace, see Brian C. Hosmer, *American Indians in the Marketplace: Persistence and Innovation Among the Menominees and Metlakatlans, 1870–1920* (Lawrence: University Press of Kansas, 1999); and Brian Hosmer and Colleen O'Neill, eds., *Native Pathways: American Indian Culture and Economic Development in the Twentieth Century* (Boulder: University Press of Colorado, 2004).

68. Johnson, *Occupation of Alcatraz Island,* 157. The Thunderbirds become known for their trafficking in heroin and for their violent tactics of enforcing street

laws to their liking. Yet for many in the Native community the Thunderbirds were a harmless gang of young toughs.

69. Weibel-Orlando, *Indian Country, L.A.*, 189. On Samoan history, see Craig R. Janes, *Migration, Social Change, and Health: A Samoan Community in Urban California* (Stanford: Stanford University Press, 1990); and Donald Denoon, Stewart Firth, Jocelyn Linnekin, Malama Meleisea, and Karen Nero, eds., *The Cambridge History of the Pacific Islanders* (Melbourne: Cambridge University Press, 1997). Mary Lee Johns, interviewed by the author, Morris, Minnesota (April 11, 2011).

70. "Many restrictions discriminate intentionally or unintentionally against the Indian renter: refusing children, limiting number of occupants, refusing to rent to welfare mothers, demanding a breakage fee along with rent that puts the price out of reach, and stringent credit checks." Sorkin, *Urban American Indian*, 68, 69.

71. Ibid., 22–23.

72. This split deserves further research. For example, how members of both urban and reservation communities perceived each other's role in shaping further federal Indian policy. Those who left their communities for relocation abandoned their allotments to further outside speculation and development, which increased the checkerboard effect on many reservations. Yet, this split is contested by scholars, "establishing rural/urban as the defining character-istic of identity is not realistic from an Indian point of view and serves to alienate Indian people from their homelands." Lobo and Peters, ed., *American Indians and the Urban Experience*, 76.

73. Hank Adams, interview by Robert Warrior (Dec. 20, 1994), 52–53, Robert Warrior's private collection (copy in possession of author).

74. Chavers interview, tape 1, side 2, 8. Hayakawa has an interesting backstory. He was born in Canada and the son of Japanese migrant workers. While his family moved back to Japan by the 1920s, Hayakawa elected to enroll in classes at the University of Manitoba and years later, despite a battle with narcolepsy he earned his PhD in English from the University of Wisconsin by 1935. His reputation in the Japanese-American community was forever tarnished over his defense of internment camps, which detained over 120,000 Japanese Americans. He himself escaped internment because he was officially a Canadian citizen. An ardent supporter of then Governor Ronald Reagan, Hayakawa soon moved into politics after hanging up his educator robes. He served only one term as a senator from California after switching his party affiliation from Democrat to Republican in order to get elected in 1976. See also Anonymous, "Ex-Sen. Hayakawa Dies; Unpredictable Iconoclast," *Los Angeles Times* (Feb. 28, 1992), n.p., available at www.latimes.com/local/obituaries/archives/la-me-si-hayakawa-19920228-story.html, accessed Aug. 6, 2015.

75. On Al Miller's application for student housing, the rental price is listed as $55 a month for a furnished apartment with no pets allowed. Also a list of expenses from the SFSC Student Financial Aid Office was for 1969–70

semesters: ". . . $256.00 married couple apartment, food costs $1,170.00, Housing Costs $495.00, other costs listed clothing, laundry, and recreation at $1,500.00 . . . the total with health insurance is $3,500.00 if married and with children add $600.00 first child, $450.00 for each additional child." I include these numbers to reveal the types of expenditures that Richard and Annie faced as a family, but it is important to also note that Richard received monies from the EOP office to curb a bulk of these aforementioned costs. "Student Notes—Miscellaneous" folder, box 4, file 27, Al Miller Papers, San Francisco Public Library, San Francisco, California. The EOP funding curbed the costs tremendously for students. The EOP financial information sheet listed the following expenses, tuition $150.00, books and supplies $150.00, rent $160.00, food $200.00, transportation $30.00, clothing $20.00, medical $40.00, and insurance $40.00. "Student Notes—Miscellaneous" folder, box 4, file 25, Al Miller Papers, San Francisco Public Library, San Francisco, California.

76. Debra Ghiringhelli, "Gatorville or Hunters Point? Married Students Offered Other Housing," *Daily Gator* (Oct. 16, 1974), n.p.; Doug Barry, "Gatorville Battle Shaping: Married Students Resist," *Daily Gator* (Oct. 24, 1973), n.p.; SFSU, Special Collections, clippings on Gatorville, San Francisco, California. The *Daily Gator* was the name of the San Francisco State College student newspaper; the Gator was the university mascot. SFSC would later change its name to San Francisco State University.

77. See Dikran Karagueuzian, *Blow It Up!* (Boston: Gambit Inc., 1971); and William H. Orrick Jr., *Shut It Down! A College in Crisis* (Washington, DC: U.S. Government Printing Office, 1969), report to the U.S. National Commission on the Causes and Prevention of Violence.

78. Kirkpatrick Sale, *SDS* (New York: Random House, 1973), 518.

79. Howard Finberg, ed., *Crisis at SF State* (San Francisco: Insight Publications, 1969), 16–18.

80. Johnson, Nagel, and Champagne, eds., *American Indian Activism*, 114–115. Al Miller (Seminole), Gerald Sam (Washoe-Paiute), Joseph "Zoe" Bill (Hooper Bay Inuit), Deanna Francis (Malecite), Mickey Gemmill (Pit River), Robert Kaniatobe (Choctaw), Ronald Lickers (Seneca), and Joyce Rice (Ho-Chunk).

81. Oakes, "Alcatraz Is Not an Island," 36–37.

82. Dean Chavers interview, tape 1, side 1, 2.

83. LaNada Boyer, "Reflections of Alcatraz," unpublished article (n.d.), 9, Robert Warrior's Personal Collection.

84. Johnson, Nagel, and Champagne, eds., *American Indian Activism*, 107. Melvin (Mel) Thom, Clyde Warrior, and Hank Adams had earned the not-so-flattering title "Red Muslims" for their radical stance on American Indian activism in the early 1960s. Each had worked with Tribes in the Pacific Northwest to support their viable protests or fish-ins to protect the treaty and fishing rights of Native nations. In recent histories of NIYC, several scholars have errone-ously given the credit for the fish-ins to NIYC leadership, but this interpreta-tion is incorrect: The fight for treaty and fishing rights had started long before

NIYC representatives decided to lend their support to the cause at Frank's Landing.

85. Richard Oakes, "Alcatraz Is Not an Island," 37–38.

86. Richard Oakes, *Native American Studies* (San Francisco: San Francisco State College, 1969), 1, San Francisco Public Library, box 4, file 32, "San Francisco State Native American Studies."

87. Anonymous, "Knife Threat Here to Senator's Wife," *San Francisco Examiner* (April 24, 1969), 22, "Newspaper Clippings" folder, box 3, file 25, San Francisco Public Library, Alcatraz Collection, San Francisco, California; Mary Lee Johns interview (April 11, 2011), Morris, Minnesota.

88. Mary Lee Johns interview. "The police never come on the street and break up any fights if you call them. They just let the Indians fight. And then they'd come late at night and arrest them, put them all in the drunk tank. Things like this are what the Indians testified to at the hearings, and I got to see it for myself." Harris and Stockel, eds., *LaDonna Harris*, 96–98. Al Miller echoed LaDonna Harris's take on the situation in the Mission. Miller in an interview had approached the San Francisco police with hiring officers to walk a beat in the neighborhood. Miller suggested that two officers who were widely known in the community were taken away and now crime had increased in the Mission. Not only did Miller want the beat cops back, but he also wanted to have two Indian center officials elected to work with the beat cops to curb violence. It was an ingenious plan to have the police linked to important cultural centers and to include diverse representation to curb violence. Anonymous, "Knife Threat Here to Senator's Wife," *San Francisco Examiner* (April 24, 1969), 22. On Alioto and the San Francisco police, see Christopher Lowen Agee, *The Streets of San Francisco: Policing and the Creation of a Cosmopolitan Liberal Politics, 1950–1972* (Chicago: University of Chicago Press, 2014).

89. Harris and Stockel, eds., *LaDonna Harris*, 96–98.

90. On NCIO, see Thomas A. Britten, *The National Council on Indian Opportunity: Quiet Champion of Self-Determination* (Albuquerque: University of New Mexico Press, 2014).

91. Johnson, *Occupation of Alcatraz Island*, 25.

92. Tim Finley, "Indians Protest Report by Cops," *San Francisco Chronicle* (April 19, 1969), n.p., "San Francsico State-NAS" folder, box 4, file 32, Al Miller Papers, San Francisco Public Library, San Francisco, California.

93. Richard Oakes, "American Indians Begin to Fight," *Daily Gator* (April 21, 1969), n.p., "Ethnic Studies-NAS-folder" folder, Hayakawa Papers, San Francisco State University Archives, San Francisco, California.

94. Other members of SCAN included David Tyler (Klamath), Patrick Genaaha (Diné), Gerald Sam (Washoe-Paiute), Gary Ray Hodge (Klamath), and Joseph "Zoe" Bill (Hooper Bay Inuit). Letter to Hayakawa from Richard Oakes, "Request for Funds," "Ethnic Studies-NAS" folder, Hayakawa Papers, San Francisco State University Archives, San Francisco, California.

95. Mary Lee Johns interviewed by author, Morris, Minnesota (April 11, 2011), in author's possession.

96. Anonymous, "M.A.N.Y. Movement of American Native Youth," "San Francisco State—NAS" folder, box 4, file 32, Al Miller Papers, San Francisco Public Library, San Francisco, Chicago. One of the first acts of this organization was to draw attention to police action or inaction with regards to Warren's Bar. In a notice posted in the Indian center the following M.A.N.Y. flyer stated, "The frequent fist fights that take place in all of the bars, the serving of minors in some of the bars in the area, the unavailability of policemen until 1:00 [a.m.] when they swoop down in numbers to harass the wrong people, bartenders looking on with indifference while people fight & the bathrooms of the bar having stopped-up, overflowing commodes. These and many other problems exist which no one seems either willing or able to do anything about." "Indian organization-American Native Youth Corp." folder, box 4, file 23, Al Miller Papers, San Francisco Public Library, San Francisco, California.

97. Richard Oakes, "Native American Critic and Review," n.d., 1, "Ethnic Studies—NAS" folder, Hayakawa Papers, San Francisco State University Archives, San Francisco, California.

98. Leonard Oakes interviews; Anonymous, "Mrs. Irene Oakes," *Massena Observer* (May 6, 1969), 5; and Eleanor Dumas, "Richard Oakes Renews Cause in East; Saved by Medicine Men," *Watertown Daily Times* (Oct. 15, 1970), 12.

99. Anonymous, "Meeting of the Committee for a Seminar," "San Francisco State-NAS" folder, box 4, file 32, Al Miller Papers, San Francisco Public Library, San Francisco, California.

100. See Rose Delia Soza War Soldier, "'To Take Positive and Effective Action': Rupert Costo and the California Based American Indian Historical Society," PhD dissertation, Arizona State University, Phoenix, Arizona, 2013. The *Indian Historian* was first published in mimeograph form from 1964 to 1967 before it was published in a bound edition that lasted from 1967 until the 1980s, after which it was known as *Wassaja/The Indian Historian*. *Wassaja* (signaling or beckoning) as a title called back to the early twentieth-century Yavapai Dr. Carlos Montezuma, who published the famed Indian rights newsletter *Wassaja* (1916–1922). Anonymous, "After 200 Years," *The Warpath* 1:4 (Fall 1969), 12, miscellaneous boxes, Murray Wax Papers, Newberry Library, Chicago, Illinois. The article identifies nine people on the advisory board for NAS: Mr. and Mrs. Rupert Costo (American Indian Historical Society); David Riesling (California Indian Education Assoc.); Earl Livermore (SF Indian Center); Adam Nordwall (Intertribal Friendship House); Lehman Brightman (United Native Americans); President of San Francisco Art Institute; David Peri (Sonoma State College); and Belva Cottier (Sioux Club and NAS Center-UC Berkeley).

101. "Under the 1868 [Fort Laramie] treaty, any male Sioux over the age of eighteen not living on a reservation can claim federal land 'not used for special purposes.' This right was also granted to other Indians in the 1887 Dawes Severalty Act. When the right was revoked in 1934, Sioux were specifically exempted. 'Claimants must make improvements worth two hundred dollars within three years.'" Importantly, the Haudenosaunee had

also rejected the 1934 Indian Reorganization Act by vote. Johnson, Nagel, and Champagne, eds., *American Indian Activism*, 118.

102. In Russell Means's autobiography he recalled that his father Walter Means and Chalk Cottier (Belva's husband and Russell's cousin), Belva Cottier, Richard McKenzie, and himself were accompanied by their lawyer Elliott Leighton. Russell Means and Marvin J. Wolf, *Where White Men Fear to Tread* (New York: St. Martin's Press, 1995), 105–106. The original wire photo (March 9, 1964, in author's possession) cites Elliott Leighton as the lawyer and Richard McKenzie is cited in the national park service website at www. nps.gov/alca/learn/historyculture/we-hold-the-rock.htm, accessed Sept. 20, 2015. "Members of the invading party, all members in good standing in the Bay Area Branch of the American Indian Council, are known in daily life as Allen Cottier, Richard McKenzie, Martin Martinez, Garfield Spotted Elk, and Walter Means." UPI, "Indians Lay Claim to Alcatraz," *Daily Independent Journal* (March 9, 1964), 3.

103. "[C]entral core of my plan would involve a high altitude observation tower—perhaps the tallest in the world . . . it would contain high-speed elevators, observation levels and a rotating restaurant which would allow the view to sweep the 360 grandeur of the horizon once each hour." Lamar Hunt, "Letter Lamar Hunt to Alioto," box 14, folder 35, Joseph Alioto Papers, San Francisco Public Library, San Francisco, California.

104. Dean Chavers had enrolled in the journalism school at UC Berkeley in 1968. After flying 158 missions in Vietnam and serving for five and a half years in the military, he decided to earn his degree from Berkeley. Chavers interview, tape 1, side 1, 2.

105. Johnson, Nagel, and Champagne, eds., *American Indian Activism*, 107.

106. LaNada Boyer, "Reflections of Alcatraz," 10, Robert Warriors Personal Collection.

107. "According to the memo out of a total of 11.3 positions allotted for Black Studies only three have been filled. Out of six positions allotted for Asian Studies 1.88 have been filled. No one has yet been approved to teach Mexican American or Native American Studies." The article then goes on to quote a Black Studies professor who recently resigned, having said, "the most effective instrument of bigotry at San Francisco State College is S. I. Hayakawa. His total insensitivity to the educational needs of non-white people has seriously crippled every program designed to meet those needs." Paul Cantor, "Ethnic Studies Flop?" *Daily Gator* 8:102 (Aug. 8, 1969), 1.

108. David Risling, "Letter to Dean Daniel Feder," "San Francisco State-NAS" folder, box 4, file 32, 1–4, Al Miller Papers, San Francisco Public Library, San Francisco, California. Risling happened to know Richard from his work with Dr. Jack Forbes at the "Far Out Labs" in Berkeley. It is little wonder that Richard was learning how to play the system with regard to university politics.

109. Richard Oakes, "Prospective Student Packet," n.d., "Ethnic Studies-NAS" folder, 1–6, Hayakawa Papers, San Francisco State University Archives, San Francisco, California. Emphasis in original.

110. Rupert Costo and Jeannette Henry, ed., *Indian Voices: The First Convocation of American Indian Scholars* (San Francisco: Indian Historian Press, 1970), 196.

111. Dr. Louis W. Ballard, "Letter to Richard Oakes," August 15, 1969. "Ethnic Studies-NAS" folder, 1, Hayakawa Papers, San Francisco State University Archives, San Francisco, California. This letter was in response to a package of information that Richard had sent to Dr. Ballard. The response was to one of the materials titled "Ten Justifiable Demands of All Native Americans of U.S. and Canada."

112. Pacifica Radio Archives, "The Occupation of Alcatraz VI–5," Bancroft Library, University of California at Berkeley (Dec. 22, 1969), vol. 1, CD 1, Berkeley, California.

113. Richard Oakes, "Letter to Helen M. Scheirbeck," August 13, 1969, "Ethnic Studies-NAS" folder, Hayakawa Papers, San Francisco State University Archives, San Francisco, California.

114. Johnson, Nagel, and Champagne, eds., *American Indian Activism*, 115.

115. Anonymous, "The White Roots of Peace—1968 or 69," *Indian Time* 33:1 (Jan. 8, 2015), n.p., available at www.indiantime.net/story/2015/01/08/blast/the-white-roots-of-peace-1968-or-69/16424.html, accessed July 17, 2015.

116. James M. Fortier, *Alcatraz Is Not an Island* (Pacifica: Diamond Island Productions, 2001), documentary movie.

117. Gambill "came to the St. Regis reservation in 1965 as a community development officer in the employ of the Canadian Department of Indian Affairs . . . [he] was adopted into the Bear clan." Dean Chavers, "Trouble at Akwesasne," *Indian Voice* 3:2 (April 1973), 11. "Gambill helped revive Ray Fadden's Akwesasne Counsellor Organization which had traveled far and wide inculcating Indian pride among Mohawk youth from the mid-1930s through the 1950s. Gambill, hoping to influence a group of young Mohawks such as Tom Porter and Francis Boots to take up leadership roles in the Mohawk Longhouse, founded White Roots of Peace. Seeing the spiritual crisis caused by the death of key elders and that many young Indians were moving away from the faith, Gambill founded this organization." Hauptman, *The Iroquois Struggle for Survival*, 224.

118. Jerry Gambill, "He Liked His Mohawk Name, Ranoies—A Big Man," *Akwesasne Notes* 4:6 (Late Autumn 1972), 6.

119. The mainland office was also in charge of sending out telegrams, approving supply runs with the General Services Administration (GSA), approval of interviews and press, writing press releases, lobbying city, state, and federal officials, sorting mail for the occupiers, and many other duties.

120. On the Alcatraz takeover, see Johnson, *Occupation of Alcatraz Island;* Paul Chaat Smith and Robert Allen Warrior, *Like a Hurricane: The Indian Movement from Alcatraz to Wounded Knee* (New York: New Press, 1996); and Johnson, Nagel, and Champagne, eds., *American Indian Activism*.

4. I'M NOT YOUR INDIAN ANYMORE

1. On the Black Panther Party, see Henry Hampton and Steve Fayer, *Voices of Freedom: An Oral History of the Civil Rights Movement from the 1950s through the 1980s* (New York: Bantam Books, 1991), 349–372, 511–538.

2. On the 1960s, see David Farber, *The Age of Great Dreams: America in the 1960s* (New York: Hill and Wang, 1994), 1–268; and David Farber, ed., *The Sixties: From Memory to History* (Chapel Hill: University of North Carolina Press, 1994), 1–316. Over twenty Asian-American activists visited Alcatraz Island on Valentine's Day, February 14, 1970. The visit inspired writer Shawn Wong to write his popular novel *Homebase* about a fictional visit to Alcatraz on Christmas Day in 1969. Recent scholarship on the novels *Homebase* and *I Hotel* places Alcatraz "as a place where Asian Americans found inspiration for their own activism." Catherine Fung, "'This Isn't Your Battle or Your Land': The Native American Occupation of Alcatraz in the Asian-American Political Imagination," *College Literature* 41:1 (Winter 2014), 150. The Red Guard operated its headquarters out of Chinatown and worked in a coalition with the Black Panther Party, the Brown Berets, and the Mission Coalition Organization and emerged as key supporter for the Alcatraz takeover.

3. Neal Starblanket and Mike Mitchell, *You Are on Indian Land* (Montreal: National Film Board of Canada, 1969), documentary movie; and Jerry Gambill, ed., *Akwesasne Notes* (April 1969), Murray Wax Papers, Newberry Library, Chicago, Illinois. The history of the December 18, 1968, protest is covered in its entirety on the documentary film *You Are on Indian Land*. The following passages on the December 18 protest were mostly pulled from the documentary footage.

4. Starblanket and Mitchell, *You Are on Indian Land;* National Film Board of Canada and Jerry Gambill, ed., "Kahn Tineta Gets Further Remand," and "Endless Remands Constitute Cruel and Needless Harassment," *Akwesasne Notes* (June 1969), n.p., miscellaneous boxes, Murray Wax Papers, Newberry Library, Chicago, Illinois.

5. Starblanket and Mitchell, *You Are on Indian Land;* Hauptman, *The Iroquois Struggle for Survival,* 148–149. *You Are on Indian Land* was shown at SFSC when the White Roots of Peace Caravan visited and stayed with Richard Oakes. Johnson, Nagel, and Champagne, eds., *American Indian Activism,* 106.

6. As early as 1934, when he was in law school at UCLA, Grossman participated in the San Francisco General Strike. Eventually he served as a lawyer with the International Longshore and Warehouse Union. In 1950, he represented Willie McGee, a Mississippi man who was sentenced to a public electrocution for allegedly raping a white woman. By the 1960s, Grossman was working to defend the rights of conscientious objectors. Tom Price, "Aubrey Grossman— Passionate Defender of Civil Liberties," *The Dispatcher* 58:1 (Jan. 2000), 1–3, available at http://archive.ilwu.org/?page_id=1606, accessed Oct. 14, 2015. "[he] had been black listed before he even passed the bar, total radical . . . [there] were very strong forces in the California Bar that were trying to keep

him from getting a license, so he always represented the underdog." Dean Chavers interview, tape 1, side 2, 11, interview in author's possession.

7. On the late Browning Pipestem, see Jane Glenn Cannon, "Attorney brings heritage to profession," *Native News* (March 1, 1999), 1–5, available on www. mail-archive.com/nativenews@mlists.net/msg00544.html, a reprint of an article from the *Norman Transcript*.

8. Don Jelinek, "Alcatraz Indians," available at www.donjelinek.com/Alcatraz_ Indians.html, accessed Sept. 25, 2015. Interview with the Bay Area publication *The Recorder* (Feb. 6, 1997; republished on Jelinek's website). Jelinek also estimated that some 40,000 to 50,000 Native peoples visited the island over the course of the entire occupation. Jelinek also revealed that the producers for Quinn and Bergen made sizeable donations to sustain the occupation and Quinn's people donated $6,000 to stage photo opportunities on the island for the film *Flap*. Photos of Quinn's visit and appearances with Richard Oakes appeared in the January 1971 issue of *Good Housekeeping* magazine. Joseph B. Bell, "America's Oldest Debt: Justice for the Indians," *Good Housekeeping* (Jan. 1971), 78, 146–150. Yet, Jelinek also mentions that IAT organizers turned down several offers including the NBC series *Ironside* with Raymond Burr, the producers of which sought to stage a Native-themed episode on the island.

9. Johnson, *The Occupation of Alcatraz Island*, 53.

10. "Some people blamed the Samoans for the fire. Others thought that a cigarette had been carelessly thrown into some trash that was piled against the rear wall of the building." Karen Ducheneaux and Kirke Kickingbird, *One Hundred Million Acres* (New York: Macmillan, 1973), 214.

11. "Indian Organization—American Indians United" folder, box 4, file 22, Al Miller Papers, San Francisco Public Library, San Francisco, California. See also Anonymous, "Urban Indians Join Forces," *The NCAI Sentinel* 14:2 (Summer 1969), 4–5.

12. Oakes, "Alcatraz Is Not an Island," 38.

13. "The Native community people who worked with us considered Adam [Nordwall] to be an opportunist and a con artist. They warned us from having anything to do with him." LaNada Boyer (Means), "Reflections of Alcatraz," n.d., p. 15, unpublished, Robert Warrior's private collection. Excerpts from this essay were later published in Johnson, Nagel, and Champagne, eds., *American Indian Activism*, 15, 88–103. "he tried to appoint himself as the leader for it [Alcatraz], and the students attitude toward Adam was get the hell out of here. Leave us alone, that was Richard's attitude, LaNada's, Dennis' [Turner], [and] all them. Oh Christ here comes Adam again you know glory hog. That's all he was. Of course he wrote that book and claimed total credit for it . . ." Chavers interview, tape 1, side 1.

14. Interview with Joe Bill, February 5, 1970, by Dennis Stanford, tape 458, side 1, 10, Doris Duke Oral History Collection, Center for Southwest Research, University of New Mexico, Albuquerque, New Mexico. Backing up Joe Bill's statement, Ross Harden said, "Both Bill and Harden indicate that an attempt to occupy the island was planned as early as September or October 1969 by

student groups but failed to materialize due to lack of logistical support."
Johnson, *Occupation of Alcatraz Island*, 53.

15. "Indian Organizations—Sonoma Co. American Indian Council, Inc." folder,
box 2, file 33, Alcatraz Collection, San Francisco Public Library, San Francisco,
California. The newsletter includes relations of Annie and briefly mentions
their involvement with the leadership on the Sonoma County American
Indian Council.

16. It is unclear exactly who the author of the Proclamation was, as it is signed
auspiciously Indians of All Tribes. Some of the evidence suggests that it was
drafted at the Indian center in a joint meeting between student leaders, Adam
Nordwall's organization United Bay Area Council of American Indian Affairs,
and other community leaders. No one person can claim authorship, and the
document remains a community document.

17. Indians of All Tribes, "Proclamation," *Indians of All Tribes Newsletter* 1:1
(Jan. 1970), 2; and Adam Fortunate Eagle, *Alcatraz! Alcatraz! The Indian
Occupation of 1969–1971* (Berkeley: Heyday Books, 1992), 44–45.

18. "the four of us swam over there [Alcatraz] . . . Richard Oak[e]s . . . Jim Bob . . .
who else . . . Ross Hard[e]n . . . and there was another guy . . . Walter Heads
and I . . . we stayed there a couple of hours because it was cold." Interview
with Joe Bill. See also Johnson, *The Occupation of Alcatraz Island*, 57. Later
accounts by both Nordwall and Findley claim that Oakes never made it to the
island; see Johnson, Nagel, and Champagne, eds., *American Indian Activism*,
81; and Fortunate Eagle, *Alcatraz! Alcatraz!* 58. However, Tim Findley states,
"Four young braves dived off the barge Monte Cristo and swam to shore
during that assault, but were taken back off again by a friendly yachtsman
after a caretaker threatened to summon United States marshals." Findley, "14
Indians Invade, Claim Alcatraz," *San Francisco Chronicle* (Nov. 10, 1969), 1.
Findley contradicts himself having changed his story almost thirty years later,
most likely an error of hindsight on the reporter's part. Richard Oakes stated,
"[T]he main boat and the press boats, well they just kept on going. They went
right on by. People on the boats saw me . . . but they just kept on going. . . . I
landed just to the left of the dock, on the rocks. I was being dragged in by the
waves or the current, or something, underneath the barge [there was a water
barge parked at the docks]. I was exhausted when I hit land. I've done a lot of
swimming, but this was the toughest swim I've ever made." Oakes, "Alcatraz
Is Not an Island," 38. The overwhelming evidence supports the conclusion
that Richard Oakes made the swim. It is possible that all the confusion
centers around Walter Heads. "Richard Oakes got the urge to dive into the
water from the Monte Cristo, and the other four followed. Walter Hatch
[Heads] was unable to finish the difficult swim, but the others made it to
shore." Johnson, Nagel, and Champagne, eds., *American Indian Activism*, 153;
and John Garvey and Troy Johnson, "The Government and the Indians: The
American Indian Occupation of Alcatraz Island, 1969–71." John Vigil interview (March 23, 2009), Snohomish Island, Washington, interview in author's
possession. Vigil also confirmed that Richard Oakes made the swim to

Alcatraz. Because of the overwhelming evidence mentioned in this footnote, I chose to conclude that Richard Oakes and others made the swim to the island.

19. The fourteen occupiers were Richard Oakes, LaNada Means, Rick Evening (Shoshone/Bannock), Jim Vaughn, John Mortal (Cherokee), Joe Bill, Kay Many Horse (Lakota), Linda Aranaydo (Creek), David Leach (Colville/Lakota), Ross Harden, Burnell Blindman (Lakota), John Whitefox (Shoshone), John Vigil (Apache), Fred Shelton (Inuit). This information was pulled from two flyers found in "Indians on Alcatraz" folder, box 3, file between 2 and 5, not marked in collection, and box 3, file 27, Alcatraz Collection, San Francisco Public Library, San Francisco, California.

20. Oakes, "Alcatraz Is Not an Island," 38.

21. Indians of All Tribes, "Proclamation," *Indians of All Tribes Newsletter* 1:1 (Jan. 1970), 2–3. See also Fortunate Eagle, *Alcatraz! Alcatraz!* 45–47. The version of the Proclamation that appears in Fortunate Eagle's text is similar to the one above, but he only lists nine points instead of the ten that appear in the newsletter.

22. Tim Findley, "Invaders Say We'll Be Back," *San Francisco Chronicle* (Nov. 11, 1969), 1, 26.

23. Johnson, Nagel, and Champagne, eds., *American Indian Activism*, 121.

24. "Nordwall's information was not firsthand because he had departed on another public relations effort to support the occupation. He had been invited to attend the first National Conference on Indian Education, which was held in Minneapolis on November 20, the same date as the planned occupation." This was the organizing conference that founded the National Indian Education Association. Johnson, *The Occupation of Alcatraz Island*, 66.

25. "It would be at night. It would be nonviolent. We had an attorney come in at the final meeting on November 19 to train people in nonviolence. He told us if we raised our arms to defend ourselves it could be called resisting arrest and could result in another charge added to the indictment." Dean Chavers, "Around the Campfire: The Indian Leader of Alcatraz," *Indian Country Today (Lakota Times)* 16:10 (Sept. 9, 1996), A5.

26. Johnson, Nagel, and Champagne, eds., *American Indian Activism*, 122.

27. Ibid., 80. Tim Findley recalls the events of the meeting. "You know [Annie] . . . was very protective of Richard . . . and she busted Shirley Keith in the mouth one night down at the bar by the bus station in San Francisco. She thought Shirley was coming on to Richard . . . I guess. She just walked in . . . picked up a beer bottle and popped [Shirley] . . . in the mouth. She was a tough little lady." Dean Chavers in his interview confirms this incident. tape 1, side 2, 4.

28. Johnson, Nagel, and Champagne, eds., *American Indian Activism*, 123.

29. Peter Bowen, "Under Cover of Darkness," *San Francisco Fault* (Nov. 24, 1971), 1–9, "San Francisco Indians-Alcatraz Indians," newspaper clips, San Francisco Public Library Archives, San Francisco, California; thanks to Benjamin V. Ryan and the Ryan family for *San Francisco Fault* © permission. See also

Peter Bowen and Brooks Townes, *The Sausalito-Indian Navy* (San Francisco: Peter Bowen and Brooks Townes, n.d.), 4–13 (a copy of this self-published book is in the author's private collection).

30. "This time the Coast Guard put up a blockade. They tried to take our boat that night, but some of us jumped on the Coast Guard boat and told them that if they tried to take our boat, we'd take theirs. They told us to get off the island, and we told them, 'No. This is Indian Land. Stay clear 200 yards.' They got out. They set up a blockade. They sailed around in circles. . . . This went on for a couple of days. . . . Also, that night, there were helicopters, circling overhead. With the Coast Guard's searchlights and all, it was quite a spectacle. The little Irish guy, the caretaker, came out and started blowing his bugle. He called up his boss on the phone and said, "The Indians are here, the Indians are here. I think they're here to stay. It's taken them thirty minutes to unload their boat." He told us that we were trespassing, but we just didn't give a damn. We told him that *he* was trespassing, and if he would cooperate, we would set up a Bureau of Caucasian Affairs and make him head of it. He laughed like hell, and later really did help us. He came over to our side." Oakes, "Alcatraz Is Not an Island," 39.

31. "The phrase *Indian Land* may have been the most ubiquitous message. The words were part of large-scale signs prominent on the barracks building facing the dock, on the water tower, and on a wall near the old warden's house. Specifically, on the side of the barracks, just above what is now the park rangers' main office, were the words *Indian Land, Indians Welcome,* and *United Indian Property.* . . . The water tower called out to bay traffic, *Welcome, Peace and Freedom,* while declaring the place *Home of the Free . . . Indian Land. You are on Indian Land* was yet another reminder written in dripping block letters along the walk up to the cell-house." Johnson, Nagel, and Champagne, eds., *American Indian Activism,* 189.

32. Tim Findley, "Invaders Claim Rock Is Theirs," *San Francisco Chronicle* (Nov. 21, 1969), 5.

33. Troy R. Johnson, *We Hold the Rock: The Indian Occupation of Alcatraz, 1969–1971* (San Francisco: Golden Gate National Parks Association, 1997), 31.

34. The mainland office also was in charge of sending out telegrams, approving supply runs with GSA, approval of interviews and press, writing press releases, lobbying city, state, and federal officials, sorting mail for the occupiers, and many other duties. As Steve Talbot remembered, "I saw what an exhausting task it was for Dean Chavers . . . when he took over the responsibility. Chavers, who was an agreeable person, became testy and rather unpleasant after working days on end with little or no sleep. Telephone and other messages, money and donated supplies, technical assistance, and many other coordination tasks for Alcatraz support took place out of this CAP storefront." Johnson, Nagel, and Champagne, eds., *American Indian Activism,* 109.

35. "The media had identified Richard Oakes as the leader on the island and he wanted the responsibility so that was agreeable with us. Richard was smart, aggressive, a handsome Mohawk who always knew what to say. We were

proud of Richard." LaNada Boyer, "Reflections of Alcatraz," unpublished essay, n.d., 18, Robert Warrior's private collection. "The women pretty well selected the leaders and we went ahead and selected Richard Oakes to represent us." Fortier, *Alcatraz Is Not an Island*. "Once the press were notified, I mostly faded into the background. This was Richard's show, and he made the most of it. For three days, the only way the media could talk to him was by telephone. Richard could talk to them via telephone from the caretakers house . . . [he] gave more press briefings than major world leaders. He handled himself really well." Dean Chavers, "Around the Campfire: The Indian Leader of Alcatraz," *Indian Country Today (Lakota Times)* 16:10 (Sept. 9, 1996), A5. Often, those writing about Alcatraz choose to avoid labeling Richard Oakes as the "leader" of Alcatraz. This is because IAT did as much as possible by "consensus" in honor of traditional forms of Native representational government. Yet, historically Native forms of "consensus" government do not lack leaders or leadership. Richard, however, was later labeled by the press as the "president" of Alcatraz, which many in IAT found offensive. This was a case of the press failing to honor or understand "consensus" government. Richard was a "Native leader" who walked alongside the people and not out in front. This was evident in his statements to the press. Oakes constantly refers to IAT first and continually uses the word *we* instead of I.

36. Fortier, *Alcatraz Is Not an Island*.
37. Ibid. Quote from Brad Patterson, White House staff member.
38. Troy Johnson, "The Occupation of Alcatraz Island: Roots of American Indian Activism," *Wicazo Sa Review* 10:2 (Fall 1994), 71. On Nixon, see Jack Forbes, *Native Americans and Nixon: Presidential Politics and Minority Self-Determination, 1969–1972* (Los Angeles: UCLA American Indian Studies Center, 1981), 1–124.
39. Joe Morris, "Nov. 20, 1969–June 11, 1971," *Alcatraz Indian Occupation Diary* (self-published, 1998), 113.
40. Oakes, "Alcatraz Is Not an Island," 39.
41. "Before it was known as the Bureau of Indian Affairs, our 'governing agency' was the War Department. We were called 'Prisoners of War' then. The two agencies are synonymous. During the Second World War, the Japanese prisoner of war camps were run by the same people that run the BIA. Somebody in Washington probably said, 'Hey, this is a natural!' We still consider ourselves prisoners of war. We'll always be at war with the values of this society!" Oakes, "Alcatraz Is Not an Island," 40. This identifies the resentment many Native people held for the Department of the Interior's Bureau of Indian Affairs (BIA). Oakes apparently held the same view of the BIA.
42. Mary Crawford, "Alcatraz Indians Call for Help," *San Francisco Examiner* (Nov. 25, 1969), n.p., "News Clippings—*Alcatraz Takeover*" folder, San Francisco State University Archives, San Francisco, California.
43. "Fish and Wildlife editor of the San Francisco Sunday Examiner-Chronicle telephoned to see if Mr. Hannon would like to go fishing in the Bay with Indian spokesman Richard Oakes to 'talk things over in private.' " GSA,

Report #2, Series: *Records Relative to the Disposal of Alcatraz Island, 1961–73*, box 15, Nov. 26, 1969, Robert Warrior's private collection, National Archives Pacific Sierra Region, San Bruno, California.

44. Tim Findley, "More Indians in Trek to Alcatraz," *San Francisco Chronicle* (Nov. 28, 1969), 30.

45. George Murphy, "Call Goes Out to Nation's Indians," *San Francisco Chronicle* (Dec. 6, 1969), 3. "I don't know what happened but I think it had started to attract so much publicity that there were reporters here from all over Europe and at one time we had reporters here from seven different countries . . . it was so obvious that in the European papers and the European TV . . . that the government was finally forced to back off and . . . leave us alone." Stella Leach, interview by Irene Silentman and Anna Boyd, Feb. 5, 1970, Special Collections: Center for Southwest Research, Doris Duke Oral History Project, American Indian Historical Research Project, University of New Mexico, Albuquerque, New Mexico, 32.

46. Associated Press, "Reagan Asks Finch for Indian Aid," *San Francisco Chronicle* (Dec. 2, 1969), n.p. Press accounts vary on the number of Native peoples visiting the island. Some state that on the weekend numbers swelled to nearly 1,000. As far as permanent settlers it averaged between 90 to 250 people. These numbers come from articles appearing in the *San Francisco Chronicle* from November 30 to December 2, 1969.

47. News photo, "Mock Trial on Alcatraz" (Nov. 26, 1969), rare photo in author's possession. Anonymous, "Indians vs US Gov't," National Park Service, Alcatraz Island Archives (accessed 2010). The jury was comprised of Bill Sears, Prissilla George, Gail Treppa, Dave Leach, Bill O'Neill, Anthony Garcia, Bill Sherman, Claudine Boyer, Carmen Christy, Freak Out, John White, Katy Evans, and Geneva Seaedy. The second flag for Alcatraz featured thirteen alternating stripes of red and white and in the far right corner the opened door lodge with fifty yellow stars—a complete reversal of the graphics found on a contemporary United States flag. Anonymous, *The Warpath* (Spring 1970), 15, miscellaneous boxes, Murray Wax Papers, Newberry Library, Chicago, Il.

48. Many Native men, before being sent off to fight in World War II, would cut off their long hair and save it. Occasionally dancers would wear their hair like a toupee in the arena. It was a symbol of sacrifice and honor.

49. Joel Tlumak, "Indians: The Rock Packing 'Em In," *San Francisco Examiner* (Nov. 30, 1969), 1.

50. "The committee is made up of regional heads for the department of Labor, Health, Education, Housing and Urban Development, Welfare, Interior, Economic Opportunity, Justice Department's Community Relations Service, Commerce Department's Economic Development Administration's Small Business Administration, and General Services Administration." Tim Findley, "Multi-Agency Talks: Week of Decisions on Indians," *San Francisco Chronicle* (Dec. 2, 1969), 1.

51. George Murphy, "Powwow on Indian Justice," *San Francisco Chronicle* (Dec. 3, 1969), 6.

52. Peter Collier, "Better Red Than Dead," *Ramparts* (Feb. 1970), 27, 28, *Ramparts* permission courtesy of Guy Stilson and Greg Stilson.

53. Lynn Ludlow, "Man in the News: Oakes Has One Goal for Alcatraz: Unity," *San Francisco Chronicle* (Dec. 7, 1969), 13. I chose to include major portions of the article because it posed a rare glimpse into Richard's life during these times.

54. Ken Michaels, "On the Warpath at Alcatraz," *Chicago Tribune Magazine* (March 22, 1970), 27, Virgil J. Vogel Research and Personal Papers, 1941–1993, Newberry Library, Chicago, Illinois. Big Rock Elementary School was managed by two state-certified teachers who also followed state curriculum standards for grades 1–7 with a typical teacher student ratio of 1 to 12.

55. "We moved onto Alcatraz Island because we feel that Indian people need a cultural center of their own. . . . And without a cultural center of their own, we are afraid that the old Indian ways may be lost. . . . We feel this is the first and most important reason we went to Alcatraz Island. . . . 'It's not just the land we want to retrieve,' explained Oakes, 'It's the life.'" Mark K. Powelson, "Alcatraz Revisited," *San Francisco Focus* (Jan. 1984), 34, News Clippings on Alcatraz, Oakland Indian Friendship House Community History Project, Robert Warrior's private collection.

56. Ramona Bennett, interview with the author (March 21, 2009), Tulalip, Washington.

57. Alvin M. Josephy Jr., *Red Power: The American Indians' Fight for Freedom*, 2nd ed. (Lincoln: University of Nebraska Press, 1999), 192–193. After the occupation, the Big Rock School continued with the opening of the American Indian Charter School in Oakland, California. On survival schools, see Julie L. Davis, *Survival Schools: The American Indian Movement and Community Education in the Twin Cities* (Minneapolis: University of Minnesota Press, 2013).

58. Dennis Banks and Richard Erdoes, *Ojibwa Warrior: Dennis Banks and the Rise of the American Indian Movement* (Norman: University of Oklahoma Press, 2004), 106–107. Banks never mentions being kicked off the island in his 2004 book; instead he stated that he stayed on the island for a couple of days. In the Dean Chavers interview, which occurred years before Banks's book was published, Chavers remembered most of the names but included Lac Courte Oreilles Anishinaabe Eddie Benton Benai and Russell Means, who were not on the island. It is likely that Eddie Benton Benai was confused with George Mitchell. Russell Means fails to mention the event in his autobiography, and it also fails to fit with his timeline for joining AIM. He first met AIM members at Jess Sixkiller's conference in October 1969 but never had direct communication with Dennis Banks and Clyde Bellecourt until January of 1970 in Detroit, Michigan. Russell Means and Marvin J. Wolf, *Where White Men Fear to Tread: The Autobiography of Russell Means* (New York: St. Martin's Press, 1995), 147–150.

59. Dean Chavers interview, tape 1, side 2, 4.

60. Ibid.

61. Robert Free interview with author (July 15, 2009), San Francisco, California. See also Morris, *Alcatraz Indian Occupation Diary*, 194–195. Joseph Morris

credited Peter Blue Cloud with creating the cover logo for the newsletter and mentioned that the printing cost was $800 an issue. Only four issues of the *IAT Newsletter* were published as the IAT council pulled funding from the newsletter to fund other projects.

62. "[Annie] said her oldest boy had been beat up two weeks before because of jealousy among the children presumably because Richard was the 'leader.' " General Services Administration, "Correspondence Confidential A," box 15, file 9A, Robert Warrior's private collection.

63. "when Oakes came back on the 'Rock' we asked him what Quinn came up with. Oakes said Quinn promised us forty teepees from a Mexican movie set he was working on and the use of his publicity setup. After that there were lots of stories floating around the island. The tribe was bullshitting that Oakes got money, a home, and a movie contract. . . . I asked Oakes if any of this was true. He told me it was a bunch of lies. No money, no home, and no contract. So all we got from Anthony Quinn the movie star was a lot of promises on top of promises." Morris, *Alcatraz Indian Occupation Diary*, 105. *Nobody Loves a Drunken Indian*, the title of Anthony Quinn's movie, derived from a western novel by author and screenwriter Clair Huffaker; the controversial movie title was later changed to *Flap*. Poster advertisements capitalized on the takeover by proclaiming, "A warning to the mayor: Flap is here! The Indians have already claimed Alcatraz. City Hall may be next. You have been warned." Original movie poster copy in possession of author.

64. Smith and Warrior, *Like a Hurricane*, 25–28.

65. Louis T. Cook, Peter Blue Cloud, and Richard Oakes, *Alcatraz Is Not an Island*, "You Are on Indian Land," a series for radio, produced by *Akwesasne Notes*, Rooseveltown, New York, 1978?, University of Wisconsin-Milwaukee Music Library, Milwaukee, Wisconsin. *Alcatraz Takeover Collection*, "Support Church" box 4, file 10, San Francisco Public Library Archives, San Francisco, California. Flyer advertising a poetry reading at Glide Methodist Church on December 19, 1969.

66. Michaels, "On the Warpath at Alcatraz," 25.

67. Troy Johnson, *The Occupation of Alcatraz Island*, 102. Pacifica Radio Archives, Bancroft Library, University of California Berkeley, "The Occupation of Alcatraz VI–5," Berkeley, California.

68. "Rep. George Brown, D-Calif., of Los Angeles, introduced legislation with 10 other congressmen in Washington D.C. calling for President Nixon to transfer title to the island to the Indians. . . . 'The occupation of Alcatraz by the Indians has been a harmless, yet effective method of bringing the attention of the American people to the fact that we have neglected the cultural needs of today's Indians,' Brown said." Anonymous, "New Support for Alcatraz Indians," *Oakland Tribune* (Dec. 24, 1969), 2, news clippings, Robert Warrior's private collection, Oakland Indian Friendship House, Community History Project. See also Anonymous, "A Hanukah Gift to the Indians," *San Francisco Chronicle* (Dec. 8, 1969), 3. Eventually, on December 23, 1969, House Joint Resolution 1042, 91st Congress first session, introduced a bill to grant title of

the island to IAT, "the resolution was referred to the Committee on Interior and Insular Affairs . . . ." Rep. Mr. Brown of California, "House Joint Resolution 1042," 91st Congress, first session, box 3, file 27, Alcatraz Collection, San Francisco Public Library Archives, San Francisco, California.

69. Tim Findley, "The Indians Claim Alcatraz Victory," *San Francisco Chronicle* (Dec. 9, 1969), n.p., Robert Warrior's private collection.

70. Ibid.

71. Anonymous, "Regional Officials to Meet With Indians on Alcatraz," *San Francisco Chronicle* (Dec. 10, 1969), n.p., Robert Warrior's private collection.

72. Susan Lydon, "Where Indians Used to Play," *Earth Times* (June 1970), 26–28.

73. Joseph Morris, *Alcatraz Indian Occupation Diary*, 106–107.

74. Oakes, "Alcatraz Is Not an Island," 40.

75. Smith and Warrior, *Like a Hurricane*, 33.

76. GSA, "Daily Reports-Mr. Don Carroll, Caretaker at Alcatraz," box 14, Robert Warrior's private collection.

77. Smith and Warrior, *Like a Hurricane*, 63–64. Quitiquit is the only source for this allegation, and no investigation was ever conducted as to whether or not Richard Oakes stole money. It is at best a rumor that had stark consequences for Richard's credibility on the island.

78. When researching the Alcatraz Collection at the San Francisco Public Library, I did find several receipts signed by Richard Oakes. It was only a handful of the total receipts acquired during the occupation, but does reveal that Richard did save receipts—he was careful about money. "Finance—Miscellaneous (Undated)" folder, box 2, file 23, Alcatraz Collection, San Francisco Public Library Archives, San Francisco, California.

79. Ed Castillo stated, "There were more and more challenges to Richard's leadership, not only were they verbal, but they became physical as well." Fortier, *Alcatraz Is Not an Island*.

80. Ibid.; Ed Willie interview. "Thomas Scott, who was the PMDS realty officer in charge of Alcatraz during the occupation, alleged that there were, in fact, eyewitnesses who saw Yvonne pushed to her death. . . . It is my opinion after having discussed Yvonne's death with a number of people who were on the island at the time, and taking into consideration the hostile atmosphere toward the Oakes family, that Yvonne Oakes was most likely pushed to her death on Alcatraz Island." Johnson, *The Occupation of Alcatraz Island*, 152–153. Paul Smith and Robert Warrior differ from Johnson when they cite only Lawana Quitiquit on the event in their book *Like a Hurricane*. Lawana speculated that Yvonne had been sniffing glue and playing carelessly and that she merely slipped and fell. Her account, which has never been corroborated by anyone else, remains an isolated opinion. The official report that Hannon would publish listed the events similar to Ed Willie's. "[Stella Leach] said she had warned the Oakes child several times away from the stairwell and corridor before the accident occurred. About three minutes after the last warning, she heard a cry outside her clinic door and went out to [find] . . . the injured child. Mrs. Leach was in the clinic with David Leach . . . and another

young Indian." GSA, "Correspondence Confidential" folder, box 15, file 9A, Robert Warrior's private collection. "There was a mystery about how a young girl like Yvonne could fall down a stairwell. She was either chased or thrown down the stairwell by her killers." Morris, *Alcatraz Indian Occupation Diary*, 107. In Paul Chaat Smith's interview with Robert Robertson, a federal negotiator revealed that "the young man's [Richard's] daughter was murdered out there . . . [i]n the old employees apartment complex [inaudible] balcony to her death. . . . I was told that by several of the people out there." Robert Robertson, interviewed by Paul Chaat Smith, Smithfield, Virginia, tape recording, Dec. 1, 1993, Robert Warrior's private collection. Also, in an interview with Sid Mills conducted over the phone by Robert Warrior on December 16, 1994, Mills stated, "You know, one of Richard's kids were killed over this [Alcatraz]." It is still uncertain if Yvonne was murdered or if her death was an accident. However, there is ample evidence that Yvonne was indeed pushed, but by whom and for what reason is left to mystery and it is highly probable that she was murdered.

81. GSA, "Correspondence Confidential A" folder, box 15, file 9A, Robert Warrior's private collection. Excerpts taken from Hannon's reflections on the day's events at the hospital. See also Robert Robertson interview (Dec. 1, 1993), Smithfield, Virginia, by Paul Chaat Smith, 9. Robert Warrior's private collection.

82. Tim Findley, "Child Badly Injured in Fall on Alcatraz," *San Francisco Chronicle* (Jan. 4, 1970), Robert Warrior's private collection.

83. Bill Boldenweck, "Death Batters Alcatraz, Indian Dream Still Intact," *San Francisco Examiner* (Jan. 9, 1970), n.p., "News Clippings—Alcatraz Takeover" folder, SFSU Archives, San Francisco, California.

84. Oakes, "Alcatraz Is Not an Island," 40.

5. ALCATRAZ IS NOT AN ISLAND, IT'S AN IDEA

1. Johnson, *The Occupation of Alcatraz Island*, 163. Later, William Oliver became the director for American Indian Studies at UCLA. On page 5 of the articles of incorporation the quorum or majority section is described thus: "Two-thirds shall constitute a quorum for the transaction of business, and no action shall be taken without the approval of at least a majority of those Council members present." Council members listed include "Stella R. Leach, Alan D. Miller, Judy Scraper, David A. Leach, Dennis Evans R. Turner, Richard Oakes, and Ray Sprang." Anonymous, "Legal Matters" folder, box 3, file 13, Alcatraz Collection, San Francisco Public Library, San Francisco, California.

2. Findley produced two articles to this effect on January 7 and 8, 1970. Some on the island viewed Findley's remarks as hearsay and rumor. Their effect was to change the course of the movement by pointing out the forces of dissent that pushed Richard Oakes away from Alcatraz. "If there is a single 'leader.' . . . It is Stella Leach, a 50-year-old [Lakota] woman with an arrow-sharp tongue and a strongly aggressive personality. She and her son, David, 22, both serve on the current seven member governing council. . . . She hides her animosities

poorly reacting sharply. . . . 'Oakes never had any particular status,' she snapped. 'He was elected spokesman for a while, and that's it. He's still on the council his status hasn't changed.' Many, perhaps, most of the original occupiers . . . have . . . left the island. Stella seemed to be the most avid member of the anti-Oakes' faction on the island. Stella Leach joined the occupation after the second day, and was not privy to the earlier occupations." Tim Findley, "Alcatraz Dissension Grows," *San Francisco Chronicle* (Jan. 7, 1970), 4. "fist fights broke out during the long cold nights on the island and sides were being formed in a dozen different personal disputes. . . . Oakes . . . was losing in a minor power struggle on the seven-member governing council. He was victimized by . . . rival jealousies and distrust. Part of the quarreling was over finances. At least some of the contributions were addressed to Oakes himself, a fact that caused added friction." Tim Findley, "Factionalism and Feuds," *San Francisco Chronicle* (Jan. 8, 1970), 4.

3. "Election of council member to replace Richard Oakes who resigned . . . Charles Dana to replace Richard's seat on council." "General Meeting," February 6, 1970, 1, box 1, file 34, Alcatraz Collection, San Francisco Public Library, San Francisco, California. This was handwritten in a notebook that contained minutes from the general meeting.

4. "To [Lawana] Quitiquit and others, it was obvious that the money was not the real issue. 'They were looking for anything,' she said. No one knew if Oakes took those letters and deposited all the money in the communal bank account or if he used the money to cover the legitimate expenses of being Richard Oakes. And that finally was what he was accused, tried, and convicted of—being Richard Oakes." Smith and Warrior, *Like a Hurricane*, 64. Warrior and Smith allege that Richard was voted off the council, but the council minutes from IAT tell a different story. According to the council minutes, Richard Oakes resigned his position and was not voted off the IAT Council.

5. Fortier, *Alcatraz Is Not an Island.*

6. "Records Relative to the Disposal of Alcatraz Island, 1961–73" folder, GSA box 15, Reports #2, National Archives Pacific Sierra Region San Bruno, California Series. On January 29, 1970, the Yvonne Oakes Memorial Fund was founded at San Francisco State College, the proceeds went to the SFSC Native American Studies department for research.

7. Anonymous, "Fishing Rights Case Won by Pomo Indian," *Ukiah Daily Journal* (Feb. 24, 1969), n.p.; Associated Press, "Pomo Indians Object to Cartoon Character in Fair Promotion," *Red Bluff Daily News* (March 13, 1970), 7; Associated Press, "Lake County Fair Drops Cartoon after Indians Sue," *Fresno Bee* (April 19, 1970), 6A; "I know that Richard Oakes and a couple of others went up to Round [Valley], must have been a couple of months ago." John Trudell, Interview by Ron J. Lujan, Feb. 5, 1970, tape 455, side 1, p. 3, Doris Duke Oral History Project, American Indian Historical Research Project-Special Collections, Center for Southwest Research University of New Mexico, Albuquerque, New Mexico. See also D.C., "Round Valley: Are Army Engineers and BIA a Conspiracy?" *Indians of All Tribes Newsletter* 1:3 (1970),

10–11. On Round Valley, see William J. Bauer Jr., *"We Were All Like Migrant Workers Here": Work, Community, and Memory on California's Round Valley Reservation, 1850–1941* (Chapel Hill: University of North Carolina Press, 2009).

8. Trova Heffernan, *Where the Salmon Run: The Life and Legacy of Billy Frank Jr.* (Seattle: University of Washington Press, 2012), 26. By the 1920s, Nisqually peoples never relied on government rations as each family annually harvested five hundred salmon. "A Beleaguered Little Band: The Nisquallys of Washington State," 201, box 83, folder 3, Frederick T. Haley Papers, University of Washington Special Collections, Seattle, Washington.

9. 1854–56, Washington Governor Isaac Stevens, who had experience as a railroad surveyor and Colonial Agent, negotiated several treaties with Indigenous nations throughout Washington. For the Nisqually, Puyallup came to be known as the Treaty of Medicine Creek—named after the Nisqually place where the treaty was negotiated. The Treaty of Medicine Creek, ratified on March 3, 1855, ignited a war throughout the region. Nisqually leader Chief Leschi led an alliance of Puyallup, Nisqually, and Klickitats to seek Seattle's destruction. The Duwamish along with several other Nations elected to remain neutral to the war. By war's end, despite protests by the Hudson Bay Company to save him, Chief Leschi was executed on February 19, 1858. After two trials and a year in jail, Leschi's last words echoed his resistance and innocence and the resolve of Native Americans. American Friends Service Committee, *Uncommon Controversy: Fishing Rights of the Muckleshoot, Puyallup and Nisqually Indians* (Seattle: University of Washington Press, 1970), 32–40; Heffernan, *Where the Salmon Run*, 17; and Vine Deloria Jr., *Indians of the Pacific Northwest: From the Coming of the White Man to the Present Day* (New York: Doubleday, 1977), 54–55. On a side note, few have studied the effects of the international boundary or medicine line upon trade, development, and resistance throughout the Puget Sound region. On the fishing rights struggle, see Alvin M. Josephy Jr., *Now That the Buffalo's Gone: A Study of Today's American Indians* (Norman: University of Oklahoma Press, 1984), 177–211.

10. By the late nineteenth century, both Canada and the United States had banned the Indigenous practice of the potlatch system; a resurgence followed after the ban was lifted in 1951. Some accounts describe the potlatch as an elaborate banking system, so the ban represented an extreme loss for many Northwest Coast Nations. On potlatch see Dennis Kelley, *Tradition, Performance, and Religion in Native America: Ancestral Ways, Modern Selves* (New York: Taylor and Francis, 2015).

11. On the Makah and whaling, see Joshua L. Reid, *The Sea Is My Country: The Maritime World of the Makahs* (New Haven: Yale University Press, 2015). On canoe journeys, see Jon D. Daehnke, *Chinook Resilience: Heritage and Cultural Revitalization on the Lower Columbia River* (Seattle: University of Washington Press, 2017), 142–174.

12. The other obvious problem with census data on Native Seattle is that it excludes the highly mobile and transient labor force that is often seasonal.

This is an unfortunate circumstance. If the 1960 Census were taken out of season, it would mean that the Indian population was not completely accounted for. Also, because of the large number of migrants living in single room occupancy hotels in and around Pioneer Square and Skid Road, these populations were more than likely excluded from an official count (because of income). Ironically, Indian centers across the country have always struggled with census officials to provide accurate measures for urban Indians. These measures have only just begun to change in recent decades. The real consequence of failed reporting is that low numbers prohibited American Indian job agencies, nonprofits, and organizations from securing competitive funding from outside grants and federal programs. Census figures for this essay were compiled from a variety of sources including: Karin M. Enloe, " 'Helping Indians Help Themselves,' An Urban American Indian Success Story: Identity, Activism, and Community Building in Seattle, 1958–1972," Master's thesis, University of Washington, 1990, 32; "During the first five months of 1962, 5,592 persons visited the center. They represented 97 tribal groups, coming from as far away as New York. Many of the tribesmen from Canada were among the visitors seeking aid." Erle Howell, "At Seattle's Indian Center: The Needy Get a Helping Hand," *Seattle Times* (Feb. 3, 1963), 3. "Only 5 percent of the patients using the Seattle Indian Health Board had health insurance. Records showed that 55 percent were transient, moving back and forth from Seattle to reservations, and 60 percent of the patients had low incomes." Fixico, *The Urban Indian Experience in America*, 117.

13. Ayer Modern MS BIA Relocation, Bureau of Indian Affairs Indian Relocation Records, 1936–1975, box 1, folders 8, 1, 15; box 2, folders 17, 20, 21; and box 3, folders 34, 37, 39, Newberry Library, Chicago, Illinois.

14. By 1957, the BIA had opened a Relocation Office for western Washington in Olympia, Washington. "Because off-reservation employment was a long-standing tradition for Indians of Puget Sound, relocation had a negligible impact on the self-definitions and associations of Indians from that region." Harmon also mentions that a national recession in the region had drastically reduced the need to encourage more labor and that it was almost impossible to advertise the "benefits" of relocation to a highly mobile population. Alexandra Harmon, *Indians in the Making: Ethnic Relations and Indian Identities around Puget Sound* (Berkeley: University of California Press, 1998), 212–223. See also Andrew Fisher, *Shadow Tribe: The Making of Columbia River Indian Identity* (Seattle: University of Washington Press, 2010). Over thirty hydroelectric dams were constructed under the auspices of the Bonneville Power Administration, including the Grand Coulee and Elwah dams. Despite fish ladders, dams had an adverse effect on fish populations and sacred sites and caused an increase in the release of toxins, which created multiple superfund sites on Indigenous lands. Construction forced the removal of Native peoples from their lands; eroded Tribal resources, medicines, and lands (infrastructure power lines, substations, and other facilities); and failed on the promise of cheap electricity for Native peoples. This is a small list of

the many complicated issues and controversies that surround dam develop-
ment throughout Indian Country. See also Douglas E. Booth, "Hydroelectric
Dams and the Decline of Chinook Salmon in the Columbia River Basin,"
Marine Resource Economics 6:3 (1989), 195–211; and Roberta Ulrich, *Empty
Nets: Indians, Dams, and the Columbia River* (Corvallis: Oregon State
University Press, 1999).

15. During the 1960s the average annual income on Indian reservations totaled
$1,500 per family versus $2,850 per Indian families in cities. In Seattle, the
average annual income grew from $2,321 in 1960 to $5,439 by 1970. See
Fixico, *Urban Indian Experience in America*, 73.

16. Harmon, *Indians in the Making*, 167, 178–180.

17. "Alaskans dominated the Seattle Indian community. . . . Seattle Indians came
from fourteen U.S. states as well as Alaska, Canada, Mexico, and Chile."
Russel Lawrence Barsh. "Puget Sound Indian Demography, 1900–1920:
Migration and Economic Integration," *Ethnohistory* 43:1 (Winter 1996), 84.
This represents Seattle as being a Pacific Rim western city, especially with
high numbers of Japanese, Chinese, and Filipino in the labor force. On page
89, Barsh offers an argument that in Seattle, the two worlds theory of
Reservation v. Urban or White v. Indian lacked any merit, "Coast Salish [the
predominant Native culture surrounding Seattle] did not have to choose
between cultures; they could work in a sawmill during the week and go to a
longhouse on the weekend, just hours away by boat or train." Most importantly, Barsh's work underscores the extremely transient nature of Seattle's
Native labor populations. Strikingly, Barsh claims that "Indians were highly
integrated into fishing and shoreworkers' unions until the 1920s, when the
postwar recession intensified competition for jobs and white-only unions
were formed," 93. This underscores a discriminatory national labor trend, as
identified in David Montgomery's *The Fall of the House of Labor: The
Workplace, the State, and American Labor Activism, 1865–1925* (Cambridge:
Cambridge University Press, 1987), 461–422. "Backed by scholarly treatises
on eugenics and 'racial traits,' congressmen like Johnson and William
Dillingham set out on a four-year quest for legislation that would exclude
people of 'undesirable' nationalities, without closing the doors to northern
Europeans. . . . By 1923, the National Industrial Conference Board's leaders
had concluded that immigration was "essentially a race question—a question
of the kind of citizenship and national life we desire to develop in the United
States. . . . In short, Congress and the Department of Labor had undertaken
the scientific management of society's entire labor force."

18. "In 1914, Pacific Northwest Indians founded the Northwest Federation of
American Indians. . . . In 1923, with the help of . . . white attorneys, the feder-
ation persuaded Congress and the Bureau of Indian Affairs to let . . . [Native
Nations] sue for claims arising from unmet treaty obligations." Matthew
Klingle, *Emerald City: An Environmental History of Seattle* (New Haven: Yale
University Press, 2007), 176–177. "Questions discussed at the convention
included the matter of tribal claims which Arthur E. Griffin, a Seattle attorney

who was representing the Indians, declared were still unsettled. . . . Senator William Bishop of Jefferson County discussed the fish, tax and citizenship questions. . . . Indians were being 'arrested for fishing without a permit.'" Anonymous, "Northwest Indians Gather in Everett: Pageant Is Feature of Redskins' Conclave," *Seattle Times* (June 6, 1926). Other articles describing this claim include Anonymous, "$400,000 to Be Paid Clallam Indian Tribe," *Seattle Times* (Feb. 1, 1926), n.p.; Anonymous, "Indians to Go on 'Warpath' for $5,000,000: Snoqualmie Tribe Will Hold Powwow on March 16; Seek Land Payment From U.S.," *Seattle Post-Intelligencer* (March 4, 1940), n.p.; Anonymous, "Indians Will Sell Seattle for 3 Million: Tribe Claims All Land in City, But Is Willing to Be Reasonable; Hires Attorney Here," *Seattle Post-Intelligencer* (Feb. 4, 1940), n.p. Coincidentally, because of the Citizenship Act of 1924, Northwest Indian Nations could use their new citizenship rights in the state and federal courts to pressure/protect land claims. This is just a random sampling of articles that demonstrate the nationalistic tone of the era.

19. Unknown. "Wigs Over Bobbed Hair Stir Wrath of Indian Beauties," *Seattle Post-Intelligencer* (Oct. 31, 1925), n.p.; and Unknown, "War Whoops Went Out with Bustles," *Seattle Post-Intelligencer* (March 31, 1938), n.p. Each article particularly deals with a side of the "modern woman" and the mass culture shift of the twenties that Indians embraced along with non-Natives. On housing and discrimination, see Thrush, *Native Seattle*, 151–161. See also Barsh, "Puget Sound Indian Demography," 89. Barsh makes a very suspect claim: "In cities they [Native peoples] were generally found in white, working-class neighborhoods, consistent with their occupational levels, which suggests that they experienced relatively little discrimination." But this account leaves out the circumstances of intermarriage or domestic service, where white males married to Native women or domestic servants could live in these predominantly white neighborhoods. If most Native peoples, or more specifically, Native men were restricted to employment in the cannery or sawmills, then their residents (if not already migratory) were forced to comply with redlined areas of Seattle, where their neighbors were predominantly Japanese, Filipino, or Chinese Americans rather than white. This was a form of racialized gender management as structured by city zoning and racially and gender restrictive covenants (Native women could only marry a white man to gain class mobility; any woman [Native or White] who married a Native man sacrificed or risked losing class/social mobility within Seattle's structure). This gendered management occurred throughout Seattle from the 1920s and well into the post–World War II era. Terry Pettus, "Seattle Is Blighted by Restrictive Covenants," *New World* 9:4 (Jan. 15, 1948), 1; and Terry Pettus, "Racial Covenants before High Court," *New World* (Jan. 22, 1948); n.p. See also Quintard Taylor, *The Forging of a Black Community: Seattle's Central District from 1870 through the Civil Rights Era* (Seattle: University of Washington Press, 1994).

20. The Garcia quote comes from Karin M. Enloe, "'Helping Indians Help Themselves,'" 32. Many of these troops were exposed to other worlds in their platoons and travels. The military proved through desegregated regiments

that Indians could actively compete on the frontlines and in their travels among soldiers from different backgrounds. The regimented life of the military and service in the wartime industry mobilized thousands of Native peoples to pursue opportunities in an urban setting after the war. Like thousands of their comrades, many Native veterans took advantage of the GI Bill to secure loans and an education, while others applied for VA loans to purchase homes or start businesses in western cities; some even relocated to the burgeoning suburbs. For some veterans, the urban environment was a place that would enrich their newfound foreign and domestic urban wartime experiences. For others, the city represented the ultimate escape, where one could get lost in the crowded streets, delight in window shopping, and experience new foods. It was a different and exciting reality, far from the pace of reservation life or life within the many rural non-reservation communities of Oklahoma. Bernstein, *American Indians and World War II*, 73. "Estimates place the number of Indian women working in war industries in 1943 at 12,000 or slightly more than one-fourth of the total population that had left the reservations for war related work." "The War Manpower Commission offered women free training in light defense jobs that could eventually pay as much as $120 a month." James B. LaGrand, *Indian Metropolis: Native Americans in Chicago, 1945–1975* (Urbana and Chicago: University of Illinois Press, 2002), 36. See also Thrush, *Native Seattle*, 163–165.

21. American Friends Service Committee, *Uncommon Controversy*, 71.
22. Robert T. Anderson, Bethany Berger, Philip P. Frickey, and Sarah Krakoff, *American Indian Law: Cases and Commentary* (St. Paul: Thomson/West, 2008), 139–143.
23. American Friends Service Committee, *Uncommon Controversy*, 90–91.
24. Harmon, *Indians in the Making*, 213–215.
25. See Lawney L. Reyes, *Bernie Whitebear: An Urban Indian's Quest for Justice* (Tucson: University of Arizona Press, 2006), 84. While no Tribes were federally terminated in Washington state, this legislation would greatly alter the political/legal rights of Tribes applying for federal-trust status. At least seven Tribes around the Seattle region fell into this non-recognized status: Chinook, Cowlitz, Duwamish, Snohomish, Snoqualmie, Snoqualmoo, and Steilacoom. Only one, the Snoqualmie, gained federal recognition in 1999. Without federal-trust status, each non-recognized Tribe is without federal protection, funding, and treaty/legal rights. This continues to be an unpromising situation that termination legislation exacerbated for non-recognized Tribes. See also Laurie Arnold, *Bartering with the Bones of Their Dead: The Colville Confederated Tribes and Termination* (Seattle: University of Washington Press, 2012). Along with Colville, the Puyallup Nation had been targeted in 1903 for disbanding by the federal government. See Harmon, *Indians in the Making*, 239.
26. "The Center is financed by donations from various churches, including Catholic, Greek Orthodox, Jewish and Protestant. A portion of the expense is provided by the United Good Neighbors. Many women's groups in churches, lodges and service clubs make regular donations in cash or commodities."

Howell, "At Seattle's Indian Center," 3; see also Enloe, "'Helping Indians Help Themselves,'" 41–43, 73. "Ramona Bennett, a Puyallup, 'My heart wasn't full. Then a friend invited me to a cultural program at the Seattle Indian Center. I went, and became involved in the American Indian [Women's] Service League. For the first time, I really belonged. The Indian Service League gave me opportunities to socialize and volunteer, and the healing began.'"

27. *Northwest Indian News* had two critical runs from 1957–1961 and 1971–1980, whereas the *Indian Center News* ran from 1960–1971, mirroring Pearl Warren's executive term as president of the American Indian Women's Service League.

28. Enloe, "'Helping Indians Help Themselves,'" 50; and Anonymous, "Greetings from Walt's Barber Shop," *Northwest Indian News* (Nov. 1971), 5.

29. Thrush, *Native Seattle*, 175. "One night . . . in one of the Indian taverns, Bernie vowed to change the image forged by the dominant culture. He pledged that he would dedicate his life to focusing the blind eyes of the U.S. government on the poverty, hardships, and needs of the Indian people living in urban areas." Reyes, *Bernie Whitebear*, 84.

30. See also Chadwick, Stauss, Bahr, and Halverson, 164, "A Tlingit attorney in Seattle, Halverson, reports that Indian clients who sought him out for assistance in a five week free-aid-program had experienced unfair mortgage foreclosures, consumer fraud, illegal evictions, serious felony charges, . . . drivers' license suspensions, insurance cancellations, and drunkenness in public." The authors identified a "six to one ratio of Indian to white arrest for Seattle . . . [or] one arrest for every four Indians, convincingly demonstrate the need . . . [for additional research] of prejudice and discrimination by law enforcement," p. 165.

31. "Many restrictions discriminate intentionally or unintentionally against the Indian renter: refusing children, limiting number of occupants, refusing to rent to welfare mothers, demanding a breakage fee along with rent that puts the price out of reach, and stringent credit checks." Sorkin, *The Urban American Indian*, 68, 69. Many Native peoples refused to live in these conditions and returned to their home communities, but for many their communities at home were often worse than conditions in the Red Ghetto: "in 1970, 46 percent of all Indian housing had inadequate plumbing facilities compared to 8 percent for urban Indians . . . 19 percent is considered crowded (more than one resident per room), compared to 44 percent for rural Indians." Sorkin, *Urban American Indian*, 22–23. As federal funding for urban Indians began to increase in the late 1960s, it led to competition for reservation communities. This was one of the sparks that created a political and cultural split between urban and rural/reservation Indians.

32. Enloe, "'Helping Indians Help Themselves,'" 68. "Only 5 percent of the patients using the Seattle Indian Health Board had health insurance." Fixico, *Urban Indian Experience*, 117. Most reservation communities have a clinic or Indian Health Service (IHS), however in urban environments most Native

people were refused service for lack of insurance. See also Reyes, *Bernie Whitebear*, 93–97.

33. Anonymous, "UW Indian Studies–New Courses," *Northwest Indian News* (Nov. 1971), 5. On the BSU strike, visit the Seattle Human Rights and Labor History Project at http://depts.washington.edu/civilr/BSU_beginnings.htm, see *The Early History of the UW Black Student Union*, by Marc Robinson.

34. American Friends Service Committee, *Uncommon Controversy*, 108. Charles Wilkenson, *Messages from Frank's Landing: A Story of Salmon Treaties, and the Indian Way* (Seattle: University of Washington Press, 2000), 49.

35. Hank Adams and Ramona Bennett interview, March 2009, Lamy, Washington. Interview in author's possession.

36. "Progress Report Regarding Disposition of Fort Lawton," box 53, file 15, Wesley C. (Wes) Uhlman Mayoral Records 1956–1978, Seattle Municipal Archives, Seattle, Washington; Angie Debo, *Geronimo: The Man, His Time, His Place* (Norman: University of Oklahoma Press, 1976), 281–298; "Letter from Fort Lawton Task Force to Wes Uhlman Jan. 19, 1970" and "Letter from American Indian Women's Service League to Wes Uhlman, September 16, 1970" box 53, file 1 & 5, Wesley C. (Wes) Uhlman Mayoral Records 1956–1978, Seattle Municipal Archives, Seattle, Washington; "Minutes May 28, 1970," box 3, file 54, Wesley C. (Wes) Uhlman Mayoral Records 1956–1978, Seattle Municipal Archives, Seattle, Washington.

37. Anonymous, "Jackson Checks Lawton Scene: Senator, Indians Powwow," *Seattle Post-Intelligencer* (March 1, 1970), 6; and Jeffery C. Sanders, "The Battle for Fort Lawton: Competing Environmental Claims in Postwar Seattle," *Pacific Historical Review* 77:2 (May 2008), 203–235.

38. Hank Adams and Ramona Bennett, interview; Stephen H. Dunphy, "Jane Fonda Uses 'Leverage' to Aid Cause of Indian Rights," *Seattle Times* (March 8, 1970), A20; and Dee Norton and Jerry Bergsman, "Indians Rally at Courthouse," *Seattle Times* (March 16, 1970), A1.

39. Grace Thorpe of Prague, Oklahoma, phone interview with author, August 28, 2001, tape 1, side 1, 7.

40. Mike Barber, "500 gather at Daybreak Star Center to Honor Northwest Indian Leader," *Seattle Post-Intelligencer* (July 21, 2000), n.p.

41. Richard Simmons, "Indians Invade, Lay Claim to Ft. Lawton," *Seattle Post-Intelligencer* (March 9, 1970), A1, B1.

42. Hilda Bryant, "MP Now Knows 'How Custer Felt' He Shouted 'Stop,' but Indians Swarmed Into Fort," *Seattle Post-Intelligencer* (April 3, 1970), B1.

43. Sid Mills, author interview, Washington; Associated Press, "Army Repels Indians at Forts Lawton, Lewis," *Bremerton Sun* (March 9, 1970), 7; Richard Simmons, "Indians Invade, Lay Claim to Ft. Lawton," *Seattle Post-Intelligencer* (March 9, 1970), A1, B1. "After being asked to leave by the military and refusing, the Indians were beaten with clubs and dragged to waiting vehicles. All tapes and photographs were destroyed by the military. The Indians were then placed in the stockade to be processed. They were put into 12-by-14-foot cells and abused and intimidated by those on duty. No one was fed for 6–8

hours. Because of personal grudges, the last 10 persons to be released were beaten by 20 unarmed MP's in their cells, resulting in two persons having dislocated shoulders and the others suffered bruises." Anonymous, "United Indians Invade Fort Lawton," *Indians of All Tribes Newsletter* 1:3 (1970), 1; and Anonymous, "Ft. Lawton MP's Accused of Beating Indian Picketers," *UW Daily* (March 11, 1970), n.p.

44. Jerry Gambill, ed., "Fonda," and "Laird Is Sued by Jane Fonda," reprinted in *Akwesasne Notes* 2:2 (May 1970), 4; Ramona Bennett interview; Anonymous, "Oh, Jane . . .," *Helix* 11:11 (March 12, 1970), 5; and Anonymous, "Indian 'Attack' on Fort Fascinates World Press," *Seattle Post-Intelligencer* (March 9, 1970), A1. The press catapulted the news of "Indians invading a U.S. military fort" as one of the top stories of the week. The popularity of the story had more to do with a Hollywood mythic image showcased around the world in hundreds of western films that dramatized a valiant frontier cavalry in opposition to the "primitive militarism" employed by Native peoples. The symbol of Fort Lawton remained a controversial target as IAT and UIAT had to dodge stereotypical portrayals in order to get their message across to the public.

45. Don Hannula and Jerry Bergsman, "Indians Drum Up Support for Fort Claim," *Seattle Times* (March 10, 1970), A1; and Don Hannuala, "Indian Picket Line Remains at Ft. Lawton," *Seattle Times* (March 11, 1970), A4. The latter article mentions Whitebear suffering from a muscle separation in his shoulder from having his arm twisted by the military police. Wayne Jacobi, "County Studies 151-Acre Claim to Fort Lawton," *Seattle Post-Intelligencer* (March 11, 1970), 1.

46. Hank Adams and Ramona Bennett interviews; Cobb, *Native Activism in Cold War America*, 178–184.

47. Hank Adams and Ramona Bennett interviews.

48. Anonymous, "Geronimo's Revenge," *Helix* 11:12 (March 20, 1970), 4. The reporters who attended this second takeover attempt noted that the early morning time prohibited them from hiring photographers to report or document the actions that day. The article appeared in *Helix*, an underground Seattle newspaper, with only drawings of the occupation force.

49. Ibid.; and UPI, "Ft. Lawton 'Invaders' Charged," *Bremerton Sun* (March 16, 1970), 4.

50. Anonymous, "Geronimo's Revenge," *Helix* 11:12 (March 20, 1970), 4.

51. Johnson, *The Occupation of Alcatraz Island*, 163–164.

52. Ibid.; Richard Simmons, "77 Indians Arrested in Lawton Invasion," *Seattle Post-Intelligencer* (March 16, 1970), 1.

53. Sid Mills, Suzette Mills, and Ramona Bennett interviews; Carol Burns, director, *As Long as the Rivers Run* (1971), documentary movie, Survival of American Indians Association, Seattle, Washington (copy in author's possession). After the second takeover attempt, UIAT met at Henderson Hall on 3004 South Alaska Street and voted in favor of keeping the occupation going. UIAT also elected a seven-member council that included Bernie Whitebear as chair, John Jimenez (Comanche), Jeanne Halliday (Duwamish/Warm

Springs), Sid Mills (Yakima), Gary Bray (Colville), Alison Bridges (Puyallup), and John Vigil (Pueblo). Anonymous, "Indians Vote to Keep Vigil at Ft. Lawton," *Seattle Post-Intelligencer* (March 23, 1970), 3. UIAT later scheduled a "work-in," in which Native laborers hired out their skilled labor in Seattle for $1.75 an hour for doing odd jobs. All proceeds went to fund and support UIAT efforts to secure Fort Lawton. Lyle Griffith, a local Seattle physician, founded a group called Fort Lawton for Indian People (FLIP) to sponsor the "work-ins." Anonymous, "Indians Seek Lawton Chapel" (March 29, 1970), 6, "Indians of North America-Land-General" folder, University of Washington Special Collections, Seattle, Washington.

54. Jerry Gambill, ed., N. Magawan, "Indians Attack Attack Army: Indians Want First Crack at Surplus Land," *Los Angeles Free Press,* reprinted in *Akwesasne Notes* 2:2 (May 1970), 5.

55. Ramona Bennett and Hank Adams interviews; Lee Maracle, *Bobbi Lee: Indian Rebel* (Toronto: Women's Press, 1990), 214–215; Bryant, "MP Now Knows," B1; Don Hannuala, "Indians Again Try to Occupy Fort Lawton; 80 Detained," *Seattle Times* (April 2, 1970), A1.

56. Sid Mills, Suzette Mills, and Ramona Bennett interviews; Anonymous, "Ft. Lawton Indian . . . Jailed Old Building Set Afire," *Seattle Post-Intelligencer* (April 3, 1970), B1; Anonymous, "Ft. Lawton Indians Capture Summit," *Community College* (April 9, 1970), 6. The source of the fire happened to be a tear gas canister fired by MPs, which triggered a fire at an older structure on the base.

57. Not everyone had been fully supportive of UIAT plans, as some in IAT believed that Whitebear had silenced their voices in the negotiations with the city. Pearl Warren remained skeptical of occupation, along with other Seattle organizations. Despite disagreement over tactic and strategies, UIAT helped win a decisive victory for Seattle's Indian City. Robert Free interview; and Sherry L. Smith, *Hippies, Indians, and the Fight for Red Power* (New York: Oxford University Press, 2012), 161.

58. Anonymous, "12 Indians Arrested in Alameda Protest," *Oakland Tribune* (March 24, 1970), 5; Anonymous, "Indians arrested in Sit-in," *The Daily Review* (March 24, 1970), 2.

59. Johnson, *The Occupation of Alcatraz Island,* 225. See also Anonymous, "Indian Leader Is Badly Beaten," *San Francisco Chronicle* (June 13, 1970), n.p., "News Clippings—Alcatraz Takeover" folder, SFSU Archives, San Francisco, California. "the Indians demanded and finally won appointment of one of their own. He is Al Trimble, who now occupies the No. 1 office in the bureau's Alameda establishment. It serves the needs of more than 32,000 Indians in the Northern California—Bay Area region." William Flynn, "Indians Seek Solidarity to Give Them Political Muscle," *San Francisco Examiner and Chronicle* (Nov. 22, 1970), 21. Anonymous, "12 Indians Arrested in Alameda Protest," *Oakland Tribune* (March 24, 1970), 5; Those arrested included Richard Oakes, Imogene Nosie, Muriel Waldon, Ramon Billy, Walter Carlin, Patrick Genecha, William Franklin, Grace Galt, Joseph Bill, Bennett Morning

Gun, Robert Bradley, Russell Waldon. Anonymous, "Indians arrested in sit-in," *Daily Review* (March 24, 1970), 2; and UPI, "Indians Sentences Suspended," *Daily Review* (June 13, 1970), 10.

6. YOU ARE ON INDIAN LAND

1. Anonymous, "Oakes Birth," *Independent Press-Telegram* (April 11, 1970), 2; and Anonymous, "Indian Leader's Wife Has Child," *Press-Courier* (April 12, 1970), 16. Little Fawn was named by Annie Oakes's mother Lillian Marrufo.
2. On the legal background at Pit River, see also M. Annette Jaimes, "The Pit River Indian Land Claim Disputes in Northern California," *Journal of Ethnic Studies* 14:4 (Winter 1987), 47–64; and Dennis Levitt, "Pit River Occupation Force," *Los Angeles Free Press* (Oct. 23, 1970), 4.
3. Jaimes, "Pit River Indian Land Claim Dispute," 50–51. Dennis Levitt, "Second Pit River Occupation Fails," *Los Angeles Free Press* (Dec. 4, 1970), 23; and Dennis Levitt, "Pit River Occupation Force," *Los Angeles Free Press* (Oct. 23, 1970), 4. The commission returned and made only cash payments that were notoriously below actual land values.
4. Chavers interview, tape 1, side 1, 5–6, 10, in author's possession.
5. Jerry Gambill, ed., John Hurst, "The Pit River Story: A Century of Genocide," *Record-Searchlight,* reprinted in *Akwesasne Notes* 3:2 (March 1971), 44. Mickey Gemmill stated, "Most Pit River Indians are unemployed for most of the year. A few make good weekly paychecks in the logging camps—but that's seasonal work for half the year. For food, a good many have to hunt and fish—even though the once salmon-filled creeks are now salmon-less and the hunters have to out fox the law in shooting deer out of season." " 'Our only weapon is the law,' declared Gemmill." Joel Tlumak, "Pit River Indians' Struggle for Land," *San Francisco Examiner and Chronicle* (June 21, 1970), 25.
6. Dennis Levitt, "Pit River Occupation Force," *Los Angeles Free Press* (Oct. 23, 1970), 4.
7. George Harwood Phillips, *The Enduring Struggle: Indians in California History* (Sparks: Materials for Today's Learning, Inc., 1996), 44; and Dolan H. Eargle Jr., *Native California: An Introductory Guide to the Original Peoples from Earliest to Modern Times* (San Francisco: Trees Company Press, 2008), 40. The U.S. military conducted the massacre as a revenge killing for two white settlers.
8. Eargle, *Native California,* 169–171.
9. "The judge limited unlicensed fishing to an area extending 1500 feet out from the rancheria. The court said that this was the only area clearly established as the historical fishing grounds of Barnes' ancestors." Anonymous, "Fishing Rights Case Won by Pomo Indian," *Ukiah Daily Journal* (Feb. 24, 1969), 5.
10. Associated Press, "Lake County Fair Drops Cartoon After Indians Sue," *Fresno Bee* (April 19, 1970), 6; and Associated Press, "Pomo Indians Object to Cartoon Character in Fair Promotion," *Red Bluff Daily News* (March 13, 1970), 7.
11. Under Section 4 of the 1790 Indian Trade and Intercourse Act it specifically states, "That no sale of lands made by any Indians, or any nation or tribe of

Indians within the United States, shall be valid to any person or persons, or to
any state, whether having the right of pre-emption to such lands or not,
unless the same shall be made and duly executed at some public treaty, held
under the authority of the United States." Francis Paul Prucha, ed., *Documents
of United States Indian Policy*, 3rd ed. (Lincoln: University of Nebraska Press,
2000), 15. See also Felix S. Cohen, *Handbook of Federal Indian Law*
(Washington, DC: U.S. Government Printing Office, 1942), 62. "Some 18
treaties with 18 California tribes were negotiated by these federal agents in
1851. . . . Other stipulations made the Indians subject to state law." The state
of California protested granting any lands to Native peoples that fell under the
purview of the president and secretary of the interior. The state's protest was
answered in 1852 when the Senate failed to ratify all eighteen treaties with
over 100 Nations. Once California Tribes relocated to new reservation lands,
they found these same lands already occupied by settlers; naturally, the
federal government never interceded on their behalf to evict these settlers.
Cohen alludes to the Indian Claim Commission proceedings "rectifying"
these claims but also explicitly states that no remedy has ever been
undertaken to correct this overt breach of treaty rights.

12. Gayle Pedersen, "40 Indians Seize Clear Lake Island," *Press Democrat* (May
17, 1970), 1, 6; Anonymous, "Indians, Boise Leaders to Talk about Island,"
Press Democrat (May 18, 1970), 1; Anonymous, "Boise: We Don't Object to
Indians," *Press Democrat* (May 19, 1970), 1, 8; Anonymous, "Living Indians
May Not Be the Only Ones on Rattlesnake Island," *Press Democrat* (May 20,
1970), 41; Bud Bigelow, "Rattlesnake Island Views—From the People
Nearby," *Press Democrat* (May 26, 1970), 3; Johnson, *Occupation of Alcatraz
Island*, 225; D.C., "Round Valley: Are Army Engineers and BIA a Conspiracy?"
Indians of All Tribes Newsletter 1:3 (1970), 10–11. Chavers interview, 13. Dean
Chavers wrote a grant for Rattlesnake Island for the Tribe to maintain the site.
"At a demonstration at Kent State University in May, Ohio National
Guardsmen panicked and shot into an angry crowd, killing four students.
A few days later, state police and National Guardsmen in Mississippi fired on
students at Jackson State College and killed two of them." David Farber, *The
Age of Great Dreams: America in the 1960s* (New York: Hill and Wang, 1994),
232. Today, Elem is still fighting to retain their protective right over
Rattlesnake Island. In 2004, John Nady, a rich Bay Area wireless microphone
manufacturer, gained title to the island. Nady, despite repeated protest from
Elem leaders and Lake County Community Development Department, has
disturbed large areas of the sacred island and destroyed hundreds of sacred
artifacts and burial sites in order to build his mega-mansion retreat. See also
Will Parrish, "The Struggle for Rattlesnake Island," *Anderson Valley Advertiser*
(Aug. 24, 2011), available at http://theava.com/archives/11866, accessed Oct.
10, 2015.

13. John Hurst, "What's Behind the Pit River Indian Occupation?" *Record-
Searchlight* (June 12, 1970), 20; and Smith, *Hippies, Indians, and the Fight for
Red Power*, 248.

14. Photo, "Pit River Indians Welcome Indians of All Tribes," *Record-Searchlight* (June 8, 1970), 18. Three photos appear on this page: Buffy Sainte-Marie, Aubrey Grossman speaking before Richard Oakes and the Pit River Council, and Oney Rhoades standing in front of the welcome sign.

15. See David Farber and Beth Bailey, *The Columbia Guide to America in the 1960s* (New York: Columbia University Press, 2001), 257. "Instead, 500,000 people poured into 600 acres outside Bethel, New York, to become part of 'Woodstock Nation.'"

16. Tari Reim, "Pith and Vinegar on Pit River," *Friends* (Sept. 4, 1970), 8–9; and Smith, *Hippies, Indians, and the Fight for Red Power*, 131, 167, 248; Wavy Gravy, *The Hog Farm and Friends* (New York: Links Books, 1974), 121–125. Inspired by other groups like the Diggers out of Haight-Ashbury whose leadership emerged from the remanences of the Mime Troupe Theater in San Francisco, organizations like the Diggers, Hog Farm, and Yippies all embraced a far left philosophy of anything goes. The Diggers managed a free food and clothing shop in the Haight which supported a massive countercultural following within this particular San Francisco district. A considerable internal migration of hippies began to arrive in the Haight after 1967. The Diggers inspired other organizations like Gravy's Hog Farm or Abbie Hoffman's Yippies to share all their food and worldly possessions. Hoffman, *Revolution for the Hell of It* (New York: Dial Press, 1968), 79–81. A book written by Abbie Hoffman chronicling the rise of the "free movement" for which the Diggers had informed the ideology of the Yippies. The term *hippie* often referred to a lifestyle and should not be confused with *Yippie*—which denotes a specific political ideology and aspiration founded by Jerry Rubin, Nancy Kurshan, Paul Krasner, and Abbie Hoffman in the months prior to the 1968 Democratic Convention in Chicago. Abbie Hoffman, *Woodstock Nation: A Talk-Rock Album* (New York: Vintage Books, 1969), 131–133, 153. See also David Farber, *Chicago '68* (Chicago: University of Chicago Press, 1988); and Peter Braunstein and Michael Doyle, eds., *Imagine Nation: The American Counterculture of the 1960s and '70s* (New York: Routledge, 2002), 71–97.

17. Reim, *Friends*, 8–9.

18. Ibid.

19. Jaimes, "Pit River Indian Land Claim Disputes," 55.

20. Dennis Levitt, "Indians Reclaim Ancestral Land: Pit River Occupation Force," *Los Angeles Free Press* (Oct. 23, 1970), 4; Reim, *Friends*, 9; Anonymous, "Pit River Tribe 'occupies' 3 Million Ancestral Acres," *Record-Searchlight* (June 5, 1970), 1; and Chavers interview, tape 1, side 2, 11.

21. Jerry Gambill, ed., John Hurst, "Little Joseph, American Indian, age 3, will endure," *Record-Searchlight* (June 8, 1970), 1, reprinted in *Akwesasne Notes* 2:5 (Sept. 1970), 27.

22. Jaimes, "Pit River Indian Land Claim Disputes," 55.

23. Gravy, *Hog Farm and Friends*, 122.

24. Ibid., 55–56; and John Hurst, "Riot-Ready Police Arrest 34 Indians near Big Bend, 'It Isn't Over Yet,'" *Record-Searchlight* (June 6, 1970), 1.

25. Grace Thorpe interview, tape 1, side 1, 8; and Dean Chavers interview, tape 1, side 1, 11.

26. Reim, *Friends*, 9; Hurst, "Little Joseph," 1.

27. Jerry Gambill, ed., Bill Slius, "Judge Refuses to Lower Bail for Arrested Indians," *Record-Searchlight* (June 9, 1970), n.p., reprinted in *Akwesasne Notes* 2:5 (Sept. 1970), 29; Anonymous, "Indian Defense Takes Offensive: 'Arrest PG&E,'" *Record-Searchlight* (June 9, 1970), 1.

28. Jerry Gambill, ed., John Hurst, "2:25 p.m.," *Record-Searchlight* (June 9, 1970), 1, reprinted in *Akwesasne Notes* 2:5 (Sept. 1970), 28.

29. Photo, "A Chat with the Law," *Record-Searchlight* (June 9, 1970), 1. The photo is of Richard Oakes squatting in front of the passenger's side of a sheriff's vehicle discussing options.

30. Jerry Gambill, ed., Bill Sluis, "11:30 p.m.," *Record-Searchlight* (n.d.), n.p., reprinted in *Akwesasne Notes* 2:5 (Sept. 1970), 28.

31. Ibid.; and Anonymous, "Indians Take Offensive: Arrest PG&E," (n.d.), 28.

32. John Hurst, "Round Three at PG&E," *Record-Searchlight* (June 10, 1970), 1.

33. Ibid.; John Hurst, "Arrests Squelch Lassen Occupation," *Record-Searchlight* (n.d.), n.p., reprinted in *Akwesasne Notes*, 31.

34. Ibid.; Anonymous, "Richard Oakes Family Needs Aid," *Record-Searchlight* (July 15, 1970), 22.

35. Ibid., "Doc Jenkins, who preceded Gemmill as Pit River chairman . . . said the Modoc County man had indeed been [Tribal] Chairman until 1965, when he 'turned renegade and joined up with the Bureau of Indian Affairs.'" Anonymous, "Pit Council Role Gets Challenge," *Record-Searchlight* (June 10, 1970), 1; and John Hurst, "PG&E Flew Leaf to Press Confab," *Record-Searchlight* (June 11, 1970), 1.

36. Grace Thorpe interview.

37. "The $5 billion claim includes $3.5 billion from an estimated land value of $1,000 per acre (they were offered 44 cents an acre in the settlement proposed by the Indian Claims Commission); land improvements of $500 million; and $1 billion in profits assuredly taken from the land since 1853." Jerry Gambill, ed., Anonymous, "$5 Billion Damage Suit: Pit Indians," *San Francisco Chronicle* (June 12, 1970), n.p., reprinted in *Akwesasne Notes* 2:5 (Sept. 1970), 30; and John Hurst, "Indian Case 'Conspiracy' Denied," *Record-Searchlight* (June 12, 1970), 1.

38. Grace Thorpe interview, tape 1, side 1, 4–5. Grace Thorpe had been with Richard Oakes all day until she, like Lego and Buckskin, decided to leave the office on California Street.

39. Anonymous, "Alcatraz Invader Beaten," *San Francisco Examiner*, n.p., News Clippings, Alcatraz Takeover, San Francisco State University Archives, San Francisco, California. "Last night . . . he was brought home unconscious by Mickey Gemmill . . . and two other Indians Louis Mitchell and a man she knew only as 'Arnold.'" I assume the "Arnold" in the quote is actually Arnold Gemmill, Mickey's brother. In October of 1970, Oakes mentions to a reporter that he had been attacked by three individuals that night at Warrens. Only

Tommy Pritchard was prosecuted and found guilty. Eleanor Dumas, "Richard Oakes Renews Cause in East: Saved by Medicine Men," *Watertown Daily Times* (Oct. 25, 1970), 12; Anonymous, "Suspect in Oakes Assault Arrested," *Oakland Tribune* (June 18, 1970), 8F; UPI, "$100,000 Bail Set in Indian Beating," *Independent Press-Telegram* (July 24, 1970), 8. Pritchard pleaded innocent to Oakes attempted murder. By 1971, Oakes sought damages from Pritchard and Warren's Bar for his injuries which prevented him from securing stable employment. UPI, "Richard Oakes seeks damages," *Ukiah Daily Journal* (May 25, 1971), 2.

40. Anonymous, "Alcatraz Invader Beaten," *San Francisco Examiner* (June 12, 1970), 3, "News Clippings—Alcatraz Takeover" folder, SFSU Archives, San Francisco, California. See also, "Mrs. Oakes said she did not act sooner because she understood from the men who brought him home that he was drunk. She realized his condition was serious at 8:15 a.m. when she noted his bloodied nose and black eye and was unable to awaken him." Ibid.; Anonymous, "Indian Leader Is Badly Beaten," *San Francisco Chronicle* (June 13, 1970), n.p.

41. "He was first taken to Alemany Emergency Hospital where spokesman said his injuries, 'were apparently serious.' Oakes was then taken to Mission Emergency where a spokesman said he was just 'beginning to be worked on.'" UPI, no title (June 12, 1970), 1, "News Clippings—Alcatraz Takeover" folder, SFSU Archives, San Francisco, California.

42. Anonymous, "Oakes in Critical Condition," *San Francisco Chronicle and Examiner* (June 14, 1970), 17.

43. "Oakes was attacked without warning by Pritchard, who apparently was still bitter about a fight two months earlier. Pritchard dropped Oakes with a single blow to the jaw with a pool cue, then smashed him again on the right side of the head as he lay on the floor . . . in the first fight, Oakes reportedly broke Pritchard's nose. Oakes was unaware that Pritchard was in the bar at the time of the attack." Anonymous, "Suspect in Attack on Oakes," *San Francisco Examiner* (June 17, 1970), 9. See also Anonymous, "Samoan Held for Attack on Oakes at Bar," *San Francisco Examiner* (June 18, 1970), 7. This article contains a photo of Tommy Pritchard. In the photo he appears to be of average build, with short, uncombed hair, a faint goatee, somewhat disheveled, and wearing a trench coat.

44. "his wife, Anne, and their six children have been in serious financial difficulties. . . . Sgt. Sol Weiner, the police fund chairman, said it is maintained to aid deserving persons in the community." Anonymous, "Police Donate $100 to Fund for Oakes Family," *San Francisco Examiner* (June 18, 1970), 7. Richard had previously worked with police to negotiate peace between the Samoan and Native community. "the families phone had been disconnected. . . . Mrs. Oakes also said the Indian Center is sending over food for her family but a relative said, 'She could use a lot more than she's getting. These kids eat a lot even if Richard isn't around to help.'" Larry Hatfield, "Hospital Vigil: Annie Oakes Keeps Hope Alive," *San Francisco Examiner and Chronicle* (June 21, 1970), 25.

45. Joe Tlumak, "'Every Indian Suffers' says Mrs. Oakes," *San Francisco Examiner* (June 13, 1970), 4.
46. "Doctors at San Francisco General Hospital admit there was a positive response Monday to the Indian Medicine. . . . Mad Bear remembered a young Mohawk in New York years ago. The 17-year-old had tried to join Mad Bear and other Indians in a confrontation with the Commissioner of Indian Affairs. But his elders wouldn't let him go along because of his age. That was Richard Oakes in 1958." Jerry Gambill, ed., Anonymous, "Medicine Men Treating Oakes," (June 25, 1970), n.p., reprinted in *Akwesasne Notes* 2:5 (Sept. 1970), 22. "Five minutes later, they continued, a red spot appeared above his heart and extended across his chest. After a second dose . . . [he] wiggled his toes and upon command yawned and made other responses." UPI, "add Oakes . . . recovery" (n.d.), 1, "News Clippings—Alcatraz Takeover" folder, SFSU Archives, San Francisco, California. "Prior to the visit by medicine men, Dr. David Bastine, a hospital resident, had told Mrs. Oakes that her husband's condition was worse and that they "should not hold out hope for recovery." Ibid.; and untitled (June 24, 1970), 1.
47. Associated Press, "White Men Say Not: 3 Indian Medicine Men Claim Leader Improved," *Abilene Reporter-News* (June 25, 1970), 3. The article mentions that Hopi citizen Thomas Banyacya administered the medicine, yet he is not actually cited with having doctored Oakes. "I remember about the time that you and Peter Mitten worked on Richard Oakes in that hospital in San Francisco. . . . Peter Mitten brought him back to life. . . . Peter Mitten did that." Doug Boyd, *Mad Bear: Spirit, Healing, and the Sacred in the Life of a Native American Medicine Man* (New York: Touchstone Books, 1994), 43–44.
48. Tim Findley, "A Traveling College: Oakes' Hunt for the Past," *San Francisco Chronicle* (Sept. 21, 1970), 2.
49. Jerry Gambill, ed., Anonymous, "Richard Oakes Family Needs Aid," *Record-Searchlight* (July 15, 1970), n.p., reprinted in *Akwesasne Notes* 2:5 (Sept. 1970), 22.
50. Anonymous, "Oakes Raps Nixon Policy on Indians," *San Francisco Examiner* (August 15, 1970), 3. "According to Grossman . . . Oakes expressed hope that Nixon would follow through with action on the new proposals, especially in the area of returning Indian land." Jerry Gambill, ed., Anonymous, no title, no source (July 21, 1970), n.p., reprinted in *Akwesasne Notes* 2:5 (Sept. 1970), 22.
51. Findley, "Traveling College," 2.
52. Sid Mills, Suzette Mills, and Ramona Bennett interview. Sid Mills stated that he and Suzette, along with Mike Mitchell from Akwesasne (a relative of Richard's), accompanied the Oakes family on the launch of the Traveling College.
53. Gambill, "He Liked His Mohawk Name," 6. "condition much improved, morale: 'I haven't began to fight!'" The family is returning to Akwesasne to work with White Roots of Peace." Jerry Gambill, ed., Anonymous, "Ann and Richard Oakes," *Akwesasne Notes* 2:6 (Oct. 1970), 38. The brief citation also

contains a photo of Annie leaning on Richard Oakes shoulder at a community meeting.

54. See also Jerry Gambill, ed., John Hurst, "Pit River Indians Seize PG&E Dam," *Record-Searchlight* (July 11, 1970), n.p., reprinted in *Akwesasne Notes* 2:5 (Sept. 1970), 32; "Pit River Indian Flag Placed atop Mt. Lassen," *Record-Searchlight* (no date), n.p., *Akwesasne Notes*, 33; and "Pit River Indians Set Forest Claim," *Record-Searchlight* (June 29, 1970), n.p., reprinted in *Akwesasne Notes* 2:5 (Sept. 1970), 32.

55. Peter Blue Cloud, ed., *Alcatraz Is Not an Island* (Berkeley: Wingbow Press, 1972), 93.

56. Jerry Gambill, ed., John Hurst, "Pit River Indian Occupation Goes On: Indian Trial to Be Moved," *Record-Searchlight* (Oct. 28, 1970), n.p., reprinted in *Akwesasne Notes* 3:1 (Jan./Feb. 1971), 4.

57. "Through Richard Oakes, many Indians from across the Nation heard of our plight and came to Pit River Country to unite with us . . . soon after we occupied, we were surrounded by law enforcement officers that were heavily armed with guns of various makes, billy clubs, police dogs, and the rest. . . . Among our people, shoulder to shoulder, stood Richard Oakes unafraid, and unarmed. Ready and willing to lay down his life if necessary for the women and little children. . . . Can any man offer more than that? He didn't give us a lot of talk about how much he thought of us and what he was trying to do for us. . . . He *showed* us how he felt." Jerry Gambill, ed., Anonymous, "An Editorial: He SHOWED US HOW he Felt," *Akwesasne Notes* 5:1 (Early Winter 1973), 34.

58. Dennis Levitt, "Second Pit River Occupation Fails," *Los Angeles Free Press* (Dec. 4, 1970), 23. Levitt also provides an account similar to that of Hurst and Blue Cloud. See also Jaimes, "Pit River Indian Land Claim Disputes."

59. Johnson, *The Occupation of Alcatraz Island*, 229. "Following the death of Annie Jarvis, Essie Parish became the spiritual leader of the Kashaya community. She had been acknowledged at the young age of six to be a Kashaya *yomta*, a term that can only be translated roughly: dreamer, seer, prophet, revelator, visionary, and healer are just a few of its implications. The Bole-Maru, a religion that developed in the 1870s and gained particular strength among the Pomo and Wintu people, relies heavily on the direction provided by a tribe's maru, or dreamer. Marus receive instructions in their dreams and they have to follow, and they frequently give orations urging others to follow them as well." L. Frank and Kim Hogeland, *First Families: A Photographic History of California Indians* (Berkeley: Heyday Books, 2007), 70–71. See also Sylvia Brakke Vane, "California Indians, Historians, and Ethnographers," *California History* 71:3 (Fall 1992), 331.

60. Donald L. Baker, "Indian Activists May Be Unified by Slaying," *Washington Post* (Nov. 26, 1972), D6.

61. Smith and Warrior, *Like a Hurricane*, 140.

62. Anonymous, "Reservation Road: Oakes in Trouble on $1 Toll Gouge," *San Francisco Examiner and Chronicle* (Nov. 22, 1970), 21. See also Jerry Gambill,

ed., Anonymous, "Armed Indians Charge Toll on Road," *Press Democrat* (Nov. 22, 1970), n.p., reprinted in *Akwesasne Notes* 3:1 (Jan.-Feb. 1971), 19. "At his trial September 1971 . . . Oakes testified that "the $1 toll was to compensate Indians for land robbed from them." Asked by his attorney, Aubrey Grossman of San Francisco, what he hoped to accomplish, Oakes said, "bring public results. We are taking action because the government has not seen fit to pay for any land they used." Oakes used the word "catalyst" to describe his role. Donald L. Baker, "Indian Activist May Be Unified by Slaying," *Washington Post* (Nov. 26, 1972), D1, D6.

63. Johnson, *The Occupation of Alcatraz Island*, 230. See also UPI (Nov. 28, 1970), 1, "News Clippings—Alcatraz Takeover" folder, SFSU Archives, San Francisco, California;., untitled (Nov. 22, 1970), 1; and, untitled (Dec. 13, 1970), 1.

64. Anonymous, "Killer of Indian Is Arraigned," *San Francisco Examiner* (Sept. 21, 1972), 6. See also UPI, untitled (Sept. 21, 1972), 1; "News Clippings—Alcatraz Takeover" folder, SFSU Archives, San Francisco, California.

65. "[Rocky] wasn't there. Besides, I won't let him use a knife. . . . Why do they want to arrest a 10 year old boy. . . . We can only reciprocate in kind. If they want to hold my kid, maybe we'll hold the sheriff." Anonymous, "Warrant Out for Oakes' 10-Year-Old Son," *San Francisco Examiner and Chronicle* (Dec. 13, 1970), 26; Anonymous, "Oakes Faces New Charge in Barricade Incident," *Press Democrat* (Nov. 27, 1970), 1, 8; and Anonymous, "'Toll-Taking' Indians Face Extortion Charge," *Press Democrat* (Nov. 27, 1970), 1.

66. Anonymous, "Oakes Threatens New Blockade," *San Francisco Examiner* (Dec. 20, 1970), 22. "He wanted to re-establish herds of deer, buffalo, elk so that the [Native] . . . people could develop an independent economy . . . a trading confederation across the continent, so that Pacific salmon could be traded for Iroquois corn and Navajo wool for Lakota cattle. . . . He was strong for [Native] . . . sovereignty and culture." Gambill, "He Liked His Mohawk Name," 6.

67. UPI, untitled (Jan. 29, 1971), 1. See also UPI, untitled (Jan. 23, 1971), 1, "News Clippings—Alcatraz Takeover" folder, SFSU Archives, San Francisco, California. On January 12, 1971, Oakes reunited with White Roots of Peace and delivered a speech alongside their event at California Lutheran College. Anonymous, "Indian Group to Appear at Cal Lutheran College," *Valley News* (Jan. 8, 1971), 37.

68. Don Hannula, "Hank Adams: Dedicated to His People's Fight for Rights," *Seattle Times* (Jan. 24, 1971), 16. Survival of American Indians Association, "Press Release" (no date), box 81, folder 2, Frederick T. Haley Papers, University of Washington Library Special Collections, Seattle, Washington. The release mentions an out of court settlement over the February 1969 shooting of fifteen-year-old Jamie Sanchez, an Indian kid who was shot inside a Yelm Federal Marshal's office by Sheriff Deputy William McCluskey. By late December of 1971, Adams had been invited to North Vietnam to establish greater solidarity with the Vietnamese and connected Native rights broadly to an international indigenous liberation movement. "Letter Lyle E. Smith, City of Tacoma to Hank Adams" (March 31, 1971); "Letter Hank Adams to Stan

Pitkin, U.S. Attorney" (April 5, 1971); Associated Press, "Police Drop Adams Case," *Daily Oregonian* (April 5, 1971), n.p.; "Letter Hank Adams to Chief Lyle E. Smith" (April 8, 1971); Stan Nast, "Adams Lie Detector Test Canceled," *Seattle Post-Intelligencer* (April 7, 1971), n.p.; Dwight Jarrell, "Hank Adams Comes Close to Taking the Lie Detector Test," *Tacoma News Tribune* (April 7, 1971), 7; and Don Hannula, "Rumors Cloud Facts in Report of Shooting," *Seattle Times* (April 11, 1971), 6, box 80, folder 8, Frederick T. Haley Papers, University of Washington Library Special Collections, Seattle, Washington. Bob Lane, "Activist Indians Plan Hanoi Visit," *Tacoma News Tribune* (Dec. 29, 1971), 1; see also Johnson, *The Occupation of Alcatraz Island*, 230–231.

69. Anonymous, "Three South Coast Brothers Are Suspects in Shooting," *Ukiah Daily Journal* (Feb. 15, 1971), 1; Anonymous, "Bartolomie, Oakes Confrontation: Sheriff Target of Bias Charge," *Ukiah Daily Journal* (Feb. 17, 1971), 1; George Hunter, " 'Contraband' Picture Results in Jailing of Journal Lensman," *Ukiah Daily Journal* (Feb. 19, 1971), 1; UPI, "Lensman Jailed in Contempt," *Daily Independent-Journal* (Feb. 20, 1971), 28; Anonymous, "Medical Tests for Marrufos," *Ukiah Daily Journal* (July 26, 1971), 2; and Anonymous, "Harold Marrufo Sentenced to State Prison," *Ukiah Daily Journal* (Oct. 5, 1971), 3.

7. FREEDOM

1. Anonymous, "Indians Fined for Trespassing," *Bakersfield Californian* (Aug. 17, 1971), 12; Anonymous, "Hearing Aug. 30 on Oakes," *Ukiah Daily Journal* (Aug. 20, 1971), 5; Associated Press, "Indians Cleared of Trespassing," *Daily Democrat* (Aug. 25, 1971), 12; and Anonymous, "Oakes Hit by Demurrer: Indian Leader's Case Returned to McCowen," *Ukiah Daily Journal* (Aug. 31, 1971), 1.

2. Anonymous, "Oakes Arrested in Lake Co.," *San Francisco Examiner* (May 3, 1971), 18. See also Johnson, *The Occupation of Alcatraz Island*, 226; AIPA-American Indian Press Association, "People in the News," 2:232 (1971), 30; FBI file, *Thomas Richard Oakes*, "At Clearlake Highlands, California" (August 28, 2001), 38, in author's possession; "those arrested besides Mrs. Barnes, were Richard Oakes, a Mohawk who lives on the Pomo reservation near the coast; Curly Buffalo, a coastal Pomo; Steven, Anthony and Calvin Brown, all of the El-Em Pomo rancheria near Clear Lake Oaks; and Irvin and Louella Miranda, both of El-Em rancheria." Anonymous, "Eight Indians Arrested at Former Army Center," *Record-Searchlight* (May 3, 1971), 13. See also Indians of All Tribes in Jerry Gambill, ed., "The Clear Lake Statement," *Akwesasne Notes* (Late Autumn, 1971), 26–27. This last article in particular spells out the terms and reasoning behind the takeover of the former Army receiving station in nearby Middletown, California. The statement clearly mirrors the objectives found within Richard Oakes's own manifesto: restoration of Tribal land base, game preserves, Native conservation, bringing orphanages and elders together, economic self-sufficiency, and a host of others. The article also states that the occupation, despite arrests, continued as select individuals

maintained hidden camps among the 640 acres. The article is attributed to Coyote and Coyote 2, trickster names associated with Indians of All Tribes. It is unclear if this is a pseudonym for Richard Oakes or if this was written by someone else. What is clear is that the ideas and ideology presented in the article are absolutely linked to Richard Oakes. Anonymous, "Indian 'Invaders' Released by Judge," *Ukiah Daily Journal* (May 4, 1971), 1; Associated Press, "Indians Held for Lake Co. 'Assault,'" *Times Standard* (May 3, 1971), 6; and Associated Press, "Indians Held in Staying at U.S. Army Facility," *Star News* (May 3, 1971), 26.

3. Anonymous, "Judge Rejects Indian Plea," *Record-Searchlight* (May 5, 1971), 1.

4. Anonymous, "Indians to Be Tried Oct. 5 for Assault," *Record-Searchlight* (May 13, 2971), 17; Anonymous, "Indian Jury to Be Selected," *Record-Searchlight* (May 17, 1971), 13; Anonymous, "Pit-PG&E Trespass Case to Resume," *Record-Searchlight* (May 24, 1971), n.p.; and "Eleven large corporations were warned today to stop logging on Pit River Indian ancestral land or the tribe would take action to stop it itself . . . the corporations warned are . . . Hearst Corp. 39,000 acres; Fruit Growers Supply Co.—81,000 acres; Diamond International—12,000 acres; U.S. Plywood—33,000 acres; Kimberly-Clark—93,000 acres; Publishers Forest Co.—107,000 acres; Southern Pacific Land Co.—166,000 acres; K.R. Walker 30,000 acres; R.G. Watt and Associates—23,000 acres; Pacific Gas and Electric Co.—53,000 acres. John Hurst, "Ultimatum to Corporations: Pit Indians Order Logging Halt," *Record-Searchlight* (May 28, 1971), 1. Once again the press was being used as a sounding board to rally public support and expose corporate trespass and misuse from a Pit River perspective.

5. Anonymous, "News Release: McCloud River Indians Hold WAR DANCE at Shasta Dam" (Sept. 2, 2004), available at http://winnememwintu.us/news_release_gary.html; see also "Wintu Tribe of Northern California and Toyon-Wintu Center," available at www.wintutribe.org.

6. John Hurst, "Indians Occupying Toyon," *Record-Searchlight* (May 21, 1971), 1; and Anonymous, "Free Indians of All Tribes: Indians Continue Toyon Occupation," *Record-Searchlight* (May 22, 1971), 1.

7. Hurst, "Indians occupying Toyon," 1. "Indians of All Tribes, including supporters from Alcatraz and activist Richard Oakes and his family, joined Wintus and Pit River Indians in the occupation of the 61-acre site." Anonymous, "Free Indians of All Tribes," 1.

8. Jerry Gambill, ed., Greg Lyon, "Indian Territory," no source, no page number, reprinted in *Akwesasne Notes* 3:5 (June 1971), 13. See also Johnson, *Occupation of Alcatraz Island*, 231; Jaimes, "Pit River Indian Land Claim Dispute," 58; and Jerry Gambill, ed., Anonymous, "Indians Ask Moral Support," June 28, 1971, no source, no page number, reprinted in *Akwesasne Notes* 3:8 (Late Autumn 1971), 28; Greg Lyon, "Negotiations Under Way in Occupation of Toyon," *Record-Searchlight* (May 26, 1971), 1.

9. Lyon, "Negotiations Under Way," 1; and Greg Lyon, "Toyon to Become Indian Territory," *Record-Searchlight* (May 27, 1971), 1.

10. John Hurst, "Indians Warned of Contempt Action," *Record-Searchlight* (June 2, 1971), 1.
11. John Hurst, "PG&E Chief Says He Didn't Order Indians Arrested," *Redding Record-Searchlight* (June 3, 1971), 1.
12. Hurst, "PG&E Chief Says," 1.
13. Anonymous, "DA Threatens Prosecution on Indians' Logging Ban," *Record-Searchlight* (June 4, 1971), 1; and John Hurst, "In Pit Indian Trial: Baker Presses Land Title Line," *Record-Searchlight* (June 4, 1971), 1; John Hurst, "Pit Indians Accuse DA of Leaping to Conclusions," *Record-Searchlight* (June 5, 1971), 1; "Wilson was sworn in with: 'Do you solemnly affirm on your honor as an Indian that the testimony you give will be the truth . . .?' Wilson objected to being sworn in with the use of the word 'God' because people use the name too loosely. Interestingly, Judge Virga allowed the change in his court." Anonymous, "Indian's Word," *Record-Searchlight* (June 4, 1971), 1.
14. John Hurst, "Indian Woman's Testimony 'Our Hearts Are in the Land,'" *Record-Searchlight* (June 9, 1971), 1.
15. John Hurst, "Indians Vow to Return," *Record-Searchlight* (June 12, 1971), 1.
16. Jerry Gambill, ed., "Indian Vows Defense of Nike Site Village," *Akwesasne Notes* (Early Summer, June 1971), 7; Jerry Gambill, ed., "Relocation Revisited: A Chicago Odyssey (Part Two)," *Akwesasne Notes* (Early Autumn, Sept. 1971), 16–17.
17. Associated Press, "Indians Occupy Nike Sites," *Record-Searchlight* (June 14, 1971), 1.
18. Jerry Gambill, ed., "Six Indians Accused of Defacing Theodore Roosevelt Statue Here," *Akwesasne Notes* (Early Summer, June 1971), 7; Associated Press, "Indians Occupy Nike Sites," *Redding Record-Searchlight* (June 14, 1971), 1; Anonymous, "Judge Rule PG&E Own Campground," *Redding Record-Searchlight* (June 14, 1971), 1; and John Hurst, "28 Indians Freed, Seven Convicted," *Redding Record-Searchlight* (June 15, 1971), 1. It is not known, besides affiliation, just how connected the Nike site takeovers were with the Pit River occupation. Two days later, on June 16, 1971, a photo appeared in the *Redding Record-Searchlight* with Mickey Gemmill at the California Nike site occupation. On the wall behind him was painted a map of the Pit River ancestral lands as he conversed with other occupiers. Anonymous, "They're Getting Comfortable in New 'Home,'" *Redding Record-Searchlight* (June 16, 1971), 27.
19. John Hurst, "Indians Plan to Lay Claim to More Corporate Land," *Redding Record-Searchlight* (June 16, 1971), 1.
20. Jerry Gambill, ed., Anonymous, "Oakes Leaves Hospital" (June 21, 1971), no source, n.p., reprinted in *Akwesasne Notes* 3:5 (Early Summer, June 1971), 12; Anonymous, "Richard Oakes Hospitalized," *Redding Record Searchlight* (June 19, 1971), 1; Anonymous, "Oakes Leaves Hospital," *Redding Record-Searchlight* (June 21, 1971), 15.
21. Eleanor Dumas, "Richard Oakes Renews Cause in East; Saved by Medicine Men," *Watertown Daily Times* (Oct. 15, 1970), n.p.

22. "There was not enough hands for all that his mind could produce, and when the winter snows came, so did a feeling of depression. He went from bar to bar . . . skirting the Mohawk reservation . . . not drinking, but trying to get everyone to forget the booze and get going on all that needed to be done, but many of his old friends were still on the same road that he had left many years back and they did not listen to him." Gambill, "He Liked His Mohawk Name," 6.

23. Geoffrey York and Loreen Pindera, *People of the Pines* (Toronto: Little, Brown, 1992), 172; Anonymous, "Powwow Sunday on Route 81 Dispute," *Syracuse Post-Standard* (Aug. 21, 1971), 6; Peter B. Volmes, "Indians, State to Talk: '81' Lane Stalled," *Syracuse Post-Standard* (Aug. 23, 1971), 6; and Anonymous, "Indians Pull Up Survey Stakes," *Syracuse Post-Standard* (Aug. 24, 1971), 17.

24. York and Pindera, *People of the Pines*, 172–173; Hauptman, *The Iroquois Struggle for Survival*, 221–222; Anonymous, "Indians Protest Upstate Highway," *New York Times* (Aug. 22, 1971), 16. Some have claimed that Richard Oakes was linked to the controversial Mohawk Warriors who broke away from the Longhouse, but this is erroneous and false. Oakes was affiliated first to Longhouse tradition at Akwesasne, the ideals of the White Roots of Peace, and not with the Warriors. Some twenty years would pass before his *cousin* Harold Oakes would work with the Warriors. The assumption by some that Richard Oakes was a supporter of, or played a role in, the Warriors movement is unfounded and circumspect at best; Peter B. Volmes, "Indians Irritated by Gravel Laying," *Syracuse Post-Standard* (Aug 25, 1971), 8; and Sean Kirst, " 'I Think He Liked Our Position': On the Birthday of John Lennon, Oren Lyons Remembers a Friend," *Syracuse Post-Standard* (Oct. 9, 2013), available at www.syracuse.com/kirst/index.ssf/2013/10/i_think_he_liked_our_position.html, accessed Oct. 9, 2015.

25. Stew Magnuson, *The Death of Raymond Yellow Thunder: And Other True Stories from the Nebraska-Pine Ridge Border Towns* (Lubbock: Texas Tech University Press, 2008), 191–193, 258–259. The notorious town of White Clay, Nebraska, is located north of Gordon. White Clay's sole economy is dependent on the sale of alcohol to Pine Ridge Reservation residents—Pine Ridge is an alcohol-free reservation. This economic exploitation, despite frequent and ongoing protest, continues to the present day. See also Mark Vasina, director, *The Battle for Whiteclay* (Glass Onion Films, 2008). See also articles in the underground Native newspaper published out of Rapid City, South Dakota, entitled *The Indian*. Anonymous, "Stop Making Fun OF INDIANS!" 1:14 (April 30, 1970), n.p., miscellaneous boxes, Murray Wax Papers, Newberry Library, Chicago, Illinois.

26. Smith and Warrior, *Like a Hurricane*, 112–117; Charles Wilkinson, *Blood Struggle: The Rise of Modern Indian Nations* (New York: W.W. Norton, 2005), 139; and Vine Deloria Jr., *Behind the Trail of Broken Treaties: An Indian Declaration of Independence* (New York: Dell, 1974), 45. See also Magnuson, *The Death of Raymond Yellow Thunder*, 191–193, 258–259; and Akim D. Reinhardt, *Ruling Pine Ridge: Oglala Lakota Politics from the IRA to Wounded Knee* (Lubbock: Texas Tech University Press, 2007), 126–129.

27. Findley, "Traveling College," 2.

28. Anonymous, "Indian Caravan to Visit," *Redding Record-Searchlight* (Aug. 9, 1972), 17.

29. Gail Hayes, "Indians Schedule Oakes Memorial," *Redding Record-Searchlight* (Sept. 23, 1972), 2; and Bony Saludes, "Oakes Death: Defense Scores Interim Victory," *Press Democrat* (March 11, 1973), n.p.

30. "Granted immunity in exchange for his testimony at Morgan's preliminary hearing, Lazore said he had been with Oakes on September 14. He said Morgan called Oakes 'a stupid Indian' and threatened 'to blow my head off.' The boy said Oakes took . . . his knife after Morgan fired a shot." Donald L. Baker, "Indian Activists May Be Unified by Slaying," *Washington Post* (Nov. 26, 1972), D6.

31. Jerry Gambill, ed.,"Ann[e] Oakes Fights Back," *Akwesasne Notes* 5:1 (Early Winter 1973), 34. In the FBI file four eyewitnesses confirm that the deputy made the derogatory remarks. When the deputy was questioned later by the FBI about the statement, he denied having made the remark. U.S. Department of Justice, Federal Bureau of Investigations, FOIA request. *File on Thomas Richard Oakes* (Aug. 28, 2001), Washington, D.C., 24, copy in author's possession.

32. "During that conversation, [the Deputy] told [Morgan], "You should have shot him (Oakes) when he had the knife in his hand." After [this the Deputy] said . . . [Morgan] asked him if he thought a white man could get off in a case like that. [The Deputy] said sure, ye[a]h, or something in the affirmative . . . [Morgan] said, "I don't want to kill him—I don't want his trouble." U.S. Department of Justice, Federal Bureau of Investigations, FOIA request. *File on Thomas Richard Oakes* (Aug. 28, 2001), unknown subject interviewed in Pennsylvania, Washington, D.C., 44, copy in author's possession.

33. Jerry Gambill, ed., "Open Season on Indians: Michael Morgan, Killer of Richard Oakes, Set Free," *Akwesasne Notes* 5:3 (Early Summer 1973), 37.

34. Bony Saludes, "Richard Oakes Slaying: Spectators Jam Hearing," *Press Democrat* (Oct. 15, 1972), 3; Bony Saludes, "The Oakes Killing: Defendant Tells How the Animosity Built Up," *Press Democrat* (March 8, 1973), 2; and Jerry Gambill, ed., "Open Season on Indians: Michael Morgan, Killer of Richard Oakes, Set Free," *Akwesasne Notes* 5:3 (Early Summer 1973), 37. This last source is attributed to Rasa Gustaitis's account of the trial and contains sketches from the courtroom that were published in this issue of *Akwesasne Notes*.

35. Bony Saludes, "Witness Says Defendant Asked Him to Give Favorable Testimony," *Press Democrat* (March 2, 1973), 2.

36. Ibid. See also Bony Saludes, "Richard Oakes Killing: Defendant Changes His Version," *Press Democrat* (March 9, 1973), 3; Jerry Gambill, ed., "Open Season on Indians: Michael Morgan, Killer of Richard Oakes, Set Free," *Akwesasne Notes* 5:3 (Early Summer 1973), 37; and Anonymous, "Trial Order in Slaying of Oakes," *Press Democrat* (Oct. 17, 1972), 1.

37. This fact is important because if Oakes had wanted to physically confront Morgan, why not take his rifle or any weapon? In each confrontation with

Morgan, Oakes was consistently unarmed. It appears that this piece of
evidence goes unnoticed in many of the documents. Especially given that
Morgan always went for a gun.

38. "five statements of county road crew workers and the forestry fire chief only
indicate that Oakes was seen on September 20, 1972, walking, running, and
yelling towards the YMCA camp sometime prior to his death." U.S.
Department of Justice, Federal Bureau of Investigations, FOIA request, *File
on Thomas Richard Oakes* (Aug. 28, 2001), Washington, D.C., 12, copy in
author's possession. Annie Oakes in an article later admitted that Richard
Oakes also had a meeting scheduled for September 20 with attorney James
King. They were to meet on Skaggs Road. Oakes was investigating the title
and deed to the YMCA camp and whether or not the camp was located ille-
gally on Kashaya land. See Anonymous, "Anne Oakes' Emotions," *Press
Democrat* (March 17, 1973), 2. Clearly, the FBI document takes a liberty with
testimony as Captain Rose later testified that Oakes seemed in good spirits as
he walked down Skaggs Springs Road.

39. Bony Saludes, "Richard Oakes Slaying: Trial Moves Slowly on Physical
Aspects of Case," *Press Democrat* (Feb. 28, 1973), 5.

40. Most of the accounts state that Morgan was returning home. But it is unclear
where Morgan's home was located. During the confrontation on September
14, in the YMCA camp parking lot, Morgan's home is there on the YMCA
property. It is also unclear if Morgan knew ahead of time about Oakes's
approach toward the camp. Road crews reported having seen Richard Oakes
yelling toward the camp. It is highly probable that Morgan was not just
returning home but was instead planning to confront and kill Richard Oakes.
Morgan's gun is equally suspicious, as this was a gun with ties to Nazi
Germany. The Walther P38 semi-automatic pistol was assigned to replace the
Luger as a sidearm for the Nazi military. These connections or associations
were never highlighted in the later trial.

41. Morgan's testimony on the event is conflicting. He gives two different
accounts, one to the Sheriff's Office and another at the trial. Morgan told the
deputy that Oakes "jumped" at him "out of a clump of redwoods." At the trial
Morgan stated, "he saw Oakes walking toward him, hands at his sides, from
the area of the redwoods." Based on Morgan's testimony, jumping and
walking are two different responses, making the claim of self-defense at best
questionable. Jerry Gambill, ed., "Open Season on Indians: Michael Morgan,
Killer of Richard Oakes, Set Free," *Akwesasne Notes* 5:3 (Early Summer 1973),
37. "Robert Meyers, a former camp employee, said he ran to the scene when
he heard the shot and 'clearly saw' Morgan with his legs slightly spread and
both hands on the pistol Oakes was a blur for a moment. . . . Meyers denied a
suggestion . . . that [he] wanted to plant a knife on Oakes' body. . . . Meyers
did say he told two other men, 'I wish Richard Oakes had a knife on him,
because it looks very bad for Mike Morgan.'" U.S. Department of Justice,
Federal Bureau of Investigations, FOIA request. *File on Thomas Richard Oakes*
(Aug. 28, 2001), Washington, D.C., 12, copy in author's possession.

42. Anonymous, "Anne Oakes' Emotions," *Press Democrat* (March 17, 1973), 1, 2.

43. Anonymous, "Richard Oakes: A Battle over Burial," *Press Democrat* (Sept. 27, 1972), 1; and Anonymous, "Oakes Burial Dispute Dropped," *Press Democrat* (Oct. 10, 1972), 8. Coincidentally, Rooseveltown was where *Akwesasne Notes* was based. It is quite possible that while the Oakes family was in New York they spent much of their time with Richard's father, Arthur Oakes.

44. Hank Adams and Ramona Bennett interviewed by author, Washington (March 20, 2009), interview in author's possession.

45. As a legal matter, Michael Morgan cannot be called a murderer or an assassin because he was never charged with, or found guilty of, murder. Morgan was charged with manslaughter, only, and was set free. An all-non-native jury found him to have acted in self-defense. Similarly, Morgan was not charged with attempted murder (or any other violent crime) for his actions on September 14 and 15. However, see all of my sources cited in this note, which support the use of the terms *assassin* and *assassination* as part of my historical argument that it was ultimately Richard Oakes's politics that led to his death. Some will claim that Richard Oakes was murdered; however, such an assertion denies that Richard Oakes was ever political. Granted not every murder is an assassination (a person's politics determines an assassination), but every assassination is also murder. "Deputy District Attorney Edward Krug argued, on the other hand, that 'there has not only been a case made out for manslaughter, but for murder in the second degree. Judge Passalacqua denied that motion, and ruled the original charge—involuntary manslaughter—should not be dismissed." Bony Saludes, "Killing of Oakes: Judge Sees Credibility Gaps in the Prosecution's Case," *Press Democrat* (Oct. 18, 1972), 5. "Her attorney, [Mrs. Oakes] Ronald Hodge of the California Indian Legal Services in Ukiah, accused Hawkes of failing to adequately investigate the case and called on the Justice Department and the California Attorney General's office to investigate the circumstances of the slaying as well as raise the charge against Morgan. 'It is our professional opinion based on our investigation of the evidence and the facts surrounding the incident that the charges unquestionably should be first-degree murder against Michael Morgan,' Hodge said." Associated Press, "Indian Leader: BIA Seeks Oakes Slaying Probe," *Sacramento Bee* (Sept. 1972), 6. "Krug rested his case after calling Anne Oakes to the stand but made a motion to increase the manslaughter charges against Morgan to second degree murder. Superior Court Judge John Moskowitz took the motion under submission for a rulling [*sic*] Tuesday, but Krug said yesterday he had decided to withdraw his request. The motion could require a new trial, he explained, and because the evidence presented by Myers' changed hestimony [*sic*] is questionable it may not warrant a new trial on that basis alone." Bony Saludes, "Oakes Widow: He Wasn't Physically Able to Attack," *Press Democrat* (March 4, 1973), 2. "Michael Morgan had a motive for killing Indian activist Richard Oakes and it was his "racial bias and prejudice" against Indians, the prosecutor told the court Friday. . . . Krug said one of the charges—voluntary manslaughter—is a

"specific intent" crime. He said part of Morgan's intent to kill Oakes was expressed when he asked Sheriff's Sgt. Mike Carver about the legal aspects of justifiable homicide. Morgan, Krug said, asked Carver about the legalities on the night of Sept. 14, six days before the killing, after Morgan and Oakes became embroiled in the first of four confrontations at the Berkeley YMCA camp, near Annapolis. . . . The defendant is charged with both voluntary and involuntary manslaughter." Bony Saludes, "Oakes Slaying Case: Race Bias Called Motive," *Press Democrat* (Feb. 25, 1973), 7. The various accounts of eyewitnesses suggest that Morgan was well aware of Oakes's politics and made overtly derogatory statements that the Native leader would be better off dead. Morgan also had two prior attempts involving an assault with a deadly weapon on September 14 and 15. Morgan never denied the prior attempts on Oakes's life, nor did he ever deny having killed Richard Oakes. He went so far as having admitted to knowing of Oakes's politics before he killed this national political figure. The quotations above lend further support to these arguments. As a historian, my professional job is to interpret the preponderance of evidence, weigh all the facts, and assert a sound and logical argument grounded in the context of past events—an act of scholarship and scholarly inquiry. My historical argument is that Michael Oliver Morgan assassinated Richard Oakes. The charge of murder is inconsequential to the definition and is why I use the term *assassination* in this biography. Similar cases abound throughout the period, including the June 12, 1963 case of civil rights leader Medgar Evers who was assassinated by Byron De La Beckwith; or Chicago Black Panther Party leader Fred Hampton who was assassinated on December 4, 1969, by the Chicago police who raided his apartment. These were tumultuous times and in some cases the term *assassination* or *assassin* has included key historical figures where no trial took place or murderer was convicted. The most famous is the assassination of President John F. Kennedy by Lee Harvey Oswald (Oswald died shortly after his arrest). Oswald never stood trial and was never convicted of murder, but he is commonly referred to as the person who assassinated President Kennedy. Two final examples: to suggest that Dr. Martin Luther King Jr. was simply murdered is to deny that he was ever a national political figure. To claim that Robert Kennedy was simply murdered is to erase his legacy as a national political figure. Had Richard Oakes not been a nationally known Indian rights leader and activist, then he might still be alive today. Ultimately, it was his political convictions that led to his untimely death. In conclusion, the term *assassination* references Oakes's earlier statement about America having a dual system of justice; one system for whites and another for Indians. Despite Morgan's eventual "not guilty" verdict, this is a national story about the travesty of justice and a failure of America's legal system. It is ironic that a Samoan, Tommy Pritchard, could be charged and sentenced on an attempted murder charge, but Morgan, an Anglo American, was only charged with manslaughter and set free. The ruling also underscores the second-class citizenship and prejudice toward Native peoples in northern California during this time period.

46. Jerry Gambill, ed., Hank Adams, "Richard Oakes . . . Alcatraz and More," *Akwesasne Notes* 4:6 (Late Autumn 1972), 7.

47. "an unforeseen event provided the needed incident. . . . Richard Oakes, leader of the Alcatraz invasion, was shot to death. . . . Indian Country was aflame with indignation, and the planners of the march decided to move." Deloria, *Behind the Trail of Broken Treaties,* 46. See also *B.I.A. I'm Not Your Indian Any More: Trail of Broken Treaties* (Rooseveltown, NY: *Akwesasne Notes,* 1974), 2. This document testifies that the death of Richard Oakes was the catalyst for the march on Washington, the spark that ignited leaders to take appropriate action. "Concerns ran high following Oakes' death. At the end of September, just a week after Oakes' death, about 50 Indians gathered at the New Albany Hotel in Denver to add flesh and bones to the concept of the Indian pilgrimage to the Capital." The eight organizations were as follows: The National Indian Brotherhood (of Canada), Native American Rights Fund, American Indian Movement, National Indian Youth Council, National American Indian Council, National Council on Indian Work, National Indian Leadership Training, and American Indian Commission on Alcohol and Drug Abuse.

48. Deloria, *Behind the Trail of Broken Treaties,* 46–47.

49. Akwesasne Notes, *B.I.A. I'm Not Your Indian Any More,* 28–29.

50. Ramona Bennett interview by author, Puyallup Reservation, Washington (March 20, 2009), interview in author's possession.

51. Bony Saludes, "Oakes Hearing Under Way," *Press Democrat* (Oct. 13, 1972), 6

52. Bony Saludes, "Richard Oakes Slaying: Spectators Jam Court Hearing," *Press Democrat* (Oct. 15, 1972), 3.

53. Anonymous, "Indian Movement Plans SR Protest," *Press Democrat* (Oct. 15, 1972), 3; Anonymous, "Indians to March in SR Tomorrow," *Press Democrat* (Oct. 29, 1972), 1, 6; and Pete Golis, "Indians Vow to Fight 'Injustices,'" *Press Democrat* (Oct. 30, 1972), 1. Approximately 200 people attended the rally.

54. Anonymous, "Trial Order in Slaying of Oakes," *Press Democrat* (Oct. 17, 1972), 1, 6.

55. Ibid.; and Anonymous, "New Charge Filed in Oakes Death," *Press Democrat* (Nov. 1, 1972), 1.

56. Jerry Gambill, ed., Anonymous, no title, *Akwesasne Notes* 4:6 (Late Autumn 1972), 6. Prosecuting attorney Edward Krug pressed for a charge of murder in the second degree, but the judge turned down the request and instead charged Morgan with manslaughter.

57. Anonymous, "Sea Ranch Is Claimed by Indians," *Oakland Tribune* (Nov. 4, 1972), 1; and Anonymous, "Pomo Indians Claim Title to Tract on Sonoma Coast," *Independent Press Telegram* (Nov. 4, 1972), 7.

58. Jerry Gambill, ed., Anonymous, "Anne Oakes Fights Back," *Akwesasne Notes* (Early Winter 1973), 34, "News Clippings—Alcatraz Takeover" folder, SFSU Archives, San Francisco, California; and Anonymous, "Oakes Widow Sues for Land," *San Francisco Examiner* (Nov. 3, 1972), 44.

59. Anonymous, "Sea Ranch Issue to Board Tuesday," *Press Democrat* (Oct. 30, 1972), 2; UPI, "Mrs. Oakes Sues to Get Indians Sea Ranch Coast," *Press*

Democrat (Nov. 3, 1972), 1; Anonymous, "Mrs. Ann Oakes: She Takes Torch from Slain Husband," *Press Democrat* (Nov. 5, 1972), 11.

60. Bony Saludes, "7 Men, 5 Women to Decide Morgan Case," *Press Democrat* (Feb. 23, 1973), 2; "The Jurors: Mrs. Lucille F. Bateman, Petaluma; Mrs. Judith Bunting, Santa Rosa; Carl L. Ipsen, Rohnert Park; Mrs. Alice M. Lee, Santa Rosa; August A. Livenais Jr., Santa Rosa; Jeannette I. Morgan, Santa Rosa; Martin J. Nelson, Petaluma; Edwin R. Skeppstorm, Fetters Springs; Mrs. Betty M. Sisson, Santa Rosa; Gordon Loy, Santa Rosa, and James S. Sparks, Sonoma. Alternates: James O. Wilson, Petaluma, and Mrs. Beverly Ritchey, Petaluma."

61. Bony Saludes, "Oakes Slaying Case: Race Bias Called Motive," *Press Democrat* (Feb. 25, 1973), 7.

62. Ibid., 7.

63. Bony Saludes, "Richard Oakes Slaying: Trial Moves Slowly on Physical Aspects of Case," *Press Democrat* (Feb. 28, 1973), 5.

64. Several outstanding questions remain about Michael Oliver Morgan's gun. The Walther P38 9mm was an automatic gun similar in design to the German Luger and was manufactured in Nazi Germany. Walther was liquidated and sold off to pay for war reparations at the close of World War II. How did Morgan come to own this rare gun: Was it a gift, inherited, or purchased? As a collectible German gun it is likely that the gun lacked any paper trail to follow, making it an untraceable gun. In the coverage of the trial it appears this line of questioning was a loose end or completely avoided by DA Krug.

65. Bony Saludes, "Defendant's Version of Why He Killed Oakes," *Press Democrat* (March 1, 1973), 1, 14.

66. Bony Saludes, "Richard Oakes Slaying: Witness Says Defendant Asked Him to Give Favorable Testimony," *Press Democrat* (March 2, 1973), 2.

67. UPI, "New Mexico Mayor Indians in Kidnap," *Press Democrat* (March 2, 1973), 11.

68. Anonymous, "Oakes Widow: He Wasn't Physically Able to Attack," *Press Democrat* (March 4, 1973), 2.

69. Bony Saludes, "The Oakes Killing Defendant Tells How the Animosity Built Up," *Press Democrat* (March 8, 1973), 2. "Morgan was on the stand a half hour under direct questioning by his lawyer, Richard Pawson, before the trial recessed for the day. Morgan spoke rapidly, but haltingly at times. He was obviously nervous and under strain. The color on his face changed back and forth from flush to pale."

70. Ibid.

71. Bony Saludes, "Richard Oakes Killing: Defendant Changes His Version," *Press Democrat* (March 9, 1973), 3.

72. Bony Saludes, "Oakes Death: Defense Scores Interim Victory," *Press Democrat* (March 11, 1973), n.p.

73. Bony Saludes, "Jury Begins Deliberations in Oakes Killing Trial," *Press Democrat* (March 14, 1973), 1, 18.

74. Bony Saludes, "Oakes Case—Not Guilty," *Press Democrat* (March 17, 1973), 1, 2; and Anonymous, "Anne Oakes' Emotions," *Press Democrat* (March 17, 1973), 1, 2.
75. Jerry Gambill, "He Liked His Mohawk Name," 6.

CONCLUSION

1. Jaimes, "Pit River Indian Land Claim Disputes," 58.
2. Ibid., 59.
3. Clara Sue Kidwell and Alan Velie, *Native American Studies* (Lincoln: University of Nebraska Press, 2005), 133.
4. Randell Roberts, "Eastwood's Tom Sullivan Works for Justice for Native Americans," *Scotsman*, n.d., 3, "News Clippings—Alcatraz Takeover" folder, SFSU Archive, San Francisco, California; and "Job Opportunity Center Opens on Northside," *The Scotsman* (Oct. 7–13, 1996), 1.
5. "Richard Oakes, through his actions and voice, promoted the fundamental idea that Native peoples have a right to sovereignty, self-determination, justice, respect, and control over their own destinies. His legacy reflects the struggles of Native people to maintain their land, identity, and lifeways." Anonymous, "Dedication of the Richard Oakes Multicultural Center," March 22, 2001, SFSU Archives, San Francisco, California.
6. "'As Long as the Grass Shall Grow!' On this day, August 1, 2010, Anna Oakes, late wife of Richard Oakes, passed away peacefully at home surrounded by her family and close friends. Now she is with her soul mate, Richard, her 'Knight in Shining Armor', who was her friend, protector, and the love of her life! She never stopped loving him, thinking of him, nor stopped talking of him. Blessings to the family and friends in this transition Anna has made in joining Richard in this long wait for them being together, and the completion of her journey and in leaving their special gifts to all who will carry on in their cherished memory." Anonymous, "Anna Oakes Obituary," *Press Democrat* (Aug. 4, 2010), n.p.; Sam Scott, "Anna Oakes," *Press Democrat* (Aug. 4, 2010), n.p.

BIBLIOGRAPHY

ARCHIVAL COLLECTIONS

Akwesasne Library and Cultural Center

Alcatraz Collection, San Francisco Public Library, Special Collections

Alcatraz Occupation Files, NPS Alcatraz Island

Al Miller Papers, San Francisco Public Library

Ayer Modern Manuscript Collection, Newberry Library, Chicago

BIA Relocation Records, Newberry Library, Chicago

Brooklyn Municipal Archives, Brooklyn Public Library

Cornell University, Archives and Special Collections

D'Arcy McNickle Papers, Newberry Library, Chicago

Doris Duke Oral History Project, Center for Southwest Research, University of New Mexico

Doris Duke Oral History Project, Western History Collections, University of Oklahoma

Hank Adams Papers, Special Collections, University of Washington, Seattle

Indian Newspapers Collection, Newberry Library, Chicago

Kahnien'kehá:ka Onkwawén:na Raotitióhkwa Language and Cultural Center

Mayor Wesley Uhlman Papers, Municipal Library of Seattle, Washington

Mayor Joseph L. Alioto Papers, Special Collections, San Francisco Public Library

McGill University, Archives and Special Collections

Murray Wax Papers, Newberry Library, Chicago

Native American Studies Papers, San Francisco State University, Archives and Special Collections

Pacifica Tape Library, Bancroft Library, Berkeley

Papers of the National Indian Youth Council, Center for Southwest Research, University of New Mexico

Puyallup Tribal Archives, Washington
Robert Warrior's Private Collection, Warrior's Research Files for *Like A Hurricane*
SFSC Strike Papers, San Francisco State University, Archives and Special
    Collections
Shirley Hill Witt Papers, Center for Southwest Research, University of New
    Mexico
S.I. Hayakawa Papers, San Francisco State University Special Collections and
    Archives
Six Nations Museum
Syracuse University, Archives and Special Collections
Underground Newspaper Collection, Center for Southwest Research, University
    of New Mexico
Underground Newspaper Collection, Special Collections, University of South
    Dakota
Virgil J. Vogel Papers, Newberry Library, Chicago

NEWSPAPERS AND NEWSLETTERS
The Abilene Reporter-News
Akwesasne Notes
Americans Before Columbus
American Press Association
Basta Ya!
Berkeley Barb
Berkeley Tribe
Brooklyn Daily Eagle
Chateaugay Record
The Citizen-Advertiser
The Eastern Door
Fort Covington Sun
The Fresno Bee
Helix
The Indian
Indian Country Today
Indian Record
Indians of All Tribes Newsletter
Indian Truth (Newsletter of The Indian Rights Association)
Los Angeles Free Press
Los Angeles Times
Many Smokes
Massena Observer
New York Times
Ogdensburg Journal
Red Bluff Daily
Redding Record Searchlight
Renegade SAIA

Rolling Stones Magazine
Sacramento Bee
San Francisco Chronicle
San Francisco Examiner
Santa Rosa Press Democrat
Seattle Post-Intelligencer
Seattle Times
SFSC The Daily Gater
The Six-Nations
Syracuse Herald-Journal
The Tribune Press
Ukiah Daily Journal
UNA Warpath
United Press International
Wampum Chronicles
Washington Post
Watertown Daily

BOOKS AND ARTICLES

Abbott, Carl. *The Metropolitan Frontier: Cities in the Modern American West.* Tucson: University of Arizona Press, 1993.

Ablon, Joan. "Relocated American Indians in the San Francisco Bay Area: Social Interactions and Indian Identity." *Human Organization* (1964), 296–304.

———. "Retention of Cultural Values and Differential Urban Adaptation: Samoans and American Indians in a West Coast City." *Social Forces* (1971), 385–393.

Ackley, Kristina, and Cristina Stanciu, ed. *Laura Cornelius Kellogg: Our Democracy and the American Indian and Other Works.* Syracuse: Syracuse University Press, 2015.

Adams, David Wallace. *Education for Extinction: American Indians and the Boarding School Experience, 1875–1928.* Lawrence: University Press of Kansas, 1995.

Agee, Christopher Lowen. *The Streets of San Francisco: Policing and the Creation of a Cosmopolitan Liberal Politics, 1950–1972.* Chicago: University of Chicago Press, 2014.

Akweks, Aren. *History of the St. Regis Akwesasne Mohawks.* Malone: Lanctot Printing Shop, 1948.

Alexander, Robert, and Kim Anderson. *Indigenous Men and Masculinities: Legacies, Identities, Regeneration.* Winnipeg: University of Manitoba Press, 2015.

Alfred, Gerald R. *Heeding The Voices of our Ancestors: Kahnawake Mohawk Politics and the Rise of Native Nationalism.* New York: Oxford University Press, 1995.

Alfred, Taiaiake. *Peace Power Righteousness: An Indigenous Manifesto.* Don Mills, Ontario: Oxford University Press of Canada, 1999.

———. *Wasase Indigenous Pathways of Action and Freedom.* Peterborough, Ontario: Broadview Press, 2005.

Allen, Chadwick, and Beth H. Piatote, eds. "The Society of American Indians and Its Legacies: A Special Combined Issue of SAIL and AIQ." *American Indian Quarterly* 37:3 (Summer 2013), 1–360.

American Friends Service Committee. *Uncommon Controversy: Fishing Rights of the Muckleshoot, Puyallup, and Nisqually Indians.* Seattle: University of Washington Press, 1970.

American Indian Press Association. "Peoples in the News." *American Indian Press Association* 2:232 (1971), 30. Robert Warrior's Private Collection.

American Policy Review Commission. *Report on Urban and Rural Non-Reservation Indians: Task Force Eight: Urban and Rural Non-Reservation Indians.* Washington, DC: U.S. Government Printing Office, 1976.

Anderson, Benedict. *Imagined Communities: Reflections of the Origins and Spread of Nationalism.* London: Verso, 2016.

Anderson, Carol. *Eyes off the Prize: The United Nations and the African American Struggle for Human Rights, 1944–1955.* Cambridge: Cambridge University Press, 2003.

Anderson, Elijah. *Streetwise: Race, Class, and Change in an Urban Community.* Chicago: University of Chicago Press, 1990.

Anderson, Robert T., Bethany Berger, Philip P. Frickey, and Sarah Krakoff. *American Indian Law Cases and Commentary.* St. Paul: Thomson/West, 2008.

Anderson, Terry H. *The Movement and The Sixties.* New York: Oxford University Press, 1995.

———. *The Sixties.* New York: Pearson/Longman, 2004

Arnold, Laurie. *Bartering with the Bones of Their Dead: The Colville Confederated Tribes and Termination.* Seattle: University of Washington Press, 2012.

Arnold, Philip P. *The Gift of Sports: Indigenous Ceremonial Dimensions of the Games We Love.* San Diego: Cognella Inc., 2012.

Bacciocco Jr., Edward J. *The New Left In America: Reform to Revolution 1956 to 1970.* Stanford: Hoover Institution Press, 1974.

Banks, Dennis, and Richard Erdoes. *Ojibwa Warrior: Dennis Banks and the Rise of the American Indian Movement.* Norman: University of Oklahoma Press, 2005.

Baritz, Loren. *The American Left: Radical Political Thought in the Twentieth Century.* New York: Basic Books, 1971.

Barker, Joanne. *Native Acts: Law Recognition, and Cultural Authenticity.* Durham: Duke University Press, 2011.

Barsh, Russel Lawrence, and James Youngblood Henderson. *The Road: Indian Tribes and Political Liberty.* Berkeley: University of California Press, 1980.

Bauer Jr., William. *"We Were All Like Migrant Workers Here": Work, Community, and Memory on California's Round Valley Reservation, 1850–1941.* Chapel Hill: University of North Carolina Press, 2009.

———. *California through Native Eyes: Reclaiming History.* Seattle: University of Washington Press, 2016.

Beck, David R. M., and Rosalyn R. LaPier. *City Indian: Native American Activism in Chicago, 1893–1934.* Lincoln: University of Nebraska Press, 2015.

Bellecourt, Clyde, and Jon Lurie. *The Thunder Before the Storm: The Autobiography of Clyde Bellecourt*. St. Paul: Minnesota Historical Society Press, 2016.

Bernstein, Alison R. *American Indians and World War II: Toward a New Era in Indian Affairs*. Norman: University of Oklahoma Press, 1991.

Blackhawk, Ned. *Violence over the Land: Indians and Empires in the Early American West*. Cambridge: Harvard University Press, 2006.

Blue Cloud, Peter, ed. *Alcatraz Is Not an Island*. Berkeley: Wingbow Press, 1972.

Bonvillain, Nancy. "Kahnawa:ke: Factionalism, Traditionalism, and Nationalism in a Mohawk Community." *American Anthropologist* 107:4 (Dec. 2005), 740–741.

Boyd, Doug. *Mad Bear: Spirit, Healing, and the Sacred in the Life of a Native American Medicine Man*. New York: Simon and Schuster, 1994.

Braunstein, Peter, and Michael William Doyle. *Imagine Nation: The American Counterculture of the 1960s and '70s*. New York: Routledge, 2002.

Britten, Thomas A. *American Indians in World War I: At War and at Home*. Albuquerque: University of New Mexico Press, 1997.

———. *The National Council on Indian Opportunity: Quiet Champion of Self-Determination*. Albuquerque: University of New Mexico Press, 2014.

Brooks, James, Chris Carlsson, and Nancy J. Peters, eds. *Reclaiming San Francisco: History, Politics, Culture*. San Francisco: City Lights Books, 1998.

Brosnan, Kathleen A., and Amy L. Scott, eds. *City Dreams and Country Schemes: Community and Identity in the American West*. Reno: University of Nevada Press, 2011.

Broussard, Albert S. *Black San Francisco: The Struggle for Racial Equality in the West, 1900–1954*. Lawrence: University Press of Kansas, 1993.

Burke, James. *Paper Tomahawks: From Red Tape to Red Power*. Winnipeg: Queenston House Publishing, 1976.

Burnette, Robert, and John Koster. *The Road to Wounded Knee*. New York: Bantam Books, 1974.

Burt, Larry W. "Roots of the Native American Urban Experience: Relocation Policy in the 1950s." *American Indian Quarterly* 10:2 (Spring 1986), 85–99.

———. *Tribalism in Crisis: Federal Indian Policy, 1953–1961*. Albuquerque: University of New Mexico Press, 1982.

Cahill, Cathleen D. *Federal Fathers & Mothers: A Social History of the United States Indian Service, 1869–1933*. Chapel Hill: University of North Carolina Press, 2011.

Cahn, Edgar S., ed. *Our Brother's Keeper: The Indian in White America*. New York: New Community Press, 1969.

Calhoun, Craig. "Nationalism and Ethnicity," *Annual Review of Sociology* 19 (1993), 211–239.

Cardinal, Harold. *The Unjust Society*. Seattle: University of Washington Press, 1999.

Carlsson, Chris, ed. *Ten Years That Shook the City: San Francisco, 1968–1978*. San Francisco: City Lights Books, 2011.

Carpio, Myla Vicenti. *Indigenous Albuquerque.* Lubbock: Texas Tech University
    Press, 2011.
Chafe, William H., Howard Sitkoff, and Beth Bailey. *A History of Our Time:
    Readings on Postwar America.* New York: Oxford University Press, 2008.
Chang, David. *The World and All the Things upon It: Native Hawaiian Geographies
    of Exploration.* Minneapolis: University of Minnesota Press, 2016.
Chávez, Ernesto. *"¡Mi Raza Primero!" (My People First!): Nationalism, Identity,
    and Insurgency in the Chicano Movement in Los Angeles, 1966–1978.* Berkeley:
    University of California Press, 2002.
Child, Brenda J. *Boarding School Seasons: American Indian Families, 1900–1940.*
    Lincoln: University of Nebraska Press, 1998.
———. *Holding Our World Together: Ojibwe Women and the Survival of Community.*
    New York: Viking, 2012.
Clarkin, Thomas. *Federal Indian Policy: In the Kennedy and Johnson Administrations,
    1961–1969.* Albuquerque: University of New Mexico Press, 2001.
Cobb, Daniel M., and Loretta Fowler, eds. *Beyond Red Power: American Indian
    Politics and Activism since 1900.* Santa Fe: School for Advanced Research,
    2007.
———. *Native Activism in Cold War America: The Struggle for Sovereignty.*
    Lawrence: University Press of Kansas, 2008.
Cohen, Felix S. *Handbook of Federal Indian Law.* Washington, DC: U.S.
    Government Printing Office, 1942.
Cohen, Lizabeth. *A Consumers' Republic: The Politics of Mass Consumption in
    Postwar America.* New York: Vintage Books, 2003.
Collier, Peter. "Better Red Than Dead: The Red Man's Burden." *Ramparts*
    (Feb. 1970), 26–38.
Connell-Szasz, Margaret. *Education and the American Indian: The Road to Self-
    Determination since 1928.* 3rd ed. Albuquerque: University of New Mexico
    Press, 1999.
———. ed. *Between Indian and White Worlds: The Cultural Broker.* Norman:
    University of Oklahoma Press, 1994.
Copeland, Alan, and Nikki Arai, eds. *People's Park.* New York: Ballantine Books,
    1969.
Cornell, Stephen. *The Return of the Native: American Indian Political Resurgence.*
    New York: Oxford University Press, 1988.
Costo, Rupert, and Jeannette Henry Costo. *Indian Voices: The First Convocation of
    American Indian Scholars.* San Francisco: Indian Historian Press, 1970.
Cothran, Boyd. *Remembering the Modoc War: Redemptive Violence and the Making of
    American Innocence.* Chapel Hill: University of North Carolina Press, 2014.
Cottrell, Robert C. *Sex, Drugs, and Rock 'N' Roll: The Rise of America's 1960s
    Counterculture.* Lanham, MD: Rowman and Littlefield, 2015.
Coulthard, Glen Sean. *Red Skin, White Masks: Rejecting the Colonial Politics of
    Recognition.* Minneapolis: University of Minnesota Press, 2014.
Countryman, Matthew J. *Up South: Civil Rights and Black Power in Philadelphia.*
    Philadelphia: University of Pennsylvania Press, 2006.

Cowger, Thomas W. *The National Congress of American Indians: The Founding Years.* Lincoln: University of Nebraska Press, 1999.

Davidson, James West, Brian DeLay, Christine Leigh Heyrman, Mark H. Lytle, and Michael B. Stoff, *Nation of Nations: A Narrative History of the American Republic Volume II: Since 1865.* Boston: McGraw-Hill Higher Education, 2008.

Davis, Julie L. *Survival Schools: The American Indian Movement and Community Education in the Twin Cities.* Minneapolis: University of Minnesota Press, 2013.

Deloria, Philip J., and Neal Salisbury. *A Companion to American Indian History.* Malden, MA: Blackwell Publishing, 2004.

———. *Playing Indian.* New Haven: Yale University Press, 1998.

———. *Indians in Unexpected Places.* Lawrence: University Press of Kansas, 2004.

Deloria, Vine, Jr. *We Talk, You Listen.* New York: Dell Publishing, 1970.

———, ed. *Jenning C. Wise: The Red Man in the New World Drama: A Politico-Legal Study with a Pageantry of American Indian History.* New York: Macmillan, 1971.

———, ed. *Of Utmost Good Faith.* San Francisco: Straight Arrow Books, 1971.

———. *Custer Died for Your Sins: An Indian Manifesto.* Second Printing. Norman: University of Oklahoma Press, 1988.

———. *Behind the Trail of Broken Treaties: An Indian Declaration of Independence.* New York: Dell Publishing, 1974.

———. *The Indian Affair.* New York: Friendship Press, 1974.

———. *God Is Red: A Native View of Religion.* Second Printing. Golden: Fulcrum Publishing, 1994.

———. *Indians of the Pacific Northwest: From the Coming of the White Man to the Present Day.* New York: Doubleday and Co., 1977.

———. *American Indian Policy in the Twentieth Century.* Norman: University of Oklahoma Press, 1985.

———. *Spirit & Reason: The Vine Deloria, Jr., Reader.* Golden: Fulcrum Publishing, 1999.

Deloria, Vine, Jr., and Clifford Lytle. *The Nations Within: The Past and Future of American Indian Sovereignty.* New York: Pantheon Books, 1984.

Denoon, Donald, Stewart Firth, Jocelyn Linnekin, Malama Meleisea, and Karen Nero, eds. *The Cambridge History of Pacific Islanders.* New York: Cambridge University Press, 1997.

Dewing, Rolland. *Wounded Knee II.* Chadron, NE: Great Plains Network, 2000.

Dickason, Olive Patricia, and William Newbigging. *A Concise History of Canada's First Nations.* Don Mills, Ontario: Oxford University Press Canada, 2010.

Diggins, John Patrick. *The Rise and Fall of the American Left.* New York: W.W. Norton, 1992.

Dimock, Marshall E. "Woodrow Wilson as Legislative Leader." *Journal of Politics* 19:1 (Feb. 1957), 3–19.

Dippie, Brian W. *The Vanishing American: White Attitudes and U.S. Indian Policy.* Lawrence: University Press of Kansas, 1982.

Donaldson, Gary A. *The Making of Modern America: The Nation from 1945 to the Present.* Lanham, MD: Rowman and Littlefield, 2009.

Dorling Kindersley Travel Guides. *San Francisco and Northern California*. New York: Dorling Kindersley, Inc., 2000.

Drinnon, Richard. *Keeper of Concentration Camps: Dillon S. Myer and American Racism*. Berkeley: University of California Press, 1987.

Ducheneaux, Karen, and Kirke Kickingbird. *One Hundred Million Acres*. New York: Macmillan, 1973.

Eargle, Jr., Dolan H. *Native California: An Introductory Guide to the Original Peoples from Earliest to Modern Times*. San Francisco: Trees Company Press, 2008.

Edmunds, David R., ed. *The New Warriors: Native American Leaders since 1900*. Lincoln: University of Nebraska Press, 2001.

Farber, David. *The Age of Great Dreams: America in the 1960s*. New York: Hill and Wang, 1994.

———, ed. *The Sixties: From Memory To History*. Chapel Hill: University of North Carolina Press, 1994.

———. *Chicago '68*. Chicago: University of Chicago Press, 1988.

Fisher, Andrew H. *Shadow Tribe: The Making of Columbia River Indian Identity*. Seattle: University of Washington Press, 2010.

Fisher, Donald M. *Lacrosse: A History of the Game*. Baltimore: Johns Hopkins University Press, 2002.

Fixico, Donald. *The Urban Indian Experience in America*. Albuquerque: University of New Mexico Press, 2000.

———. *Termination and Relocation: Federal Indian Policy, 1945–1960*. Albuquerque: University of New Mexico Press, 1986.

———. *The American Indian Mind in a Linear World: American Indian Studies and Traditional Knowledge*. New York: Routledge, 2003.

Fogleman, Billye Y. Sherman. *Adaptive Mechanisms of the North American Indian to an Urban Setting*. Ph.D. dissertation, Anthropology Department, Southern Methodist University, 1972.

Forbes, Jack D. *Native Americans and Nixon: Presidential Politics and Minority Self-Determination, 1969–1972*. Los Angeles: University of California American Indian Studies Center, 1981.

Fortier, James, dir. *Alcatraz Is Not An Island*. San Francisco: Diamond Island Productions. Documentary, 2001.

Fortunate Eagle, Adam. *Alcatraz! Alcatraz! The Indian Occupation of 1969–1971*. Berkeley: Heyday Books, 1992.

Fortunate Eagle, Adam, and Tim Findley. *Heart of the Rock: The Indian Invasion of Alcatraz*. Norman: University of Oklahoma Press, 2002.

Fox, Rona Marcia Fields. *The Brown Berets: A Participant Observation Study of Social Action in the Schools of Los Angeles*. Ph.D. dissertation, University of Southern California, 1970.

Frakes, George E., and Curtis B. Solberg, eds. *Minorities in California History*. New York: Random House, 1971.

Franco, Jere' Bishop. *Crossing the Pond: The Native American Effort in World War II*. Denton: University of North Texas Press, 1999.

Frank, Thomas. *The Conquest of Cool: Business Culture, Counterculture, and the Rise of Hip Consumerism*. Chicago: University of Chicago Press, 1997.

Galperin, Patricia O. *In Search of Princess White Deer: A Biography*. Sparta, NJ: Flint & Feather Press, 2012.

Garcia, Matthew. *From the Jaws of Victory: The Triumph and Tragedy of Cesar Chavez and the Farm Workers Movement*. Berkeley: University of California Press, 2012.

Gedicks, Al. *The New Resource Wars: Native and Environmental Struggles against Multinational Corporations*. Boston: South End Press, 1993.

Genetin-Pilawa, C. Joseph. *Crooked Paths to Allotment: The Fight over Federal Indian Policy after the Civil War*. Chapel Hill: University of North Carolina Press, 2012.

Getches, David H., Charles F. Wilkinson, and Robert A. Williams Jr. *Cases and Materials on Federal Indian Law*. St. Paul: West/Thomson, 2005.

Gitlin, Todd. *The Sixties: Years of Hope, Days of Rage*. New York: Bantam Books, 1987.

Gosse, Van. *Rethinking the New Left: An Interpretative History*. New York: Palgrave MacMillan, 2005.

Gravy, Wavy, and Hugh Romney. *The Hog Farm and Friends*. New York: Links Books, 1974.

Haas, Ernst B. "The Attempt to Terminate Colonialism: Acceptance of the United Nations Trusteeship System." *International Organization* 7:1 (Feb. 1953), 1–21.

Hagan, William T. *The Indian Rights Association: The Herbert Welsh Years 1882–1904*. Tucson: University of Arizona Press, 1985.

Hampton, Henry, and Steve Fayer. *Voices of Freedom: An Oral History of the Civil Rights Movement from the 1950s through the 1980s*. New York: Bantam Books, 1991.

Harmon, Alexandra. *Indians in the Making: Ethnic Relations and Indian Identities around Puget Sound*. Berkeley: University of California Press, 1998.

Harris, LaDonna, and Henrietta Stockel, eds. *LaDonna Harris: A Comanche Life*. Lincoln: University of Nebraska Press, 2000.

The Harvard Project on American Indian Economic Development. *The State of The Native Nations: Conditions under U.S. Policies of Self-Determination*. New York: Oxford University Press, 2008.

Hauptman, Laurence M. *The Iroquois and the New Deal*. Syracuse: Syracuse University Press, 1981.

———. *The Iroquois Struggle for Survival: World War II to Red Power*. Syracuse: Syracuse University Press, 1986.

———. *In the Shadow of Kinzua: The Seneca Nation of Indians since World War II*. Syracuse: Syracuse University Press, 2014.

Heffernan, Trova. *Where the Salmon Run: The Life and Legacy of Billy Frank Jr.* Seattle: University of Washington Press, 2012.

Heins, Marjorie. *Strictly Ghetto Property: The Story of Los Siete de la Raza*. Berkeley: Ramparts Press, 1972.

Hertzberg, Hazel W. *The Search for an American Indian Identity: Modern Pan-Indian Movements.* Syracuse: Syracuse University Press, 1971.

Hill, Rick. "Skywalkers: The Legacy of Mohawk Ironworkers." *Turtle Quarterly* 1:4, 2–9.

Hine, Robert V., and John Mack Faragher. *The American West: A New Interpretive History.* New Haven: Yale University Press, 2000.

Hippler, Arthur E. *Hunter's Point: A Black Ghetto.* New York: Basic Books, 1974.

Hogeland, L. Frank, and Kim Hogeland. *First Families: A Photographic History of California Indians.* Berkeley: Heyday Books, 2007.

Holm, Tom. *Strong Hearts, Wounded Souls: Native American Veterans of the Vietnam War.* Austin: University of Texas Press, 1996.

———. *The Great Confusion in Indian Affairs: Native Americans & Whites in the Progressive Era.* Austin: University of Texas Press, 2005.

Hosmer, Brian, ed. *Native Americans and the Legacy of Harry S. Truman.* Kirksville, MO: Truman State University Press, 2010.

Hosmer, Brian, and Larry Nesper, eds. *Tribal Worlds: Critical Studies in American Indian Nation Building.* Albany: State University of New York Press, 2013.

Howell, Ocean. *Making the Mission: Planning and Ethnicity in San Francisco.* Chicago: The University of Chicago Press, 2015.

Hoxie, Frederick E. *The Campaign to Assimilate the Indians, 1880–1920.* Lincoln: University of Nebraska Press, 2001.

———. *This Is Indian Country: American Indian Activists and the Place They Made.* New York: Penguin, 2012.

Issel, William. "Liberalism and Urban Policy in San Francisco from the 1930s to the 1960s." *The Western Historical Quarterly* 22:4 (Nov. 1991), 440.

Isserman, Maurice, and Michael Kazin. *America Divided: The Civil War of the 1960s.* New York: Oxford University Press, 2008.

Iverson, Peter. *"We Are Still Here": American Indians in the Twentieth Century.* Wheeling, IL: Harlan Davidson, 1998.

———, ed. *The Plains Indians of the Twentieth Century.* Norman: University of Oklahoma Press, 1985.

———. *Carlos Montezuma and the Changing World of American Indians.* Albuquerque: University of New Mexico Press, 1982.

Jaimes, Annette M., ed. *The State of Native America.* Boston: South End Press, 1992.

———. "The Pit River Indian Land Claim Disputes in Northern California." *Journal of Ethnic Studies* 14:4 (Winter 1987), 47–64.

Janes, Craig R. *Migration, Social Change, and Health: A Samoan Community in Urban California.* Stanford: Stanford University Press, 1990.

Jasen, Patricia. "Native People and the Tourist Industry in Nineteenth-Century Ontario." *Journal of Canadian Studies* 28:4 (Winter 1993/1994), 5–27.

Jensen, Gary F., Joseph H. Stauss, and V. William Harris. "Crime, Delinquency, and the American Indian." *Human Organization* 36:3 (Fall 1977), 252.

Johansen, Bruce E., and Willard Bill Sr. *Up from the Ashes: Nation Building at Muckleshoot.* Seattle: Muckleshoot Indian Tribe, 2014.

———. *Life & Death in Mohawk Country.* Golden, CO: Fulcrum Publishing, 1993.

Johnson, Troy R. *The Occupation of Alcatraz Island: Indian Self-Determination and the Rise of Indian Activism.* Urbana: University of Illinois Press, 1996.

———. *We Hold The Rock: The Indian Occupation of Alcatraz, 1969–1971.* San Francisco: Golden Gate National Parks Association, 1997.

———. *Alcatraz: Indian Land Forever.* Los Angeles: American Indian Studies Center, University of California, 1994.

———. *You Are on Indian Land! Alcatraz Island, 1969–1971.* Los Angeles: American Indian Studies Center, University of California, 1995.

———, ed. *Contemporary Native American Political Issues.* Lanham, MD: Altamira Press, 1999.

———. *Red Power: The Native American Civil Rights Movement.* New York: Chelsea House Publishers, 2007.

Johnson, Troy R., Duane Champagne, and Joane Nagel. *American Indian Activism: Alcatraz to the Longest Walk.* Urbana: University of Illinois Press, 1997.

Johnston, Basil H. *Indian School Days.* Norman: University of Oklahoma Press, 1989.

Jorgensen, Joseph G., ed. "Indians and the Metropolis." In *The American Indian in Urban Society,* ed. Jack O. Waddell and O. Michael Watson. Boston: Little, Brown and Company, 1971.

Josephy, Alvin M., Jr. *Red Power: The American Indians' Fight for Freedom.* Lincoln: University of Nebraska Press, 1971.

———. *Now That the Buffalo's Gone: A Study of Today's American Indians.* Norman: University of Oklahoma Press, 1984.

Karagueuzian, Dikran. *Blow It Up!* Boston: Gambit, 1971.

Katznelson, Ira. *City Trenches: Urban Politics and the Patterning of Cities in the United States.* Chicago: University of Chicago Press, 1981.

Kauanui, J. Kehaulani. *Hawaiian Blood: Colonialism and the Politics of Sovereignty and Indigeneity.* Durham, NC: Duke University Press, 2008.

Kelly, Casey Ryan. *The Rhetoric of Red Power and the American Indian Occupation of Alcatraz Island (1969–1971).* Ph.D. dissertation, University of Minnesota, 2009.

Kinbacher, Kurt E. *Urban Villages and Local Identities: Germans from Russia, Omaha Indians, and Vietnamese in Lincoln, Nebraska.* Lubbock: Texas Tech University Press, 2015.

Kirk, Andrew G. *Counterculture Green: The Whole Earth Catalog and American Environmentalism.* Lawrence: University Press of Kansas, 2007.

Klingle, Matthew. *Emerald City: An Environmental History of Seattle.* New Haven: Yale University Press, 2009.

Koch, Karl, III, and Richard Firstman. *Men of Steel: The Story of the Family that Built the World Trade Center.* New York: Three Rivers Press, 2002.

Koppes, Clayton R. "From New Deal to Termination: Liberalism and Indian Policy, 1933–1953." *Pacific Historical Review* 46:4 (1977), 544.

Koster, John, and Robert Burnette. *The Road to Wounded Knee.* New York: Bantam Books, 1974.

Krouse, Susan Applegate, and Heather A. Howard, eds. *Keeping the Campfires Going: Native Women's Activism in Urban Communities.* Lincoln: University of Nebraska Press, 2009.

Kruse, Kevin M. *White Flight: Atlanta and the Making of Modern Conservatism.* Princeton: Princeton University Press, 2005.

Kruse, Kevin M., and Thomas J. Sugrue, eds. *The New Suburban History.* Chicago: University of Chicago Press, 2006.

LaDuke, Winona. *All Our Relations: Native Struggles for Land and Life.* Cambridge: South End Press, 1999.

LaGrand, James B. *Indian Metropolis: Native Americans in Chicago, 1945–1975.* Urbana: University of Illinois Press, 2002.

Landsman, Gail H. *Sovereignty and Symbol: Indian-White Conflict at Ganienkeh.* Albuquerque: University of New Mexico Press, 1988.

Lawson, Michael L. *Dammed Indians Revisited: The Continuing History of the Pick-Sloan Plan and the Missouri River Sioux.* Pierre: South Dakota Historical Society Press, 2009.

Leuchtenburg, William E. *Franklin D. Roosevelt and the New Deal 1932–1940.* New York: Harper and Row, 1963.

Lewis, Randolph. *Alanis Obomsawin: The Vision of a Filmmaker.* Lincoln: University of Nebraska Press, 2006

Lincoln, Kenneth. *Native American Renaissance.* Berkeley: University of California Press, 1983.

Litwak, Leo, and Herbert Wilner. *College Days in Earthquake Country: Ordeal at San Francisco State, a Personal Record.* New York: Random House, 1971.

Lobo, Susan. *Urban Voices: The Bay Area American Indian Community.* Tucson: University of Arizona Press, 2002.

Lobo, Susan, and Kurt Peters, eds. *American Indians and the Urban Experience.* Walnut Creek, CA: Altamira Press, 2001.

Lobo, Susan, and Steve Talbot, eds. *Native American Voices.* New Jersey: Prentice Hall, 2001.

Lomawaima, K. Tsianina, and David Wilkins. *Uneven Ground: American Indian Sovereignty and Federal Law.* Norman: University of Oklahoma Press, 2001.

———. *They Called It Prairie Light: The Story of Chilocco Indian School.* Lincoln: University of Nebraska Press, 1994.

Lonetree, Amy. *Decolonizing Museums: Representing Native America in National and Tribal Museums.* Chapel Hill: University of North Carolina Press, 2012.

Lowery, Malinda Maynor. *Lumbee Indians in the Jim Crow South: Race, Identity, and the Making of a Nation.* Chapel Hill: The University of North Carolina Press, 2010.

Lurie, Nancy Oestreich, and Stuart Levine, eds. *The American Indian Today.* Baltimore: Penguin Books, 1968.

Lyman, Richard W. *Stanford in Turmoil: Campus Unrest, 1966–1972.* Stanford: Stanford University Press, 2009.

Lyons, Scott Richard. *X-Marks: Native Signatures of Assent*. Minneapolis: University of Minnesota Press, 2010.

Lytle, Mark Hamilton. *America's Uncivil Wars: The Sixties Era from Elvis to the Fall of Richard Nixon*. New York: Oxford University Press, 2006.

Maddox, Lucy. *Citizen Indians: Native American Intellectuals, Race, and Reform*. Ithaca, NY: Cornell University Press, 2005.

Maestas, John R., ed. *Contemporary Native American Address*. Provo, UT: Brigham Young University Press, 1976.

Magnuson, Stew. *The Death of Raymond Yellow Thunder: And Other True Stories from the Nebraska-Pine Ridge Border Towns*. Lubbock: Texas Tech University Press, 2008.

Malone, Michael P., and Richard W. Etulain. *The American West: A Twentieth Century History*. Lincoln: University of Nebraska Press, 1989.

Manbeck, John B. *The Neighborhoods of Brooklyn*. New Haven: Yale University Press, 1998.

Mankiller, Wilma, and Michael Wallis. *Mankiller: A Chief and Her People*. New York: St. Martin's Press, 1993.

Maracle, Lee. *Bobbi Lee: Indian Rebel*. Toronto: Women's Press, 1990.

Margon, Arthur. "Indians and Immigrants: A Comparison of Groups New to the City." *Journal of Ethnic Studies* 4:4 (Winter 1977), 18.

Martinez, David. *Dakota Philosopher: Charles Eastman and American Indian Thought*. St. Paul: Minnesota Historical Society Press, 2009.

Marx Jr., Herbert L., ed. *The American Indian: A Rising Ethnic Force*. New York: The H.W. Wilson Company, 1973.

Matthiessen, Peter. *In the Spirit of Crazy Horse*. New York: Penguin, 1992.

McFarlane, Peter. *Brotherhood to Nationhood: George Manuel and the Making of the Modern Indian Movement*. Toronto: Between The Lines, 1993.

McKenzie-Jones, Paul. *Clyde Warrior: Tradition, Community, and Red Power*. Norman: University of Oklahoma Press, 2015.

McMillen, Christian. *Making Indian Law: The Hualapai Land Case and the Birth of Ethnohistory*. New Haven: Yale University Press, 2007.

McNenly, Linda Scarangella. *Native Performers in Wild West Shows: From Buffalo Bill to Euro Disney*. Norman: University of Oklahoma Press, 2012.

McNickle, D'Arcy. *Native American Tribalism: Indian Survivals and Renewals*. New York: Oxford University Press, 1973.

———— and Harold E. Fey. *Indians and Other Americans: Two Ways of Life Meet*. New York: Harper Brothers, 1959.

Means, Russell, and Marvin J. Wolf. *Where White Men Fear to Tread*. New York: St. Martin's Press, 1995.

Metcalf, Ann. "Indians in the San Francisco Bay Area." *Urban Indians*. Chicago: Newberry Library, 1980.

Metoyer, Cheryl A. *Perceptions of the Mohawk Elementary Students of Library Services*. Ph.D. dissertation, Indiana University, 1976.

Miller, J. R. *Skyscrapers Hide the Heavens: A History of Indian-White Relations in Canada*. Toronto: University of Toronto Press, 1989.

————. *Shingwauk's Vision: A History of Native Residential Schools.* Toronto: University of Toronto Press, 2009.

Miller, Mike. *A Community Organizer's Tale: People and Power in San Francisco.* Berkeley: Heyday Books, 2009.

Momaday, N. Scott. *House Made of Dawn.* New York: Harper and Row, 1968.

Morris, Joseph. *"Indian Joe": Alcatraz Indian Occupation Diary.* Self-published, 1998.

Muñoz, María L. O. *Stand Up and Fight: Participatory Indigenismo, Populism, and Mobilization in Mexico, 1970–1984.* Tucson: University of Arizona Press, 2016.

Nagel, Joane. *American Indian Ethnic Renewal: Red Power and the Resurgence of Identity and Culture.* New York: Oxford University Press, 1997.

Navarro, Armando. *La Raza Unida Party: A Chicano Challenge to the U.S. Two-Party Dictatorship.* Philadelphia: Temple University Press, 2000.

Needham, Andrew. *Power Lines: Phoenix and the Making of the Modern Southwest.* Princeton: Princeton University Press, 2014.

Neils, Elaine M. *Reservation to City: Indian Migration and Federal Relocation.* Chicago: Department of Geography, University of Chicago, 1971.

Nesper, Larry. *The Walleye War: The Struggle for Ojibwe Spearfishing and Treaty Rights.* Lincoln: University of Nebraska Press, 2002.

Nichols, Roger L. *The American Indian Past and Present.* New York: McGraw Hill, Inc., 1992.

North American Indian Traveling College. *Tewaarathon (Lacrosse): Akwesasne's Story of our National Game.* Cornwall, Ontario: North American Indian Traveling College, 1978.

Oakes, Richard. "Alcatraz Is Not an Island." *Ramparts* (Dec. 1972), 35–40.

Orrick, William H., Jr. *Shut It Down! A College In Crisis.* Washington, DC: U.S. Government Printing Office, 1969.

Parker, Dorothy. *Singing an Indian Song: A Biography of D'Arcy McNickle.* Lincoln: University of Nebraska Press, 1994.

Perlstein, Rick. *Nixonland: The Rise of a President and the Fracturing of America.* New York: Scribner, 2008.

————. *The Invisible Bridge: The Fall of Nixon and the Rise of Reagan.* New York: Simon & Schuster, 2014.

Philip, Kenneth R. *Termination Revisited: American Indians on the Trail to Self-Determination, 1933–1953.* Lincoln: University of Nebraska Press, 1999.

Phillips, George Harwood. *The Enduring Struggle: Indians in California History.* Sparks, NV: Materials for Today's Learning, Inc., 1996.

Phillips, Stephanie. *The Kahnawake Mohawk and the St. Lawrence Seaway.* M.A. Thesis, Department of Anthropology, McGill University, 2000.

Piatote, Beth H. *Domestic Subjects: Gender, Citizenship, and Law in Native American Literature.* New Haven: Yale University Press, 2013.

Poliandri, Simone, ed. *Native American Nationalism and Nation Re-building: Past and Present Cases.* Albany: State University of New York Press, 2016.

Pommersheim, Frank. *Broken Landscape: Indians, Indian Tribes, and the Constitution.* New York: Oxford University Press, 2009.

Pritzker, Barry M. *A Native American Encyclopedia: History, Culture, and Peoples.* New York: Oxford University Press, 2000.

Prucha, Francis Paul. *The Great Father: The United States Government and the American Indian.* Lincoln: University of Nebraska Press, 1984.

Quiñones, Juan Gómez. *Chicano Politics: Reality and Promise, 1940–1990.* Albuquerque: University of New Mexico Press, 1990.

Rae, Heather, dir. *Trudell.* Apaloosa Pictures. Documentary, 2004.

Ramirez, Renya K. *Native Hubs: Culture, Community, and Belonging in Silicon Valley and Beyond.* Durham, NC: Duke University Press, 2007.

Ranson, Mort, dir. *You Are on Indian Land.* Canada: National Film Board of Canada. Documentary, 1969.

Rasenberger, Jim. *High Steel: The Daring Men Who Built the World's Greatest Skyline.* New York: Harper Collins, 2004.

Reid, Joshua L. *The Sea Is My Country: The Maritime World of the Makahs.* New Haven: Yale University Press, 2015.

Reinhardt, Akim D. *Ruling Pine Ridge: Oglala Lakota Politics from the IRA to Wounded Knee.* Lubbock: Texas Tech University Press, 2007.

Reyes, Lawney L. *Bernie Whitebear: An Urban Indian's Quest for Justice.* Tucson: The University of Arizona Press, 2006.

Richter, Daniel K. *The Ordeal of the Longhouse: The Peoples of the Iroquois League in the Era of European Colonization.* Chapel Hill: The University of North Carolina Press, 1992.

Rickard, Clinton, and Barbara Graymont. *Fighting Tuscarora: The Autobiography of Chief Clinton Rickard.* Syracuse: Syracuse University Press, 1973.

Roediger, David R., and Elizabeth D. Esch. *The Production of Difference: Race and the Management of Labor in U.S. History.* New York: Oxford University Press, 2012.

Rorabaugh, W. J. *Berkeley at War: The 1960s.* New York: Oxford University Press, 1989.

Rosales, Arturo F. *Chicano! The History of the Mexican American Civil Rights Movement.* Houston: Arte Publico Press, 1996.

Rosenthal, Nicolas G. "Repositioning Indianness: Native American Organizations in Portland, Oregon, 1959–1975." *Pacific Historical Review* 71:3 (Aug. 2002), 415–438.

———. *Reimagining Indian Country: Native American Migration and Identity in Twentieth-Century Los Angeles.* Chapel Hill: University of North Carolina Press, 2012.

Rosier, Paul C. *Serving Their Country: American Indian Politics and Patriotism in the Twentieth Century.* Cambridge: Harvard University Press, 2009.

———. "'Modern America Desperately Needs to Listen': The Emerging Indian in an Age of Environmental Crisis." *Journal of American History* 100:3 (Dec. 2013), 711–735.

Ruiz, Vicki L. *From Out of the Shadows: Mexican Women in Twentieth-Century America.* New York: Oxford University Press, 2008.

Sale, Kirkpatrick. *SDS.* New York: Random House, 1973.

————. *The Green Revolution: The American Environmental Movement 1962–1992.*
New York: Hill and Wang, 1993.

Sanchez, George J. *Becoming Mexican American: Ethnicity, Culture, and Identity in Chicano Los Angeles, 1900–1945.* New York: Oxford University Press, 1993.

Sandoval-Strausz, A. K. "Latino Landscapes: Postwar Cities and the Transnational Origins of a New Urban America." *Journal of American History* 101:3 (Dec. 2014), 804–831.

Schulman, Bruce J. *The Seventies: The Great Shift In American Culture, Society, and Politics.* Cambridge: Da Capo Press, 2001.

Schusky, Ernest L., ed. *Political Organization of Native North Americans.* Washington, DC: University Press of America, 1980.

Self, Robert O. *American Babylon: Race and the Struggle for Postwar Oakland.* Princeton: Princeton University Press, 2003.

————. *All in the Family: The Realignment of American Democracy since the 1960s.* New York: Hill and Wang, 2012.

Sheffield, R. Scott. *The Red Man's on the Warpath: The Image of the "Indian" and the Second World War.* Vancouver: University of British Columbia Press, 2004.

Shepherd, Jeffrey P. *We Are an Indian Nation: A History of the Hualapai People.* Tucson: University of Arizona Press, 2010.

Sheyahshe, Michael A. *Native Americans in Comic Books: A Critical Study.* Jefferson, NC: McFarland, 2008.

Shreve, Bradley G. *Red Power Rising: The National Indian Youth Council and the Origins of Native Activism.* Norman: University of Oklahoma Press, 2011.

Silva, Noenoe K. *Aloha Betrayed: Native Hawaiian Resistance to American Colonialism.* Durham, NC: Duke University Press, 2004.

Simpson, Audra. *To the Reserve and Back Again: Kahnawake Mohawk Narratives of Self, Home and Nation.* Ph.D. dissertation, Anthropology Department, McGill University, 2003.

————. *Mohawk Interruptus: Political Life across the Borders of Settler States.* Durham, NC: Duke University Press, 2014.

Simpson, Leanne. *Dancing on Turtle's Back: Stories of Nishnaabeg Re-Creation, Resurgence, and a New Emergence.* Winnipeg: Arbeiter Ring Publishing, 2011.

Singer, Beverly R. *Wiping the War Paint off the Lens: Native American Film and Video.* Minneapolis: University of Minnesota Press, 2001.

Smith, Sherry L. *Hippies, Indians, and the Fight for Red Power.* New York: Oxford University Press, 2012.

Sorkin, Alan L. *The Urban American Indian.* Lexington: Lexington Books, 1978.

Spicer, Edward H. *A Short History of the Indians of the United States.* New York: D. Van Nostrand, 1969.

Steiner, Stan. *The New Indians.* New York: Delta Books, 1968.

————. *The Vanishing White Man.* New York: Harper & Row, Publishers, 1976.

————. *La Raza: The Mexican Americans.* New York: Harper Colophon Books, 1970.

Stonechild, Blair. *Buffy Sainte-Marie: It's My Way.* Markham, Ontario: Fifth House Publishers, 2012.

Strickland, Rennard. *Tonto's Revenge: Reflections on American Indian Culture and Policy.* Albuquerque: University of New Mexico Press, 1997.

Sturtevant, William C., ed. *Handbook of North American Indians: Indians in Contemporary Society.* Washington, DC: Smithsonian Institution, 2008.

Sugrue, Thomas J. *The Origins of the Urban Crisis: Race and Inequality in Postwar Detroit.* Princeton: Princeton University Press, 1996.

Suri, Jeremi. *Power and Protest: Global Revolution and the Rise of Détente.* Cambridge: Harvard University Press, 2003.

Sutton, Mark O. *An Introduction to Native North America.* Boston: Pearson Education, 2008.

Tarbell, Reaghan, dir. *To Brooklyn and Back: A Mohawk Journey.* Documentary, Vision Maker Media, 2008.

Taylor, Graham, D. *The New Deal and American Indian Tribalism: The Administration of the Indian Reorganization Act, 1934–45.* Lincoln: University of Nebraska Press, 1980.

Taylor, Quintard. *The Forging of a Black Community: Seattle's Central District from 1870 through the Civil Rights Era.* Seattle: University of Washington Press, 1994.

Terkel, Studs. *American Dreams: Lost and Found.* New York: Ballantine Books, 1980.

Teuton, Sean Kicummah. *Red Land, Red Power: Grounding Knowledge in the American Indian Novel.* Durham, NC: Duke University Press, 2008.

Thompson, Heather Ann. *Blood in the Water: The Attica Prison Uprising of 1971 and Its Legacy.* New York: Pantheon Books, 2016.

Thornton, Russell, ed. *Studying Native America: Problems and Prospects.* Madison: University of Wisconsin Press, 1998.

Thrush, Coll. *Native Seattle: Histories from the Crossing over Place.* Seattle: University of Washington Press, 2007.

Trahant, Mark N. *The Last Great Battle of the Indian Wars: Henry M. Jackson, Forrest J. Gerard and the Campaign for Self-Determination of America's Indian Tribes.* Fort Hall, ID: Cedars Group, 2010.

Trask, Haunani-Kay. *From a Native Daughter: Colonialism and Sovereignty in Hawai'i.* Honolulu: University of Hawai'i Press, 1999.

Troutman, John W. *Indian Blues: American Indians and the Politics of Music, 1879–1934.* Norman: University of Oklahoma Press, 2009.

Vennum, Thomas. *American Indian Lacrosse: Little Brother of War.* Baltimore: Johns Hopkins University Press, 1994.

Vigil, Ernesto B. *The Crusade for Justice: Chicano Militancy and the Government's War on Dissent.* Madison: University of Wisconsin Press, 1999.

Villarreal, Arturo. *Black Berets for Justice.* M.A. thesis, Department of Social Science, San Jose University, 1991.

Wagner, Jean Katharine. *An Examination and Description of Acculturation of Selected Individual American Indian Women in an Urban Area.* Ph.D. dissertation, Anthropology Department, New York University, 1972.

Warrior, Robert Allen, and Paul Chaat Smith. *Like a Hurricane: The Indian Movement from Alcatraz to Wounded Knee.* New York: New Press, 1996.

Warrior, Robert Allen, Craig Womack, and Jace Weaver. *American Indian Literary Nationalism*. Albuquerque: University of New Mexico Press, 2006.

Washburn, Wilcomb E. *The Indian in America*. New York: Harper Colophon Books, 1975.

———, ed. *Handbook of North American Indians: History of Indian-White Relations*, vol. 4. Washington, DC: Smithsonian Institution, 1988.

Wax, Murray. *Indian Americans: Unity and Diversity*. Englewood Cliffs, NJ: Prentice-Hall, 1971.

Weibel-Orlando, Joan. *Indian Country, L.A.: Maintaining Ethnic Community in Complex Society*. Urbana: University of Illinois Press, 1999.

Weitzman, David. *Skywalkers: Mohawk Ironworkers Build the City*. New York: Roaring Brook Press, 2010.

Weston, Mary Ann. *Native Americans in the News: Images of Indians in the Twentieth Century Press*. Westport, CT: Greenwood Press, 1996.

Weyler, Rex. *Blood of the Land: The Government and Corporate War Against First Nations*. Philadelphia: New Society Publishers, 1992.

Whalen, Kevin. *Native Students at Work: American Indian Labor and Sherman Institute's Outing Program, 1900–1945*. Seattle: University of Washington Press, 2016.

White, Louellyn. *Free to Be Mohawk: Indigenous Education at Akwesasne Freedom School*. Norman: University of Oklahoma Press, 2015.

White, Richard. *"It's Your Misfortune and None of My Own": A New History of the American West*. Norman: University of Oklahoma Press, 1991.

———. *The Organic Machine: The Remaking of the Columbia River*. New York: Hill and Wang, 1995.

Wilkins, David E. *The Hank Adams Reader: An Exemplary Native Activist and the Unleashing of Indigenous Sovereignty*. Golden, CO: Fulcrum Publishing, 2011.

Wilkins, David E., and Heidi Kiiwetinepinesiik Stark. *American Indian Politics and the American Political System*. 3rd ed. Lanham, MD: Rowman & Littlefield Publishers, Inc., 2011.

Wilkinson, Charles. *Blood Struggle: The Rise of Modern Indian Nations*. New York: W.W. Norton, 2005.

———. *Messages from Frank's Landing: A Story of Salmon, Treaties, and the Indian Way*. Seattle: University of Washington Press, 2000.

Willard, William. "Outing, Relocation, and Employment Assistance: The Impact of Federal Indian Population Dispersal Programs in the Bay Area." *Wicazo Sa Review* 12:1 (Spring 1997), 29–46.

Willensky, Elliot. *When Brooklyn Was the World, 1920–1957*. New York: Harmony Books, 1986.

Wilson, Edmund. *Apologies to the Iroquois*. New York: Vintage Books, 1960.

Wirt, Fredrick M. *Power in the City: Decision Making in San Francisco*. Los Angeles: University of California Press, 1974.

Wolin, Sheldon S., and John H. Schaar. *The Berkeley Rebellion and Beyond: Essays on Politics and Education in the Technological Society*. New York: Random House, 1970.

Wright-McLeod, Brian. *The Encyclopedia of Native Music: More Than a Century of Recordings from Wax Cylinder to the Internet.* Tucson: University of Arizona Press, 2005.

Wunder, John R. *"Retained by The People": A History of American Indians and the Bill of Rights.* New York: Oxford University Press, 1994.

York, Geoffrey, and Loreen Pindera. *People of the Pines: The Warriors and the Legacy of Oka.* Toronto: Little, Brown, 1992.

Young Bear, Severt, and R. D. Theisz. *Standing in the Light: A Lakota Way of Seeing.* Lincoln: University of Nebraska Press, 1994.

Zhou, Min, and J. V. Gatewood. *Contemporary Asian America: A Multidisciplinary Reader.* 2nd ed. New York: New York University Press, 2007.

Zimmerman, Bill. *Airlift to Wounded Knee.* Chicago: Swallow Press, 1976.

INDEX

Richard Oakes is referred to as "RO" in the subentries of this index. Italicized page numbers refer to illustrations.